Hierarchical Topology Control for Wireless Networks

Hierarchical Topology Control for Wireless Networks
Theory, Algorithms, and Simulation

Jiguo Yu, Xiuzhen Cheng, Honglu Jiang, and
Dongxiao Yu

CRC Press
Taylor & Francis Group
Boca Raton London New York

CRC Press is an imprint of the
Taylor & Francis Group, an **informa** business

CRC Press
Taylor & Francis Group
6000 Broken Sound Parkway NW, Suite 300
Boca Raton, FL 33487-2742

First issued in paperback 2020

© 2018 by Taylor & Francis Group, LLC
CRC Press is an imprint of Taylor & Francis Group, an Informa business

No claim to original U.S. Government works

ISBN-13: 978-0-367-57217-4 (pbk)
ISBN-13: 978-1-4822-9869-7 (hbk)

Visit the Taylor & Francis Web site at
http://www.taylorandfrancis.com

and the CRC Press Web site at
http://www.crcpress.com

Contents

Preface

The thought of sending information by radio waves (i.e. wireless communication) has 100 years of history. That is, when a plurality of wireless transceiver devices sharing part of wireless spectrum can send messages to each other, it can be a wireless communication network. Therefore, wireless networks focus on the general mechanism of effectively sharing all wireless spectrum, procedures and algorithms, making all kinds of communication instances between different devices achieve the desired quality of service. The wireless network can be divided into two kinds: wireless networks based on fixed infrastructure (Wireless Personal Area Network WPAN, wireless metropolitan area network WMAN, Wireless Local Area Network WLAN and wireless wide area network WWAN); wireless networks without fixed infrastructure (wireless self-organizing network Ad Hoc, wireless sensor network WSN and wireless mesh network WMN).

The research object of this book is the wireless Ad Hoc network and the wireless sensor network (in the following part, we call wireless network for short). At present, the wireless network obtains rapid development in the aspects of both theory and practice. The wireless network provides the strong power especially as the branch of physical systems (e.g., CPS) and Networking (e.g., IoT). It has been more and more applied directly to information collection of real life. Common applications include agricultural systems, intelligent buildings, security monitoring, military operation, intelligent transportation and other fields.

In the future, wireless networks especially wireless sensor networks will be developed in the following two possible directions.

1. More powerful the sensor device is, more scenarios the wireless sensor network will be used in. It can handle the traffic load which cannot imagine today, can do more computing and can store more data. The battery energy resource is more powerful, so that the lifetime of wireless sensor networks will be longer.
2. Wireless sensor networks, which are designed by nanotechnology, will be brought into the world of another application, and it can be widely used in the environment and geographical conditions that cannot be imagined today.

The two kinds of circumstances above will bring new research challenges.

Our focus is on topology control algorithms of wireless networks.

Topology control is an important technology in wireless networks, whose goal is to effectively utilize energy and extend network lifetime without affecting the important performance of networks such as connectivity and coverage.

Now, there are different definitions and classification methods for the topology control of wireless networks.

Xue Zhang et al. defined the topology control as obtaining an optimized network structure that ensures the quality of the network connectivity and coverage, to prolong the network lifetime as the main target, considering the communication interference, network latency, load balancing, simplicity, reliability, scalability and other performances. The authors divided topology control into power control and sleep scheduling. In addition, there are three other different classification methods. Paolo Santi defined that topology control is a mechanism to coordinate the nodes according to the transmission range, which can generate the network with desired properties, at the same time it can reduce energy consumption, improve the capacity of the network. That is, the topology control is the power control. Miguel A. Labrador et al. presented the definition: topology control is the identification and management of the node parameters and operation mode to revise the topology constantly; the goal is to extend the network lifetime, ensuring the important features (such as network connectivity and coverage). The author divided the topology control into power adjustment and hierarchical topology control. The latest research result of Azrina Abd Aziz et al. provided the definition that topology control is a kind of technology which controls the generation of network parameters and maintains an optimized topology; this topology can reduce the energy consumption, and can obtain the desired network properties. The topology control is divided into power adjustment, power mode and clustering technology.

This book focuses on hierarchical topology control of wireless networks: to present a comprehensive and systemic introduction of hierarchical topology control of wireless networks; to introduce the new classification method of clustering algorithms; to give a detailed introduction of the typical clustering algorithms of each classification, the latest research results and problems needed to be solved; to give a scientific summary on connected dominating set algorithms; to present a general classification of distributed algorithms; to provide a comparative analysis of network simulation tools used in algorithm design; and to give the simulation instances using different simulation tools

This book includes five chapters.

In the first chapter, a brief introduction of wireless networks is provided, and the wireless Ad Hoc network and the sensor network are described in detail.

In Chapter 2, we introduce the concept of topology control of wireless networks, and present the general classification and introduction of classical power control algorithms of wireless networks.

In Chapter 3, we mainly introduce the clustering technology of the hierarchical topology control of wireless networks. A detailed classification of clustering algorithms, the typical clustering algorithms and related research are introduced, presenting the latest clustering algorithm and our own research results, and also putting forward further research problems.

In Chapter 4, we focus on the construction of virtual backbone based on the dominating set of the hierarchical topology control in wireless networks. We begin with the classical construction algorithms of maximal independent set, then successively introduce the important results of connected dominating set under different models and the deformation algorithms. The latest mobility model, interference model, and the partition results of dominating set are provided in detail, which includes the latest research and our own results, and the problems needed further research of related fields. As an important method of constructing the hierarchical topology control, we also supplement the definition and the general design principles of distributed algorithms, the classification of distributed algorithms, emphasizing the important role and the application of the local computation in wireless networks.

The last chapter simply introduces many kinds of simulation tools of wireless networks, presenting the important network simulation tool NS2, with the detailed introduction of typical simulation examples (including source code). Meanwhile, this chapter also introduces how to realize the simulation process of hierarchical topology control using C language and under Java environment. In the end, we give the simulation tool developed by Labrador et al.

This book presents a good example for the design of local distributed algorithms in wireless networks, providing theoretical basis to further study on solving the problem of clustering and dominating set design under more realistic physical models. The problems needed to be solved involving in our book point out the next research direction of this area.

This book is the first monograph on the hierarchical topology control of wireless networks, which can be the textbooks and reference books for the students of computer science and technology, network engineering, communication engineering, electronic engineering, internet of things and others, and the references for graduate students, but also can be used as the reference books for the above related researchers.

I am grateful to my graduated students Nannan Wang, Yingying Qi, Xin Gu, Kang Wang, Wenjun Liu, Qingbo Zhang and other students for their excellent research works. I would like to express my sincere gratitude to my cooperative partners Xiuzhen, Dongxiao and Lu for their hard work. I thank Qufu Normal University, and NSF of China, for offering the support and help of the scientific research.

Especially, I would like to appreciate Richard O'Hanley, the editor and Alexandra Andrejevich, the associate project manager of the book in CRC, for their excellent work.

It should be noted that the book cites a large number of references, we are extremely grateful to all the authors. In addition, due to the space limitations, some important references did not be cited, and we apologize to the authors.

Due to time constraints, coupled with our limited level, the errors of this book are inevitable, we would greatly appreciate the criticism and the corrections of the experts and scholars.

Contact Email: jiguoyu@sina.com.

Jiguo Yu
March 2017

Acknowledgments

The work was supported by NSF of China under Grants 61672321, 61373027, 61602195 and 61771289.

Authors

Jiguo Yu received the PhD degree in School of Mathematics from Shandong University in 2004. From 2007, he has been a professor in the School of Computer Science, Qufu Normal University, Shandong, China. He is currently a professor in the School of Information Science and Engineering, Qufu Normal University. His main research interests include wireless networks, privacy-aware computing, distributed algorithms, peer-to-peer computing and graph theory. In particular, he is interested in designing and analyzing algorithms for many computationally hard problems in networks. He has published 100+ papers including top journals and conferences such as IEEE/ACM Transactions on Networking, IEEE Transactions on Vehicular Technology, IEEE Internet of Things Journal, IEEE Transactions on Big Data, IEEE Transaction on Cloud Computing, IEEE INFOCOM, IEEE ICDCS and so on. He is an editor of Journal of Network and Computer Applications and International Journal of Sensor Networks, and a senior member of IEEE and CCF (China Computer Federation).

Xiuzhen Cheng received the MS and PhD degrees in computer science from the University of Minnesota–Twin Cities, Minneapolis, MN, USA, in 2000 and 2002, respectively. She is a Professor with the Department of Computer Science, The George Washington University, Washington, DC, USA. She was a Program Director for the U.S. National Science Foundation in 2006 for six months (full time) and from 2008 to 2010 (part time). She has authored or co-authored over 200 peer-reviewed papers. Her current research interests include Fog computing, privacy-aware computing, mobile handset networking systems (mobile health and safety), wireless and mobile security, smart cyber-physical systems, and algorithm design and analysis. Dr. Cheng is the Founder and the Steering Committee Co-Chair of the International Conference on Wireless Algorithms, Systems, and Applications (WASA, launched in 2006), and the Co-Founder of the IEEE Symposium on Privacy-Aware Computing (PAC, launched in 2017). She has served on the Editorial Boards of several technical journals such as the IEEE Transactions on Parallel and Distributed Systems and IEEE Wireless Communications and on the Technical Program Committees of various professional conferences/workshops such as ACM MobiHoc, MobiCom, ACM MobiSys, IEEE INFOCOM, IEEE ICDCS,

IEEE ICC, and IEEE/ACM IWQoS. She has also chaired several international conferences such as IEEE CNS and WASA. She is a fellow of the IEEE.

Honglu Jiang received her BS and MS degrees in computer science from Qufu Normal University in 2009 and 2012, respectively. She is currently a PhD Candidate in Qufu Normal University. She is also an engineer in Shandong Polytechnic. Her research interests include wireless networks, distributed computing and privacy-aware preserving.

Dongxiao Yu received the BSc in 2006 in the School of Mathematics from Shandong University, and the PhD degree in 2014 from the Department of Computer Science, The University of Hong Kong, respectively. He is currently an Associate Professor with the School of Computer Science and Technology, Huazhong University of Science and Technology. His research interests include wireless networks and distributed computing. He has published 50+ papers including top journals and conferences such as IEEE/ACM Transactions on Networking, IEEE Transactions on Parallel and Distributed Systems, IEEE INFOCOM, IEEE ICDCS, ACM PODC, IEEE IPDPS and so on.

Chapter 1

Wireless Networks

1.1 Introduction

1.1.1 Introduction to Wireless Networks

The wireless network includes global voice and data networks that allow users to establish long-range wireless connections, as well as infrared and radio frequency (RF) technologies optimized for short-range wireless communication. The uses of wireless and wired networks are very similar. The biggest difference between wireless networks and wired networks is in the different transmission media. Wireless networks use radio technology instead of network cable, but the wireless network can be a backup for wired networks.

A wireless network is designed to construct a ubiquitous computing environment that truly realizes 6As: anyone can use a wireless network at any time, at any location by any means with any other person for anything. Wireless network technology is the core technology for achieving the 6As dream—mobile computing and ubiquitous computing (Figure 1.1).

1.1.1.1 Development History of Wireless Networks

The origins of wireless networks can be traced back to World War II, when the US Army used radio signals to transmit data. The Army developed a set of radio transmission technologies, using encryption technology with high intensity, which was widely used in both the US military and the allied military. In 1971, researchers at the University of Hawaii created the first radio communication network based on the packet technology. This is called the **ALOHAnet**, also known as the **ALOHA system** or simply **ALOHA**; it was a pioneering computer networking system

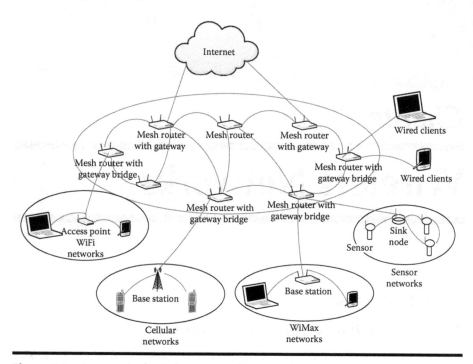

Figure 1.1   A canonical wireless network.

developed at the University of Hawaii. ALOHA originally stood for Additive Links On-line Hawaii Area. Generally, we call it ALOHAnet directly.

The ALOHAnet can be regarded as the wireless local area network (WLAN) of the early stage. It includes seven computers that use a bidirectional star topology across four Hawaiian Islands, while the central computer is put on the Oahu Island. From that point, the wireless network can be said to be officially born.

1. First-generation (1G) mobile communication system

   The simulative cellular mobile communication system was born in the 1970s. The 1G system uses the analog signal transmission mode to achieve voice service, using frequency division multiple access (FDMA) technology to divide the channel.

   Representative: The mobile phone system "Advanced Mobile Phone Service" (AMPS) was first scheduled to commence commercial service in 1983; it was developed by AT&T Bell Labs in the United States in 1976. In the AMPS, the communication area is divided into hexagonal cells, called "One Cell" (10–20 km), with a low-power radio base station, as shown in Figure 1.2. The base station is linked to the mobile telephone switching center and then linked with the local public center network or another mobile telephone switching center, which completes the call link.

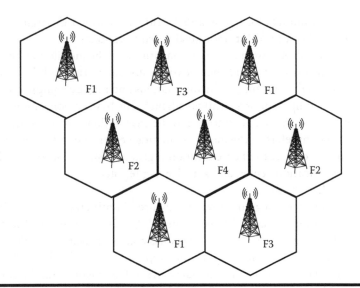

Figure 1.2   Hexagonal honey comb.

The process of making mobile subscriber calls is as follows: the user requests the channel from the base station. The base station assigns the idle channel to the user if there is an idle channel at this time. When the mobile phone in the talking state is handed over, the switching center notifies the new cellular structure to take over this mobile phone and then selects one available channel, so that the call will not be interrupted. When the roaming phenomenon occurs (i.e., a move to another cellular structure that does not belong to the supervision of unified switching center), the new switching center will be responsible for establishing communication connection.

2. Second-generation (2G) mobile communication network

Since the 1G system has deficiencies such as low spectrum efficiency, poor voice quality, low access capacity, poor security, and no data communication services, it has been replaced by a digital cellular mobile communication system, forming the 2G mobile communication network.

The 2G mobile communication system currently has two major mobile communication standards: global system for mobile communication (GSM) and code division multiple access (CDMA) system. At present, the mainstream technology of global mobile communication among them is the digital mobile phone system.

Representative: GSM of digital cellular mobile communication standard and CDMA.

1. GSM communication

GSM was jointly developed in 1990 by the European Conference of Postal and Telecommunications Administrations and the European

Telecommunications Standards Institute, for which the signal transmission is the same as for traditional wired telephones.

The GSM system is mainly constituted by the mobile station, the base station subsystem, and the network subsystem. The mobile station may be a portable station or vehicular stations and may be equipped with a terminal equipment or a terminal adapter. The base station subsystem refers to the base transceiver station and the base station controller; the network subsystem refers to the mobile switching center, the operation and maintenance center, the home location registers, visiting location register, an authentication center, and a device flag register.

2. CDMA system

CDMA technology has been widely used in military anti-jamming communication research. In November 1989, Qualcomm's field tests in the United States proved that CDMA has a large capacity for cellular mobile communications, making it a hot topic in the world. In 1995, CDMA public network entered commercial use in Hong Kong and the US. Global CDMA users had reached more than 5 million by 1998 and 20 million by 1999. China's CDMA development was not behind with its long-term military research and technology accumulation; 863 national programs of CDMA cellular technology research had been carried out by 1993.

At present, the international common CDMA standard is the IS series of standards mainly developed and promulgated by the American National Standards Institute and the Telecommunications Industry Association. The Telecommunications System Bulletin file, increased to 14.4 kb/s rate group on the basis of IS95A, assigned or switched to the personal conference standard, 1900 MHz, band, and so on.

3. Third-generation (3G) cellular mobile networks

The International Telecommunications Union (ITU) put forward the third generation (3G) mobile communication prototype as early as 1985. Therefore, the uniform standard and frequency band, improving the spectrum efficiency and supporting multimedia mobile communication, is the main difference between 3G mobile communication and 2G. Broadband Wideband Code Division Multiple Access (WCDMA) proposed in Europe uses the frequency division duplex channel. The supporters of WCDMA are mainly in Europe and Japan, as well as in the GSM network operators and manufacturers. The WCDMA can gradually change over to 3G mobile communication based on the existing GSM via General Packet Radio Service (GPRS). The ITU proposed the concept of the 3G mobile communication system in 1985 and named it the "Future Public Land Mobile Telecommunication System." In 1996, the ITU changed its name to "International Mobile Telecommunications-2000" (IMT-2000).

The 3G technology works in 2000 MHz, with a maximum transmission rate of 2000 kbps, which entered commercial use in 2000.

1. Functions of 3G: To support the broadband digital mobile network with voice data integration and mobile multimedia services. To provide higher capacity and faster data transmission rate and achieve the integration of mobile phones, the Internet, computers, and a variety of household appliances. To provide mobile network, video on demand (VOD), videophone, distance education, and other personalized, global, and multimedia communication services. It constitutes four function subsystems: core network (CN), radio access network (RAN), mobile station (MS), and user identification module, in which the CN and the RAN are the important contents of the 3G mobile communication systems.

2. Main features of 3G: It integrates the functions of cellular, cordless communication, paging, clustering, wireless spread spectrum, wireless access, mobile data, mobile satellite, personal communication, and other mobile communications. It provides high-quality service compatible with fixed telecommunication networks, supporting for low-rate voice and data services, and asymmetric data transmission. The three major services of mobility, interaction, and distribution can be realized through the connection of global satellite network from micro microcell, to microcell, then to macrocell, until it reaches the point of "anytime, anywhere."

3. The main standard of 3G is IMT-2000 CDMA-DS (Direct-Spread Spectrum (DSSS) CDMA technology), WCDMA, which can directly spread the signal within the frequency bandwidth of 5 M, jointly submitted by Europe and Japan; IMT-2000 CDMA-multi-carrier (MC), CDMA2000, was submitted by the US technology companies represented by Qualcomm that a number of 1.25 M narrowband DSSS systems are assembled into a broadband system; IMT-2000 CDMA-time division duplex (TDD), TD-SCDMA, proposed by China Datang Telecom, is the only 3G communication standard approved by ITU based on TDD.

4. Fourth-generation (4G) mobile communication system
   While the world's major network operators were planning the next-generation network, the Nordic TeliaSonera first completed the 4G (fourth-generation) network construction using Long-Term Evolution (LTE) technology and began to provide 4G service in the Swedish capital, Stockholm, and the Norwegian capital, Oslo, which is the first official commercial 4G network worldwide. The LTE project is the evolution of 3G; it improves and enhances the 3G air access technology, using orthogonal frequency division multiplexing (OFDM) and multiple-input, multiple-output (MIMO) as the only standard of the evolution of wireless networks.

   China Mobile also invested about 180 billion Yuan to start a comprehensive 4G network construction in mid-2012. It includes the equipment procurement for TD-LTE (China's 4G technical standards) in 100 cities of China in 2013. The size of the completion of TD-LTE base stations is more than 200,000. That is, 180,000 new base stations were constructed in 2013.

4G mobile communication is the ideal mode for supporting high-speed data (2–20 Mb/s) connection, also known as the broadband access and distribution network, with an asymmetric data transmission capacity of more than 2 Mb/s and an automatic switching capability of different rates from 2 to 100 Mb/s.

The 4G mobile communication system is a multifunction integrated broadband mobile communication system, which is different from the 3G system in terms of service, function, and frequency band. It provides wireless services in different fixed and wireless platforms and network operation across different frequency bands, which is closer to personal communication than the 3G mobile communication.

The 4G mobile communication technology can increase the Internet speed to 50 times greater than 3G mobile technology and can achieve three-dimensional image transmission of high quality. The information transmission series of the 4G mobile communication technology is one level higher than the 3G mobile communication technology. The use efficiency of wireless frequency is much higher than that in the 2G and 3G systems, with better anti-signal fading performance. In addition to high-speed information transmission technology, it includes a high-speed mobile wireless information access system, the pull technology of mobile platform, encryption technology, and inter-terminal communication technology with high security. The 4G terminals can also be used for positioning, alarm, and so on.

The 4G system can automatically manage and dynamically change its structure to meet the system changes and requirements of development. Users may use a variety of mobile devices to access the 4G system. Several different access systems combine into a common platform; the systems can complement each other to meet different business requirements. While mobile network services tend to be diversified, they ultimately will evolve and become a bridge for communication in multiple industries, sectors, and societies.

Prior to the deployment of 4G communication network systems, most of the global wireless infrastructure was built on the 3G mobile communication system. Many of the world's wireless infrastructures would have to go through a significant amount of change and updates if they were to migrate to 4G communication technologies. So far, 4G technology has not been universally used, and the 3G technology still has a longer life cycle. The LTE technology is seen as an extension of the 3G technology.

1.1.1.2 Standards for Wireless Networks

The common standards for wireless networks are as follows:

IEEE 802.11a: It uses the 5 GHz frequency band, with the transmission speed of 54 Mbps, and is not compatible with 802.11b.

IEEE 802.11b: It uses the 2.4 GHz frequency band, with the transmission speed of 11 Mbps.

IEEE 802.11g: It uses the 2.4 GHz frequency band, with the transmission speed of 54 Mbps, and is compatible with 802.11b.

IEEE 802.11n draft: It uses the 2.4 GHz frequency band, with the transmission speed of up to 300 Mbps. The current standard is still the draft, but the product has emerged in an endless stream.

IEEE 802.11b is currently the most commonly used, but 802.11g has the ability to be the next generation of IEEE standard. The 802.11n is also in rapid development.

The standard of IEEE 802.11b contains two parts that ensure access control and encryption, which must be configured on each device in the wireless local area network (LAN). Companies with hundreds of WLAN users need reliable security solutions that can be managed from a single control center. The lack of centralized security control is the fundamental reason WLANs are used only in relatively small businesses and specific applications.

The standard of IEEE 802.11b defines two mechanisms to provide access control and privacy for WLANs: Service Set Identifier (SSID) and Wired Equivalent Privacy (WEP). There is also a mechanism for encryption through a transparent virtual private network running on a WLAN.

The feature commonly used in WLAN is that SSID is a named number that provides access control at a low level. The SSID typically is the network name of the device in the WLAN subsystem that is used to split the subsystem locally.

The standard of IEEE802.11b stipulates a kind of optional encryption scheme called WEP (Wired Equivalent Privacy), which provides a mechanism to ensure data flow of WLAN. WEP uses a symmetric scheme that uses the same key and algorithm for encrypting and decrypting data.

1.1.2 Classification of Wireless Networks

As shown in Figure 1.3, we classify the wireless network based on its infrastructure.

The infrastructure-based wireless network can be divided into wireless personal area network (WPAN), wireless metropolitan area network (WMAN), WLAN, and wireless wide area network (WWAN).

1. Wireless personal area network

    WPAN is a new wireless communication network technology that is proposed to realize wireless and seamless rich service in a small radius for specific groups. It can effectively solve the problem of "last few meters of cable," allowing the network to carry through to the end.

    WPAN is a wireless network that ranks with the WWAN, WMAN, and WLAN with a relatively small coverage area. In the network structure, WPAN is located at the end of the entire network chain to achieve the connection

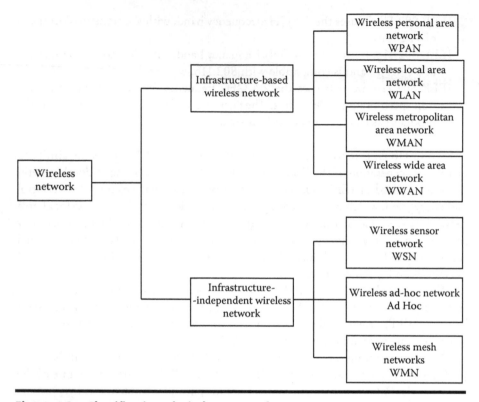

Figure 1.3 **Classification of wireless networks.**

between terminals in the same location, such as connecting a phone and a Bluetooth headset. The coverage of WPAN is generally within the scope of 10 m, which must be run in the licensed wireless band. WPAN devices are inexpensive, small, and easy to operate, and have low power consumption.

The key technologies of WPAN are Bluetooth (Blue Tooth), Infrared Data Association (IrDA), home radio frequency (HomeRF), ultra wideband (UWB), and Zigbee.

2. Wireless local area network

WLAN is a wireless network, communicating by wireless media in a local area, working in the 2.4 or 5 GHz band. It is a convenient data transmission system that uses RF technology to replace the LAN formed by an old twisted-pair copper (coaxial), so that the WLAN can make use of a simple access architecture to allow users to use it to achieve the ideal state of Information portable, convenient to walk the world.

The WLAN includes WMAN and WPAN (Table 1.1).

3. Wireless metropolitan area network

WMAN provides an Internet-oriented high-speed connection to a metropolitan area. As the 802.11 standard for WLAN, IEEE launched the 802.16

Table 1.1 Several Common Standards of 802.11 WLAN

Standard	Brand	Data Rate	Physical Layer	Advantages and Disadvantages
802.11b	2.4 GHz	Up to 11 Mb/s	HR-DSSS	The highest data rate is lower with the lowest price and the furthest signal transmission distance and is not easily hindered.
802.11a	5 GHZ	Up to 54 Mb/s	OFDM	The highest data rate is higher supporting more users online at the same time, with the highest price and shorter signal transmission distance; can easily be hindered.
802.11g	2.4 GHz	Up to 54 Mb/s	OFDM	The highest data rate is highest supporting more users online at the same time, with moderate price and longest signal transmission distance; not easily hindered.

standard for the WMAN, while the industry has also set up a worldwide interoperability for microwave access (WiMAX) forum similar to the WiMAX alliance.

The promotion of WMANs is to meet the growing market demand for broadband wireless access (BWA). Although 802.11x technology has been used and obtained great success in BWA for many years with many other proprietary technologies, the overall design of the WLAN and the features are not well suited for outdoor applications of BWA. When it is used outdoors, the bandwidth and the number of users are limited, and there are other issues such as communication distance. Based on this, the IEEE decided to develop a new and more complex global standard that should solve the problems of both the physical layer and quality of service (QoS) aspects to meet the BWA and the needs of the "last mile" access market (Figure 1.4). The **last mile** refers to the portion of the telecommunications network chain that physically reaches the end-user's premises.

4. Wireless wide area network
   WWAN refers to the wireless network covering national or global scope providing a wider range of wireless access. Compared with WPAN, WLAN

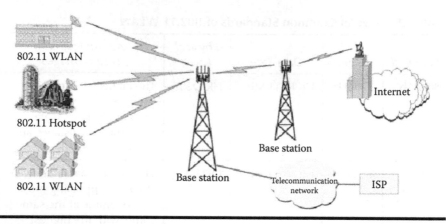

Figure 1.4 The structure of WMAN.

and WMAN, it emphasizes fast mobility with the transmission rate of about 3 Mbps. IEEE802.20 is an important standard for WWAN.

WWAN adopts communication that connects the LAN to extremely dispersed physical locations using wireless networks. WWAN connections are geographically larger, often covering a country or a continent. Their purpose is to allow the interconnection of distributed LAN, whose structure is divided into a terminal system (the user set of two terminals) and a communication system (the intermediate link).

Infrastructure-independent wireless networks can be divided into wireless ad hoc networks, wireless sensor networks (WSNs), and wireless mesh networks (WMNs).

1. Wireless ad hoc network (ad hoc)
   A mobile ad hoc network (MANET) consists of a group of wireless mobile nodes. It can be used rapidly without the existing fixed communication network infrastructure. It is a self-organizing, self-healing network requiring minimum human intervention and no central entity. Network nodes cooperate with each other through the wireless link to communicate, exchange information, and share the information and services. Network nodes are able to enter and leave the network dynamically, arbitrarily, and frequently, without prior warning or notification and without disrupting the communication of other nodes in the network.

   Different from the technology of traditional wireless communication networks, wireless self-organizing networks do not need to support fixed equipment. In ad hoc work, the node working as the user terminal is self-networking and communicates with other user nodes for data forwarding. This kind of network form breaks through the geographical limitation of the traditional wireless cellular network and can be deployed more quickly, conveniently, and efficiently. It is also suitable for the communication needs of some emergency situations, such as individual soldier communication systems on the battlefield. However, wireless ad hoc networks are also limited by the network bandwidth, poor support for real-time services, and low security. The ad hoc network is the foundation and predecessor of the WSN and WMN.

2. Wireless sensor network

WSN is a wireless network composed of a large number of stationary or mobile sensors in the form of self-organization and multihop. The goal is to collaboratively sense, collect, process, and transmit the monitoring information of the sensing objects in the geographic coverage area of the network. A large number of sensor nodes will probe the data through the aggregation node and send it to the user through other networks.

3. Wireless mesh network

WMN is a special form of ad hoc network; its early research is derived from the research and development of the mobile ad hoc network (MANET). It is a high-capacity and high-speed distributed network, which is different from the traditional wireless network. It can be regarded as a fusion of WLAN and an ad hoc network and produce the advantages of both. It also can solve the bottleneck problem of the new network structure. WMAN is written in the standards of IEEE802.16 WMAN.

In the wireless network technology, the most important research is on the wireless ad hoc network, WSN, and WMN at present.

In the remainder of this chapter, we will focus on wireless ad hoc networks and WSNs.

1.2 Wireless Ad Hoc Network

1.2.1 Introduction to Wireless Ad Hoc Networks

"Ad hoc" comes from Latin, meaning "for this" and "for this purpose only." The literal meaning is "for a specific purpose or occasion" or "only for this case." The ad hoc network is the foundation and predecessor of WSN and WMN.

According to the definition of IEEE, the ad hoc network is a special wireless mobile network with the characteristics of self-organization, peer to peer, and multihop, and is also known as a mobile ad hoc network (MANET). MANETs can work independently or with an Internet or cellular wireless network. In the latter case, a MANET is usually connected to an existing network in the form of a terminal subnet (stump network). Taking into account the limitations of bandwidth and power, MANETs are generally not suitable as intermediate transmission networks, which only allow the information generated or destined for the internal nodes of the network to enter and exit; other information is not able to travel through the network. Thus, it greatly reduces the routing overhead of the existing Internet interworking. Figure 1.5 is a simple ad hoc network consisting of three nodes.

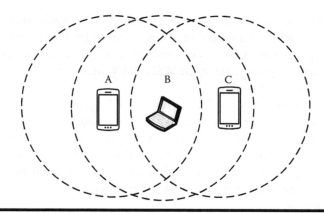

Figure 1.5 A simple ad hoc network.

Host C is not within the wireless coverage of host A (represented by a ring around host A), and host A is not within the range of host C's wireless coverage. If hosts A and C need to exchange information, they need host B to forward their packets. Because host B is within the wireless coverage of hosts A and C, host B serves as a router for the communication between hosts A and C.

As mentioned previously, the wireless network can be divided into an infrastructure-based wireless network and an infrastructure-independent wireless network. Thereinto, an infrastructure-based mobile wireless network has a fixed wired gateway, bridging the mobile terminal through the base station. When the mobile terminal strides across the wireless coverage area of a certain base station, it is connected with another adjacent base station by switching the mode so as to realize seamless communication of the whole network. As the base station and the mobile terminal are only one hop distance, the infrastructure-based mobile wireless network is also known as a single-hop wireless network such as cellular digital packet data (CDPD), general packet radio service (GPRS), wireless Asynchronous Transfer Mode (ATM), and mobile Internet protocol (IP).

Figure 1.6 shows a typical single-hop wireless network (GSM network). As shown in the figure, the source and destination users (mobile phones) are connected to the nearest base station by wireless means. The two base stations connect to the public telephone network through their own switching subnetworks and establish the contact channel between two terminal users, whereby two terminal users can make a call. In this system, each terminal only connects with the base station closest to itself; this is called a single-hop wireless network.

Infrastructure-independent mobile wireless networks do not have a fixed gateway and router, and the node itself has the function of routing and maintenance, so that all mobile terminals can be dynamically added to and leave the network. In the infrastructure-independent mobile wireless network, due to the limited wireless transmission range, two nodes that cannot communicate directly need to use multiple intermediate nodes for relaying communication, so this type of network

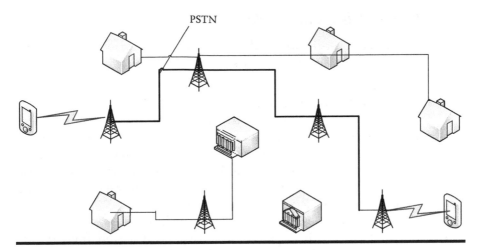

Figure 1.6   A diagram of single-hop wireless network.

is called a multihop wireless network or MANET. The nodes of an ad hoc network coordinate and realize self-organization and self-running through the layered network protocol and distributed algorithm. It is also called a multihop wireless network, self-organized network, or an infrastructure-independent network.

Figure 1.7 shows a typical structure of a MANET. The nodes of the network can be notebook computers with wireless interface, PDAs, smartphones, and other mobile terminals. Each node has an equal status, which can be seen from the figure. There is no central control node, and the nodes are connected by a wireless channel. The topology of the network changes dynamically with the movement of the nodes. The nodes in the network have the function of host and router at the same time. As a host, they should complete human–computer interaction tasks; as a router, they run routing protocols for routing discovery and routing maintenance. As the wireless transmission range of nodes is limited, two wireless nodes that cannot communicate directly achieve communication through the relay nodes. As shown in Figure 1.7, the communication between source A and destination F relies on the multihop mechanism.

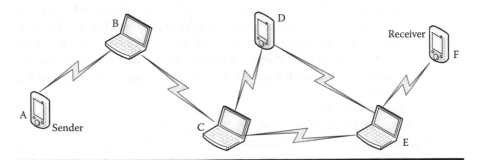

Figure 1.7   A diagram of multihop MANET.

1.2.2 Characteristics of Ad Hoc Networks

Compared with other traditional wireless networks and fixed networks, ad hoc networks have the following characteristics.

1. They are centerless and have an automatic configuration.

   The ad hoc network has no central structure, and there is no absolute control center in the network. The user terminals in the ad hoc network have independent routing and host functions. In the cellular mobile communication system, there are many centralized entities, such as base stations and mobile switching centers. Without the preexisting network infrastructure, all nodes are equal in status. So, it is called a peer-to-peer network.

2. They have a dynamically changing network topology.

   The network topology is a logical view of the physical network from the perspective of the network layer. In the MANET, the mobile user terminal can be randomly moved in the network, as can the power change of wireless transmitters, interference factors of wireless channel, terrain, and other factors. So the network topology formed by the mobile terminals through the wireless channels may change at any time, and the way and speed of changes are difficult to predict. It is specifically reflected by the increase or disappearance of the mobile terminal nodes, the increase or disappearance of the wireless channel, and the segmentation and merging of the network topology structure. For the traditional wired network, the network topology has more stable performance.

3. They share characteristics of wireless transmission.

   The ad hoc network uses the wireless transmission technology. Due to the characteristics of the wireless channel itself, the provided network bandwidth is much lower than the cable channel, and the quality of the wireless channel is poor. The traditional shared channel is one-hop-shared, while the sending power of the nodes in the ad hoc network is limited. The channel is shared by multiple hops: the sending of a node can be heard only by its one-hop neighbors; the nodes outside this range are not aware. This feature improves the spatial reuse of the channel, and, on the other hand, the collision of the message is related to the geographical position of nodes. In addition, there may exist unidirectional links between nodes. That is to say, node A can send packets to node B successfully. However, node A may not receive the packets sent by node B because the coverage range of the two nodes is not the same.

4. They have multihop routing.

   As the transmission power of the mobile terminal is not very large, the coverage of one single node is limited. When it communicates with the nodes outside its coverage area, it needs the intermediate nodes to forward, that is, it needs to go through multiple hops. Unlike the ordinary network, the forwarding in the ad hoc network is done by the normal nodes, not by a dedicated routing device (such as a router). That is to say, in an ad hoc network, each node has the functions of both the host and the router. It needs to run the corresponding routing protocol to participate in packet forwarding and route maintenance according to routing policies and routing information. Conversely, if multihop routing can be used, the transmit power of the node can be very low, thus saving energy.

5. They share the limitations of mobile terminals.

Usually personal digital assistants (PDAs), notebook computers, are the main forms of wireless terminals in ad hoc networks. Relative to desktops, their inherent characteristics include that the energy relying on the battery can be exhausted, they have small memory and low performance, they have the benefits of mobility and smartness, and they are lightweight, among others. They bring a certain degree of difficulty in the application, development, and promotion of the programming. What's more, smaller peripherals such as the screen are not conducive to carrying out more complex business. Also, in view of cost and portability, a mobile node cannot be equipped with too many wireless transceivers; it generally relies on the battery power with limited energy.

6. They have poor security.

The ad hoc network is a special kind of wireless mobile network. It is more vulnerable to network attacks such as passive eavesdropping, active intrusion, and denial of service due to the wireless channel, limited power, and distributed control technology. The wireless link makes the ad hoc network vulnerable to attacks of link layer, including passive eavesdropping and active counterfeiting, information replay, and information destruction. Nodes roaming in a hostile environment (such as the battlefield) lack physical protection, so the network is vulnerable to the attacks of the leaked internal nodes and external nodes. The topology and membership of the network are often changed, and the trust relationship between the nodes often changes as well.

7. They have limited wireless transmission bandwidth.

The ad hoc network uses the wireless transmission technology as the underlying means of communication. Due to the physical characteristics of the wireless channel itself, it can provide much lower network bandwidth than the cable channel. In addition, there are many factors, such as collision, signal attenuation, noise, and interference between channels, that make the actual bandwidth of the mobile terminal far less than the theoretical maximum bandwidth, changing with time dynamically.

8. They have a short network lifetime.

The ad hoc network lifetime is short compared to that of the fixed network. The differences between ad hoc networks and traditional networks are summarized in Table 1.2.

Table 1.2   The Differences between Ad Hoc Networks and Traditional Networks

Comparison/Network type	Traditional Network	Ad Hoc Network
Infrastructure	Yes	No
Node ability	Strong	Weak
Network survivability	Low	High
Configuration speed	Slow	Fast
Network flexibility	Bad	Good
Control mode	Centralized	Distributed
Energy supply	Sufficient	Limited
Route selection/maintenance	Simple	Difficult
Communication reliability	Reliable	No guarantee
Node reliability	Reliable	Suspicious
Network topology	Fixed	Dynamic
Communication mode	Fixed	Peer to peer
Communication forwarding	Center, one-hop	Centerless, multihop
Transmission equipment and media	Base station and wired network	Node and wireless network

1.2.3 The Structure of the Nodes in Ad Hoc Networks

The nodes of ad hoc networks and the nodes of general networks are very different, in addition to the functions of ordinary nodes, which also have the function of the router.

Each node of the ad hoc network can be roughly divided into three parts: host, router, and radio. The host will complete the general function of mobile terminals, including human–machine interface and data processing applications. The router part is mainly responsible for maintaining the network topology and routing information to complete the message forwarding. The radio section provides wireless channel support for information transmission.

In view of the physical structure, ad hoc network nodes can be divided into the following categories: single-host single radio, single-host multiradio, and multihost single/multiradio (Figure 1.8).

The most important feature of a single-host single radio is the simple structure, so the general handset uses such structure.

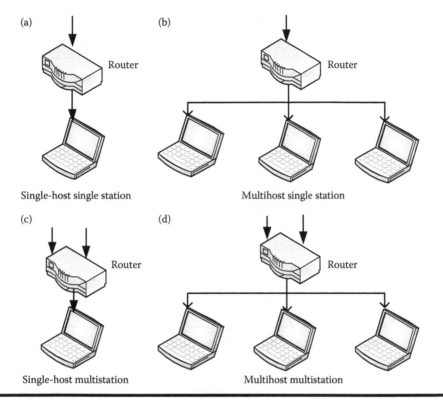

Figure 1.8   A diagram of ad hoc network nodes.

Single-host multiradio structure is more complex than the former. It needs to set up relay nodes to interconnect in two or more networks.

Multihost single/multistation nodes may include multiple hosts. Multiple hosts share one or more stations whose direct benefit is its use in building an overlay type of network. It can also be used as a gateway node to interconnect multiple ad hoc networks and to access other networks.

1.2.4 The Architecture of Ad Hoc Networks

Ad hoc networks have more special properties and characteristics than the past networks. Therefore, distributed control is often used for networking, and each node in the network has a self-organizing function. The feature of distributed control means that the control function of the original network is distributed to multiple nodes or even all nodes in the autonomous network. The self-organizing function of the ad hoc networks means that the nodes can automatically sense changes in the network topology, so as to adaptively modify the original routing information and working parameters, to achieve the network's self-management and self-control.

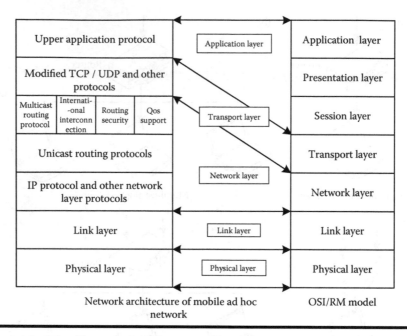

Upper application protocol	Application layer	Application layer
Modified TCP / UDP and other protocols		Presentation layer
Multicast routing protocol / Internati-onal interconnection / Routing security / Qos support	Transport layer	Session layer
Unicast routing protocols		Transport layer
IP protocol and other network layer protocols	Network layer	Network layer
Link layer	Link layer	Link layer
Physical layer	Physical layer	Physical layer
Network architecture of mobile ad hoc network		OSI/RM model

Figure 1.9   The diagram of ad hoc network structure.

The ad hoc network architecture can generally be divided into five layers: physical layer, data link layer, network layer, transport layer, and application layer. Their specific distinction and the corresponding relationship with the transmission control protocol/Internet protocol (TCP/IP) system are shown in Figure 1.9.

1. Physical layer
   In the architecture of the ad hoc network, the physical layer provides a physical connection for the wireless transmission access control through the transmission medium of wireless communication. It completes the encoding and decoding of the wireless signal and carries out the signal transmission and reception. The main functions include channel discrimination and selection, wireless signal monitoring, modulation/demodulation, and so on. Because of multipath fading caused by multipath propagation, intersymbol interference, and interference caused by spatial broadcast characteristics of wireless transmission, the bandwidth capacity of transmission link in an ad hoc network is reduced. Therefore, the design goal of the physical layer is to overcome the transmission loss of wireless media with relatively low loss of function, to obtain a larger link capacity. To achieve the design goals of the physical layer mentioned previously, the key technologies commonly used include modulation and demodulation, channel coding, multiantennae, adaptive power control, and adaptive rate control.

2. Data link layer

   The data link layer of the ad hoc network can be divided into two sublayers: the logical link control (LLC) sublayer and the media access control (MAC) sublayer. The data link layer mainly provides reliable and error-free data information for the network layer. It establishes, maintains, and removes one or more data links with no transmission errors between the two layers. The LLC sublayer has nothing to do with the media. Its main functions are to provide addressing, sorting, error control, and flow control.

   The MAC sublayer provides the function of media access control, which includes two parts: (1) the division of the channel, that is, how to divide the spectrum of different channels, and (2) channel allocation, that is, how the channel is assigned to different users. We can use the random access mechanism (carrier sense multiple access (CSMA), IEEE802.11), access mechanism based on channel partitioning (time division multiple access (TDMA), frequency division multiple access (FDMA), code division multiple access (CDMA), or space division multiple access (SDMA)), and channel partitioning. The token ring mechanism can be adopted when traffic is heavy. In ad hoc networks, exposed terminals and hidden terminals must be overcome.

3. Network layer

   The network layer is the key point of the ad hoc network. The main functions include neighbor discovery, packet routing, congestion control, and internetworking. The routing protocol is the main function of the network layer. The role of the routing protocol is to discover and maintain the route to the destination node. The unicast routing protocol is responsible for maintaining the routing table and keeping it consistent with the current topology. The multicast routing protocol provides the underlying support for group communication. International interconnection can bridge the ad hoc network and the existing network, expanding the coverage and application range of the existing network.

4. Transport layer

   The transport layer of the ad hoc network is based on the transport layer in wired networks. The TCP/user datagram protocol (UDP) is modified based on wireless environments to adapt and complete the function of transmission. The transport layer mainly provides reliable end-to-end services for the application layer, isolating the upper layers from the lower layers and efficiently utilizing the network resources according to the characteristics of the network layer. Traditional TCP will make the loss of ad hoc network packets very serious. Concerning wireless error and node mobility, all packet loss is attributed to congestion; thus congestion control and avoidance algorithms were created. The direct use of TCP protocol will lead to the unnecessary reduction of end-to-end throughput. Therefore, the traditional TCP must be improved.

5. Application layer

   The application layer of the ad hoc network specifies various types of services, including real-time applications (emergency control information) with strict latency and loss rate limits, and datagram services without any guarantees of service quality. In practical applications, a variety of protocols and standards of the application layer can be used. Ad hoc network-based services are the same as in other types of networks, mainly including traditional services and data services, which require the ad hoc network to consider practical issues when providing business services.

1.2.5 The Application of Ad Hoc Networks

The application field of ad hoc networks is distinguished from ordinary communication networks. Ad hoc networks are suitable for situations in which it is not possible or easy to prepopulate the network infrastructure or the network needs to be deployed quickly. The self-organization of ad hoc networks provides the possibility of deploying networks and communicating immediately in a special environment. The forwarding characteristics of multihop and intermediate nodes can keep the network coverage unchanged and reduce the transmission power of each terminal, so that the mobile terminal can be increasingly miniaturized to achieve energy savings. In the short term, military communications will continue to be the focus of technology applications in the ad hoc network. To allow the ad hoc network to be widely used in the civil field, it is necessary to find a suitable place to show its characteristics. As part of the application of ad hoc networks, we will introduce the applications in the WSN.

1.3 Wireless Sensor Network

1.3.1 Introduction to the WSN

Advances in microelectronics, computing, and wireless communications led to the rapid development of low-power multifunctional sensors that can integrate information acquisition, data processing, and wireless communications in a small space, and thus WSN emerged. WSN is a multihop self-organizing network system formed by a large number of inexpensive micro-sensor nodes deployed in the monitoring area. The purpose of WSN is to cooperatively sense, collect, and process the information of objects in the covering area and then launch it to the observers. Sensors, sensing objects, and observers constitute a sensor network. WSN is an interdisciplinary research field involving sensor technology, computer network technology, wireless transmission technology, distributed information processing technology, microelectronics manufacturing technology, software programming technology, and so on; it has distinct characteristics of interdisciplinary research. The technology in the military and civil fields has important application prospects, which will have a significant impact on the political, military, and industrial development of countries. *Bloomberg Businessweek* and the *MIT*

Technology Review consider the WSN one of the most influential technologies in the twenty-first century and one of the top 10 technologies to change the world, in a report predicting future technology developments. Sensor networks, plastic electronics, and bionic human organs are also known as the future of the three major high-tech industries.

With the rapid development of communication technology, embedded computing technology, and sensor technology, a variety of micro-sensors with the ability of perception, computing power, and communication have been developed. The fact that the WSN is composed of many micro-sensors raised a major concern. WSN integrates the sensor technology, embedded computing technology, distributed information processing technology, and communication technology, which can collaborate with real-time monitoring, sensing, and collecting information of various environments or monitoring objects in the distribution area. This information is then processed to be more detailed and accurate, which is sent to the users. WSNs enable people to access a large amount of detailed and reliable information about the physical world at any time and place and under any environmental condition, which can be widely used in military operation, country security, environmental monitoring, traffic management, medical and health fields, the manufacturing industry, the monitoring of terrorism and disaster, and other fields. The WSN is a revolution in information perception and acquisition, which plays a key role in the new generation network.

In 2003, the US National Science Foundation established a WSN research program and invested 34 million dollars to support relevant fundamental theory research. The US Department of Defense and the military give the WSN high priority and consider it an important research area; they have set up a series of research projects. Intel, Microsoft, and other information industry giants have also set up or started the corresponding action plan; many countries in the world, including China, have started research in this field.

1.3.2 The Structure of Nodes in WSNs

1. Sensor node structure
   Some of the sensor nodes in modern applications are shown in Figure 1.10.
   Sensor nodes are generally composed of four parts: sensor module, processor module (calculation module), wireless communication module (RF module), and energy module, which are as shown in Figure 1.11. The processor module includes an analog-to-digital conversion module, a data processing module, and a data storage module. The brief introduction is as follows:
   Sensor module: It is used for information awareness. All the sensing nodes in the network should use this module to realize the data acquisition of environment information.
   Analog-to-digital conversion module: It transforms the perception of analog into data for subsequent data processing, storage, and forwarding.

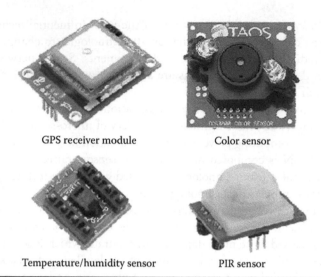

GPS receiver module   Color sensor

Temperature/humidity sensor   PIR sensor

Figure 1.10   Common sensor nodes.

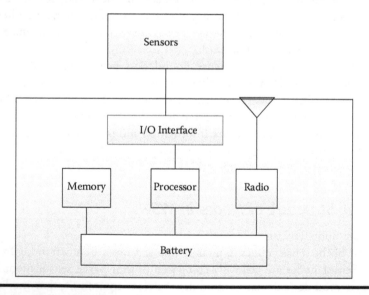

Figure 1.11   The architecture of sensor nodes.

Data processing module: It completes noise reduction or information extraction process of the data.

Data storage module: It temporarily stores and then periodically sends data.

Wireless communication module: It achieves internode communication and data transmission.

Energy (power) module: It is the energy source of the node.

2. The characteristics of sensor nodes
   1. Limited energy
      The sensor nodes are small in size and usually battery powered, so the energy is very limited. In the practical application of sensor nodes, with a large number of sensor nodes, low cost, wide distribution range, and complicated deployment environment, even in some areas that cannot be reached otherwise, the current method of replenishing the batteries of sensor nodes is unrealistic. The efficient use of limited energy to maximize the network lifetime is the most important challenge of the WSN.

      The modules of sensor nodes that consume energy include the sensor module, processor module, and wireless communication module, especially the latter. As shown in Figure 1.12, the wireless communication module has a sending state, a reception state, an idle state, and a sleep state. The wireless communication module in the idle state monitors the use of wireless channels and checks whether data are sent in the sleep state when the communication module is closed. The wireless communication module consumes the most energy in the transmission state, followed by the idle state, and then the reception state; the least energy is consumed in the sleep state.
   2. Poor communication capacity
      The relationship between energy consumption and the communication distance of wireless communication is

$$E = kd^n \tag{1.1}$$

The parameter n satisfies $2 < n < 4$. The value of n depends on many factors. For example, when the deployment of sensor nodes is closer to the ground, interference will be caused by large obstructions and the value of

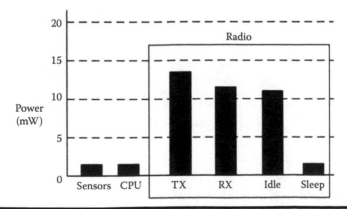

Figure 1.12   Comparison of energy consumption of sensor nodes.

n will be large. The quality of the antenna has a great impact on the quality of the signal transmission. Normally, the value of n is 3. As can be seen from Equation 1.1, the farther the communication distance, the greater the energy consumption will be. With the increase in communication distance, energy consumption will increase dramatically. Therefore, in the premise of satisfying the network connectivity, the one-hop distance communication should be reduced. Therefore, the communication range of the sensor nodes is usually only tens to hundreds of meters, and the communication range will change frequently under different environments. Generally speaking, the wireless communication radius of sensor nodes is less than 100 m.

3. Restricted computing and storage capacity

The sensor node is a kind of microembedded device and requires less cost and consumes less power, which inevitably leads to relatively small storage capacity. In order to complete tasks, sensor nodes need to complete the acquisition and conversion of monitoring data, data management, and data processing, and then respond to the node request and node control.

1.3.3 The Architecture of WSNs

1. The structure of sensor networks

The basic structure of the sensor network is shown in Figure 1.13. The sensor network system usually includes the sensor node, the sink node (usually called a base station), and the managed node. A large number of sensor nodes are randomly deployed within or near the sensor field, which can form the network by self-organization. Sensor nodes will transmit the monitoring data

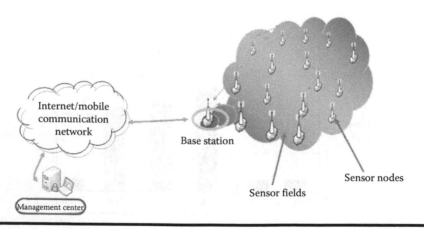

Figure 1.13 Basic structure of WSNs.

along the other sensor nodes hop by hop. The monitoring data in the transmission may be processed by a number of nodes. Then the data will be sent to the convergence node by multihop routing and finally through the Internet or satellite to reach the managed node. The user configures and manages the sensor network through the managed node, releases monitoring tasks, and collects monitoring data. The three basic elements of the sensor network are the sensors, the sensing objects, and the observers. Its basic function is to cooperatively perceive, collect, process, and distribute perceptual information. Figure 1.14 is a practical scenario of the applications of WSNs.

The sensor node is usually a miniature, embedded system, whose processing power, storage capacity, and communication capacity are comparatively weak. It is powered by a battery with limited energy. In terms of network functions, each sensor node takes into account the dual functions of the traditional network node's terminals and routers. In addition to local information collection and data processing, it stores, manages, and integrates data forwarded from other nodes. Each node collaborates with other nodes to perform specific tasks. At present, the hardware and software technologies of sensor nodes are the focus of sensor network research.

The storage capacity and communication capacity of the sink node are relatively strong. It connects the sensor network with the external network such as the Internet, realizes the protocol conversion between the two protocol stacks, releases the monitoring task of the managed node, and collects the data forwarded to the external network. A sink node can be either a sensor node with enhanced functionality, sufficient power supply, and more memory and computing resources or a special gateway device with only a wireless communication interface and no monitoring capability.

2. The protocol stack of sensor networks

With the deep research of sensor networks, researchers proposed a number of protocol stacks for the sensor network. An early proposed protocol stack includes the physical layer, data link layer, network layer, transport layer, and application layer, corresponding to the five-layer protocol of the Internet protocol stack. Moreover, the protocol stack includes an energy management platform, a mobile management platform, and a task management platform. These management platforms enable sensor nodes to work together in an energy-efficient manner, forward data across node-moving sensor networks, and support multitasking and resource sharing. The functions of each layer protocol are as follows.

1. Physical layer: It provides a simple but robust signal modulation and wireless transceiver technology.

    The main technology of the wireless communication physical layer includes the medium selection, modulation technology, and spread spectrum technology.

    Medium selection: The medium of wireless communication includes an electromagnetic wave and a sound wave. Electromagnetic wave is the most important wireless communication medium, whereas sound wave is generally only used for underwater wireless communication. According to the different wavelengths, electromagnetic waves are divided into radio waves, microwaves, infrared waves, millimeter waves and light waves, among which radio waves are the most widely used in the wireless network.

Modulation technology: Modulation and demodulation technologies comprise one of the key technologies of wireless communication systems. Usually the coding information of signal source contains the direct current (DC) component and the frequency component with low frequency, known as the baseband signal. The baseband signal is often unable to be considered a transmission signal, and thus, it is converted to a bandpass signal with high frequency relative to the baseband frequency in order to facilitate channel transmission. The bandpass signal is usually referred to as a modulated signal, whereas the baseband signal is called a modulation signal.

Modulation has a great impact on the effectiveness and reliability of the communication system. Modulation and demodulation often determine the quality of the communication system to a great extent. According to the type of baseband signal used in modulation, modulation can be divided into analog modulation and digital modulation. Analog modulation uses the analog baseband signal to control a parameter of the high-frequency carrier, so that the high-frequency carrier changes with

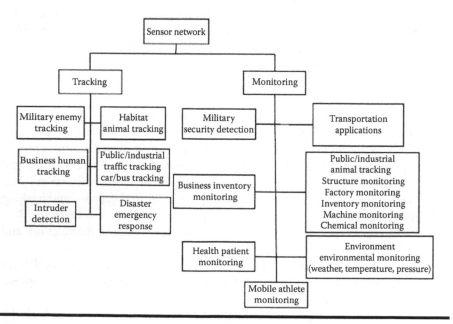

Figure 1.14 Application scenario of WSNs.

the analog baseband signal. Digital modulation is a digital baseband signal that controls the parameters of the high-frequency carrier, so that the high-frequency carrier changes with the digital baseband signal. At present, communication systems are in transition from the analog to the digital format; digital modulation has become the mainstream modulation technology.

Modulation is divided into amplitude modulation, frequency modulation, and phase modulation according to the different parameters controlled by the original signal.

Since the 1980s, people have paid a lot of attention to the application of modulation technology in wireless communication systems, in order to seek a digital modulation method with higher spectrum utilization and a better spectrum. As the anti-noise performance of the amplitude-shift keying signal is not ideal, the modulation methods widely used in wireless communication are frequency-shift keying and phase-shift keying.

Spread spectrum technology: Spread spectrum is an information transmission mode. The bandwidth occupied by the signal is much larger than the minimum bandwidth required for the transmitted information. The band expansion of the frequency is completed through an independent code sequence, achieved by the encoding and modulation method regardless of the information transmitted. At the receiver, the same code is used for relevant synchronous receiving, despreading, and restoring of information.

Spread spectrum technology can be divided into three categories: Frequency-hopping spread spectrum, time-hopping spread spectrum, and broadband chirp spread spectrum.

Compared with general wireless communication systems, spread spectrum communication mainly increases the spread spectrum modulation at the transmitting terminal, whereas it increases the spread spectrum demodulation at the receiver. The advantages of spread spectrum technology include the ease of repeating the use of frequency, improvement of the wireless spectrum utilization, strong anti-interference, low bit error rate, and good concealment. The interference to a variety of narrowband communication systems is very small; it can achieve CDMA and anti-multipath interference. It has accurate timing and ranging, which is suitable for digital voice and data transmission, and a variety of communication services. The installation is simple, and it is easy to maintain.

WSN is a type of wireless communication network, so it contains the previously described characteristics of the physical layer technology for wireless communication.

At present, the main transmission media of WSNs are radio waves, infrared rays, and light waves. The radio waves are less restrictive, so the industrial, scientific, and medical (ISM) band is usually chosen. The advantage of ISM frequency is that it has a free frequency band, there is no need to register, and it has a big range of optional spectrum, flexibility, and convenience. Limited power and the mutual interference of wireless communication applications are the main shortcomings of the ISM frequency band.

Although the sensor network can be realized through other means of communication, such as electromagnetic waves (e.g., RF and infrared) and sound waves, radio wave is the current main communication method of sensor networks and has been widely used in many areas.

2. Data link layer: It is responsible for data framing, frame detection, media access, and error control. It ensures point-to-point and point-to-multipoint connections of the WSN.

The wireless spectrum is the medium of wireless communication, and this broadcast media is a scarce resource. In WSNs, multiple nodes may simultaneously access the channel, resulting in conflicts among the packets, so that the recipient has difficulty distinguishing the received data, thus wasting the channel resources, resulting in decreased network throughput. In order to solve these problems, we need to design a MAC protocol. The so-called MAC protocol is intended to make effective, orderly, and fair use of shared media through a set of rules and processes. The MAC layer protocol is mainly responsible for two functions. The first is the establishment of the network structure. Because thousands of sensor nodes are densely distributed in the area to be measured, the MAC layer mechanism needs to provide effective communication links for data transmission and propose a network organization structure for the multihop transmission of wireless communication and self-organization. The second is to allocate the resources reasonably and efficiently for the sensor nodes.

At present, the MAC protocol of WSNs can be classified according to the following conditions: whether to use distributed control or centralized control; whether to use a single shared channel or multiple channels; and whether to use a fixed allocation channel or a random access channel. According to the third classification method, the MAC protocol of sensor networks is divided into the following three kinds:

a. Time-division multiple access noncontention access mode. The wireless time-division multiple access method allocates fixed usage periods of wireless channel use for each sensor node to avoid mutual interference between nodes.

b. Stochastic contention access. If the random access method of the wireless channel is adopted, the nodes randomly use the wireless channel when the data need to be transmitted, so as to minimize the interference between the nodes. A typical approach is to use the carrier sense multiple access (CSMA) protocol.

c. Competition and fixed allocation of the combination of access. By using frequency-division multiplexing or code-division multiplexing, wireless channel assignment without collision between nodes can be realized.

The IEEE 802.11 MAC protocol is divided into distributed coordination function (DCF) and point coordination function (PCF); DCF is the basic access control mode of the IEEE 802.11 protocol.

In the DCF mode, the carrier sense mechanism determines the state of the wireless channel by physical carrier sensing and virtual carrier sensing. The physical carrier sense is provided by the physical layer, while the virtual carrier sense is provided by the MAC layer.

The IEEE 802.11 MAC protocol specifies three types of inter-frame space (IFS), which are used to provide priority for accessing wireless channels: shortest IFS (SIFS), IFS used by nodes in PCF mode (PIFS), and the IFS used by nodes in DCF mode (DIFS).

3. Network layer: It is mainly responsible for routing and routing generation.

Routing refers to the act of selecting an internetwork to transfer information from a source node to a destination node, while the information is passed through at least one intermediate node. The routing protocol is responsible for forwarding data packets from the source node to the destination node through the network. It includes two functions: (1) to find the optimal path between the source node and the destination node, and (2) to correctly forward the data packet along the optimized path.

Compared with the routing protocols of traditional networks, WSNs have features of energy-based routing protocols and local topology-based information and are data-centric and application-related. Therefore, energy efficiency, scalability, robustness, and fast convergence must be satisfied when routing protocols are designed according to specific applications.

For a variety of applications, the routing protocols of WSNs can be divided into the energy-aware routing protocol, query-based routing protocol, geographical position-based routing protocol, and reliable routing protocol.

a. Energy-aware routing protocol

Efficient use of network energy is a significant feature of routing protocols in sensor networks. In order to emphasize the importance of the efficient use of energy, here they are divided into energy-aware routing protocols. Energy-aware routing protocols start with the energy consumption of data transmission and discuss the issues of minimum energy consumption and maximum network lifetime, such as the maximum effective power routing algorithm, the minimum energy consumption routing algorithm, the minimum hop-based routing, the maximum and minimum effective power node routing, and so on.

b. Query-based routing protocol

In applications such as environmental monitoring and field estimation, it is necessary to constantly query the data collected by the sensor nodes. A task query command is released in the sink node (query node); then the detection node terminal of sensor networks reports the collected data to the monitoring center. In these types of monitoring and detection applications, communication flow is mainly caused by the command and data transmission between the query node and the sensor detection node. Meanwhile, data fusion usually has to be conducted in the formation acquisition of the sensor node by reducing communication traffic to save energy. Namely, data fusion technology and the design of the routing protocol are combined into directed diffusion routing and rumored routing.

c. Geographical position-based routing protocol

In application problems such as target tracking, it is often necessary to wake up sensor nodes that are closest to the tracked target in order to obtain more accurate information about the target. In such application problems related to the coordinate position, it is usually necessary to know the exact or approximate geographical position of the destination node. The routing information of nodes can be used as the basis of routing, which can not only complete the routing function of nodes, but also reduce the energy consumption of the system to maintain the routing protocols. The main examples include geographic and energy aware routing (GEAR), graph embedding (GEM) routing, and boundary location geographical routing.

d. Reliable routing protocol

Some applications of sensor networks have high requirements on the quality of service and may have special requirements in terms of reliability and real time. For example, in the use of video sensors for battlefield environmental monitoring, the transmission of video images should be as smooth as possible. However, the stability of the wireless network is usually difficult to guarantee. The quality of the communication channel is low, and the network topology changes frequently. To meet the service quality of some aspects of the user, consideration must be given to reliable routing protocol design technology such as multipath routing based on disjoint paths, ReInForM routing, and SPEED routing.

4. Transport layer: It is responsible for the transmission control of the data flow. Ensuring the quality of communication services is an important part.

For a WSN, the transport layer is not required if information is only passed inside. When the WSN connects with other networks, the transport layer protocol is necessary.

The TCP of the Internet is an end-to-end transmission protocol based on a global address. The attribute-based naming in the design thought is not necessary for the scalability of the sensor network, so the transport layer protocol, which is suitable for the sensor network, should be more similar to the UDP protocol. The study of WSN transmission protocol and the research results are relatively small. At present, the research work on WSN transport protocol focuses on congestion control and reliable guarantee. Congestion control can be divided into flow control, multiplexing, data aggregation, and a virtual gateway. A reliable guarantee includes data retransmission and redundant transmission.

In the flow control, the ERST, PORT, and IFRC protocols are congestion control protocols based on report rate regulation. Fusion and CCF are congestion control protocols based on forwarding rate adjustment. They are suitable for networks with high requirement of data fidelity. Buffer-based, PCCP, and CODA are based on integrated rate regulation.

A multichannel shunt spreads traffic through multichannel forwarding to solve the problem of congestion. The ARC protocol is intended to construct a new forwarding path by using redundant nodes in the network. The CAR is similar to the ARC method. The BGR increases the direction deviation range in the geographic route to expand the optional range of the forwarding path.

Data fusion includes CONCERT and PREI. The former uses adaptive aggregation, while the PREI divides the network into same-sized pieces to aggregate the data from the same grid.

Concerning reliability, the data retransmission protocol includes three categories: the guarantee of gateway to node, the guarantee of node to gateway, and the two-way reliable guarantee.

Redundant transmissions include copy-to-send (AFS, ReInForM, MMSPEED, and GRAB) and coding redundancy.

5. The application layer includes a series of application layer software applications based on monitoring tasks.

In addition, the functions of each platform are as follows:

1. The energy management platform manages the sensor node's use of energy. Each protocol layer needs to consider energy saving.
2. The mobile management platform detects and registers the movement of sensor nodes and maintains the route to the sink node so that sensor nodes can dynamically track the location of their neighbors.
3. The task management platform in a given area completes the balance and schedules monitoring tasks.

1.3.4 Technologies of WSNs

WSN research is interdisciplinary, and there are many key technologies to be researched. We briefly introduce some key technologies that are critical points supporting the sensor network.

1. Node location

   In many application problems of sensor networks, monitoring data without node location information is meaningless. For example, when detecting various environmental characteristics in the deployed area, the sensing data tend to have no practical meaning without corresponding position information. In applications such as natural disaster monitoring and forest fire prevention, node location information is particularly important.

   The WSN location problem is providing node location information in a self-organizing network through a specific method. This self-organizing network location is divided into node self-location and target location. Node self-location is the process of determining the coordinate position of a network node and the network itself. It can be done by manual calibration or with various node self-location algorithms. Target location is the network coverage area of an event or the coordinates of a specific location. Target location is based on a known network node as a reference to determine the location of the event or target within the network coverage.

   Location information can be divided into two major categories: physical location and symbol location. Physical location refers to the value of the location of the target under a specific coordinate system, indicating the relative or absolute position of the target. Symbol location refers to the information about the degree of proximity of a target to a base station or multibase stations, indicating a connection relationship between a target and a base station and providing the rough range of the target located.

   According to different basis, the positioning method of the WSN can also be classified as follows:

   1. According to whether to rely on measuring distance, the positioning methods can be divided into distance-based positioning and positioning without distance. Distance-based positioning technology measures the distance between nodes and calculates the location of the network according to node geometry. There are several ways to determine the position of a point in parsing geometry. The most common methods are multilateral positioning and angle location.
   2. According to the deployment of different occasions, the positioning methods can be divided into indoor positioning and outdoor positioning.
   3. According to the way of collecting information, the network collecting of sensor data is called passive location. The node actively sends out information, which is used for positioning, called active location.

2. Topology control

For the wireless self-organizing sensor network, the network topology control is very important. A good network topology automatically generated by topology control can improve the efficiency of routing protocols and MAC protocols. It can lay a foundation for data fusion, time synchronization, and target location. It is also helpful for saving the energy of nodes to prolong the lifecycle of the network.

The main research problems for topology control of sensor networks are eliminating unnecessary wireless communication links between nodes and generating a highly efficient data forwarding network topology control through the power control and backbone network node selection under the premise of meeting network coverage and connectivity. Topology control can be divided into two aspects: node power control and hierarchical topology formation. The power control mechanism adjusts the transmit power of each node in the network. When the network connectivity is satisfied, the transmit power of the node is reduced, and the number of neighbors that can be reached in one hop is equalized. The hierarchical topology control mechanism constructs the CDS and clustering algorithm.

3. Energy management

The energy of the sensor nodes is limited; thus, how to use the limited energy to maximize the lifetime is a major constraint on WSN applications. Good energy management improves energy efficiency. The realization methods mainly include dormancy mechanism and data fusion.

The main idea of the dormancy mechanism is that the calculation and communication units are in an idle state, and these components are turned off or transferred to a state of lower power consumption when there is no event of interest around the node; this is called the sleep state.

The energy-saving effect of data fusion is mainly embodied in the implementation of routing protocols. The intermediate node of the routing process does not simply forward the received data. Because the data sent by the nodes in the same area have great redundancy, the intermediate nodes need to perform data fusion on these data. After local fusion processing, the data are routed to the convergence point and forward only useful information. Data fusion effectively reduces the data traffic in the whole network.

4. Data fusion

Data fusion is also called information fusion. It is a multisource information processing technology that can obtain more accurate and complete estimates or judgments than a single information source by optimizing multisource data from the same target. Data fusion can improve the accuracy and comprehensiveness of information, reduce the uncertainty of information, improve the reliability of the system, and increase the real time of the system.

Because of the limited resources of the sensor network nodes, it is inappropriate to transmit data directly to the sink nodes in the process of collecting information, which will waste communication bandwidth and energy and reduce information collection effectiveness. Therefore, in applications of WSNs, the purpose of data fusion is to reduce network traffic and improve the efficiency of network bandwidth. How to eliminate interference and how to reduce data redundancy are the main focus of data fusion. Data fusion technology can be implemented in multiple layers of the sensor network protocol stacks, both in MAC protocol and in routing protocol, or application layer protocol. Through data fusion, energy can be saved, the accuracy of the collected data will be enhanced, and the efficiency of data collection will be improved.

The data fusion technology of sensor networks can be classified from different perspectives. For example, according to the information content of data before and after the fusion, the data fusion can be classified into two types: lossless fusion and lossy fusion. According to the relationship between data fusion and the semantics of application layer data, it can be divided into application-dependent data fusion, application-independent data fusion, and data fusion based on these two technologies. Based on fusion operation level, data fusion can be classified into data-level, feature-level, and decision-level fusion.

5. Network security

In most civil applications of sensor networks, such as environmental monitoring, forest fire prevention, and migration tracking, security is not an issue of paramount importance. However, in other areas, such as the wireless security network of the commercial community, the sensor network of monitoring an enemy's military deployment, we need to consider the security issues of data sampling, transmission processes, and even the physical distribution of nodes. A lot of information cannot be understood by unrelated personnel or enemy personnel.

How to ensure that the network is not affected by the intruder, how to effectively prevent the spread of harmful data within the network, and how to ensure that the information being transmitted cannot be used for illegal users are important in the field of security research of WSNs. As a new type of wireless network originated from military application, WSN mainly adopts the RF wireless communication network, whose security issues are very important.

The design of sensor network security technology includes two aspects, namely, communication security and information security. Communication security is the foundation of information security. Communication security ensures the data collection, integration, and transmission of the basic functions of sensor networks, which is a network-oriented security. Information security focuses on the authenticity, integrity, and confidentiality of the information transmitted in the network, which is user-oriented application security.

The sensory protocol for information via negotiation (SPIN) security protocol suite is one of the earliest security frameworks of WSNs and includes two secure protocols, secure network encryption protocol (SNEP) and microtimed efficient streaming loss-tolerant authentication protocol (μTESLA). The SNEP protocol provides security services such as point-to-point communication authentication, data confidentiality, integrity, and freshness. The μTESLA protocol provides data authentication services for broadcast messages.

6. Time synchronization

WSN synchronization management mainly refers to time synchronization management.

In a distributed application of WSNs, each sensor node has its own local clock. The crystal oscillator frequency of different nodes has deviation, and humidity and electromagnetic interference will result in run-time deviation between the network nodes. Sometimes the capacity of a single node of a sensor network is limited. Alternatively, the needs of some applications require the entire system, and all nodes within the network to cooperate with each other when achieving the functional requirements. The collaborative work of distributed systems needs time synchronization between nodes. So the time synchronization mechanism is a key point of the infrastructure framework of distributed systems.

In distributed systems, time synchronization involves two different concepts of "physical time" and "logical time." "Physical time" represents the absolute time of human society. "Logical time" reflects the sequence of events, which is a relative concept. A distributed system usually requires a global time that represents the overall system time. The global time may be physical or logical time, as desired.

The significance and role of the time synchronization mechanism of WSNs are mainly reflected in the following two aspects. First, the sensor nodes usually need to work with each other to complete complex monitoring and sensing tasks. Data fusion is a typical example of cooperative operation, and the final fusion of data collected by different nodes forms a meaningful result. Second, some energy-saving program of the sensor network is achieved by time synchronization.

At present, there are several mature time synchronization protocols for sensor networks. Among them, RBS, TINY/MINI-SYNC, and TPSN are considered the most basic time synchronization mechanisms. The basic idea of the RBS synchronization protocol is that multiple nodes receive the same synchronization signal and then synchronize multiple nodes that receive the synchronization signal. This synchronization algorithm eliminates the time uncertainty of the synchronization signaling side. The disadvantage of this type of synchronization protocol is that the overhead is large. TINY and MINI-SYNC are two simple, lightweight time synchronization mechanisms. The TPSN time synchronization protocol adopts the hierarchical structure to realize the time synchronization of the entire network nodes.

1.3.5 Applications of the WSN

1.3.5.1 Military Application

WSN has the characteristics of rapid deployment, self-organization, strong concealment, and high fault-tolerance, so it is very suitable for military application. Enemy forces and equipment monitoring, real-time monitoring of the battlefield, target positioning, battlefield assessment, nuclear and biochemical attack monitoring, and search functions can be achieved by the WSN. At present, many topics of international organizations are studied on the needs of the battlefield as the background such as the US Command, Control, Communications, Computers, Intelligence, Surveillance, Reconnaissance (C4KISR) program, smart sensor web, smart sensor network communication, unattended ground sensor group, sensor networking system, mesh sensor system CEC, and so on.

In the field of military applications, the long-range target of technology is as follows: A large number of low-cost sensor nodes in accordance with a certain density in the area are deployed by the use of aircraft or artillery and other launch devices. The nodes test on the surrounding parameters such as temperature, humidity, sound, magnetic field, infrared ray, and so on. Each kind of information is gathered and transmitted to the information center through the constructed network formed by the sensor itself, passing the gateway, the Internet, the satellite, and other channels.

The technology can be used to monitor an enemy's military situation. Sensor nodes are installed in the friendly force's equipment and arms for identification, controlling their own situation at any time. Understanding an enemy and oneself and the feature of preemption can be achieved through the deployment of various sensors in enemy positions. In addition, the technology can be used for guiding smart weapons, as well as for radar, satellites, and other cooperation. The characteristic of being close to the environment can prevent blind spots and greatly improve the efficiency of weapons.

At the present stage, the following system has been successfully applied based on the technologies of software, hardware, communications, sensors, and other features.

Example: In 2005, the US military successfully tested the gun positioning system organized by the products of United States Crossbow. The nodes were placed around the building, effectively forming a network in accordance with certain procedures to detect emergencies (such as gunshots, explosion sources, etc.) and providing a powerful method for use by ambulances and counterterrorism.

Example: The Science Applications International Corporation built an electronic perimeter defense system that provided military defense and intelligence information to the US military through WSNs. In this system, multiple micrometer sensor nodes are used to detect whether a person is carrying a gun and whether a vehicle is coming. Meanwhile, the system can monitor a vehicle or a moving crowd with an acoustic sensor.

1.3.5.2 Agricultural Application

China is a large agricultural country, so the crop quality and high yield have great significance in the country's economic development. In these areas, WSNs have superior technical advantages. They can be used to monitor irrigation, soil air change, livestock, poultry environmental conditions, and large area surface inspections. A typical system is composed of environmental monitoring nodes, base stations, communication systems, the Internet, and hardware and software monitoring systems. It is possible to place sensors with different functions in the area to be tested and form a network to monitor long-term and large-scale climate changes, including temperature, humidity, wind, atmosphere, rainfall, the collection of humidity relative to the land, nitrogen concentration, and soil pH value. It can also carry out scientific forecasting to help farmers in disaster reduction, scientific cultivation, and increasing crop yields. In the "Ninth Five-Year Plan," "factory efficient agricultural engineering" has called the intelligent sensor and sensor network development national key projects. Several attempts in this area (domestic and foreign) are shown in the following (Figure 1.15).

Example: In 2002, Intel took the lead in setting up the world's first wireless vineyard in Oregon. Sensor nodes were distributed in every corner of the vineyard, detecting the soil temperature, humidity, or the number of harmful substances in the region every minute to ensure the healthy growth of the grapes. The researchers found that subtle changes in vineyard climate can greatly affect the quality of wine. Through the years of data records and correlation analysis, the exact relationship between the wine texture and the sunshine, temperature, and humidity in the grape-growing process can be accurately grasped. This is a typical example of precision farming, intelligent farming.

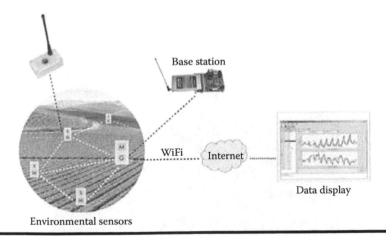

Figure 1.15 Structure of agricultural ecological environment monitoring example.

Example: The program of "The Research and Application of Intelligent Vegetable Production Network Sensor System," conducted by the Beijing Municipal Science and Technology Commission formally applies agricultural WSNs to greenhouse vegetable production. In the greenhouse environment, a single greenhouse can become a measurement and control area for WSNs. Sensor nodes form a wireless network to measure soil moisture, soil composition, pH value, precipitation, temperature, air humidity and air pressure, light intensity, CO_2 concentration, and so on. It can obtain the best conditions for crop growth and provide a scientific basis for the precise control of the greenhouse. Ultimately, with the greenhouse sensors, the implementing agency can acquire standardization, digitization, and networking and achieve increased crop yields and improved economic efficiency (Figure 1.16).

WSNs have the advantage of convenient communication and deployment, which can be applied in the control of water-saving irrigation. At the same time, the node has the ability to measure soil and meteorological parameters. Combining with the Internet and GPS technology, the node can easily realize the dynamic management of the irrigation area, the establishment of crop water demand information collection, and precision control of the expert system and then achieve efficient, low energy consumption, low investment, and a multifunctional agricultural water-saving irrigation platform. It can be used to quantify, standardize, model, and integrate agricultural and ecological water-saving technologies in the greenhouse, garden greenbelt, high-speed road isolation zone, and farmland irrigation area. It will promote the rapid and healthy development of water-saving industry.

Example: Digital Sun's development of an automatic sprinkler system, s. sense wireless sensor, currently obtained a number of international reports. It used a wireless sensor to sense soil moisture. If necessary, it would communicate with the

Figure 1.16 Feedback loops in a greenhouse control system. (From http://www. klbict.co.uk/gcse/theory/5_3/5_3_3_feedback.htm.)

receiver and control the valve of the irrigation system to achieve automatic, water-saving irrigation.

A professor believes that the advantages of WSNs are particularly applicable to the following aspects of production and scientific research: indoor and soil greenhouse temperature, humidity, light monitoring, precious economic crop growth analysis and measurement, grape quality, breeding, and production, and so on. It can bring high-tech auxiliary means of rural development and income-generating projects to the Yangling demonstration area. In addition, the technology provides powerful information for growth and simulations of precious medicinal herbs and orchards, condition analysis of high-value crops, manual intervention, and forest fire prevention.

For example, the growth law of many rare medicinal herbs in the Shaanxi Qingling—Bashan mountain area can be accurately measured and transmitted to the control center through wireless channels, satellites, or the Internet. The growth cycle, moisture, humidity, light, rain, and other information can be accurately monitored. Using the results, agricultural workers can create simulated environments and increase production and improve the status of scarce rare medicines.

We use the WSNs to construct agricultural environment automatic monitoring system. Data collection and environmental control of wind, light, water, electricity, heat, and pesticide can be accomplished with the same network equipment. It can effectively improve the degree of intensive agricultural production, simplify system complexity, and reduce equipment costs.

1.3.5.3 Industrial Application

1. Industrial safety

   "The sensor network can be used in hazardous working environments where employees at coal mines, oil rigs, nuclear power plants and assembly lines can be monitored at all times," said Pete Casal, president of British Petroleum. These sensor networks can tell the work site what employees are working, what they are doing, their security, and other important information. The corresponding wireless nodes are installed at each discharge port of the relevant factory to complete the monitoring of the plant wastewater and pollutants, the collection, analysis, and flow measurement of the sample.

   The costs of monitoring staff safety in the coal, petrochemical, and metallurgical industries and the monitoring of flammable, explosive, toxic substances have been high. WSNs extricate some of the operating personnel from a high-risk environment while improving the accuracy and speed of the response to dangers.

   China has more than 600 large coal mines, more than 2000 medium-sized coal mines, and more than 10,000 small and medium-sized coal mines. The requirements of an advanced underground production security system in the coal industry are huge. Sun Binjian, the engineer of the Shaanxi Bin

Chang mining area, believes that the tracking of moving targets and the multisensor fusion monitoring of the surrounding environment create lots of room for many aspects of production safety development underground.

Example: Researchers at the Beijing University of Posts and Telecommunications carried out research of a coal mine gas alarm and miners positioning WSN system. A node included temperature and humidity sensors, gas sensors, and dust sensors. After explosion-proof processing and technical optimization, the sensor network can be used in a dangerous working environment, so that the staff working in the coal mine and the surrounding environment will be monitored at all times (Figure 1.17).

2. Advanced manufacturing

With the development of the manufacturing technology, all kinds of production equipment are more sophisticated. Now the staff is trying to install the appropriate sensor nodes from the production line to the complex machinery and equipment, in order to keep abreast of the health of the work equipment, to obtain early detection and early treatment so as to effectively reduce the loss and accident rate.

Example: Researchers at the University of Electronic Science and Technology of China, China Aerodynamics Research and Development Center (CARDC), and the Beijing Aerospace Command and Control Center conducted environmental monitoring of a large wind tunnel with WSNs. It can be also used for all-round detection of the rotation mechanism, air source system, wind tunnel operation system, other infrastructure, and the wired

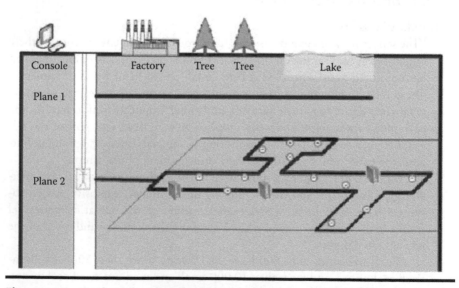

Figure 1.17 Coal mine safety detection and location system (Beijing University of Posts and Telecommunications).

sensor systems that are not convenient to install or unsafe for the application environment.

Example: US Intel Corporation installed 200 wireless sensors for a chip factory in Oregon to monitor the vibration of some equipment and to provide monitoring reports when the results of the measurements were exceeded. "The program has a significant effect although it covers only a handful of components in the 4000 testable parts," says Hans Mundell, assistant director of the Intel Research Center. Today, researchers no longer need to visit the machine every two or three months.

China's high-tech enterprises, such as integrated circuit chip production, state monitoring of large-scale precision equipment, have huge technical needs and market. The WSN technology in these areas will contribute a lot.

3. Traffic management control

Example: In 1995 the US Department of Transportation proposed the "National Functional Transportation System Project Plan," expected to be fully operational by 2025. The system integrates a large number of sensor networks, with the global positioning system (GPS), regional network system, and other resources. The purpose is to enable all vehicles to be maintained efficiently, with low consumption and in good condition, to automatically keep a good distance between cars, to give the best directions, and sound alarms for potential faults. Such a traffic information system has been built in Pittsburgh, Pennsylvania, and has a certain commercial value.

Example: Wuhan University of Technology conducts the monitoring and control applications for trains through the WSN. The air quality inside the car and hidden safety hazards can be detected.

Example: Shenyang Institute of Automation of Chinese Academy of Sciences carried out the study of expressway traffic monitoring system based on WSNs. The use of the technology can replace traditional equipment for image monitoring systems, low-visibility situations, and road icing conditions when effective monitoring of high-speed sections is not possible. It can also overcome the impact of traffic caused by the closure of highways and other negative factors. In addition, for some areas of hazardous weather, the technology can greatly reduce vehicle rear-end collisions and other traffic accidents.

4. Security and defense system

Example: A museum in the United Kingdom used WSN to design an alarm system that placed nodes at the bottom or back of precious artifacts or artworks. It ensures the safety of exhibits by detecting whether the brightness of the light changes, measuring whether items are affected by vibrations and other factors.

5. Products storage circulation management

This can be used for temperature, humidity control, central air conditioning system monitoring, and control of the plant environment for the storage of grains, vegetables, fruits, and eggs by the use of the features such as the high integration of multisensors, easy deployment, and flexible networking. It can also be used for workshop environment control, special laboratory environment control to provide solutions to protect the safety of inventory quality, and energy reduction.

Example: The famous Wal-Mart chain has invested money in installing wireless sensor nodes and RF identification bar-code chips (RFID) on its cargo to ensure that it is in the best possible storage environment. Meanwhile, it allows the company and the supplier to track the flow of goods from production to cashier

1.3.5.4 Environmental Observation and Forecasting System

China has a vast territory, numerous species, and environmental and ecological problems. WSNs can be widely used in ecological environment monitoring, biological population research, meteorology, geography research, and flood and fire detection. Here are some common application areas:

1. It can research endangered species by tracing the rare birds', animals', and insects' habitats, feeding habits, etc.
2. Sensor nodes can be deployed in subareas along the river to monitor information about water levels and information about associated water resources.
3. Nodes can be placed in mountainous areas prone to the debris flow, landslides, and other natural disasters to issue early warnings to prepare officials to take appropriate measures to prevent further malignant accidents.
4. We can lay a large number of nodes in key protected areas to monitor the internal fire situation at any time. If there is a danger, they can immediately alert and give the specific location and the current size of the fire as shown in Figure 1.18.
5. They are deployed in earthquake, flood, severe tropical storm disaster areas, and remote areas and are used for emergency and temporary emergency communications.

Example: In 2002, scientists from Intel's team and University of California Berkeley and Bar Harbor Atlantic University used WSN technology to monitor the habitat of seabirds in Main Duck Island. The swallow located on the Main Duck Island on the Maine coast was so wary of the environment that the researchers were unable to adopt the usual method for tracking observations. So they used hundreds of nodes including nearly 10 sensors for light and humidity, barometers, infrared sensors, and a camera. The system transmits the data to the base station computer 300 feet away by a self-organized wireless network. Then it is transmitted to a server in California via satellite. After that, researchers all over the world can view the data of each node in the area through the Internet, grasp firsthand environmental data, and provide an extremely effective and convenient platform for ecological environment researchers.

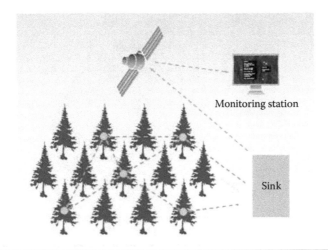

Figure 1.18 Fire monitoring.

Example: In 2005, Australian scientists used WSNs to detect the distribution of toads in North Australia. For the toad's loud and unique yell, the use of sound as a detection feature is very effective. Researchers collected the signal and process on the node, and then a small amount of processed data was sent back to the control center. We can generally understand the distribution of toads' habitats through the process (Figures 1.19 and 1.20).

Example: University of Hawaii lay sensor networks in Hawaii Volcanoes National Park to monitor the microclimatic changes in the areas in which the endangered species were located.

Figure 1.19 The picture of cane toad. (From http://deography.com/cane-toad-bufo-marinus-bufonidae/.)

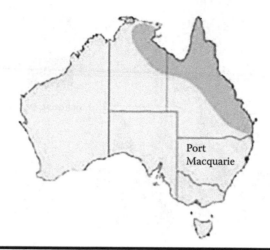

Figure 1.20 The map of cane toad's distribution in Australia.

Example: The Oregon Graduate School set up 13 stations on the Columbia River to monitor the flow rate, salinity, temperature, and water level of each station area.

Example: US ALERT system uses a variety of sensors to monitor rainfall, river water level, and soil moisture and thus predict the possibility of the outbreak of flash floods.

Example: The CSIRO ICT Research Center in Australia locates the nodes in animals to monitor their physiological condition (pulse, blood pressure) and the external environment and develop a complete model of grassland grazing and animals.

Example: Department of Automation of Shanghai Jiaotong University carried out a gas source prediction and location system based on the attenuation model of gas pollution sources. The technology can be extended to the tracking and positioning of radioactive elements and chemical elements.

The researchers believe that China has many outstanding natural scenic areas and complex terrains; large areas bring great difficulties to scenic area management or search and rescue work. If the sensor network nodes are widely laid in the scenic area, and each visitor goes into the area with an active node, it is not only easy to manage, but also the visitor's location can be found and timely resolution delivered if the visitor encounters problems. It brings a win-win for improving the quality of service and personnel security.

1.3.5.5 Building Condition Monitoring

When China is in a peak period of infrastructure construction, all kinds of large-scale safety constructions and monitoring are a long-term concern for architectural design organizations. The completed Three Gorges Project, Sutong Bridge, a large number of offshore platforms in Bohai Sea and submarine pipelines, and the 2008 Olympic venues are examples. The WSNs can make buildings and bridges, and other buildings sense their conditions. Intelligent buildings with sensor networks can automatically tell the management about their status, allowing management to conduct maintenance work in good order.

Example: A three-dimensional protection detection network can be constructed efficiently using appropriate sensors, such as piezoelectric sensors, acceleration sensors, ultrasonic sensors, and humidity sensors. The system can be used to monitor bridges, viaducts, highways, and other road environments. For many old bridges, the piers have been exposed to water erosion for a long time. Sensors can be placed at the bottom of the piers to sense the pier structure. They can also be placed on either or both sides of the bridge to collect temperature, humidity, vibration, and erosion degree, which reduces the loss of life and property caused by a broken bridge.

Example: In 2003, a group of researchers from Harbin Institute of Technology developed a WSN for the health monitoring of a marine platform and other civil engineering structures. The structure of the building is monitored by a variety of intelligent sensors, such as fiber grating sensors, fiber reinforced polymer-fiber grating ribs and their strain sensors, piezoelectric thin film sensors, shape memory alloy sensors, fatigue life wire sensors, and acceleration sensors.

Example: In 2004, the research group of Ou Jinping Academy in the Harbin Institute of Technology applied WSNs to develop a new system for the dynamic testing of super high-rise buildings. It is also applied to the environmental noise and acceleration response test of the Shenzhen Diwang Building. Diwang Building is 81 floors high, and the mast is 384 m high. In the field test, the wireless sensors were arranged vertically on the outer surface of the building. The system successfully measures the distribution of ambient noise along the building height and the acceleration response to the wind-induced vibration of the structure.

Example: The protection of precious ancient buildings has long been a focus of heritage conservation work. Nodes with temperature, humidity, pressure, acceleration, lighting, and other sensors are placed in the protected object, and long-term monitoring of buildings can be effectively carried out without cable drilling (see Figure 1.21). In addition, for precious cultural relics, monitoring whether temperature and humidity exceed the safe value at the location of the corners, ceilings, and other places can better protect the quality of exhibits.

Example: Beckett, the largest engineering and construction company in the United States, has adopted a wireless sensor in the London subway system and hopes to further apply it to intelligent buildings, defense constructions, and chemical plants. "These applications are just starting out, and future applications are expected to be much deeper and broader," said Fred Weitling, the manager of corporate infrastructure.

Figure 1.21 WSNs used in the protection of precious cultural heritage areas. (From Xiaojiang Chen, Dingyi Fang, Xueqing Huang, *J. Sensor Technol.***, 1(4), 91, 2011.)**

Example: Japanese technology giant Fujitsu announced in December 2004 that it had signed a research agreement with the US-based Xerox Palo Alto Research Center to study how to install a networked seismic sensor in a building to provide better monitoring and early warning for the residents.

In addition, WSNs have good application prospects for preventing large-scale disasters in large-scale projects. Taking China's West-East Gas Pipeline and the construction of pipelines as an example, because these pipes have to cross large uninhabited areas, pipeline monitoring has been a problem. If the sensor network technology is mature, the West-East Gas Pipeline project alone may save billions of dollars.

1.3.5.6 Medical Nursing

WSNs play an important role in the detection of human physiological data, the health status of the elderly, hospital drug management, and telemedicine. With the placement of sensors of temperature collection, breathing, blood pressure, and other measurement sensors on the patient's body, the doctor can remotely understand the patient's situation. Physiological data can be collected by the long time use of sensor networks. The data is also very useful in the development of new drugs.

Intel Corporation is currently developing a home-care WSN system. The system is a department to deal with the aging social technology project of the United States. According to the demonstration, the system embedded sensors in shoes, furniture, and home appliances to help the elderly and patients with disabilities enjoy independent family life. When necessary, the sensors can alert that the users need to be helped by the medical staff and social workers.

Example: Researchers have developed WSN systems based on multiple accelerometers for human behavior monitoring, such as sitting, standing, lying, walking, falling, and crawling. This system uses multiple sensor nodes, which are installed in several characteristic parts of the human body. The system extracts, fuses, and classifies the three-dimensional acceleration information generated by the action of the human body in real time. Then the behavior pattern of the detected person will be displayed on the monitoring interface. The system will be a safety helper for some elderly and disabled patients if it can become a little more product oriented. At the same time, the system can be applied to rehabilitation centers for people with disabilities, with accurate measurements of the progress of various types of limb restoration, thus providing a valuable reference for the design of rehabilitation programs (Figure 1.22).

Example: Researchers can use WSNs to implement telemedicine monitoring. In an apartment, 17 sensor nodes are distributed in all directions, including the bathroom. Each sensor node includes the temperature, humidity, light, infrared sensors, and sound sensors when another node uses the ultrasonic node. According to the information collected by these nodes, monitoring interfaces a real-time display of the activities of personnel. According to the multisensor information fusion,

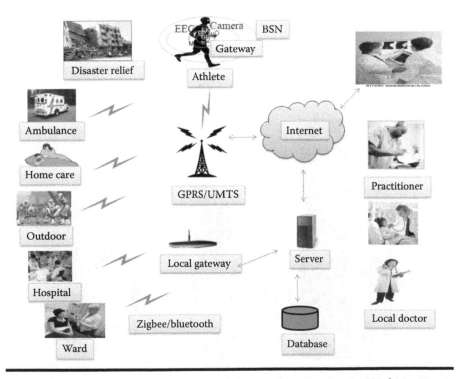

Figure 1.22 Healthcare application using WSNs. (From Kumar Pardeep, Hoon-Jae Lee, *Sensors*, 12(1), 55–91, 2012.

the activities of the person under surveillance (cooking, sleeping, watching TV, showering, and so on) can be judged quite accurately. So the health condition of the elder, such as Alzheimer's disease can be accurately detected. Because the system does not use a camera, it's relatively easy to make patients and their families accept it (Figures 1.23 and 1.24).

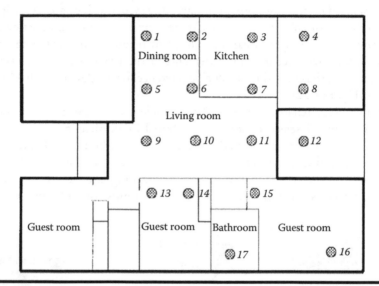

Figure 1.23 The distribution of wireless sensor bathroom.

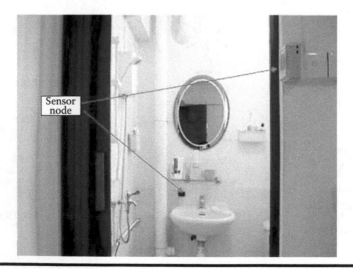

Figure 1.24 The distribution of nodes in the apartment.

1.3.5.7 Smart Home

Smart home systems are designed to connect the various home devices so that they can run automatically to provide residents with as much convenience and comfort as possible.

Example: The traditional water meter and electricity meter can be read by meter readers. With the development of society and the popularization of high-rise buildings, the traditional operation brings more and more trouble to meter readers. The researchers of the Department of Computer Science in Zhejiang University developed a wireless water meter system based on WSN, with a high degree of automation, allowing meter reading staff to read the meters without access to each household. You can get all of the building's water meter readings just by pressing the meter key downstairs.

Example: Fudan University, University of Electronic Science and Technology, and other organizations developed a smart building system based on WSN. The typical structure includes lighting control, alarm access control, and a home appliance-controlled PC system. Each part can communicate with the others and ultimately publish information on the network by the PCs through the Internet. The owner can detect any family situation through the Internet terminal. The system can detect and make an alarm for fire, theft, and other security risks and can achieve centralized meter readings.

Example: Electronic camphor is a typical smart home product, which is actually a WSN device with a temperature and humidity sensor. It cannot replace the mothproof effect and the mildew-fighting effect of camphor, but when it detects that the temperature and humidity in the wardrobe is unsuitable for clothing preservation, it can notify the owner for appropriate treatment by short message service (SMS) or telephone message.

1.3.5.8 Space and Ocean Exploration

Exploring the external planet has always been the dream of mankind, with the help of sensor nodes deployed by spacecraft to achieve the long-term, close monitoring and exploration of a large range of surface planets. It is an economically viable option. NASA's JPL Labs developed sensor webs for the future of Mars exploration, selecting the landing site and other technical requirements for preparation. The project is now being tested and perfected at the Florida Aerospace Center's Environmental Monitoring Program (Figure 1.25).

The twenty-first century is a century in which mankind has deepened the exploitation and utilization of marine resources. Highly intelligent, strong, autonomous, distributed, all-weather information collection, transmission, processing, and integration technology is imperative for marine physics research, data collection, traffic navigation, resource exploration, pollution monitoring,

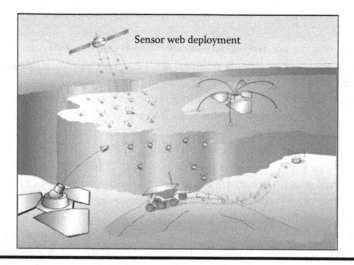

Figure 1.25   The WSN application model in space exploration program.

disaster prevention, and monitoring, positioning, tracking, and classification of underwater military targets. After the Indian Ocean tsunami, global leaders held a summit in Jakarta, Indonesia. The first agenda item was planning and building sensor networks in the Indian Ocean, in order to allow for the early warning of future sea bottom earthquakes.

In the view of these requirements, underwater distributed information collection, network communication, and information processing technology based on multisensors has been a hot topic in recent years, with the rapid development of communication technology, digital signal processing (DSP) technology, microelectro-mechanical system (MEMS) sensor technology, and other related fields. Research and development of important issues have become urgent in the fields of national economy, the military, and national defense (Figure 1.26).

Figure 1.26   The underwater WSN technology. (From http://mooring.ucsd.edu/ projects/corc/corc_intro.html.)

According to the references of the research projects in current European and American countries, the institutions using underwater sensor networks can be roughly divided into the following categories:

1. Based on the surface buoy (RF + underwater acoustic communication), arbitrary lifting three-dimensional underwater sensor network system.

    Advantages: easier to deploy, able to use solar energy, can use GPS and wireless communication on water, avoid and reduce the difficulties of underwater communications.

    Disadvantages: impedes the waterways, easily found and damaged, easily follows the crowd and location unfixed.

2. The three-dimensional network system that can be arbitrarily lifted and lowered by a node fixed at a submarine base station. The connection with surface gateway, node connection, and data transmission to the base station can be achieved through the optical cable or acoustic communication.

    Advantages: does not affect the navigation.

    Disadvantages: maintenance is difficult.

3. Three-dimensional system based on the surface buoy node (RF + underwater acoustic communication), underwater autonomous navigation (underwater acoustic communication), and underwater fixed node (underwater acoustic communication).

    Advantages: is full coverage, has flexible configuration, and is powerful.

    Disadvantages: system is complex and has high cost.

    Compared with the ground WSNs, the underwater sensor network still has many difficulties such as the limited effective bandwidth, the underwater channel has bad conditions, and so on.

1.3.6 Characteristics and Challenges of WSNs

Many problems need to be solved in order to effectively run WSNs in practical applications. The main challenges are as follows:

1. Limited power

    The volume of the sensor node is small, and it is usually battery-powered, so energy is very limited. The requirement of sensor nodes is large and of low cost and wide distribution. Even the environment of the deployment area may be complicated, and some areas cannot be reached, so replenishing the sensor node battery energy is unrealistic. How to most efficiently use limited energy to maximize the network life cycle is the biggest challenge for WSNs.

    The modules of sensor nodes consuming energy include the sensor module, processor module, and wireless communication module, especially the latter. The wireless communication module has four states: sending, receiving, idle, and sleep. The wireless communication module in the idle state monitors the use of wireless channels and checks whether data has been sent; in the sleep state, the communication module is closed. As mentioned earlier, we know that the energy consumption of the wireless communication module in the transmission state is the largest; it is slightly less in the sending state. How to make network communication more efficient, how to reduce unnecessary forwarding and receiving, and how to move into the sleep state as soon as possible when communication is unnecessary are the important problems needed to be focused on in the sensor network protocol design.

2. Limited communication capacity

   The wireless communication bandwidth of the sensor node is limited, usually only a few hundred kbps rate. Due to changes in the node energy, coupled with the effect of high mountains, buildings, wind, thunder and lightning, and other obstructions in natural and urban environments, wireless communication performance may change frequently, resulting in frequent interruptions of communication. Therefore, how to finish the query, analysis, mining, and transmission of perceptual data with high communication quality and limited communication capacity is one of the challenges of sensor networks. In academia, the goal is to find the mechanism with minimum communication complexity in the sensor network environment, which is the first challenge we are facing.

3. Limited computing and storage capacity

   The sensor node is a kind of microembedded device, requiring a low price and low power consumption. These restrictions will inevitably lead to its relatively weak carrying capacity of the sensors and relatively small storage capacity. In order to complete various tasks, sensor nodes need to complete the acquisition and conversion of monitoring data, data management and processing, response to the task request of the sinking node, node control, and other work. How to use a limited number of computing and storage resources to complete the collaborative tasks becomes a challenge for the sensor network design.

   With the development of low-power circuit and system design technology, a lot of ultra-low-power microprocessors have been developed. In addition to reducing the processor's absolute power consumption, the modern processor also supports modular power supply and dynamic frequency regulation. With the characteristics of these processors, the dynamic energy management and the dynamic voltage regulation modules are designed by the operating system of the sensor nodes, which can make more efficient use of nodes' resources. Dynamic energy management means that some modules are idle when the nodes are not interested in the events nearby, and these components are turned off or transferred to the sleep state with a lower power consumption. Dynamic voltage regulation is intended to save the microprocessor power consumption by reducing the operating voltage and frequency of the microprocessor when the calculated load is low. Many processors, such as strong acorn RISC machine (ARM), support voltage-frequency regulation.

4. Communication mode

In the application of WSNs, the data transmission can be greatly saved due to multihop routing compared to single-hop routing. Therefore, multihop routing is usually adopted. In addition, a large number of sensor nodes spreading in the monitoring area will simultaneously send their own monitored data to the same sink node, that is, multiple sources point to a target node. Therefore, a multisource information transmission requires multiple paths composed of multiple sensor nodes. How to choose the optimal communication path for multisource information transmission is the fourth challenge, which is the optimal or nearly optimal routing protocol for different WSNs in the application environment.

For different sensor network applications, different routing protocols have been put out, such as energy-aware routing protocols. Because the efficient use of network energy is a significant feature of routing protocols of sensor networks, some of the early proposed routing protocols tend to consider the energy factor. Energy-aware routing protocols start from energy consumption in data transmission and discuss the optimal energy consumption path and network life cycle maximization problem. In the query-based routing protocol, communication traffic is mainly caused by the commands and data transmission between the query node and the sensor node. At the same time, data fusion is usually performed of the sampling information of sensor nodes on the transmission path, which also saves energy by reducing communication traffic. There are also robust routing protocols designed for link stability, communication channel quality, and frequent topology changes, as well as geolocation routing protocols designed for applications such as target tracking. So far, due to various practical application environments and different goals, there is no complete and clear classification of routing protocols. In order to meet different application requirements, increasingly practical routing protocols are needed.

5. Dynamic network

First, in a sensor network with mobile nodes, some nodes move frequently. When the nodes move beyond the transmission range of other nodes, the communication between the mobile node and other nodes fails, and the topology of the network is destroyed. In addition to the sensor nodes, sensing objects and observers of these two elements may also have mobility, which will affect the network topology. Second, as we have already said, because the node energy is limited, when the node energy is exhausted, the communication of this node as the routing node between the others will be interrupted. On the other hand, because nodes are often affected by mountains, buildings, obstacles, and other city landscapes and wind, thunder, lightning, and other natural environments, the performance of wireless communication will often change, leading to frequent interruption of communication. Some sensor nodes may be out of the network for a long time; the offline work also causes the damage of network topology. Third, in some sensor network applications, with the joining of a new node, the original topology of the network should adapt to this change and make appropriate changes. In these cases, it is necessary to reconstruct the communication path among nodes in the network. The adaptability and fault tolerance also need to be considered when designing the routing algorithm. Therefore, how to establish the data theory of random connectivity of a network, laying a solid foundation for the reconstruction of a communication path, and the design of an adaptive routing algorithm are the fifth challenge we are facing.

6. Acorn RISC Machine

In order to obtain accurate information, a large number of sensor nodes are usually deployed in the monitoring area. The number of sensor nodes may reach tens of thousands or even more. On the one hand, the sensor nodes are distributed in a large geographical area, such as the sensor network for forest fire prevention and environmental monitoring, so we need to deploy a large number of sensor nodes. On the other hand, a large number of sensor nodes deployed in a smaller space will also form a large-scale network. Large-scale sensor networks have their advantages. For example, a greater signal-to-noise ratio of information can be obtained through different spatial perspectives. Massive information collection through the distributed processing can improve monitoring accuracy. A large number of nodes can also increase the coverage of the monitoring area.

However, we cannot ignore the fact that, because the sensor network is widely distributed, most of them are distributed in a dangerous environment where people cannot reach them. These nodes may work in the open air environment, exposed to the hot sun and rain, under the destruction of personnel or animals, which requires the sensor node to be very strong, resistant to damage, and suitable for a variety of harsh environmental conditions. Due to the characteristics of a large number of sensors, wide distribution will make network maintenance very difficult. The communication confidentiality and security of sensor networks are also very important for preventing the monitoring data from being stolen and accessed. Therefore, how to make the hardware and software of sensor networks with high robustness and fault tolerance is the sixth challenge.

7. Large scale distributed trigger

The sensor network not only monitors the sensing objects, but it also needs real-time control. The sensor nodes must configure control devices and control software, which are described as triggers. The sensor network will have to possess sufficient capacity to coordinate and manage thousands of triggers. Therefore, how to manage thousands of distributed triggers is the seventh challenge we are facing.

8. Infinite perceptual data flow

Because each node in the sensor network can generate infinite data flow with high real-time performance, each sensor node has only limited memory and computing resources, which is hard to deal with in these huge real-time data streams. Therefore, how to design energy efficient, real-time, mass-sensing data flow query, analysis, and mining of distributed algorithms is the eighth challenge.

9. Data-centric

In the current Internet, the IP address is the only identification for network equipment. The resource location and information transmission depend on the IP address of terminals, routers, servers, and other network equipment. If we want to access Internet resources, we must first know the IP address of the server storing resources. Therefore, the current Internet is an address-centric network, but the sensor network is not such a network. In the sensor network, the user is interested in data rather than the network and sensor hardware. Users rarely ask: "How do I achieve the connection between node A and node B?" They often ask: "Which areas of the network are poisonous?" The sensor network is not address-centric. Users do not ask: "What is the temperature of the sensor of address 27?" But they ask, "What is the temperature at a particular location?" In a sensor network, the data transmission is done in an aggregated manner, not an address-to-address route. So the theory and technology of the sensor network data management system is the ninth challenge we are facing, that is, how to build a data-centric sensor network. Based on the perceptual data management and processing, we can integrate data management, processing technology, and network technology, to provide users with an effective perception of data space or perception database. Users can use the sensing data freely as they use the usual database and data processing systems.

10. Requirement of a variety of sensors

In many sensor network applications, a variety of sensors is required, such as physical perceptron, biosensors, and chemical perceptron. Therefore, how to build a new perceptron concept, theory, technology, and a variety of new perceptrons is the tenth challenge.

11. Other challenging issues

Theory and Technology of the Delivery and Deployment of Sensor Nodes.
The Location of Sensor Nodes.
Research on Reliability of Networking Connectivity and Detection of Coverage
Sensor Network Security and Anti-interference

References

1. L. Sun, J. Li, Y. Chen, H. Zhu. *Wireless Sensor Network*. Tsinghua University Press, Beijing, 2005 (in Chinese).
2. R. Hekmat. *Ad-Hoc Networks: Fundamental Properties and Network Topologies[M]*. Springer, Dordrecht, the Netherlands, 2006.

3. Z. J. Haas, J. Deng, B. Liang, P. Papadimitratos, S. Sajama. Wireless Ad Hoc Networks. *IEEE Journal on Selected Areas in Communications*, 2002, 17(8): 1329–1332.
4. F. Ren, H. Huang, C. Lin. Wireless sensor network. *Journal of Software*, 2003, 14(14): 1513–1525 (in Chinese).
5. Z. Shaoren, W. Haitao, Z. Zhifeng. *Adhoc Network Technology*. Posts & Telcom Press, Beijing, 2005 (in Chinese).
6. H. Yu. *Wireless Mobile Ad Hoc Network*. Posts & Telcom Press, Beijing, 2005 (in Chinese).
7. M. Barbeau, E. Kranakis. Principles of Ad-hoc networking[J]. *Personal Indoor & Mobile Radio Communications IEEE International Symposium on*, 2007, 5: 3428.
8. J. Chen. *Wireless Sensor Network Application Examples*. Xi'an Cheng Feng Technology Co. Ltd, 2009 (in Chinese). https://wenku.baidu.com/view/3b1fc4e2172ded630b1cb6e7.html.
9. E. H. Callaway. *Wireless Sensor Network: Architectures and Protocols[M]*. Publishing House of Electronics Industry, Beijing, 2007 (in Chinese).
10. C. L. J. Hailing, M. Yong. Overview of wireless sensor networks. *Journal of Computer Research and Development*, 2005, 42(001): 163–174 (in Chinese).
11. G. Anastasi, M. Conti, M. Di Francesco, A. Passarella. Energy conservation in wireless sensor networks: A survey. *Ad Hoc Networks*, 2008, 7(3): 537–568.
12. G. Mao, B. Fidan, B. D.O. Anderson. Wireless sensor network localization techniques. *Computer Networks*, 2007, 51(10): 2529–2553.
13. C. F. Garcia-Hernandez, P. H. Ibargüengoytia-González. Wireless sensor networks and application: A survey[J]. *Journal of Computer Science and Network Security*, 2008, 21: 157–209.
14. L. Jianzhong, G. Hong. Survey on sensor network research. *Journal of Computer Research and Development*, 2008, 1: 1–15 (in Chinese).
15. J. Yick, B. Mukherjee, D. Ghosal. Wireless sensor network survey. *Computer Networks*, 2008, 52(12): 2292–2330.
16. A. A. Abbasi, M. Younis. A survey on clustering algorithms for wireless sensor networks. *Computer Communication*, 2007, 30: 2826–2841.
17. H. Alemdar, C. Ersoy. Wireless sensor networks for healthcare: A survey. *Computer Networks*, 2010, 54(15): 2688–2710.
18. S. K. Singh, M. P. Singh, D. K. Singh. Routing protocols in wireless sensor networks—A survey. *International Journal of Computer Science and Engineering Survey (IJCSES)*, 2010, 1(2): 63–83.

Chapter 2

Topology Control of Wireless Networks

2.1 Introduction of Topology Control

Once a wireless network is deployed, each node in the network can communicate with a set of nodes within a certain distance, and communication links can be established between the nodes to ensure that transmitted signals can be detected by one another. The topology of the network is determined by these nodes and links that can communicate directly.

As discussed in Chapter 1, wireless networks have many characteristics that are different from traditional wired networks. For example, wireless signals interfere with each other. There are many possible routes in the network. If a node uses a large amount of power to communicate directly with a remote node, it will consume a lot of unnecessary node energy and limit the reuse of wireless bandwidth. Even for nodes with small mobility, the routing protocol has to recalculate to construct a new topology.

These characteristics of wireless networks make topology control a very challenging problem. We need to control the node by a certain parameter, changing the mode of operation of the node to achieve network topology changes to extend the life of the network.

For topology control, there are three different international definitions and classification methods. Santi [1] in Italy defined topology control as a mechanism for coordinating nodes according to the transmission range of a node that can generate a network with the desired properties by reducing energy consumption and increasing network capacity. That is, topology control is power control. In the United States, Labrador [2] defined topology control as the identification and management of node parameters and operating modes; it constantly corrects the topology of the network. Its goal is to expand the network's survival time under the premise of guaranteeing the important characteristics of the network (such as connectivity and coverage). In Labrador's work, topology control is divided into power control and hierarchical topology control. The newest research of Aziz et al. (2012) [3] defined topology control as follows: It is a technology that generates and maintains optimal network topology by controlling network parameters; it can reduce energy consumption and obtain desired network properties. Aziz et al. divided topology control into power adjustment, power mode, and clustering technology.

Zhang Xue et al. [4] defined topology control as a technique that refers to extending the lifetime of the network as the main goal, taking into account factors such as communication interference, network delay, load balancing, simplicity, reliability, scalability, and so on, in the case of ensuring network coverage and connectivity. An optimized and improved network topology can be formed by setting or adjusting the parameters and operating modes of the nodes: setting or adjusting the transmission power of the nodes or using certain principles to select the appropriate nodes to be backbone nodes to participate in network processing and transmission. This topology can be formally described as a graph transformation as shown in Equation 2.1.

$$G = (V, E) \xrightarrow{\text{topology, control}} T = (V_T, E_T) \qquad (2.1)$$

$G=(V, E)$ represents the original network topology, and V contains all sensors deployed in the network and not dead. If node a can send data to node b using the maximum power transmission, then $\langle a,b \rangle \in E$ is the directed edge. T is the network topology after topology control, and $V_T \subseteq V$, $E_T \subseteq E \cdot V_T$ is the set of active sensor nodes of the network, and E_T is the edge set of E after it is simplified by topology control.

The traditional and common definitions of topology control often emphasize power control and backbone control while ignoring the important topological control mechanism of clustering. In Reference [3], Aziz et al. emphasized the importance of clustering algorithms in topology control. The topology control definition is supplemented as follows: "It is considered to be the topology control as long as the network topology is configured by controlling parameters to achieve energy savings." Obviously, clustering technology satisfies this definition.

Therefore, we divide topological control into power control and hierarchical topology control. Hierarchical topology control is divided into hierarchical topology control based on backbone network and hierarchical topology control based on clustering, as shown in Figure 2.1.

Power control technology studies the transmission power of the sensor nodes. This technology minimizes the degree of connectivity between nodes and their neighboring nodes, the overall link weights of the network nodes, and network interference by adjusting the transmission power of the nodes. It is necessary to ensure that all nodes in the network are interconnected.

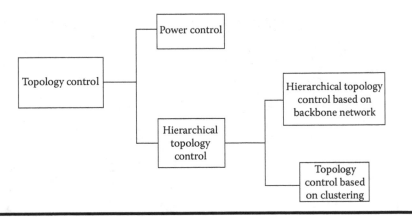

Figure 2.1   The classification of topology control.

Hierarchical topology control mainly studies the role assignment of network nodes and divides the network nodes into hierarchical layers by selecting the backbone nodes. The nonbackbone nodes go into sleep state to save energy when the routing is designed. In the cluster topology control, the network nodes are divided into cluster head nodes and cluster member nodes, and the network is divided into several clusters. All cluster member nodes can transmit data to the cluster head in one-hop or multihop mode, while the cluster head node can transmit the collected data to the base station through one-hop or multihop after data fusion. If noncluster head nodes do not communicate, the communication module can be closed in order to achieve the purpose of saving energy. In the backbone network topology control technology, the general heuristic algorithms or coloring algorithms are used to select the backbone nodes. This section is discussed in more detail in Chapters 3 and 4.

With the help of three types of topology control methods, three main topologies can be formed in the network. Suppose the original topology of a wireless sensor network (WSN) is shown in Figure 2.2a, wherein the black squares represent base stations. Figure 2.2b is a planar topology after a power topology control of Figure 2.2a. In this kind of structure, the nodes in T are usually equal. Figure 2.2c is a hierarchical topology controlled by the cluster topology control. Usually, all nodes in V are divided into several disjointed subsets. Each subset is called a cluster composed of a cluster head node and several cluster member nodes. There are two kinds of intra-cluster structures. When a member node has only one hop to the cluster head, only the edges from the members to the cluster head are retained. When a member node has multiple hops to the cluster head, the cluster node keeps all the edges on the path from the member node to the cluster head. Cluster structure is also divided into two kinds: direct communication between cluster head and base station and communication between cluster head and base station in the multihop mode through other cluster heads. Thus, the corresponding edges will be reserved. Figure 2.2d shows the backbone network after topology control. These backbone

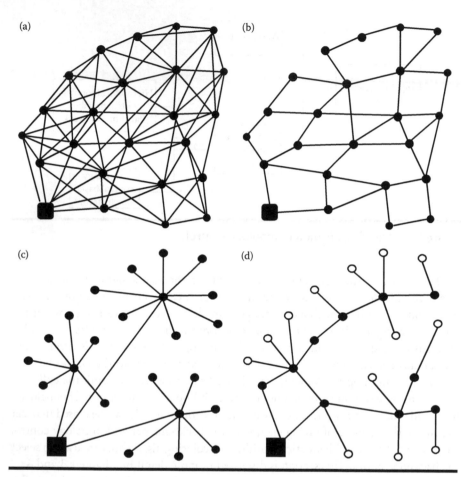

Figure 2.2 The mainstream topology structure after topology control. (a) Original network topology, (b) planar topology structure, (c) clustered hierarchical topology, and (d) backbone network topology.

networks conform to certain rules. For example, if the structure is a dominating set topological structure, a subset of connected nodes D is called the dominating set, such that either any node u in V is in D or there is a one-hop neighbor node v of u in D. If any two nodes are not in D, there is no edge belonging to E_T. In Figure 2.2d, the black nodes constitute a connected dominating set.

According to different practical applications, wireless network topology control has the corresponding goal. General design objectives and related concepts in topology control are described in the following [4].

1. Coverage: This can be viewed as a measure of the quality of service of a sensor network. In the coverage problem, the most important factor is the network's perception of the physical world [5]. Coverage problems can be divided into

area coverage, point coverage, and barrier coverage [6]. Area coverage studies the coverage or monitoring of target areas. Point coverage focuses on the coverage of discrete object points. Barrier coverage studies the probabilities of the detection of moving objects across a network's deployed area. Relatively speaking, the area coverage is studied more. If any point in the target area is monitored by k sensor nodes, the network is said to be k-covered, or it is said that the coverage of the network is k. It is generally required that each point of the target area be monitored by at least one node, or 1-covered. Since it is often difficult to discuss complete coverage of a target area, partial coverage is also sometimes studied, including partial 1 coverage and partial k coverage. Asymptotic coverage is also sometimes discussed. When the number of nodes in the network tends toward infinity, the probability of completely covering the target area tends to 1, which is called asymptotic coverage. For a deployed static network, coverage control is implemented mainly through sleep scheduling. The Voronoi diagram is a commonly used coverage analysis tool. For the dynamic network, the mobility of the nodes can be utilized to realize the redeployment of the nodes according to the requirements of the network coverage after the initial random deployment. The virtual potential field method is an important redeployment method. Overlay control is the basic problem of topology control.

2. Connectivity: For large-scale wireless networks, the data sensed by the sensor nodes are generally transmitted in a multihop manner to the base station to save energy. This requires topology control to ensure network connectivity. If removing k sensor nodes can render the network unconnected, we say the network is k connected, or the network connectivity is k. Topology control in general ensures that the network is connected (1 connected). Some applications may require network configuration to a specified degree of connectivity. As in the case of asymptotic coverage, we sometimes discuss the asymptotically connected issues. That is, when the deployment area tends toward infinity, the possibility of network connectivity tends to 1. Power control and hierarchical topology control must ensure network connectivity, which is the basic requirement of topology control.

3. Sparsity: This requires that the number of links in the network topology be linearly related to the number of nodes. This is usually expressed as the average node degree, which is consistent with the node degree mentioned in a later section. Many of a WSN's routing protocols are based on flooding [7] and keeping fewer links to reduce the overhead, which is also beneficial to the scalability of WSNs [8].

4. Node degree: Average node degree can reflect the sparsity of the network. An excessively high node degree indicates serious interference and conflict between the signals. The message may need to repeatedly retransmit and consume a lot of unnecessary energy. When the node degree is too low, the communication between the ends needs a longer transmission path, resulting in

increased energy consumption. In Reference [9], a theoretical analysis of the node degree shows that the static wireless network has the best performance when the node degree is 6.

5. Symmetry: This requires that all links in the network topology are bidirectional. On the asymmetric link, communication is difficult to achieve; even if it is possible to be achieved, the cost is very high [10]. Thus, many communication protocols are required to have this characteristic. For example, many multiple access control (MAC) protocols require a direct reply to the clear to send (CTS) when the receiver receives the sender's request to send (RTS).

6. Planarity: This requires that the network topology is drawn on a two-dimensional plane and that no two edges intersect, except at the ends.

7. Network lifetime: There are multiple definitions; network lifetime is generally defined as the length of time before the percentage of dead nodes is below a certain threshold [11]. It is also possible to define the lifetime of a network by measuring the quality of service of the network [12]. We can assume that the network survives only when it satisfies certain coverage quality, connectivity quality, and some other quality of services. Power control and hierarchical topology control are very effective techniques for prolonging the network lifetime. Maximizing the lifetime of a network is a very complex problem, and it has been the main goal of topology control research.

8. Interference and competition: Reducing communication interference, reducing the MAC layer of competition, and extending the life of the network are basically the same. Power control can adjust the transmission range, while the hierarchical topology control can adjust the number of working nodes. These can change the number of one-hop neighbor nodes (that is, the number of nodes competing for channels). In fact, for power control, the size of the competition area of the network radio channel is proportional to the transmission radius r of the node. So, reducing r can reduce the competition. Hierarchical topology control can also obviously reduce interference and contention by leaving as many nonbackbone nodes as possible in a sleep state.

9. Network delay: When the network load is high, low transmit power will bring less end-to-end delay. For low-load conditions, low transmit power will bring more end-to-end delay [13]. An intuitive explanation for this is that when the network load is low, the high transmit power reduces the number of hops from the source node to the destination node, thus reducing the end-to-end delay. When the network load is high, the node competition is intense, and low transmit power reduces network delay by mitigating competition. This is a rough relationship between power control and network delay.

10. Topological properties: In fact, for the network topology, it is difficult to directly give a quantitative measurement based on the ultimate goal of topology control. Therefore, in the design of a topology control (especially power control) program, good topological properties are often pursued as the next best thing.

In addition, topology control should consider other aspects such as load balancing, simplicity, reliability, scalability, and so on. There are intricate relationships between the various design goals of the topology control. The study of these relations is an important part of topology control research.

2.2 The Classification of Topology Control

In the earlier part of this chapter, we introduced the classification of topology control in wireless networks. In this section, we give more details to this classification and the specific algorithms in each category.

At present, there is a lot of research on topology control, which mainly aims at maximizing the lifetime of the network and focusing on power control and hierarchical topology control. Hierarchical topology control can be based on backbone network construction or on clustering. In Sections 2.2.1 and 2.2.2, we will introduce the concrete algorithms.

2.2.1 Power Control

Power control technology refers to reducing network energy overhead, mitigating competition for shared space channels, reducing interference to neighboring nodes, and increasing network capacity by adjusting the transmit power of the node signal, under the premise of the hardware supporting variable transmit power.

Power control technology is one of the main research directions of topology control. Adjusting the node's transmit power enables efficient use of network energy. In general, when a node is transmitting with a higher power, the signal sent by the node can reach more neighbor nodes, and the network topology is strongly connected. In this way, packets can go to the destination node with fewer hops; however, this results in more energy consumed, additional collisions due to more nodes competing for use of the wireless channel, and additional energy consumption and network delay due to data retransmission. In addition, the use of higher power transmission introduces more network interference. Although higher power makes the information transmission delay small, strong interference still greatly reduces the reuse rate of network bandwidth and network capacity. When the transmission power is very small, network topology is divided into islands without connectivity. Moreover, while the network capacity becomes larger, the data transmission delay becomes serious. Therefore, it is necessary to optimize the transmit power of the nodes and automatically adjust the transmit power of each node in the network to maximize the network lifetime under the premise of satisfying the basic properties of the wireless network (such as connectivity).

Power control is a very complex issue. Kirousis et al. reduced it to the range problem [14], referred to as range assignment (RA), and discussed the computational complexity of the problem in detail. Let $N = \{u_1, u_2, \ldots, u_n\}$ be a set of points representing the position of the network node in the $d(d = 1, 2, 3)$ dimension space, $r(u_i)$ denoting the emission radius of the node u_i. The RA problem is to make the network transmission power (the sum of the transmit power of each node) smallest, that is, to minimize $\sum_{u_i \in N} (r(u_i))^\alpha$, while ensuring network connectivity, where α is a constant greater than 2. In the one-dimensional case, the RA problem can be solved in the polynomial $O(n^4)$ time, whereas in two-dimensional and three-dimensional cases, the RA problem is NP-hard. The actual power control problem is more complex than the RA problem.

This conclusion tells us in theory that trying to find an optimal solution for the power control problem is unrealistic and that we should find practical solutions to power control from actual cases. Many solutions have been proposed. The basic idea is to extend the network lifetime by adjusting the transmit power. We list and discuss a few typical representative power control algorithms in the following sections.

2.2.1.1 Minimize the Maximum Transmit Power

CONNECT and BICONN are two centralized topology control algorithms [15] proposed by R. Ralnanathan et al. for power control. They are intended to minimize the maximum transmit power of each node, that is, as the optimization criterion for the network topology under the premise of network connectivity. The algorithm steps are as follows:

Step 1: The network is composed of only nodes, no edges. Initially, each node is its own component.

Step 2: According to the nondecreasing order of their mutual distance, choose edges in the network sequentially. That is, increase the transmit power of the node. If the selected edge can join different connected components when joining the network, these components are merged together to form one connected component. If the selected edge is already connected to one of the connected components, it is discarded because each connected component is a tree. If this already connected edge is added to the tree, it will create a loop, and the connected component of the network will be gradually reduced. Repeat this process until all the nodes in the network are on the same connected component.

Step 3: If the network topology generation is complete, define the edge that is not added to the network of other nodes as the side-effect edge. This step is the post-processing stage of the algorithm. It is designed to adjust the side-effect edge and reduce the transmit power of the node. The side-effect edges are mined and processed so that the transmit power allocated by each node is minimized. First, remove the edges outside the range of the wireless signal coverage and then sort the lengths of the edges in nonincremental order and select the longer side sequentially. A binary search is used to find whether there is an alternative side-effect edge to ensure network connectivity.

In Figure 2.3, the 6 nodes of A-F illustrate the process of CONNECT constructing the network topology. The nodes are described in the form of *s-p*, while *d(s)* is used to describe the edges, and *s* is the order of nodes adding to the network. *p* is the power used in this step; *d* is the length of the edge. In the figure, the dotted edge is a side-effect edge.

Since the nodes are in the form of wireless communication, adding the side-effect edge of CD in Step 6 of Figure 2.3 to the topology will not increase the transmit power of the nodes. The transmission power of each node is minimal, and the network is still connected while reducing the edges between nodes A and B. Eventually, the transmit power of each node in the topology of Step 7 in Figure 2.3 is the minimum.

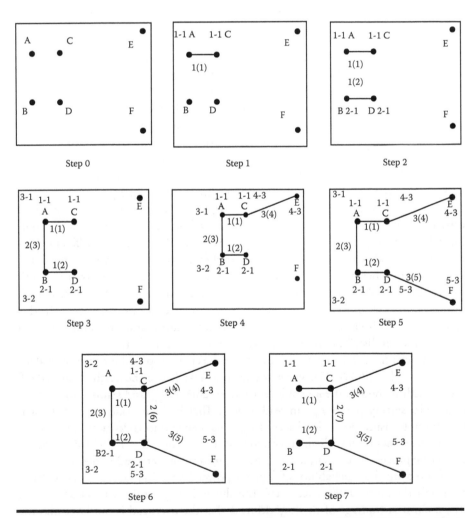

Figure 2.3 The network topology constructing process of CONNECT algorithm.

The algorithm BICONN also uses a greedy technique to modify a connected network into a biconnected network, which is similar to the algorithm CONNECT. We first identify the biconnected components in the graph induced by the power assignment from algorithm CONNECT. Then, node pairs are selected in the non-decreasing order of their mutual distance and joined only if they are in different biconnected components. This is continued until the network is biconnected.

CONNECT and BICONN algorithms are both centralized. Focusing on the calculation of the optimal transmit power, a centralized algorithm needs to obtain global information such as network topology, link status, and node location. Due to the large amount of communication overhead and computational overhead, they are clearly not suitable for the scale of WSNs.

2.2.1.2 Common Power Allocation

Narayanaswamy et al. of the University of Illinois proposed and implemented a simple method COMPOW [16] of combining power control with routing protocol. The basic idea is that all sensor nodes use the same transmit power to minimize the power while ensuring network connectivity. COMPOW establishes the routing table on each power level. At the power level p_i, the routing table RT_{P_i} is established by using the power exchange Hello message. All reachable nodes are entries in the routing table. COMPOW selects the minimum transmit power p_{com} so that $RT_{P_{com}}$ and $RT_{P_{max}}$ have the same number of entries, where p_{max} is the maximum transmit power. Thus, the entire network uses common transmit power p_{com}. In short, in the algorithm process each node maintains multiple routing tables, corresponding to different transmit power levels, and the same level between the nodes of the routing table exchange control messages. By comparing the entries in different routing tables, a node can determine the minimal common power level to ensure the maximum number of connected nodes and then use that power to transmit uniformly. COMPOW has better performance when the nodes are evenly distributed. However, in cases of uneven distribution, some isolated nodes will appear. In this case, a relatively isolated node will cause all nodes to use a lot of transmit power. In cases of uneven distribution of nodes, algorithm flaws are obvious.

Aiming at the defect of COMPOW, Kawadia et al. proposed the improved algorithm CLUSTERPOW [17]. When forwarding a packet to the destination node d, the algorithm chooses the lowest level routing table $RT_{P_{min}}$ and sends it to the next hop node, setting power p_{min} instead of p_{com}. That is, each node chooses its own minimum transmit power level according to its own connectivity with the destination node, rather than with all other nodes in the network. In CLUSTERPOW, the clustering process is implicit; it does not require any cluster head nodes. Clustering is achieved by the reachability of a given power level. The cluster level is determined by the number of power levels. The cluster is a dynamic distributed process. The main disadvantage of this algorithm is that the overhead is too large and the scalability of the protocol is poor.

2.2.1.3 Direction-Based Power Control

Wattenhofer, of Microsoft Research Asia, and Li et al., of Cornell University, proposed the CBTC to ensure that network connectivity is based on direction [18]. The basic idea of the algorithm is that node u selects the minimum power $P_{u,\rho}$ to ensure that in every cone of degree ρ around u, there is at least one neighbor. The author proves that the connectivity of the network can be ensured at that time of $\rho \leq 5\pi/6$.

The steps of CBTC algorithm are as follows.

Step 1: Node u broadcasts a Hello message using low transmission power p_0. It gradually increases the transmission power to discover more neighbors. If the node u finds a new neighbor v in this process, then v joins the set $N(u)$ [$N(u)$ denotes the set of neighbor nodes of node u] and records its direction relative to v and the required power p_k. If the points in $N(u)$ cover all the cone area of degree ρ around u, or the maximum transmission power P is reached, then go to the second step.

Step 2: The algorithm eliminates the redundant edges without affecting the connectivity. This process reduces the number of nodes to help (not guarantee) reductions in interference and collisions and increases network throughput. Redundant edge removal can be done when it will not worsen the network minimum power routing. If node u has two neighbor nodes $v, w \in N(u)$, and $p(u,v) + p(v,w) \leq p(u,w)$, then w is removed from $N(u)$, where $p(u, v)$ denotes the required transmit power from node u to v, $p(v, w)$ denotes the required transmit power from node v to w, and $p(u, v)$ denotes the transmission power required from node u to w.

Simulation results show that about 90% of the nodes in the network are still working in the algorithm CBTC, when 80% of nodes in the network with the maximum transmit power are dead.

Bahramgiri et al. of the Massachusetts Institute of Technology have extended it to three-dimensional space and proposed fault-tolerant CBTC [19]. The problems to be solved of the CBTC algorithm include how to gradually increase the power; due to the differences in energy consumption of nodes, how to protect nodes with low energy; and so on. The direction-based algorithm does not need to obtain its own position information through global positioning system (GPS), but it needs reliable direction information. So it needs to solve the problem of arrival angle. The node needs to be equipped with multiple directional antennas, so it has higher requirements for sensor nodes.

2.2.1.4 Power Control Based on Node Degree

The core idea of the algorithm based on the node degree is to give the upper and lower demands of the node degree, to dynamically adjust the node's transmit power, making the degree of the node rest in a reasonable range. A node degree-based algorithm uses local information to adjust the connectivity between adjacent nodes, thus ensuring the connectivity of the entire network, while ensuring that the node's link has a certain degree of redundancy and scalability. The typical node degree-based power control algorithms of the local neighbor average algorithm LMA and the local average algorithm LMN algorithm are proposed by Kubisch et al. [20], as well as the algorithms LINT and LILT proposed by Ramanathan et al. [21]; they are briefly described in the following section.

2.2.1.4.1 LMA and LMN

The steps of LMA algorithm are as follows.

In the first step, all nodes start with the same transmission power of TransPower, and each node periodically broadcasts a LifeMsg with its own ID.

In the second step, if the node receives a LifeMsg message, it sends a LifeAckMsg reply message, which contains the node ID.

In the third step, when each node again sends LifeMsg, the node first checks the received LifeAckMsg message, then uses these messages to count the number of its neighbors—NodeResp.

In the fourth step, if NodeResp is less than the lower bound of NodeMinThresh, then the node will increase the transmission power in this round of transmission, but the transmission power cannot exceed B_{max} times of the initial transmission power, as shown in Equation 2.2. Likewise, if NodeResp is greater than the maximum number of neighbors NodeMaxThresh, then the node will reduce the transmission power as shown in Equation 2.3, where B_{max}, B_{min}, A_{inc}, and A_{dec} are the four parameters, which will affect the power adjustment accuracy and scope.

$$TransPower = \min\{B_{max} * Transpower,$$

$$A_{inc} * (NodeMinThresh - NodeResp) * TransPower\} \qquad (2.2)$$

$$TransPower = \min\{B_{min} * Transpower,$$

$$A_{dec} * (1 - (NodeResp - NodeMaxThresh) * TransPower\} \qquad (2.3)$$

LMN algorithm and LMA are similar, but the calculation method of NodeResp is different. In the LMN algorithm, when each node sends a LifeAckMsg message, the node puts the number of the neighbors to this message. After collecting all the LifeAckMsg messages of the nodes sending the LifeMsg message, the node averages the sum of its own neighbors and the number of neighbors contained in all LifeAckMsg messages as its own number of neighbors. The simulation results show that the convergence and network connectivity of the two algorithms can be guaranteed, and a certain degree of optimization effect can be achieved through a small amount of local information. However, there are still some imperfections in the algorithm, such as the need to further study the rational decision conditions of neighbor nodes and the allocation of different weights using the information from the neighbor nodes according to the strength of the signal.

2.2.1.4.2 LINT and LILT

LINT and LILT are two kinds of heuristic topology control algorithms. Nodes increase or decrease power according to the dynamic topology of the mobile network to make the node degree close to the ideal node degree.

The procedure of the LINT algorithm is as follows.

The algorithm sets three main parameters for each node: the ideal node degree d_d, the upper limit of the node degree d_h, and the lower limit of the node degree d_l. The node periodically checks the active node degree in the neighbor table established by the routing mechanism. If the degree is greater than d_h, the node reduces the working power. If the degree is less than d_l, the node increases the transmission power. Otherwise, the node does nothing. Let γ denotes loss in units of dB, then:

$$\begin{cases} \gamma(r) = \gamma(r_{thr}), & r < r_{thr} \\ \gamma(r) = \gamma(r_{thr}) + 10 * \varepsilon * \log_{10}(r/r_{thr}), & r \geq r_{thr} \end{cases} \tag{2.4}$$

where, $2 < \varepsilon < 5$ depending on the surrounding environment. r is the propagation radius, r_{thr} is a limit, and the limit of propagation loss is constant γ $(r > r_{thr})$. The transmission power P_d at the ideal node degree can be obtained by the following equations.

$$d_c = D * \pi * r_c^2 \tag{2.5}$$

$$d_d = D * \pi * r_d^2 \tag{2.6}$$

$$p_c - (\gamma(r_{thr}) + 10 * \log(r_c/r_{thr})) = T \tag{2.7}$$

$$p_d - (\gamma(r_{thr}) + 10 * \log(r_d/r_{thr})) = T \tag{2.8}$$

Substituting 2.5 and 2.6 into 2.7 and 2.8:

$$p_d = p_c - 5 * \varepsilon * \log(d_d/d_c) \tag{2.9}$$

where, d_c and p_c denote the current degree and the current transmission power in the network with the node density D and derive an expression of reaching the ideal node degree d_d for the new transmission power p_d, r_c denoting the propagation radius of the node with the transmission power p_d. r_d denotes the propagation radius at the target transmission power. The nodes are randomly distributed in the plane, and T represents the sensitivity of radio reception.

LINT and LILT are zero-overhead protocols that do not require specialized control information. The difference is that the types of feedback information and network characteristics to be maintained are different. LILT can also use effective global network topology information, according to some of the link-state routing protocols.

2.2.1.5 Power Control Based on Proximity Graph

The basic idea of the power control algorithm based on proximity graph is that all nodes use the maximum transmission power forming the topology G. The proximity graph G' of G is obtained according to a certain neighbor decision condition, and each node determines the transmit power with the furthest adjacent node. This is an approximate algorithm intended to solve the power problem. The classical proximity graph models are relative neighborhood graph (RNG), Gabriel graph, Delaunay graph, Yao graph, and minimum spanning tree (MST); refer to Chapter 4 for more details. Typical algorithms for power control based on proximity graph are the DRNG and DLSS algorithms proposed by Li and Hou [22] (based on directed RNG and directed local MST, respectively), the XTC algorithm proposed by Wattenhofer [23], Asymmetric Link proposed by Liu [24], and MTCP based on minimum cost spanning tree MST, which is proposed by Wieselthier et al. [25]. They are introduced as follows.

1. DRNG and DLSS

   DRNG and DLSS are the topology control algorithms proposed for heterogeneous WSNs with different transmission ranges. In the two algorithms, each node uses local information to establish its own neighbor set and adjust its own transmit power. Its purpose is to shorten the transmit radius of the node and to reduce the transmit power, thus saving node energy and prolonging the network lifetime.

   The process of building a network topology of DRNG and DLSS algorithms consists of three stages: the information collection phase, the topology construction phase, and the topology construction of two-way connection phase.

   Information collection phase: The information required for each node u to build a topology is its reachable neighbor set N_u^R, which can be obtained by collecting local information. Each node periodically broadcasts a Hello message with its own maximum transmit power, which includes at least its own ID, maximum transmission energy, and location. It is assumed that each node can obtain its own position information with a self-matching positioning device or GPS positioning. Each node then determines its own set N_u^R of reachable neighbors by receiving the Hello message.

   Topology construction phase: After obtaining the reachable neighbor set N_u^R, the two algorithms determine the neighbor nodes according to the following criteria: For DRNG algorithms: As shown in Figure 2.4, if $v \in N_u^R$ and there is no other node that satisfies $w(u, p) < w(u, v)$, $w(p, v) < w(u, v)$,

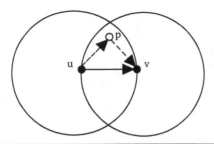

Figure 2.4 DRNG algorithm.

and $d(p,v) \le r_p$, the node v is selected as the neighbor node of the node u, denoted as $u \xrightarrow{DRNG} v$.

The criteria of DLSS algorithm determining the neighbor nodes is as follows: Assume the known node u and its reachable neighbor subgraph G_u^R, when the node v in the node u is on the direct local generation graph S_u, which is the output of DLSS (u). The node u is only at one-hop distance, node v is the neighbor of node u, denoted as $u \xrightarrow{DLSS} v$.

DLSS is an extension of LMST in heterogeneous networks [26]. In the LMST algorithm, the energy costs of all the edges in the direct local MST are calculated, but the connectivity of the network cannot be maintained in the heterogeneous network. In the LMST algorithm, each node u computes a direct local generation graph, minimizing the maximum energy consumption of all edges in the graph and taking the one-hop node as its neighbor node.

After this phase is completed, the node u determines its own neighbor set and then adjusts the transmitting radius to the distance to the farthest neighbor node.

Two-way link topology construction stage: In the topology after the topology construction, some links may not be two-way connected. In this stage, the network topology can be connected in both directions by adding or deleting edges.

The performance of DRNG and DLSS: (1) Both DRNG and DLSS algorithms can maintain heterogeneous network connectivity; (2) Both DRNG and DLSS algorithms guarantee the two-way connectivity of the network after the addition and deletion of the network topology; (3) The output node degree of DRNG and DLSS is bounded.

Figure 2.5 shows an example of optimized topology through DRNG and DLSS. In this experiment, 50 nodes are evenly distributed in the range 1000 m × 1000 m, and the transmission range of the nodes is evenly distributed in [200 m, 250 m]. Figure 2.5a is the original topology that each node is transmitting with the maximum power. Figure 2.5b is the topology optimized by the DRNG algorithm, while Figure 2.5c is optimized by the DLSS algorithm. It can be seen that both the DRNG algorithm and the DLSS

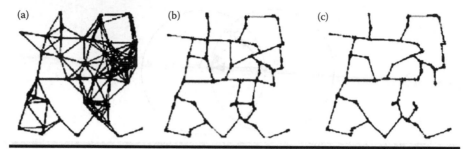

Figure 2.5 Algorithm optimization graph of DRNG and DLSS. (a) The original topology, (b) the optimization diagram of DRNG, and (c) the optimization diagram of DLSS. (From Li, N. and Hou J. C., Topology control in heterogeneous wireless networks: Problems and solutions, *Proceedings of the IEEE Conference on Computer Communications (INFOCOM),* **IEEE Press, New York, 2004, 232–243.)**

algorithm reduce the number of edges in the network topology and reduce the transmission power of the nodes, while reducing the communication interference between the nodes.

The DRNG and DLSS algorithms focus on the connectivity of the network, fully considering the theory of neighbor graph. Taking the characteristic of the sensor network into consideration, they make the topology connected under the premise of the bidirectional connected original network. In the average power and node degree, they both have good performance.

2. XTC

XTC is a novel topology control algorithm based on the sequence of link quality of neighbor nodes. It does not need to know the exact coordinates of the node, which can work in the mountains or in an environment with obstacles.

The basic idea of XTC is to use the strength of the received signal as the distance measurement of RNG. XTC algorithms can be divided into the following three steps.

The first step is neighbor ordering. The node u computes a total order over all its neighbors in the network graph. From an abstract point of view, this order is intended to reflect the quality of the links to the neighbors. The link to a neighbor appearing early in the total order is regarded as being of higher quality than the link to a neighbor that is placed later. A neighbor w appearing before v in the order means the link quality of w is better than that of v.

The second step is information exchange. The node u broadcasts its own neighbor order while receiving the orders established by all of its neighbors.

The third step is edge election. A node u traverses the total order with decreasing link quality. "Good" neighbors are considered first; "worse" ones, later. Informally speaking, a node u only builds a direct communication link to a neighbor v if u has no "better" neighbor w that can be reached more easily from v than u itself (Figure 2.6).

Figure 2.6 Edge selection diagram of XTC. (From http://dcg.ethz.ch/members/ wroger.html.)

XTC does not need the position information and too high request to sensor nodes, so it is suitable for the heterogeneous network and for the three-dimensional space. Compared with other algorithms, XTC is simpler and more practical. However, XTC still has a certain distance to practical requirements. For example, XTC does not take into account the changes of communication link quality.

3. Asymmetric link

The purpose of the algorithm is to obtain the minimum energy topology, that is, the reachability between any two nodes is guaranteed to be the same as the initial topology. The nodes are heterogeneous, which can automatically adjust the wireless power. The algorithm is divided into three steps.

The first step is establishing the vicinity topology. Node i broadcasts a message, referred to as the initialization request (IRQ) message, using its maximum transmission power. The nodes that receive the IRQ message are referred to as the vicinity nodes of node i. The IRQ message includes the location of node i as well as the maximum power information. Upon receiving such an IRQ message, each node j in the vicinity nodes of node i replies to node i with an initialization reply message. Having the knowledge of the locations and the maximum transmission powers for itself and all its vicinity nodes, node i may derive the existence of the vicinity edges.

The second step is deriving the minimum-power vicinity tree. With the knowledge of the weighed, directed topology, a directed path and all available paths from node i to j are found.

The third step is the propagation of transmission powers. In this phase, node i needs to calculate the transmission power for itself and for each vicinity node, to ensure that all its minimum-power paths exist in the final minimum-power network topology. Specially, for node i itself and each node in the set of V_i, the transmission power is assigned as the power required to reach the furthest one-hop downstream nodes in i's minimum-power vicinity tree. Node i first adopts the minimum power assigned to itself and then sends the minimum power required for each vicinity node with an explicit PR message. Upon receiving the PR message, a vicinity node j compares the power requirement from i with its current power setting. If i requires a stronger transmission power at node j, node j increases its power accordingly. Otherwise, it discards the PR message.

The simulation results show that the algorithm can save more than 50% energy, increase network density, and increase energy efficiency to 80%–90% for small networks with only 10 nodes.

4. MTCP algorithm based on MST

First, $G = (V, E)$ is defined as a graph with a maximum range R. V is a set of sensor nodes, and E is a set of inter-node links. The elements of E are denoted by $l(u, v)$, where $u, v \in V$. Figure 2.7 shows the original network topology of 100 nodes when all nodes have the maximum transmit radius R. This is expressed as $G = (V, E)$. Let G be strongly connected. The edge load is defined by the selected energy consumption model. Constructing an MST requires the distance between nodes. The $MST(G) = (V, E_{mst})$ represents the MST constructed on graph $G = (V, E)$, and each node in V can be the root node of the spanning tree. It is obvious that $MST(G)$ is also connected to the strongly connected graph G. Thus, in the algorithm, an adjustable transmission range $r(u)$ is defined,

$$\forall u \in V, r(u) = \max\{d(u,v) | v \in V \wedge (u,v) \in E_{mst}\} \qquad (2.10)$$

This means that each node in the MST can reduce its wireless transmission coverage, just needing to cover all the neighbors. Through the use of greedy algorithms such as Prim, one can construct an MST. The Prim algorithm creates an MST by selecting multiple edges at a time. The greedy criterion for selecting the next edge is to choose the least costly edge from the remaining edges that have not yet been added to the tree and join so that all the selected edges are still a tree. Finally, the edges selected in all steps form a tree, as shown in Figure 2.8.

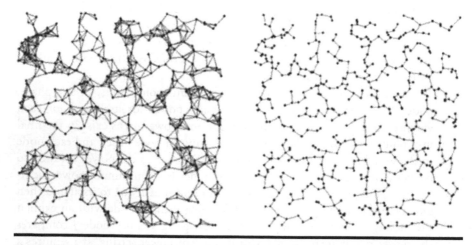

Figure 2.7   XTC algorithm. (From http://dcg.ethz.ch/members/wroger.html.)

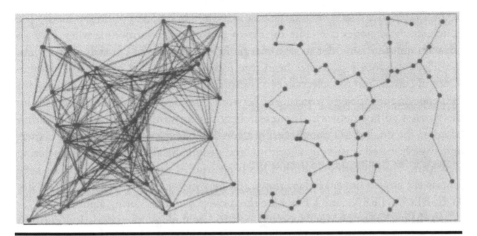

Figure 2.8 Network topology constructed by MTCP algorithm. (From Wieselthier, J. et al., On the construction of energy-efficient broadcast and multicast trees in wireless networks, *Proceedings of the IEEE Infocom 2000*, Tel Aviv, Israel, 2000, 585–594.)

MTCP algorithm is based on MST. The topology control algorithm follows the traditional broadcast algorithm, for all nodes to establish a shared broadcast tree. The information is transmitted on the shared tree; it arrives at all tree members. The advantage of this kind of algorithm is that only some of the tree members participate in the data forwarding after the spanning tree is established. The other member nodes do not forward the data packets and only need to receive and send back the data, thus reducing energy consumption. For large-scale WSNs, it is a centralized algorithm, which needs the global information of the network. It needs a great deal of computational overhead and information overhead to build the topology. At the same time, because some key nodes in the tree need to communicate with more neighbors, it leads to more energy consumption. The topology cannot guarantee that the energy consumption of each node is even or guarantee the balance of the entire network energy consumption.

2.2.2 Hierarchical Topology Control

Hierarchical topology control technology is a very important technology in topology control research; it mainly includes clustering topology control technology and backbone network topology control technology.

In the clustering topology control, the network nodes are divided into cluster head nodes and cluster member nodes, and the network is divided into multiple clusters. For the WSN, all cluster member nodes can transmit data to the cluster head node in one-hop or multihop mode. The cluster head nodes transmit the data in the cluster after data fusion to the base station in one-hop or multihop mode. The noncluster head nodes can close their own communication module when they do not communicate, in order to save energy. In the research of clustering algorithm, the selection process of cluster head, the forming process of cluster, the maintenance of cluster, and the selection of a transmission route of data all have important influence on the topology structure of network. The algorithm research begins from the wireless ad hoc network. The researchers put forward the clustering algorithm based on the smallest ID, the clustering algorithm based on the highest node degree, node weight-based clustering algorithm, and geographical location based clustering algorithm. The clustering algorithm has been studied extensively. Researchers have proposed a large number of algorithms, among which LEACH, HEED, PEGASIS, ACE, EEUC, TEEN, and TTDD are the most popular clustering algorithms.

In the backbone network topology control technology, the heuristic algorithm or the coloring algorithm is usually adopted to select the backbone nodes. There are many kinds of backbone node selection, such as the node selection algorithm based on node energy, the node selection algorithm based on energy consumption, backbone node selection algorithm based on distance, node degree-based backbone node selection algorithm, and so on. Different selection criteria will have different effects on the network topology, the energy of the network nodes, and the execution efficiency of the routing strategy. These algorithms have also been extensively studied in wireless ad hoc networks and WSNs.

Chapters 3 and 4 of this book give a detailed introduction of the clustering algorithm and the backbone network construction algorithm.

References

1. P. Santi. Topology control in wireless ad hoc and sensor networks. *ACM Computing Survey*, 37(2): 164–194.
2. M. A. Labrador, P. M. Wightman. *Topology Control in Wireless Sensor Networks*. Springer Science+Business Media B.V., Heidelberg, 2009.
3. A. A. Aziz, Y. A. Sekercioglu, P. Fitzpatrick, M. Ivanovich. A survey on distributed topology control techniques for extending the lifetime of battery powered wireless sensor networks. IEEE Communications Surveys and Tutorials, 2013, 15: 121–144.
4. X. Zhang, S. Lu, G. Chen, X. Chen Dao, L. Xie. Topology control for wireless sensor networks. *Journal of Software*, 2007, 18(4): 943–954 (in Chinese).
5. S. Meguerdichian, F. Koushanfar, M. Potkonjak, M. B. Srivastava. Coverage problems in wireless ad-hoc sensor networks. In: Bauer F, Cavendish D, eds. *Proceedings of the IEEE Conference on Computer Communications (INFOCOM)*, IEEE Press, New York, 2001, 1380–1387.
6. M. T. Thai, F. Wang, D. Z. Du. Coverage problems in wireless sensor networks: Designs and analysis. *International Journal of Sensor Networks* (Special Issue on Coverage Problems in Sensor Networks), 2008, 3(3): 191–200.
7. K. Akkaya, M. Younis. A survey on routing protocols for wireless sensor networks. *Ad Hoc Networks*, 2005, 3(3): 325–349.

8. X. Y. Li, P. J. Wan, Y. Wang et al. Sparse power efficient topology for wireless networks. In: *Proceedings of the 35th Annual Hawaii International Conference System Sciences (HICSS)*, Big Island, Hawaii, 2002, 9, 3839–3848.
9. L. Kleinrock, J. Silvester. Optimum transmission radio for packet radio networks or why six is a magic number. *NTC 1978; National Telecommunications Conference*, 1978, 1: 4.
10. R. Prakash. Unidirectional links prove costly in wireless ad-hoc networks. In: *Proceedings of the 3rd International Workshop on Discrete Algorithms and Methods for Mobile Computing and Communications (DIAL-M)*, Seattle, WA, 1999, 15–22.
11. J. Deng, Y. S. Han, W. B. Heinzelman, P. K. Varshney. Scheduling sleeping nodes in high density cluster-based sensor networks. *ACM/Kluwer Mobile Networks and Applications (MONET)*, 2005, 10(6): 825–835.
12. K. Wu, Y. Gao, F. Li, Y. Xiao. Lightweight deployment-aware scheduling for wireless sensor networks. *ACM/Kluwer Mobile Networks and Applications (MONET)*, 2005, 10(6): 837–852.
13. V. Kawadia. Protocols and architecture for wireless ad hoc networks. PhD Thesis. University of Illinois at Urbana–Champaign, 2004.
14. L. M. Kirousis, E. Kranakis, D. Krizanc, A. Pelc. Power consumption in packet radio networks. *Theoretical Computer Science*, 2000, 243, 289–305.
15. R. Ramanathan, R. Rosales-Hain. Topology control of multi-hop wireless networks using transmit power adjustment. In: *Proceedings of the 9th Joint Conference on IEEE Computer and Communications Societies (INFOCOM)*, Tel-Aviv, Israel, March 2000.
16. S. Narayanaswamy, V. Kawadia, R. S. Sreenivas, P. R. Kumar. Power control in ad-hoc networks: Theory, architecture, algorithm and implementation of the COMPOW protocol. In: Proceedings of the European Wireless Conference, Florence, 2002, 156–162.
17. V. Kawadia, P. R. Kumar. Power control and clustering in ad-hoc networks. In: Mitchell K, ed. *Proceedings of the IEEE Conference on Computer Communications (INFOCOM)*, IEEE Press, New York, 2003, 459–469.
18. L. Li, Y. H. Joseph. A cone-based distributed topology-control algorithm for wireless multi-hop networks. *IEEE/ACM Transactions on Networking*, 2005, 13(1): 147–159.
19. M. Bahramgiri, M. T. Hajiaghayi, V. S. Mirrokni. Fault-tolerant and 3-dimensional distributed topology control algorithms in wireless multihop networks. *Wireless Networks*, 2006, 12(2): 179–188.
20. M. Kubisch, H. Karl, A. Wolisz, L. C. Zhong, J. Rabaey. Distributed algorithms for transmission power control in wireless sensor networks. In: Yanikomeroglu H, ed. *Proceedings of the IEEE Wireless Communications and Networking Conference (WCNC)*, IEEE Press, New York, 2003, 16–20.
21. R. Ramanathan, R. R. Hain. Topology control of multihop wireless networks using transmit power adjustment. In: *Infocom 2000*, Tel Aviv, Israel, 2000, 404–413.
22. N. Li, J. C. Hou. Topology control in heterogeneous wireless networks: Problems and solutions. In: *Proceedings of the IEEE Conference on Computer Communications (INFOCOM)*, IEEE Press, New York, 2004, 232–243.
23. R. Wattenhofer, A. Zollinger. XTC: A practical topology control algorithm for ad-hoc networks. In: Panda DK, Duato J, Stunkel C, eds. *Proceedings of the International Parallel and Distributed Processing Symposium (IPDPS)*, IEEE Press, Santa Fe, NM, 2004, 216–223.

24. J. Liu, B. Li. Distributed topology control in wireless sensor networks with asymmetric links. In: *Proceedings of Global Telecommunications Conference, GLOBECOM'03*, IEEE, 3, 1257–1262.
25. J. Wieselthier, G. Nguyen, A. Ephremides. On the construction of energy-effieient broadeast and multicast trees in wireless networks. In: *Proceedings of the IEEE Infocom 2000*, Tel Aviv, Israel, 2000, 585–594.
26. A. Clementi, P. Penna, R. Silvestri. On the power assignment problem in radio networks. *ACM/Kluwer Mobile Networks and Applications (MONET)*, 2004, 9(2): 125–140.

Chapter 3

Clustering Algorithms

3.1 Clustering Routing Protocols in Wireless Ad Hoc Networks

3.1.1 Outline

The ad hoc network, which was introduced in Chapter 1, is a new wireless network without infrastructure. It consists of dramatic nodes with wireless devices under the support of various protocols. Because of mobile nodes, the topology will change quickly in an unpredictable way along with the movement of nodes. The nodes can have the function of both host and router: As a host, a node can send and receive data; as a router, the node needs to switch the routing information, construct a routing table, and forward the corresponding data according to the routing protocol configured in advance. Compared with the wireless network based on the base station or the AP, the characteristics of the ad hoc network bring a lot of difficulties for scalability and management, such as noncenter structure and the mobility of nodes. Clustering is proposed as a popular solution to these difficulties and was first proposed in ad hoc networks. Mobile nodes with the same property (e.g., similar geographic position, similar motion behavior) use a clustering method. The cooperative work among the nodes in a cluster can improve the whole performance of the network. Generally, nodes in the same cluster are regarded as an autonomous domain. In a cluster, the node with the strongest ability will be chosen as a cluster head to manage the other nodes in the cluster. When it needs inter-cluster communication, the corresponding nodes will be responsible for communication and provide reliability for the ad hoc network. Figure 3.1 shows the clustering topology of the ad hoc network.

Generally, the clustering algorithm in an ad hoc network completes the cluster formation and connection in the topology probe.

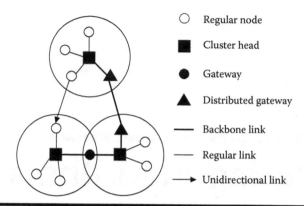

Figure 3.1 The clustering topology of the ad hoc network.

The topology probe obtains the information of neighbors and the topology of the whole network by sending or receiving probe packets. A node, periodically or on demand, sends a probe packet to declare its presence. Meanwhile, it listens in the channel and updates its neighbor table by receiving the probe packets from its neighbors. When the node sends the probe packet again, it will include the information of all of its neighbors. The node will realize that it is disconnected from one of its neighbors if the probe packet from this neighbor includes its own information. Therefore, after a round of probe packets, each node knows which nodes are its neighbors. After the second round of probe packets, a node will master the information of the nodes two hops away because the node's neighbor shows the information of its neighbor. In this way, a node will obtain the information of the whole network.

Cluster forming refers to the process of electing the cluster head and dividing the clusters according to a rule. Without the loss of generality, a node with strong function and power will be elected as the cluster head.

Cluster connection refers to the process that adjacent clusters select the associated nodes. In order to decrease the control overhead of associated nodes, gateway nodes and distributed gateway nodes can be selected by the rule of minimum degree: If two adjacent clusters overlap and more than one node that can directly communicate with two cluster heads exist, the node with the minimum degree should be chosen as the gateway node; if two clusters are adjacent but do not overlap, choose one node from each cluster respectively to construct a distributed gateway according to the rule of minimum degree. If the degree is the same in these two scenarios, choose the node with minimum ID or choose randomly. However, when the node density is high and packet flow is heavy, one needs to choose more associated nodes to balance the traffic and try to utilize virtual backbone network to reduce the number of nodes participating in the flooding broadcast.

The goal of the clustering algorithm is to establish and maintain a set of clusters that are connected with each other and can overlap the whole network and support resource management and routing protocols with less overhead of calculation and communication. The clustering mechanism needs to maintain a stable topology, to reduce the possibility of reclustering and optimize the connection among the clusters. Moreover, it needs to consider other aspects, such as the energy of nodes, workload balance of the network, and the support of routing algorithms or channel access protocols.

3.1.2 Classic Clustering Algorithms in Wireless Ad Hoc Networks

3.1.2.1 Minimum ID Clustering Algorithm

Minimum ID heuristic algorithm [1] is a simple clustering algorithm proposed by Gerla et al. The algorithm is described as follows.

1. First, assign a unique ID to each node in the network and mark each node as white.
2. If a node finds its ID minimum among its neighbors, it will mark itself black and become a cluster head.
3. Then the node marks all its neighbors gray, which means these gray nodes are the members of this cluster.
4. Repeat steps (2) and (3) until there are no white nodes in the network.
5. Finally, all the cluster heads connect to each other through gateways; thus, cluster heads and gateways constitute a connected virtual backbone network.

The advantages of the algorithm include small calculation, it is easy to realize, the frequency of cluster head updating is slow, and there is little overhead of maintaining a cluster.

However, there are some disadvantages. Only choosing the nodes with minor IDs as cluster heads will cost more energy for these nodes, which tends to bottleneck nodes and leads to the function partition of network (Figure 3.2).

3.1.2.2 Maximum Degree Clustering Algorithm

The maximum degree algorithm is also proposed by Gerla et al. Compared with the minimum ID clustering algorithm, the maximum degree algorithm is mainly different in step (2): If a node has not participated in clustering and finds that it is the maximum degree node among its neighbors, it will be the cluster head and be marked as black (choose the node with the minor ID when the degrees are same). The algorithm draws on the same method as for choosing a router in the Internet; the principle is to minimize the number of routers. Therefore, the goal of the algorithm is to minimize the number of clusters. A node can obtain the number of its neighbors by exchanging control messages; the node with the maximum degree

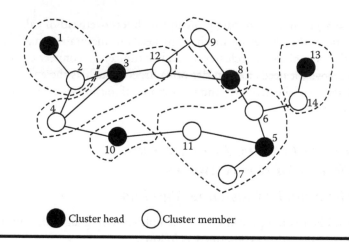

Cluster head   ○ Cluster member

Figure 3.2   Minimum ID clustering algorithm. (From Lin, C. H. R., Gerla, M., *A Distributed Architecture for Multimedia in Dynamic Wireless Networks*, IEEE GLOBECOM, 1468–1472, 1995.)

among its neighbors will be the cluster head. The node with the minimum ID will be the cluster head when the degrees are the same. Then the one-hop neighbor of the cluster head will be the regular member in the cluster. This process is repeated until all nodes join a cluster.

The algorithm is characterized by the use of node degree as a clustering standard to form a small cluster structure. Fewer clusters also reduce the time for packet delivery, and the channel reuse efficiency decreases. The throughput of a region will be reduced seriously when the node density of the region is too high, because it cannot achieve workload balance and channel sharing. Besides, the cluster heads change quickly if the nodes have strong mobility, which increases the overhead of maintenance. Therefore, the algorithm is adapted to the network with lower density (Figure 3.3).

3.1.2.3 Motion-Based Clustering Algorithm

The MOBIC algorithm is proposed by Basu et al. The basic idea is to select the nodes with relatively stable motion as cluster heads. Each mobile node can calculate the difference of speed between itself and its neighbors. The lower the difference is, the more stable the node is. The node with the minimum difference in the local area will be chosen as a cluster head.

Specifically, each node calculates the relative mobility between itself and the source node by receiving Hello messages continuously from the same source in the MOBIC algorithm. The node can calculate its average local mobility when it obtains relative mobility between itself and all of its neighbors. Then it will attach the average local mobility to the Hello message and broadcast it to its neighbors. With this way of clustering, the next steps are similar to the LID algorithm.

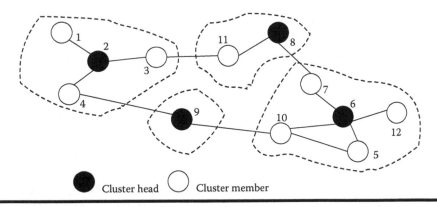

Figure 3.3 Maximum degree clustering algorithm. (From Lin, C. H. R., Gerla, M., *A Distributed Architecture for Multimedia in Dynamic Wireless Networks*, IEEE GLOBECOM, 1468–1472, 1995.)

The calculation of relative mobility does not rely on location information. Thus, it is better than methods using distance or speed.

3.1.2.4 Weight-Based Clustering Algorithm

Weight-based heuristic clustering algorithm [4] is proposed as a new clustering algorithm by Basagni in 1999. The main idea is to select the node with the higher weight that has not participated in clustering as the clustering head (consider using the node with lower ID when the weights are the same).

The selection of weight is not unique. Generally, however, it adapts a factor as a basis. It is common to use the mobile speed of a node as the factor. The faster the node moves, the lower the weight is; otherwise, the larger the weight is.

The WCA algorithm [5] is a clustering algorithm proposed by Chatterjee and Das in 2002; it considers multiple factors based on the previous algorithms. The description is as follows:

1. Calculate the degree d_n of node n.
2. Calculate the difference between the ideal degree M and the degree d_n of node n; note as $D_n = |d_n - M|$.
3. Calculate the sum p_n of the distance between node n and its one-hop node.
4. Calculate the mobile ability M of node n.
5. Calculate the consumed battery energy M_n of node n.
6. Calculate the weight of node n: $I_n = c_1 D_n + c_2 P_n + c_3 M_n + c_4 T_n$, in which c_1, c_2, c_3, and c_4 are weight factors and satisfy $c_1 + c_2 + c_3 + c_4 = 1$.
7. Select the node with minimum I_n as the cluster head by comparing it with its neighbors. Other aspects are the same as the previously described algorithms.

The steps in the algorithm are consistent with the previously described weight-based algorithm, but it differs in weight selection. The weight-based algorithm already mentioned considers only a certain influential factor, such as mobile speed and node degree, not multiple factors that can affect clustering in the network. The authors believe that four factors of a node must be considered in the determination of node weight: mobile ability, ideal degree, transmission power, and battery level. The other characteristic of this algorithm is that weight calculation and cluster head selection are carried out as desired.

The algorithm will start when these two scenarios occur: (1) network initialization and (2) the dominating set cannot cover all the nodes when a node is added into or leaves the network. Although the algorithm considers multiple factors to make the cluster head selection more reasonable, it has greatly increased the calculation overhead because it needs to calculate the value of weight frequently due to the frequent change of network topology. Besides, the weights of multiple factors are not completely reasonable. Thus, a more optimal method is needed to improve the algorithm.

3.1.2.5 Clustering Algorithm Based on Geographical Location

All the clustering algorithms mentioned previously are based on topology without using the information of location. In the clustering algorithm based on geographical location, mobile nodes can confirm their current locations by Global Positioning System (GPS). The nodes can also estimate distances to their neighbors according to the strength of a received signal, then confirm their coordination positions by the triangulation method.

Neighbor nodes confirm local network topology by exchanging the information of location, then select the cluster head and form a cluster according to the distribution of neighbor nodes. For example, the number of local neighbor nodes is m, and each node knows the position of its neighbors, so then the center of these nodes can be obtained. Thus, the node closest to the center can be chosen as the cluster head, and the network topology of the cluster can be confirmed. This method can reduce overall power needed and average transmission delay of the communication between the cluster head and nodes in the cluster because the sum of the distance between the center and nodes in the cluster is minimal. The size of the cluster can be adjusted according to density, mobility, and transmission power, so that the performance of the network can be optimized. The algorithm can manage the nodes better, but the overhead of the message is larger. The clustering algorithm based on topology rather than the algorithm based on geographical location tends to be chosen when the transmission range of the node changes dynamically because the latter cannot adapt to this situation well. The position and function of clustering algorithm in routing protocols are gradually highlighted along with the development of hierarchical topology control. A large number of clustering routing protocols emerged when the clustering algorithm was introduced into the hierarchical topology control research in wireless sensor networks (WSNs). Therefore, on the basis of the outline of clustering algorithms in ad hoc networks that have already been mentioned, we will propose a detailed introduction of classic clustering algorithms and related works.

3.2 Clustering Routing Protocol in a WSN

3.2.1 Outline

Routing protocols in WSNs can be divided into flat routing and hierarchical routing based on network topology. In flat routing, nodes are in equal positions with the same function and responsibility. The best characteristic is that all of the nodes are the same, so that routing protocols are strong and data flows in the network are well distributed. The major drawback is low scalability; the scale of the network has to be limited if the algorithm is not strong enough. Classic flat routing protocols, such as flooding [6] and gossiping [7], don't need to use any routing protocol or maintain network topology in the process of data forwarding. In the flooding protocol, each node broadcasts the data from the adjacent router to all of its neighbor nodes (except the node that sends the data). It ends when data is sent to the destination node or the data has not been sent to the destination node but arrives at the maximum hop of data transmission. The Sensor Protocol for Information via Negotiation (SPIN) [8] is a data-centric routing protocol. In order to overcome the defects of implosion, overlapping, and resource abuse in traditional routing protocols, SPIN protocol introduces two key technologies: innovation negotiation and resource adaption. Directed diffusion (DD) routing is a classic data-centric routing protocol, of which the process of implementation consists of three steps: interest diffusion, initial gradient establishment, and data transmission. A lot of data-centric algorithms are modified versions of the DD routing. There are other classic flat routing protocols, such as rumor [10], greedy perimeter stateless routing (GPSR) [11], trajectory based forwarding [12], energy-aware routing [13], gradient-based routing [14], and sequential assignment routing [15]. Flat routing protocol is effective in small-scale networks. However, its use is unimaginable in large-scale networks, because a lot of nodes generate more data and occupy a lot of bandwidth with limited resources. Moreover, flat routing protocol does not possess any manager node and as a result may lack optimization management of resources and be slow to respond to dynamic changes in the network.

Different from the flat routing protocol, the hierarchical routing protocol divides the network hierarchically. As a kind of hierarchical routing technology, clustering is a proven basic mechanism and can prolong the lifetime and improve the scalability of a WSN.

Clustering divides the nodes into a lot of so-called clusters, each of which consists of a cluster head (CH) and many cluster members. Generally, clustering makes the network a double-layer structure, in which the cluster head is located at the higher layer and the cluster members are located at the lower layer (the cluster head of the lower layer is regarded as a cluster member of the cluster head of the higher layer in multilayer clustering). Cluster members send collected data to the cluster head, and the cluster head fuses the data and sends it directly to or through other cluster heads to the base station, as shown in Figure 3.4. Since the cluster head needs to receive and fuse the data from cluster members and then transmits

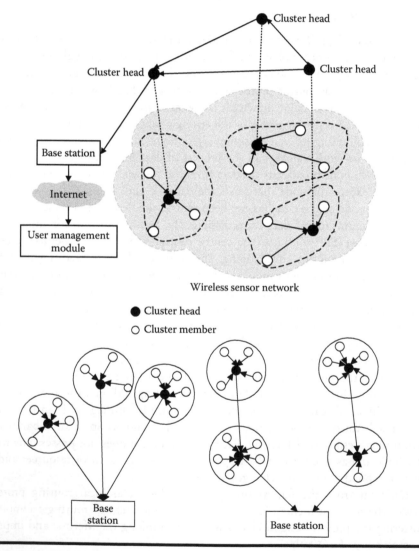

Figure 3.4 **The logical structure and physical structure of general clustering topology.**

the fused data a long distance, it consumes much more energy than the cluster members do. Clustering algorithms mostly execute by rounds to solve this problem. The role of cluster heads can be taken in turns periodically to balance energy load. Clustering can not only improve the scalability of the network and reduce delay, but can also support data fusion and prolong the lifetime of the network.

3.2.2 The Advantages and Goals of Clustering Algorithms

Compared with flat routing protocol, clustering protocols have a lot of advantages, such as better scalability, less workload, less energy consumption, and stronger robustness. In this section, we summarize the advantages and goals of clustering algorithms in WSNs.

Scalability: The sensor nodes are divided into a hierarchical structure in the clustering mechanism. The cluster head needs to collect, aggregate, and fuse the data from the nodes in the cluster and then broadcast the data to the base station; it also manages the cluster members. The cluster members are responsible for sensing the environment and collecting the information from the environment. Routing is established by clusters in the topology of the clustering network. This mechanism creates routing localization, so the routing tables in the sensor nodes are reduced greatly, which means the function of the cluster members is simple. They only need to maintain the routing information of their own cluster instead of the maintaining complicated routing information with large scale by the large routing table. Since the clustering algorithm is suitable for the distributed algorithm and can respond quickly to the change in the system, it can be adapted in a large-scale network with good scalability.

Data aggregation/fusion: Since resources are limited in a WSN, problems arise when each node sends the data directly to the base station in the process of collection: It wastes communication bandwidth and energy because there may be redundancy in the collected data; also, it may cause a jam due to mass communication and collisions, which reduce efficiency and the accuracy of the information. Data aggregation/fusion refers to the process of sending data to the base station after being collected and fused, which is an effective method of saving energy. Data aggregation/fusion, the most popular method, has each cluster head collect data from cluster members, then fuse and send it to the base station. Generally, a routing tree will be constructed among the cluster heads, sending data to the base station by multiple hops. Communication traffic will be reduced, thereby saving the energy of the network.

Less workload: As we mentioned earlier, sensor nodes will produce a great amount of redundant data when the nodes send data simultaneously. Data aggregation/fusion technology is generated as an important technology and goal of WSNs. Data aggregation/merging fuses data from different source nodes to reduce the transmission of redundant data and provides a more accurate and comprehensive view for the monitored target. In the topology of clustering networks, all cluster members need only to collect data and send it to the cluster head, while the cluster head fuses the data and sends it to the base station. It can reduce the transmission of redundant data, thereby saving the energy. Also, the routings are established by clusters, so routing tables in the sensor node can be decreased greatly. As it is not necessary to maintain a lot of routing information, it is easy to manage the network.

Less energy: Data aggregation and fusion can reduce a lot of redundant data transmission and data traffic in the network, thereby saving energy in the clustering routing mechanism. Transmission consists of the intra-cluster transmission and inter-cluster transmission. In a multihop routing mechanism, each cluster member only needs to send the data to the nearest cluster head, which then sends it to the base station through multiple cluster heads. Energy consumption can be reduced by decreasing a lot of long distance transmission in this way. Besides, cluster heads are responsible only for transmitting data, which can also reduce energy consumption. Moreover, cluster members send data in their own slots and the transmission module is closed most of the time, while the cluster heads are responsible for routing forwarding.

Robustness: Since the management of clustering network topology is based on clusters, it is easier for the clustering routing mechanism to manage the network topology and the change of topology caused by adding nodes, moving nodes, or premature deaths. Each cluster deals with the change of topology alone, so that the network has better robustness and easier manageability. Generally, the cluster head shifts periodically in all of the sensor nodes to balance energy consumption between the cluster head and regular nodes. Thus, function interruption of the network caused by premature deaths can be avoided.

Collision avoidance: In a multihop flat model, all nodes are the same and share all of the wireless media. Thus, resource efficiency is low in this kind of model. However, WSNs are regarded as cluster structures in the multihop flat model. Transmission among the sensor nodes consists of intra-cluster and inter-cluster communication, which achieves data collection and data transmission, respectively. Therefore, the resource is assigned to each cluster to reduce collisions in inter-cluster transmission. Every cluster head assigns a transmission slot for cluster members after cluster construction. Each cluster member can transmit data only in its own slot, time division multiple access (TDMA) scheduling. Cluster members will not conflict with each other in this way. Besides, since the ratio of cluster heads to nodes is low, communication traffic is not heavy when cluster heads transmit data to the base station, even simultaneously. Thus, there is less collision, and the multihop clustering model is more suitable for large-scale WSNs compared with the multihop flat model.

Less delay: Only the cluster heads are responsible for the inter-cluster transmission when WSNs are divided into clusters. As mentioned previously, the inter-cluster transmission can avoid collisions among the nodes. Thus, the retransmission mechanism is not needed, and data delays are reduced. Besides, inter-cluster transmission is executed by a flooding mode like the flat routing mechanism. Since the number of cluster heads is much less than the number of all nodes and only the cluster heads are responsible for the transmission, the number of hops from the source node to the base station can be reduced, thereby decreasing the delay.

Workload balance: Workload balance is an essential factor and goal when we consider how to prolong the lifetime of WSNs. In cluster construction, clusters are usually uniform in size and energy balance. In addition, cluster heads are put at the center-of-gravity position, so that all cluster members can be close to the cluster head, and the energy for each will be similar as well. Moreover, in order to consider energy consumption among cluster heads, the scale of the cluster that is far away from the base station is larger than that of the one close to the base station in the inter-cluster single-hop clustering network, thus the cluster head of the former can save more energy when transmitting a long distance. It is opposite in the inter-cluster multihop clustering network; that is, the scale of the cluster close to the base station is smaller, so the cluster head away from the base station can save some of the energy used to manage the nodes in the cluster to carry out long-distance data transmission. In addition, whether intra-cluster or inter-cluster transmission, multi-path routing is a way to achieve workload balance, which can avoid premature deaths caused by the overuse of an optimal path.

Fault tolerance: Fault tolerance is a major challenge in WSNs. In the process of communication, nodes will be dead when the energy is used up or they are damaged in a severe environment. In order to avoid the data loss of the key nodes, it is necessary to have fault tolerance in a clustering mechanism. Thus, the solution to fault tolerance must be considered in the design of clustering algorithms. Periodical reconstruction is the most direct way to recover from a transmission failure, even though it may disrupt the operation of the algorithm and interrupt the function of the network. Since the failure of a cluster head may cause function interruption in the local network, designing backup cluster heads is a feasible way to avoid network reconstruction on a large scale. Besides, designing a multiple backup path is a feasible way to avoid failure in the optimal path.

Connectivity: It is important to maintain connectivity in WSNs. Sensor nodes transmit data to one or more base stations by single hop or multiple hops. Therefore, transmission success depends on the connectivity between each node and its next-hop node. Besides, a sensor node is isolated if it cannot communicate with any node, and its data can never transmit to the base station. As a result, connectivity is an essential goal in WSNs. In clustering WSNs, connectivity problems occur in the connectivity of cluster members to cluster heads (intra-cluster communication) and cluster heads to the base station (inter-cluster communication). Generally, intra-cluster connectivity is achieved by cluster forming algorithms, while inter-cluster communication is achieved by adjusting the transmitting power and setting gateway nodes. For networks with fixed transmitting power, this can be achieved by a condition such as the increased density of cluster heads to satisfy the coverage requirement and connectivity among the cluster heads.

Avoiding energy holes: Generally, multihop mode is adapted to transmit collected data to the base station. Each node transmits the data it collected and forwards the data from other nodes. Sensor nodes that are closer to the base station can transmit more data than those farther from the base station, without considering MAC protocols. Thus, the nodes closer to the base station use the energy, leading to a hole around the base station. The nodes far from the base station can then not transmit data to it. This is the so-called energy hole problem. The energy balance method, which can avoid the energy hole problem, considers the situation from three perspectives: node deployment, workload balance, and energy mapping and assignment. For example, heterogeneous clustering is a workload balance method. In this method, the shorter the distance between the cluster and base station, the smaller the cluster is, and the energy consumed by cluster heads is less in a small-scale cluster. Therefore, cluster heads in distant clusters have more energy to forward data. However, one needs to analyze the optimal value of cluster radius in theory. Obviously, it is common to choose nodes with more energy as cluster heads, which means that choosing nodes with higher abilities as cluster heads is an effective method of energy balance.

Maximizing network lifetime: Lifetime is an important factor in WSNs. The energy, calculation ability, storage ability, and transmission bandwidth of sensor nodes are limited, especially in some severe environments. Therefore, minimizing the energy used in intra-cluster communication is optimal. For example, put the cluster head at the center-of-gravity position as far as possible to reduce the overhead of the communication between the cluster members and the cluster head. Select the best path by energy sensing in the inter-cluster communication; maximize lifetime by selecting the path whose energy is the highest and the energy consumption is lowest. In the clustering mechanism, the energy balance method is usually adapted to maximize the network lifetime by making full use of limited energy. The lifetime of a network is not defined clearly yet, but three common definitions in the algorithm are as follows: (1) the time from deployment until the first node dies, (2) the time from deployment until a percentage of nodes are alive, and (3) the time from deployment until the last node dies [113].

Improve quality of service: Generally, less delay and higher accuracy are quality of service (QoS) requirements. It is difficult to satisfy all QoS requirements for all routing protocols, because some requirements go against the rules of protocols. The current clustering routing algorithms of WSNs mainly consider improving energy efficiency rather than the QoS requirements. However, QoS must be taken into consideration in many real-time applications, such as combat target tracking and urgent event monitoring.

3.2.3 The Classification of Clustering Algorithms

This section will introduce some characteristics of clusters (such as shape, number, and routing), the characteristics of the cluster heads (such as whether they exist, their mobility and role), property in the process of clustering (such as control method, convergence time, and goals of cluster algorithms), and the comprehensive classification of clustering algorithms in the whole process of clustering algorithms (i.e., the different stages of algorithms) [16]. Figure 3.5 shows the classification of clustering algorithms based on clustering property. We will provide a detailed introduction in the next parts.

3.2.3.1 The Characteristics of Clusters

As shown in Figure 3.6, clustering algorithms can be classified according to six characteristics of the cluster: the shape, the number of clusters, whether the size is uniform, intra-cluster routing, inter-cluster routing, and the number of cluster layers.

The shape of the clusters: Clustering routing in WSNs can be classified into three categories based on the shape of the clusters: block-based clustering routing, grid-based clustering routing, and chain-based clustering routing. A block-based clustering routing algorithm forms the network into clusters and manages the network with the cluster as a unit; a grid-based clustering routing algorithm divides the network areas into grids of the same size and forms the clusters with the grid as a unit; a chain-based clustering routing algorithm organizes the nodes as a chain topology by rules to transmit the data.

The number of clusters: The clustering mechanism can be divided into two categories based on the constant number of clusters: fixed constant number of clusters and unfixed variable number of clusters. For the former, the set of cluster heads is determined in advance and the number of clusters is fixed in the clustering process, which generally adapts centralized clustering algorithms. However, the cluster heads are selected by random probability or some other rules, which generally adapts distributed clustering algorithms.

Uniformity of cluster size: Clustering routing can be divided into two categories, which are the clusters with uniform size and the clusters with heterogeneous size. In the uniform clustering routing, the cluster heads are distributed evenly and randomly in the network. Regular nodes join the closest clusters and become cluster members. The size of the Voronoi region composed of cluster heads and member nodes is the size of the cluster. Therefore, the scale of the cluster is uniform. In the single-hop network, the cluster head can communicate with the base station directly; thus, the cluster head that needs to transmit for a long distance will run out of energy. In a multihop network, cluster heads can communicate with the base station through intermediate nodes; thus, the nodes closer to the base station may run out of energy forwarding data from other clusters. The premature death of local nodes may cause the division of the network, reducing network lifetime. This problem is regarded as a "hot pot" problem or an "energy hole" problem. The heterogeneous clustering algorithm is an efficient way to solve the energy hole problem. In the heterogeneous clustering algorithm, energy consumption among cluster heads can be balanced by controlling the size of clusters. In the single-hop network,

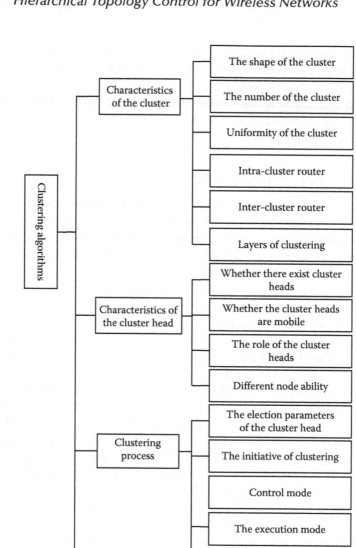

Figure 3.5 The classification of clustering algorithms.

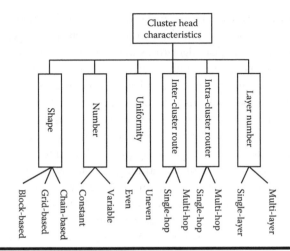

Figure 3.6 **The classification of clustering algorithms based on the characteristics of clusters.**

the cluster far away from the base station has a smaller scale, so the cluster head can have enough energy to execute a long-distance transmission; in the multihop network, the cluster close to the base station has a smaller scale, so the cluster head can have enough energy to forward data from other cluster heads.

Intra-cluster routing: Clustering routing can be divided into two categories based on the routing method for the transmission from cluster members to cluster heads: single-hop intra-cluster routing and multihop intra-cluster routing. All cluster members transmit data directly to their corresponding cluster heads with the single-hop intra-cluster method, which is easy to realize and manage and suitable for the small-scale scenario. For the multihop intra-cluster, cluster members need other nodes to forward the data to the cluster heads, which can save the energy of cluster members to a certain degree and is suitable for when the cluster scale is large and the cluster head is far away from the cluster members. However, the method is complicated to execute because nodes in the cluster need to maintain more routing information and the management of the cluster head is relatively complicated.

Layers of clustering: Clustering-based routing can be divided into single-layer clustering routing and multilayer clustering routing according to the number of clustering layers in the network. In single-layer clustering routing, the network is divided into two layers, in which the high layer includes the cluster head and the low layer includes the cluster members. All nodes in the network consist of cluster heads and cluster members, which are assigned to the cluster heads. Most of the clustering routings are only one layer of cluster head. This algorithm has the advantages of simple implementation and management, relatively small control overhead, and less delay. Multilayer clustering, which is based on single-layer clustering, clusters nodes according to real applications. In multilayer clustering, cluster heads in lower layers are cluster members of cluster heads in the higher layer. Multilayer clustering can reduce energy further and fuse data. This kind of algorithm can generally be classi-fied into top-down hierarchical algorithms and down-top hierarchical algorithms. However, algorithms need to execute iteratively. Thus, algorithms are not suitable for environmental monitoring in real applications because this is complicated and the overhead is large; also, transmissions may cause large delays when there are large numbers of clustering layers. Some researchers believe that ideal energy saving and complexity are achieved when the number of clustering layers is 2 or 3.

Inter-cluster routing: Clustering routing protocol includes two categories based on the routing method of transmission among the cluster heads: single-hop inter-cluster route and multihop inter-cluster route. All cluster heads can communicate with the base station directly in the single-hop inter-cluster routing method. Thus, it will cost great energy when the cluster head transmits data to the base station, and it is not suitable for the large-scale network. On the contrary, in multihop inter-cluster routing, communication between the cluster head and the base station is realized through other cluster heads and therefore saves more energy than single-hop routing.

3.2.3.2 The Characteristics of Cluster Heads

As shown in Figure 3.7, when we classify the clustering mechanism further based on the characteristics of the cluster head, it can be analyzed from four aspects: whether there are cluster heads, whether cluster heads are mobile, the relationship between the node ability and the cluster heads, and the role of the cluster heads.

Whether there exist cluster heads: According to the existence of cluster heads, the clustering mechanism can be divided into two categories: with cluster heads and without cluster heads. In the former scenario, each cluster in the network has at least one cluster head. There is only one cluster head in most clustering algorithms. In the latter scenario, however, there is no head in the cluster; examples are some chain-based clustering algorithms.

Whether cluster heads are mobile: According to the mobility of the cluster head, clustering mechanisms can be divided into clustering in the mobile scenario and clustering in the static scenario. In the former scenario, the cluster head is mobile and the relationship among the nodes is changeable instead of fixed, so that each cluster needs to continuously maintain the cluster structure. On the con-trary, the cluster is fixed and the structure of the cluster stays stable in the latter scenario. Obviously, it is easy to manage once the relationship remains unchanged after being determined, but the cluster head cannot stay static in this scenario; it can obtain better network performance by relocation.

Different node ability: According to the different energy of the nodes, clustering mechanisms can be divided into homogeneous and heterogeneous modes. In the homogeneous clustering mechanism, the cluster head is selected at random or by some other rules. In the heterogeneous mechanism, however, each sensor node has a different ability. Thus, the role and the geographical position of the cluster head

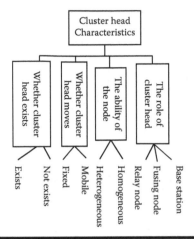

Figure 3.7   The classification of clustering algorithms based on the characteristic of cluster heads.

can be predetermined by calculation of the base station in a centralized algorithm. It means that super nodes with strong ability will afford more duty to balance the energy among the nodes, so that these nodes are usually selected as the cluster heads. In the process of the cluster head election, nodes with higher abilities will run for the cluster heads with the priority if the distributed algorithm is adapted.

The role of the cluster heads: The clustering mechanism can be classified into three categories according to the different duties of the cluster heads: whether the cluster head is only responsible for forwarding the data, the cluster head collects the data from its cluster members and fuses the data, or the cluster head can be a base station based on environmental monitoring and goals. In general, however, cluster heads usually have more than one role. In the most common clustering algorithm, the cluster head needs to collect and fuse the data from cluster members, as well as forwarding data from other cluster heads.

3.2.3.3 The Process of Clustering

As shown in Figure 3.8, from the view of property, the clustering process can be classified as the election parameters of the cluster head, whether the clustering process is initiative or responsive or hybrid, the control mode of the algorithm, the execution mode of the algorithm, the convergence time of the algorithm, whether the clustering is static or dynamic, and the numerous goals of clustering.

The election parameters of the cluster heads: According to the parameter property of the cluster heads selection, the clustering mechanism can be classified into determined mechanism, adaptive mechanism, and random mechanism. In determined mechanism, the algorithms mainly consider the intrinsic property of the nodes, such as the ID and the neighbor number of a node. In adaptive

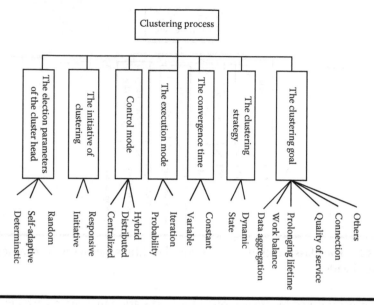

Figure 3.8   The classification of the clustering algorithm based on the clustering process.

mechanism, the node with the higher weight can be selected to be the cluster head. The types of weight include residual energy of nodes, relative residual energy (the ratio of the average residual energy of the neighbor nodes to its own residual energy), and the cost of communication. Random clustering mechanism is mainly used in safety clustering algorithms. The cluster head is selected at random in the election process without considering factors such as the residual energy and the cost of communication.

The initiative of clustering: According to the initiative of clustering, clustering routing algorithms can be classified into the initiative algorithm, the responsive algorithm, and the hybrid algorithm. In the initiative algorithm, all the routings between the source node and the destination base station are calculated and maintained before routing is executed, which does not consider whether there is data flow or data needs to be transmitted. Once data arrives, it can be transmitted to the base station in the predetermined routing. On the contrary, the routing between the source node and the base station is not predetermined in the responsive clustering network. Routing is established only when data needs to be transmitted to the base station. Hybrid clustering combines the initiative and responsive methods. In this kind of network, it can adapt initiative clustering and responsive clustering modes according to the real application. For example, The Adaptive Threshold sensitive Energy Efficient Sensor Network (APTEEN) is a classic hybrid method. The clustering protocol adjusts the corresponding parameters based on the real application, achieving data transmission by switching between initiative and responsive modes.

Control mode: Based on whether there is a central control node, the clustering algorithm can be divided into the centralized algorithm, the distributed algorithm, and the hybrid algorithm. In general, the central control node has the ability of continuous battery supply, better storage, and calculation, and it can obtain the overall information of the network (such as position and residual energy of each node). It can adapt a complicated algorithm to get the optimal result of clustering. However, the ability of calculation and communication is not strong because of the limited energy. Therefore, for large-scale WSNs, centralized algorithms have some defects in flexibility, scalability, and robustness. For example, many centralized algorithms require obtaining the residual energy of nodes. Since the energy of sensor nodes keeps decreasing in the operation, the nodes need to update the central control node concerning residual energy; this will cause a great deal of transmission and large overhead. Different from the centralized algorithm, a node only needs to switch the information with its neighbors to obtain the local information in the distributed algorithm. It can even make judgments independently without considering the neighbors. This kind of algorithm is easy, efficient, and flexible; thus, it is more suitable for large-scale WSNs. Currently, the mostly classic clustering algorithms in WSNs are distributed algorithms. The hybrid algorithm combines the centralized algorithm and the distributed algorithm. In this method, the centralized method is used to construct the clustering topology, while the distributed algorithm is used to coordinate the relationship among the cluster heads.

The execution mode: According to the execution mode of the algorithm in the clustering process, the clustering method can be divided into two types: that based on probability and that based on iteration. In the clustering method based on probability, all nodes calculate an election probability according to the information they obtained; then, they determine the role based on probability. In other words, each node can determine its role in an independent and distributed way. However, in the clustering method based on iteration, each sensor node has to determine its role after a certain number of iterations of the algorithm.

Convergence time: The clustering method can be divided into two categories considering the convergence time of the algorithm: with variable convergence time or with constant convergence time. In the method with variable convergence time, the convergence time depends on the number of nodes in the network. The more nodes there are the longer the convergence time is. The less nodes there are the shorter the convergence time is. Therefore, this kind of algorithm is suitable only for a small-scale network. In the method with constant convergence time, the algorithm is completed after a certain number of iterations. Thus, it can be finished in a constant convergence time, having no concern for the number of nodes and the scale of network.

The clustering strategy: It can be divided into static clustering and dynamic clustering according to the clustering strategy. Static clustering refers to the formation of static clusters at the initial stage of the network. The role of each cluster head only rotates in their own cluster. This algorithm often uses energy-driven based cluster head rotation mechanism. On the one hand, it avoids the huge overhead of cluster reconstruction; on the other hand, it can balance the energy consumption of the nodes in the cluster through the rotation of cluster heads. In the dynamic clustering mechanism, the cluster head rotates periodically to balance the node's energy consumption. It has to consume some energy for constructing cluster after each completion of cluster head election. This method can get a better balanced energy consumption. Since each cluster head rotation must be carried out in the entire network, the overhead for topology construction is too large, resulting in a lot of unnecessary waste of energy. In [33], it is analyzed and proved that energy-driven based cluster head rotation strategy is superior to time-driven based cluster head rotation strategy.

The goals of clustering: As mentioned above, in the process of clustering, the requirements of the network are different in different real applications. Thus, there are different clustering goals such as data aggregation/fusion, workload balance, fault tolerance, the guarantee of connectivity, extension of network lifetime, and the guarantee of quality of service. Therefore, the clustering method can be divided into more and different categories based on different goals. In general, each clustering algorithm has more than one clustering goal.

3.2.3.4 The Whole Process of the Algorithms

Generally, each complete clustering routing algorithm includes three basic stages: generating the cluster head, forming the cluster, and data transmission. The generation of the cluster head is the basis of forming the cluster, and the nodes that transmit data rely on the structure of the clustering. These three parts are closely related but relatively independent. Different methods can be used in generating cluster heads and forming the cluster. Also, one cluster can adopt different data transmission mechanisms. All clustering algorithms in WSNs are designed according to how to select the cluster head, how to form the cluster, and how to transmit data. The selection of the cluster head and the process of forming the cluster are the basis of the data transmission. Existing algorithms have different emphases on research in general, a part of which is aimed at the three stages together and another part of which is aimed at one or two of the three stages. In Section 3.2.4, we will further discuss existing clustering algorithms and introduce other related algorithms in the area.

3.2.4 Classic Clustering Algorithms and Related Works in WSNs

3.2.4.1 LEACH

The Low Energy Adaptive Clustering Hierarchy (LEACH) protocol [17] is the most classic clustering routing protocol, proposed by Heinzelman et al. of the Massachusetts Institute of Technology. It is an early hierarchy routing protocol for WSNs, using adaptive clustering mechanism and cluster head cycle mechanism.

Therefore, it receives a lot of attention. Many clustering routing protocols learn from the ideas of the LEACH algorithm, improving the shortcomings of the LEACH protocol.

Compared with flat routing protocol, LEACH can save a lot of energy, since short-distance transmission can save more energy. In LEACH, most of the communications are the intra-cluster communication, while only cluster heads need to communicate with the remote base station. LEACH coordinates and controls cluster forming and operations in a distributed way and uses cluster head cycle mechanism to rebuild the cluster. Therefore, the workload of the network is more balanced. Moreover, the cluster head aggregates data from cluster members and removes redundant data-by-data fusion technology. Then the cluster head sends data to the base station, thereby reducing the overall traffic in the network. Although some energy is used in the process of dealing with data, this energy consumed by calculation is far less than the energy consumed by communication; thus, it can save a lot of energy. The simulation shows that LEACH can prolong the lifetime of a network about 15% over the general flat routing protocol. The clustering mechanism can balance the assignment of resources and optimize energy. Following is a concrete analysis of LEACH.

For simplicity, LEACH protocol makes the assumption for the network model as follows:

1. The base station is outside and far away from the monitoring area of the WSN. All nodes and the base station in the network are static.
2. The transmission power of all nodes in the network can be adjusted.
3. All nodes in the network are energy homogeneous, and the nodes need enough energy to communicate.
4. The calculation ability of the node needs to satisfy bidirectional communication.

LEACH protocol adapts the first order radio model as the energy model for communication, as shown in Figure 3.9. This model is based on the following assumption:

1. All nodes in the network are homogeneous with limited energy.
2. The energy consumption in all directions is the same.
3. The base station is static and far away from the monitoring area of the WSN.

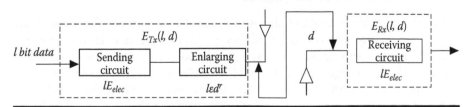

Figure 3.9   The energy model of WSN.

If the 1-bit information is transmitted for distance d, the energy consumption of the sender is

$$E_{Tx}(l,d) = \begin{cases} l * E_{elec} + l * \varepsilon_{fs} d^2 & (d < d_0) \\ l * E_{elec} + l * \varepsilon_{mp} d^4 & (d \geq d_0) \end{cases}, \tag{3.1}$$

in which, E_{elec} represents the energy consumed by the transmitter circuit. If the distance of data transmission is lower than threshold d_0, the power amplifier consumption uses the free space model; if the distance data transmission is greater than or equal to the threshold d_0, the power amplifier consumption uses the multipath-fading model. ε_{fs} and ε_{mp} represent the energy required by the amplifier power in these two models, respectively.

The energy consumed by the receiver is

$$E_{Rx}(l) = l * E_{elec}. \tag{3.2}$$

LEACH protocol can be described as follows: The operation of LEACH is executed by cycle, each of which includes two stages of the cluster construction and stable data transmission. In the stage of the cluster construction (i.e., the stage of forming the cluster), all the sensor nodes execute the LEACH algorithm to form the cluster. The data transmission stage is divided into repeatable frames, in which the cluster members send the collected data to the cluster head in their own slot; then, the cluster fuses the data and transmits it to the base station. Since the cluster construction stage will cost a lot of energy, generally, the data transmission stage should be much longer than the cluster construction stage to reduce the additional overhead of the cluster reconstruction.

Figure 3.10 shows the flow of two stages in each cycle of the LEACH protocol. The cluster construction stage is divided into two stages of the cluster head election and cluster forming. Therefore, we will introduce the LEACH protocol according to three key steps of the algorithm: the cluster head election, the process of forming the cluster, and data transmission.

3.2.4.1.1 The Cluster Head Election

The cluster head of the LEACH algorithm is selected at random. The cluster head rotates periodically to share responsibility for communication in the network. Since there is no central node to control the election or a node to coordinate, the cluster head election algorithm of LEACH is distributed; each node can determine the cluster head dependently. The cluster election has two bases; that is, whether each node has been the cluster head until this point and the sum of cluster heads needed in the network. The specific method is that each node generates a random

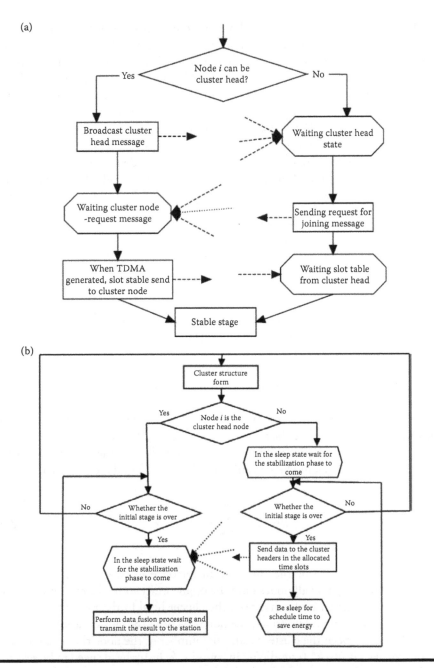

Figure 3.10 **The algorithm flow of each cycle in LEACH protocol. (a) The stage of forming the cluster. (b) The stage of data transmission. (From Heinzelman, W. B. et al., An application-specific protocol architecture for wireless microsensor networks.** *IEEE Transaction on Wireless Communication,* **1, 660–670, 2002.)**

number from 0 to 1, then the node whose random value is lower than the threshold $T(n)$ will be selected as the cluster head by itself and broadcasts the information to all nodes in the network to declare that it is the cluster head. In each round of a cycle, a node will set the value of the threshold $T(n)$ as 0 if it has been the cluster head, thus it will not be selected as the cluster head again; if it has not been the cluster head, it will participate in the election with probability $T(n)$. As the number of the node that has been the cluster head grows larger and larger, the value $T(n)$ of other nodes will be larger, thus the probability that a node generates a random value lower than $T(n)$ will be larger. $T(n)=1$ when only one node has not been the cluster head, which means this node will be selected as the cluster head. The threshold $T(n)$ is calculated as follows:

$$T(n) = \begin{cases} \dfrac{p}{1-p\,(r \bmod 1/p)} & n \in G \\ 0 & others \end{cases}, \tag{3.3}$$

in which p refers to the percentage of cluster heads in the total number of nodes in the network; r is the current number of cycles; G indicates the set of nodes that have been cluster heads.

$T(n)$ is the average probability that a node that has not been a cluster head will become the cluster head in the round r. Mathematical method can prove that as follows:

Assume that there are N sensor nodes with the same initial energy in the network. k cluster heads need to be selected in each round. Every node will be selected as the cluster head with probability $T_i(t)$ in the round $r+1$. The expectation of the cluster head number should be k in this round when the node selects $T_i(t)$.

$$E[CH] = \sum_{i=1}^{N} T_i(t) * 1 = k. \tag{3.4}$$

Each node needs to be the cluster head for once in N/k rounds of the same period to make sure that all nodes have the opportunity to be the cluster head. Let $C_i(t)$ represent whether node i has been the cluster head in the $r \bmod (N/k)$ round of the recent N/k round. If $C_i(t)=1$, the node has been the cluster head; if $C_i(t)=0$, the node has not been the cluster head. The number of the node that has not been the cluster head is $N-k*(r \bmod N/k)$ in round r. k cluster heads need to be selected in this round; thus, the node I, which has not been the cluster head in round r, will be selected as the cluster head with probability $T_i(t)=k/N-k*(k \bmod N/k)$. Therefore, it holds that

$$T_i(t) = \begin{cases} \dfrac{k}{N - k * \left(r \bmod \dfrac{N}{k} \right)}, & C_i(t) = 0 \\[4ex] 0, & C_i(t) = 1 \end{cases} \tag{3.5}$$

Since $C_i(t)$ represents whether node i can be the cluster head at time t: It can be if the value is 1; it cannot be if the value is 0. Thus, $\sum_{i=1}^{N} C_i(t)$ indicates the sum of nodes that can be the cluster head at time t. Therefore, the expectation of $\sum_{i=1}^{N} C_i(t)$ is

$$E\left[\sum_{i=1}^{i} C_i(t) \right] = N - k * (r \bmod N / k). \tag{3.6}$$

Therefore, the residual energy of each node is basically the same after N/k rounds. The expectation of the node that can be the cluster head is

$$E[CH] = \sum_{i=1}^{N} T_i(t) * 1$$

$$= (N - r * (r \bmod N / k)) * \dfrac{k}{N - k * \left(r \bmod \dfrac{N}{k} \right)}$$

$$= k. \tag{3.7}$$

These assumptions for probability are based on the condition that all nodes have the same initial energy and data transmission for every frame. We can see that if the initial energy of the node is not equal or there is data to be transmitted only when an event occurs, the probability is that the node with more energy will be the cluster head to balance energy consumption and prolong the lifetime of the network.

3.2.4.1.2 The Process of Forming the Cluster

Some nodes will be selected as cluster heads when each round finishes. These nodes inform all other nodes in the network that they are the cluster heads in this round. The specific process is that each cluster node uses nonpersist carrier sense multiple access (CSMA) MAC protocol to broadcast a message, which includes the ID of the node and the head indicating the message type. Each node that is not the cluster head chooses the corresponding cluster head and adds into the cluster. The choice is based on minimum cost of communication. The measurement of the communication cost is judged by the strength of received information at each cluster head. If a node that is not the cluster head receives the strongest signal from some cluster head, the communication cost between this node and the cluster head is minimum; then it should choose this cluster head as its cluster head and add into this cluster. The node that is not the cluster head chooses a cluster randomly if the signal strength is equal.

When each node that is not the cluster head determines its cluster head, it will send a request message to inform the cluster head that it wants to be a cluster member. The message includes the ID of the node and the ID of the cluster head. The process uses the nonpersist CSMA MAC protocol as well.

Then, the cluster head will build a TDMA scheduling table for coordinating the intra-cluster transmission, and it will broadcast the table to all cluster members. This scheduling can make sure that different nodes send the message in different slots; thus, the messages will not collide. The cluster member will shut down the communication module if the slot is not for it, thereby reducing energy consumption. The stage of forming the cluster finishes when all cluster members receive the TDMA scheduling table. The next stage is data transmission.

3.2.4.1.3 Data Transmission

The cluster head will generate a TDMA scheduling table and broadcast the table to all cluster members when it receives the request from all cluster members. Once the cluster is formed and the TDMA scheduling is determined, the data transmission begins. Assume that the sensor nodes always have data to transmit and the cluster members transmit data to the cluster head in their own slots. The cluster member will shut its communication module if the slot has not arrived. However, the wireless communication module of the cluster head is open all the time to receive the data from different cluster members continuously. When a round of data transmission is completed, the cluster head will compress the received data to a new message by fusion technology. The Code-Division Multiple Accessing (CDMA) method is adopted in the cluster to reduce interference. In order to avoid interference from adjacent clusters, the cluster head determines the CDMA codes of all cluster members as the identification of the cluster and transmits the CDMA codes to the intra-cluster nodes with the TDMA scheduling table. Therefore, the signal of other clusters will be leached in the intra-cluster communication.

A new round will begin after a period time, and the network enters a next period, in which it needs to select cluster heads and loop the process. Since the cluster head needs to complete the work such as data fusion and communication with the base station, the energy consumption is large. The cluster head election algorithm of LEACH can make sure that each node has the same probability of being the cluster head, so that nodes in the network consume energy relatively evenly.

Figure 3.11 is the basic cluster topology that the LEACH algorithm can build.

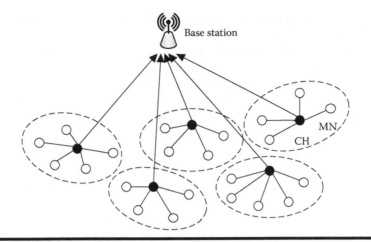

Figure 3.11   The network topology of the LEACH protocol.

Some of the main advantages of the LEACH protocol are as follows:

1. All nodes become the cluster head periodically, thereby equalizing the high energy consumption of the cluster head to each node, so that the energy of all the nodes in the network can be evenly consumed.
2. First, divide the cluster; then, the cluster head fuses the data from the cluster members; finally, the aggregation mechanism used by the cluster head for transmitting data to the base station can reduce the number of nodes that need to transmit over a long distance and can decrease the data traffic in the network, thereby reducing the energy consumption of the overall network. There is high redundancy when the cluster head deals with the data using fusion technology, especially when data has high relativity. The redundant data will be greatly reduced in this way and thereby also the energy consumption.
3. The TDMA scheduling mechanism can avoid unnecessary collision in data transmission. It can stay in the sleeping state when the node does not work, thereby saving a lot more energy.
4. The hierarchical structure of LEACH makes the routing information simple. The node does not need to maintain a lot of routing information, which can reduce the requirement of node ability and is more suitable for real applications.

However, the LEACH protocol inevitably has many shortcomings.

1. The node in the network forms the cluster by self-organizing in LEACH protocol, and the cluster head is selected randomly. This method cannot make

sure that the cluster heads are well distributed; thus, it cannot ensure the validity of the cluster size.

2. The selection of threshold $T(n)$ does not consider the residual energy of nodes. Thus, each node has a probability of being the cluster head even if it has little residual energy. Since the energy consumption of the cluster head is large, the node will quickly run out of energy. Once the cluster head has died, the whole cluster managed by it will be in the unmanaged state for a long time in the current round. This monitoring area will experience problems such as failing to report, lack of, or delay of monitoring data.

3. All cluster heads send data collected from the cluster members to the base station by single-hop communication mode. In the real network, however, the base station is beyond the monitoring area and far away from the network. If data fusion is not strong enough, cluster heads will need to transmit more data to a more remote base station. Frequent long-distance communication will cause the node to quickly run out of energy, thereby reducing the lifetime of the network.

4. Each cluster member communicates with the cluster head directly by single-hop mode instead of forwarding through other nodes. Although this method and the mechanism are simple and convenient, the size of each cluster is limited as a result. If the size of the cluster is too large, the cluster member will run out of energy. Therefore, this single-hop mechanism is not beneficial to the extension of large scale WSNs.

5. LEACH adopts the MAC-layer mechanism of TDMA scheduling. In fact, not every node uses every slot with data for the cluster head all the time. This kind of communication mechanism cannot utilize bandwidth efficiently and thereby wastes energy.

6. LEACH uses periodic rotation for cluster reconstruction. It will use a lot of energy in every overall reconstruction. Moreover, it may cause the periodical interruption of the network function.

Researchers propose many modified algorithms in an effort to correct the disadvantages of the LEACH protocol and based on the ideas of the LEACH algorithm. Most of the existing clustering algorithms follow the idea of the LEACH algorithm. In the next part of this chapter, we will conclude the discussion of various clustering algorithms based on the emphasis of algorithm design as comprehensively as possible. We will give a detailed introduction about the representative clustering routing protocol of each classification and summarize other similar protocols.

3.2.4.2 Centralized and Hybrid Clustering Algorithms (LEACH-C)

LEACH-C (LEACH-Centralized) [18] is proposed by Heinzelman et al. and is a centralized algorithm based on the base station control on the basis of the LEACH protocol. It is the most classic of the improved LEACH algorithms, dividing the stage of forming the cluster and the stage of stable data transmission. In the stage of forming the cluster, the LEACH-C algorithm has a major difference from the LEACH algorithm. It makes good use of the high capacity of the base station. The process of the algorithm is as follows.

1. In the initial stage of the network, each node sends the information about its energy and location to the base station via a positioning device.
2. The base station confirms the location of each node.
3. The base station clusters the network by simulated annealing algorithm. It determines the optimal cluster head and balances the number of nodes in each cluster according to some rules. Now the probability of being the cluster head is proportional to the current energy, rather than with equal probability. The probability of being the cluster head is larger when the node has more energy. The probability $P_i(t)$ that node i can be selected as the cluster head at time t can be calculated as follows:

$$P_i(t) = \min\left\{\frac{E_i(t)}{E_{total}(t)}k, 1\right\}, \tag{3.8}$$

in which, k is the number of cluster heads in round 1; $E_i(t)$ is the current energy of node i; $E_{total}(t)$ is the sum of energy of all the nodes.
4. The base station broadcasts the message including the information of the cluster head, CDMA extended code of each cluster, and TDMA scheduling calculated by the members in each cluster. All nodes receive the information to confirm their own roles.
5. The nodes and the cluster head confirm their relative distance according to their own positions.
6. Each node sends the collected data and the information of its current energy to the cluster head in its slot.
7. The cluster head fuses the data and transmits to the base station directly after receiving data from the cluster members. If the cluster head does not receive the data, it judges the residual energy of the node. The cluster head determines that the node is dead if the energy of the node is lower than the threshold. If the node energy is still greater than the threshold, but no data is transmitted, it is determined that the node is moving, and return to step 5.
8. The LEACH-C algorithm is similar to LEACH in the next step of data transmission; thus, we do not repeat that (Figure 3.12).

In LEACH protocol, each node judges independently whether it becomes the cluster head according to the random value and threshold value; thus, the cluster head generated in each round cannot be confirmed as to the number and exact position. While LEACH-C adopts a centralized algorithm for selecting the cluster head, the

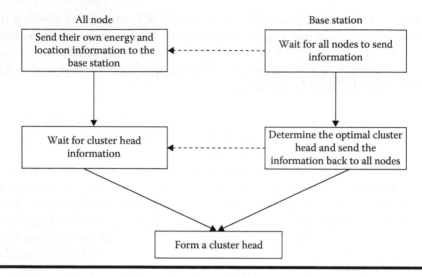

Figure 3.12 The flow of cluster head election in LEACH-C.

algorithm selects the optimal cluster heads according to the overall information of the network, then the optimal cluster structure is obtained, which means a node can be selected as the cluster head only when its residual energy is higher than the average residual energy of all nodes in the network. In LEACH-C protocol, the base station calculates the average residual energy of all nodes according to the received information of energy and position from the nodes; then it selects optimal cluster heads. Therefore, the number of cluster heads is stable. Moreover, the cluster heads are well distributed, and the number of nodes in each cluster is roughly the same. The nodes can obtain a better workload balance as a result. Therefore, LEACH-C outperforms LEACH.

The cluster head in LEACH-C has higher residual energy, but the cluster head needs to bear a larger workload and may run out of the energy more quickly. That is because the cluster head needs to collect and aggregate the data from the cluster members; then it sends the fused data to the base station. Also, the cluster head is responsible for scheduling the sending slot of the cluster members and broadcasts the scheduling table to all cluster members. In order to balance the energy consumption between the cluster head and regular nodes, LEACH-C needs to convert the role of the cluster head. As a result, it will use additional overhead in the process of establishing a new cluster, the network function may be interrupted, and the transmission of monitoring data may be delayed.

LEACH-F [18] makes some adjustment on the basis of LEACH as well. The process of forming the cluster is similar to LEACH, with the use of a simulated annealing algorithm by the base station. Meanwhile, the base station generates a list of the heads for each cluster and broadcasts it to all cluster members, informing them of the sequence of being the cluster head. The topology stays unchanged after forming the cluster. The cluster members will become the cluster head according to the sequence in the list. Compared with LEACH and LEACH-C algorithms, this algorithm does not need to rebuild the cluster in the overall network. Rebuilding the cluster in a local area can greatly reduce the additional overhead of forming the cluster in the overall network. The disadvantage, however, is that LEACH-F is just an ideal algorithm. It can be proved in theory, but it cannot be applied in real networks. For example, the algorithm cannot deal with the situation when a node adds into the network, moves, or prematurely dies.

In the hybrid energy-aware sensor network (HYENAS) [19], the process of generating the cluster is realized by the base station in a centralized algorithm, similar to LEACH-C. The LEACH algorithm needs to form the cluster again in each round of cycle. Unlike LEACH, however, the structure of HYENAS does not change in each round. Whether the structure of the cluster needs to be rebuilt depends on the similarity of the cluster. The judgment of the similarity is a machine learning process. The specific process is as follows.

HYENAS adopts case-based reasoning technology to generate the appropriate number for the cluster. Meanwhile, it generates a list named "blacklist." In each round, blacklist will record the cluster as a bad cluster and record its information if the average energy consumption of the cluster is higher than double the average energy threshold of the overall network. The information includes

1. the number of intra-cluster nodes
2. the sum of squares of the distance from the cluster head to each cluster member
3. the distance between the cluster head and the base station
4. the average energy consumption of each node in the cluster

In each round, the protocol calculates the similarities between the clusters and records bad clusters in blacklist by *k-NN* algorithm successively. If the similarity is higher than a certain threshold, the base station reselects the cluster head by a centralized algorithm and rebuilds the cluster; if the similarity is not high enough, the structure of the cluster does not need to change, and the base station just needs to reselect the cluster head for the cluster. In order to avoid successive comparison of *k-NN* algorithm, HYENAS proposes a relaxation algorithm to replace the similarity calculation, thereby accelerating the convergence of the algorithm. HYENAS avoids the periodical reconstruction of the cluster, saving the overhead of forming the cluster in each round.

Base Station Controlled Dynamic Clustering Protocol (BCDCP) [20] is a centralized clustering algorithm controlled by the base station as well. The main idea of BCDCP is dividing the network into uniform-sized clusters, so that cluster heads are well distributed in the network. The data is forwarded to the base station through cluster heads.

In BCDCP, first, the base station collects the residual energy of all nodes and calculates the average energy of all nodes in the network. Then the base station chooses the nodes whose residual energy is more than the average to form the set S. Since the route is built by the communication among the cluster heads in BCDCP, the cluster head has to possess more energy. The nodes that do not belong to S become cluster members. These nodes will execute the tasks with low energy consumption. Cluster generation is achieved by iterative dividing of the algorithm in the base station. The base station divides the network into two unique size clusters, then divides these two clusters into more small clusters until the number of clusters reaches the predetermined number. In order to balance the workload of each cluster, dividing algorithm adopts the balanced clustering algorithm in Reference [21] to divide the cluster into two uniquely sized subclusters; thereby, the clusters in the network are well distributed. The specific process of the cluster-dividing algorithm is as follows:

Step 1: Select two nodes with the furthest distance from the set S, noted as nodes *i* and *j*.

Step 2: Divide the current cluster into two sets. The nodes nearer to the node *i* will join the set of node *i*, while the nodes nearer to the node *j* will join the set of node *j*.

Step 3: Make two sets with similar number of nodes via a balance algorithm.

Step 4: The set S is divided into two subsets S1 and S2 according to the grouping situation of the third step and the attribution of the nodes in the set S.

BCDCP adopts a multihop routing mechanism for sending data to the base station. Once the cluster and the cluster head are determined, the base station chooses the route with the lowest energy consumption then sends the result of clustering and the selected cluster heads to all the nodes. When transmitting the monitoring data, the route among the cluster heads is generated by minimal spanning tree algorithm, which can minimize the energy consumption of each cluster head. Then the cluster head chooses a cluster head randomly for forwarding data to the base station. Since the cluster head is selected at random, the workload of sending the data can be assigned to all cluster heads. Figure 3.13 shows the topology of clustering network constructed by BCDCP.

BCDCP uses the base station with high energy to build the cluster and connects the clusters by minimal spanning tree algorithm. Then it selects a cluster head randomly, transmitting the monitoring data to the base station.

The advantages of BCDCP are as follows.

1. The structure of the cluster and the route of transmission are built by the base station, so that BCDCP solves the problem of cluster head distribution and makes sure that the energy consumption among the cluster heads is similar.

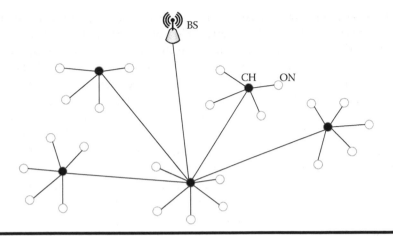

Figure 3.13   The clustering topology built by the BCDCP algorithm.

2. The cluster head schedules the cluster members by TDMA mechanism, so that nodes open the communication module only in the transmitting slot and stay in sleeping state in other slots, which can save a lot of energy.

However, BCDCP protocol has many disadvantages.

1. BCDCP is a centralized algorithm with poor scalability and robustness, which is not suitable for a large-scale network.
2. In the process of forming the cluster, each node needs to send the message to the base station, which increases the complexity of designing and energy consumption.
3. BCDCP is not suitable for the responsive network.

Dynamic/Static Clustering protocol (DSC) [22] is also an extensive algorithm of LEACH-C. In DSC, each node collects the information of its position via a GPS positioning device then sends the information of position and energy to the base station. The base station determines the optimal cluster heads based on the collected data then broadcasts the clustering result to all nodes. Every cluster head divides the transmitting slots for the cluster members in the cluster by TDMA mechanism of the LEACH algorithm. Compared with LEACH-C, the number of messages received by the base station in DSC protocol is reduced greatly, but DSC cannot avoid the other drawbacks of LEACH-C.

The LEACH-completely Controlled by Base station (LEACH-CCB) protocol is proposed in Reference [23]. The protocol uses 5% nodes to communicate with the base station. Meanwhile, 10% nodes stay in sleeping state. The base station schedules the state switch of the nodes, and the cluster head that has been selected in the last round cannot participate in the next round.

Analytical Hierarchy Process (AHP) [24] is also an algorithm in which the cluster head is selected by the base station. However, AHP supports the mobility of the node, so that it is more complicated than the LEACH-C algorithm. The algorithm needs to consider three factors in the selection of the cluster head: the energy of the node, the mobility of the node, and the distance between the node and the center of the cluster. The AHP algorithm uses these factors to calculate the local weight and overall weight then combines two weights to select the cluster head. In the process of maintaining the cluster, the cluster head will be selected again only when the current cluster head dies or moves to another cluster. Compared with LEACH, AHP postpones the time of death of the last node. Compared with LEACH-C, AHP needs to transmit more messages between the network and the base station, thereby causing higher energy consumption for more communication between the node and the base station.

LMSSC [25] is a hybrid clustering algorithm, that is, the clustering process is operated by the cooperation of the base station and the nodes. LMSSC algorithm mainly includes two stages: forming the cluster and selecting the cluster head. The algorithm generates all the clusters first then selects a cluster head for each cluster. This kind of mechanism is different from the other process in which it first selects the cluster head then forms the cluster.

1. The stage of forming the cluster: In this stage, the base station divides the network into a certain number of clusters based on the initial topology of the network. The specific method is as follows: the base station calculates the weight W of the distance between the node that has not been clustered and its neighbors. W is calculated as follows:

$$W = \frac{1}{n} \sum_{i=1}^{n} d_i^2, \tag{3.9}$$

in which, n is the number of neighbors; d_i is the distance between the node and its neighbor i. The base station selects the node with the lowest weight and forms the cluster as the center of the node, deleting the nodes in the cluster from the set of the nodes that have not been clustered. The base station executes the generation algorithm iteratively until at least 80% of nodes have entered the clusters.

2. The stage of selecting the cluster head: After forming the cluster, the base station will select an appropriate cluster head for each cluster. The base station determines the cluster head according to two parameters: distance and energy. The distance parameter includes the square of the distance between the node and all of its neighbors and the square of the distance between the node and the base station. The energy parameter is the residual energy of the node. The base station calculates the CH weight based on these two parameters. CH can be calculated as follows:

$$CH(i) = E_{r_i} \times \left[1 / \left(\sum_{j=1}^{n} d_j^2 + d_{BS}^2 \right) \right], \qquad (3.10)$$

in which, n is the number of neighbors; d_j is the distance between the node i and its neighbor j; d_{BS} is the distance between node i and the base station. The base station will choose the node with the maximum CH value as the cluster head. If the cluster head becomes invalid or dies, the base station will select a new cluster head based on the value of CH.

Jae-hwan Noh et al. proposed the Multihop Routing Protocol based on Super-Cluster Header [26], in which the stage of clustering is executed by the base station in a centralized method, and the cluster members adopt a multihop mode to transmit data to the cluster head in the stage of stable data communication. Different from LEACH-C protocol, the cluster head does not transmit data to the base station directly. The protocol introduces a super cluster head. This node is responsible for collecting data from all cluster heads, then fusing and forwarding it to the base station. The three-layer structure of data fusion can save energy and prolong the lifetime of the network, but it increases delay.

The energy-conscious message routing (ECMR) [27] algorithm is applicable for energy-heterogeneous WSNs. The algorithm assumes that the cluster head is predetermined; the energy of the cluster head is sufficient and unlimited; the nodes in the cluster communicate with the cluster head by multihop mode; the protocol needs to build multiple optimal routes from the cluster members to the cluster head. The ECMR algorithm assumes that the base station gives the cluster head information from all cluster members (including the ID and position of nodes). The cluster head adopts the Dijkstra algorithm in a centralized way based on the received information to calculate the minimum cost route between the source and the destination. The calculation of the weight of the link considers factors such as the residual energy of the node, the cost of communication, data delay, and the workload of the link. The cluster head estimates the residual energy of the node according to the energy consumption model and recalculates the route regularly. Since the calculation considers factors such as energy, the cost of communication, and so on, ECMR has greater energy saving, higher throughput, and lower delay.

3.2.4.3 Iterative Clustering Algorithms

Younis et al. proposed an energy-efficient clustering algorithm, hybrid energy-efficient distributed (HEED) clustering [28]. The authors pointed out that longer lifetime, extension, and workload balance are three critical requirements. Balancing energy consumption throughout a network can prolong its lifetime.

The clustering election is different in HEED and LEACH. First, the cluster head selection in HEED considers the residual energy of the node, rather than energy at random. Second, the selection in HEED is based on two parameters. The main parameter is the residual energy of the node. That is, the node with higher residual energy has higher probability of being the candidate cluster head, so that the algorithm has a faster convergence. Whether the candidate cluster head becomes the cluster head depends on whether its residual energy is much higher than its neighbors' (i.e., whether the convergence is faster than the neighbors' in the iterative process). The second parameter is the cost of intra-cluster communication, which is used to determine which nodes within the broadcast area of multiple cluster heads enter which cluster at the end. This parameter can balance the workload among the cluster heads. HEED takes average minimum reachability power (AMRP), that is, the intra-cluster average reachable energy, as the standard of cost of balancing intra-cluster communication. The average reachable energy AMRP of a cluster can be calculated by the formula 3.11.

$$AMRP = \frac{\sum_{i=1}^{M} MinPwr_i}{M}. \tag{3.11}$$

The specific process of HEED algorithm is as follows.

1. Initial stage: In this stage, HEED needs to determine the ratio of the number of the cluster heads against the number of all nodes in the network at first. Each node counts the number of its neighbors and calculates its AMRP value. Then each node calculates the probability CH_{prob} of being the cluster head and judges whether it can be the candidate cluster head based on that probability. The calculation of CH_{prob} is as follows:

$$CH_{prob} = C_{prob} \frac{E_{residual}}{E_{max}}, \tag{3.12}$$

in which, $E_{residual}$ is the residual energy of the node; E_{max} indicates the maximum initial energy of the node in the network. The maximum initial energy of all nodes is the same. According to the formula 3.12, the higher the residual energy of the node, the higher the probability of being the cluster head.

2. Iterative process: In this stage, the algorithm is executed in a periodic iterative way. After a certain number of times of iteration, if the node finds out that there is a temporary cluster head, it will compare its AMRP with the AMRP of the temporary cluster head. If the node itself is also the temporary cluster head and its AMRP is the minimum, it will declare itself the cluster head; else, the algorithm executes the next iteration. If there is no neighbor of the node to declare itself the temporary cluster head, the node will be the temporary cluster head with a certain probability. If a temporary cluster head has the maximum AMRP among the temporary cluster heads of its neighbors or there

is no temporary cluster head of its neighbors, the temporary cluster head will declare itself the cluster head. If the node cannot find the final cluster head among its neighbors, it will declare itself the cluster head, or it will be the temporary cluster head with the minimum AMRP. At the end of each iteration, each node in the network will double CH_{prob}; then the next iteration will be executed. The nodes will end the iteration when the value of CH_{prob} equals 1.

3. Final stage: In this stage, each node finds an adjacent cluster head at first, which can make the cost the minimum. If the node can find the cluster head, it sends a request message to add into the cluster, and it will become a cluster member with the permission of the cluster head. Otherwise, the node will decide to be a cluster head by itself if it cannot find any cluster head in the neighbor area.

The pseudocode of HEED algorithm is as follows [28].

I. Initialize

1. $S_{nbr} \leftarrow \{v : v \text{ lies within my cluster range}\}$

2. *Compute and broadcast cost to* $\in S_{nbr}$

3. $CH_{prob} \leftarrow \max\left(C_{prob} \times \dfrac{E_{restdual}}{E_{max}}, P_{min} \right)$

4. $is\_final\_CH \leftarrow FALSE$

II. Repeat

1. $if ((S_{CH} \leftarrow \{v : v \text{ is a cluster head}\}) \neq \Phi)$

2. $\quad my\_cluster\_head \leftarrow least\_cost(S_{CH})$

3. $\quad if (my\_cluster\_head = NodeID)$

4. $\qquad if (CH_{prob} = 1)$

5. $\qquad\quad Cluster\_head\_msg(NodeID, final\_CH, cost)$

6. $\qquad\quad is\_final\_CH \leftarrow TRUE$

7. $\qquad Else$

8. $\qquad\quad Cluster\_head\_msg(NodeID, tentative\_CH, cost)$

9. $\qquad ElseIf (CH_{prob} = 1)$

---

10. $Cluster\_head\_msg(NodeID, final\_CH, cost)$

11. $is\_final\_CH \leftarrow TRUE$

12. $ElseIf\ Random(0,1) \leq CH_{prob}$

13. $Cluster\_head\_msg(NodeID, \text{tentative}\_CH, cost)$

14. $CH_{previous} \leftarrow CH_{prob}$

15. $CH_{prob}\ min(CH_{prob} \times 2, 1)$

Until $CH_{previous} = 1$

III. Finalize

1. $if\ (is\_final\_CH = FALSE)$

2. $if\ ((S_{CH} \leftarrow \{v : v\ is\ a\ final\ cluster\ head\}) \neq \Phi)$

3. $my\_cluster\_head \leftarrow least\_cost(S_{CH})$

4. $join\_cluster\_head\_msg(cluster\_head\_ID, NodeID)$

5. $Else\ Cluster\_head\_msg(NodeID, final\_CH, cost)$

6. $Else\ Cluster\_head\_msg(NodeID, final\_CH, cost)$

HEED has a lot of advantages.

1. The generation of the cluster head is based on two hybrid parameters, which consider the residual energy of the node and also introduce multiple constrain conditions by owner-membership for the selection process of the cluster head. The process of cluster head generation is totally distributed.
2. The generation of the cluster head is realized in a limited iteration with fast convergence.
3. The control message has little complexity and low overhead.
4. The generation of the cluster head can be well distributed in the whole network with more reasonable topology.
5. The communication between the cluster head and the base station (i.e. intracluster communication adopts multihop mode, which can save more energy than single-hop mode).

HEED also has a lot of disadvantages.

1. The nodes that are the candidate cluster head but not selected as the final cluster head will be forced to be a cluster head. This kind of cluster head may be within the transmission range of other cluster heads or become an isolated node without any cluster members. As a result, there may be cluster heads out of the expected number, thereby causing unbalance of energy consumption.
2. Similar to LEACH, the periodical cycle for rebuilding the cluster will consume a great deal of energy, thereby certainly shortening the lifetime of the network.
3. Since the structure of the cluster can be formed after multiple iterations, it needs to consume the energy continuously. In each iteration, many messages need to be broadcasted, which can cause higher complexity.
4. The cluster head closer to the base station needs to forward messages from other cluster heads, so it may prematurely die and cause an energy hole due to its heavy workload.

DWEHC [29] is a distributed clustering algorithm similar to HEED; it was proposed by Ding et al. DWEHC modifies HEED in two aspects, one of which is forming the cluster with unique size and the other is optimizing the intra-cluster topology by sensing the position of the node. The commonality between DWEHC and HEED is that the size of network and the density of node are not assumed, and the residual energy is considered in the process of the cluster election as well. Each node executes DWEHC in a distributed way, and the algorithm ends after a certain amount of iterations.

Different from LEACH and HEED, DWEHC builds a multilayer structure for intra-cluster communication and limits the number of father nodes. Besides, in the process of cluster head election, DWEHC defines a parameter weight that can be calculated in a local distributed way. Each node calculates its weight by sensing the position of its neighbors according to the formula as follows.

$$W_{weight}(t) = \frac{E_{residual}(s)}{E_{initial}(s)} \times \sum_{u} \frac{R-d}{6R}, \tag{3.13}$$

in which, $E_{residual}(s)$ and $E_{initial}(s)$ refer to the residual energy and initial energy of a node, respectively; R is the range of cluster size, that is, the distance between the node and the cluster head in a cluster; d is the distance between node s and its neighbor node u. According to formula 3.13, in an adjacent area, the node with the maximum weight will be selected as the cluster head, and other nodes will be cluster members. In this stage, cluster members are considered as 1-level nodes, which can communicate with the cluster head directly. Each cluster member can adjust the relationship with other cluster members gradually, so that it can use the least energy to communicate with the cluster head. Assume that a node can estimate whether it still is a 1-level cluster member or has become an h-level cluster member if it knows the distance between itself and its neighbors (h is the number of hops from the node to the cluster head). If a cluster member can save energy by reaching the cluster head through multiple hops, it can become an h-level cluster member. Continue this process until all nodes can achieve the energy-efficient topology. The energy consumption of each cluster can be calculated by the distance between the node and its neighbors. In order to limit the level, each cluster has a range *R*. The multilayer cluster structure of DWEHC is shown as Figure 3.14. After executing DWEHC, each node becomes a cluster head or a cluster member. Moreover, each node can be covered by only one cluster head.

Intra-cluster communication adopts TDMA scheduling. Each father node polls its direct child node and fuses the packets from its child node with its own packets into one packet, then forwards it to its father node until all data arrives at the cluster head. For inter-cluster communication, the cluster head polls its first-layer child node then fuses the collected data with its own data and sends it to the base station.

DWEHC has a lot of advantages.

1. Similar to HEED, it is an absolute distributed clustering algorithm; the election of the cluster head is based on the residual energy and position of the node.
2. The consideration of residual energy in the cluster head election can make the distribution of the cluster head generated by DWEHC more balanced, which

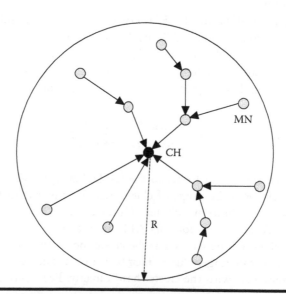

Figure 3.14   Clustering unit constructed by the DWEHC algorithm.

can greatly reduce energy consumption in intra-cluster and inter-cluster communication.

3. The clustering process of DWEHC can be completed in a few iterations, which has nothing to do with the topology and scale of the network.

DWEHC has some disadvantages.

1. Similar to LEACH, the inter-cluster communication of the protocol is in a single-hop mode, that is, inter-cluster data is transmitted from the cluster head to the base station directly. Therefore, it will cause a lot of energy consumption, so that the protocol is not suitable for the large-scale network.
2. Similar to HEED, the iteration process will generate high overhead of control messages.

The energy-saving distributed clustering algorithm EEDC [30] previously proposed is also an improved algorithm for HEED. The algorithm is executed by cycles, each of which can be divided into the process of forming the cluster and the process of data transmission. The process of forming the cluster can be divided into three stages: the predetermination of the cluster head, the determination of the cluster head, and the formation of the cluster.

1. The predetermination of the cluster head: In this stage, the node with higher residual energy needs to be selected as a candidate cluster head. At the beginning of the stage, all nodes are marked as "Plain." The specific selection is that each node decides whether it becomes a candidate cluster head according to its predetermined probability P_{tch}. The candidate cluster head will be marked as "Tentative_CH." The formula of P_{tch} is as follows.

$$P_{tch} = \alpha \times \frac{E_{current}}{E_{max}}, \tag{3.14}$$

in which, $E_{current}$ is the current residual energy of the node; E_{max} is the maximum initial energy of the node. The value of α is within $(0, 1)$, indicating the initial probability of being a candidate cluster head. The number of the candidate cluster heads can be changed by adjusting the value of α. $E_{current}$ is reduced with the operation of the network. Thus, the value of α should be improved continuously to make sure that P_{tch} will not be decreased because of the residual energy of the node, so that it will not affect the number of the candidate cluster heads and quality of the cluster head eventually.
2. The determination of the cluster head: In this stage, the candidate cluster head participates in the election of the final cluster head. In order to reduce energy consumption, the cost of intra-cluster communication is used as the competition parameter W for the candidate nodes to compete with the final

cluster head. The election parameter W of the candidate cluster head v is calculated as follows:

$$W_v = \frac{\sum_{i=1}^{d(v)} dist(v, v_i)}{d(v)}, \tag{3.15}$$

in which, v_i is a neighbor of node v in the range of R_c; $dist(v, v_i)$ is the distance between nodes v_i and v; $d(v)$ is the degree of node v, that is, W_v is the average distance between node v and its neighbors; the smaller the W_v, the less the energy consumption of cluster head v.

Each candidate cluster head broadcasts a message "Compete_Msg," which includes the communication cost w with radius R_c. Meanwhile, it will receive a "Comepete_Msg" message from its neighbors. Each candidate cluster head builds a list of candidate cluster heads according to received "Comepete_Msg" messages. Besides, the node itself can be within its list of candidate cluster heads. If the communication cost of candidate cluster head v is lower than any neighbor cluster head in its list, v will become the final cluster head and inform its neighbors by broadcasting a message "Head_Msg" with radius R_c. When there are multiple nodes with minimum communication cost, the node with minimum id has priority. The candidate cluster head that receives the message "Head_Msg" will be the regular node and broadcasts a message "Quit_Msg" with radius R_c to inform its neighbors about its decision to quit the election. The neighbor cluster head receiving the message "Quit_Msg" updates its list of candidate cluster heads and deletes the coordinating node; it then joins the next cycle of election. The process will not end until all the candidate cluster heads determine whether they are final cluster heads or the regular nodes. The pseudocode of the stage is as follows.

1. **If** state==Tentative_CH

2. w =average communication cost

3. Broadcast Comepete_Msg

4. Update tentative CH neighborhood table TCHNT[ ]

5. **While**(state==Tentative_CH)

6. **If** TCHNT[]==

7. state Final_CH

8. Broadcast Head_Msg

9. **Else**

10. Myhead[] the node has the least w in TCHNT[ ]
11. **If** MyID==least_id(Myhead[ ])
12. state Final_CH
13. Broadcast Head_Msg
14. **End if**
15. **End if**
16. **If** receive a Final_CH
17. state Plain
18. Broadcast Quit_Msg
19. **End if**
20. **If** receive a Quit_Msg
21. Update tentative CH neighborhood table TCHNT[ ]
22. **End if**
23. **End while**
24. **End if**
25. **If** state==Plain && have not received a Head_Msg
26. state Final_CH
27. Broadcast Head_Msg
28. **End if**

Lines 2 to 4 of the pseudocode comprise the ready process of the stage. The final cluster head is generated by a "while" cycle. When all candidate cluster heads determine their roles (final cluster heads or regular nodes), a node has not been covered by a cluster head if it does not receive "Head_Msg." It will then be forced to become a cluster head and broadcasts a "Head_Msg."

The formation of the cluster is similar to LEACH, so we will not introduce it.

Theory analysis and simulation prove that EEDC possesses all of the characteristics of an effective clustering algorithm: (1) absolutely distributed; (2) the cluster head is well distributed; (3) the algorithm has small overhead; (4) it can deal with the energy heterogeneous problem. The simulation result proves that EEDC is more effective for prolonging the lifetime of the network than LEACH and HEED.

3.2.4.4 Chain Clustering Algorithms (PEGASIS)

PEGASIS [31] protocol is an extension of LEACH protocol, proposed by Lindsey et al., which follows the clustering idea of the LEACH algorithm. The difference is that the nodes in PEGASIS only communicate with their closest neighbors, and only one node communicates with the base station as the leader in each cycle. The node sends a test signal with diminishing energy and determines its closest neighbor by monitoring the replies. All of the nodes in the network can master the relationship of each other in this way.

PEGASIS protocol uses the Greedy algorithm to form a chain. It builds a chain construction before communication in each cycle to make sure that each node has its neighbors. The chain is built from the node that is the farthest from the base station. Each node finds the closest node. A node that is already in the chain cannot be accessed again. In this way, the chain can eventually include all of the nodes in the network. Then it selects a leader in each cycle. A token mechanism is adopted for data transmission after the leader selection. At first, the token signal is transmitted by the nodes on two sides of the chain; then the nodes at the sides send data to the next nodes, which fuse the data with their own and send the fused data to the next nodes; finally the leader node fuses the data from two sides to send to the base station. The chain needs to be rebuilt if one of the nodes in the chain dies.

Generally, the key ideas of the PEGASIS algorithm are:

1. The base station is static and far away from the monitoring area of the wireless network.
2. The sensor nodes stay unmoved once they are deployed.
3. Each node knows the position of other nodes and can communicate with the base station directly with enough calculation ability to support signal processing and route calculation.
4. All sensor nodes in the network are homogeneous; the node has the ability to control transmitting power and uses the minimum necessary power to communicate with the base station.

The energy model adopted by the PEGASIS algorithm is the same as that for LEACH, so we will not describe it again here.

The algorithm process of the PEGASIS protocol can be divided into three parts: the stage of forming a chain, the stage of leader node election, and the stage of data transmission. The details are as follows.

3.2.4.4.1 The Stage of Forming a Chain

The PEGASIS protocol adopts the Greedy algorithm to form the sensor nodes into a cluster chain, which ensures that each node consumes the least energy with minimal communication distance.

Forming the chain is the key of the PEGASIS protocol. The whole process is divided into slots. The chain is built before transmitting data. It starts from the node that is the farthest from the base station. The beginning node is the initial head node of the chain. In every slot, the node beyond the chain and closest to the head node joins the chain and becomes the new head node of the chain. The process will be repeated until all nodes join the chain. In the real network, the node sends an energy diminishing test signal and determines which neighbor is the closest by monitoring the replies. All nodes can master their relative positions in this way and find the closest node. A node only communicates with its neighbor nodes in each cycle.

Since a node already in the chain cannot be accessed in the Greedy algorithm, the distance among neighbors will be larger with the addition of a node. Therefore, starting from the node that is farthest from the base station can ensure that a node finds its closest neighbor and can avoid premature death due to long-distance communication. When a node dies, it will be deleted and other nodes will be rebuilt for a new chain according to the Greedy algorithm. Figure 3.15 shows the chain topology formed in the stage of forming the chain.

3.2.4.4.2 The Stage of Leader Node Election

The difference between the PEGASIS protocol and the LEACH protocol is that only one needs to be selected to communicate with the base station in PEGASIS protocol while multiple cluster heads need to be selected to communicate with the base station in LEACH protocol, as shown in Figure 3.16.

The method of leader node election in the PEGASIS protocol is as follows: assign id from 1 to N to all N nodes in the wireless network; then calculate the value of i mod N (i is the number of the current cycle) and find the node whose ID is i mod N as the leader node. This kind of election method makes sure that all the nodes have been the leader after N cycles, avoiding excessive energy consumption because of being the leader all the time. Besides, each node is distributed in the chain randomly (i.e., node i may be at position j), which can make sure that the position of the leader is random. Once a node dies, the position of the dead node is random, improving the robustness of the network.

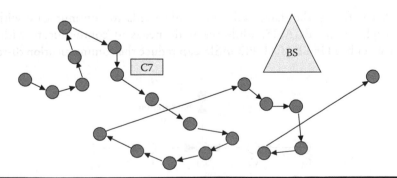

Figure 3.15   Chain topology formed by PEGASIS.

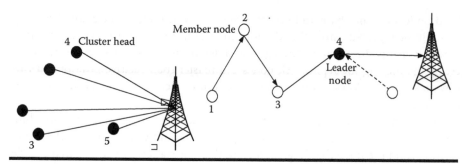

Figure 3.16 The communication mode with the base station in LEACH and PEGASIS.

3.2.4.4.3 The Stage of Data Transmission

The stage of data transmission starts after the formation of the chain and the election of the leader node. The data transmission in PEGASIS algorithm uses token control mechanism. The token is small, so it consumes little energy. Assume that there are five sensor nodes in the network, and remark the number of each node as C_0, C_1, C_2, C_3, C_4. The chain is shown as Figure 3.17, in which C_2 is the leader node. In each cycle, the leader node controls and sends data from two sides by a token. First, the token is sent to C_0 along the chain; then C_0 sends data to C_1. C_1 fuses the data from C_0 with its own into a new packet and sends it to C_2. After that, C_2 sends the token to C_4. C_2 collects the data of C_3 and C_4 in the same way. As shown in the figure, C_0 and C_4, which are located at the sides of the chain, only need to transmit the data to their neighbors; C_1, C_2, and C_3, which are located in the middle of the chain, need to collect data from their neighbors first; then they need to fuse the data from the neighbors with their own data and transmit the new packet to their neighbors on the other side. Continue like that until the data arrives at the leader node C_2. Finally, C_2 sends the fused data to the base station.

Compared with the LEACH protocol, the advantages of PEGASIS are as follows.

1. When fusing the data, each node only needs to communicate with its neighbor in PEGASIS, while the node needs to communicate with the cluster head in LEACH. PEGASIS can reduce the communication distance

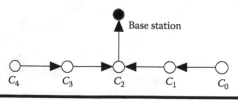

Figure 3.17 The token mechanism of PEGASIS.

of each node in every cycle, thereby decreasing the energy consumption in every cycle.

2. In LEACH, each cluster head receives data from multiple cluster members. The more cluster members there are, the more data the cluster head needs to receive. In the PEGASIS algorithm, a leader node only receives packets from two nodes at most in every cycle, which can greatly reduce the energy consumption of the leader node; compared with the reconstruction of cluster in LEACH, the reconstruction of chain in PEGASIS consumes less energy. The simulation result shows that PEGASIS can double the lifetime compared with LEACH.

3. In each cycle, PEGASIS only needs a leader node to communicate with the base station, while LEACH needs multiple cluster heads to communicate with the base station, and the distance between the cluster head and the base station is large. The larger the number of cluster heads that need to communicate with the base station, the more energy is consumed. Therefore, LEACH can save a lot of transmission energy compared with PEGASIS.

However, PEGASIS has some disadvantages.

1. In the process of forming the chain, each node needs to know global information. The protocol is not suitable in the situation where global information cannot be obtained.

2. The protocol assumes that each sensor node can communicate with the base station directly. In real networks, however, the sensor node adopts a multihop mode to arrive at the base station generally.

3. PEGASIS assumes that all sensor nodes have equal energy, so nodes may die at the same time.

4. The protocol avoids the overhead of rebuilding the cluster, but the topology still needs to be adjusted dynamically because the sensor node needs to know the energy status of its neighbors for data transmission. For the network, which is highly efficient or is easily damaged in severe conditions, a great deal of overhead will be needed to rebuild the chain frequently.

5. In the chain built by the protocol, long-distance nodes will cause too much data delay. Besides, the uniqueness of the leader node makes the chain head become a bottleneck. Once the leader node becomes abnormal, communication with the base station will be interrupted, thereby causing a failure in monitoring the overall network.

Lindsey et al. proposed a solution of binary and three-layer data fusion aiming at the fifth disadvantage [32]. The binary fusion algorithm in which the node has CDMA function is that data fusion is executed at the same time among the adjacent nodes in a PEGASIS chain; then the data goes up layer by layer until it is sent to the base station (as shown in Figure 3.18). The layer level is log N (N is the number of nodes).

When the node does not have CDMA functions, the three-layer fusion algorithm should be as follows: Multiple adjacent nodes in the PEGASIS chain constitute a group and fuse the data in sequence to reduce signal collisions. The protocol has three layers. Finally, the cluster head sends data to the base station.

Concentric ring clustering system (CCS) [33], proposed by Jung et al., aims to reduce the energy hole caused by the PEGASIS protocol. The main idea of CCS considers the position of the base station to improve the performance of the algorithm, so that the lifetime of the network can be prolonged. In the CCS mechanism, the network is divided into multiple concentric-ring tracks. Different concentric-ring tracks refer to different clusters, and each ring track is marked by a layer value. The track closest to the base station is marked as level 1. The level increases along with the distance to the base station. Thus, each node has its own level in the network. Besides, the ring track in each layer builds a chain topology like the PEGASIS protocol. Each cluster sends its position information to the cluster head in the higher layer and the lower layer after the cluster head election. In the stage of data transmission, all nodes in each level send data to their closest node along the chain. The node that receives data fuses it with its own data and sends the fused data to the cluster head in the lower level. Finally, the cluster head in level 1 sends data to the base station. The process of data transmission is shown in Figure 3.19.

Compared with PEGASIS, CCS has the following advantages:

1. The distance between the cluster head and the base station is shortened, so a lot of energy can be saved.
2. The network is divided into a series of concentric-ring clusters, so that data flow returning from the base station is reduced, which can save a lot of energy.

However, CCS has some disadvantages.

1. The node in each level is not well distributed; the level with less nodes will run out of energy quickly. In this kind of level, the probability of being the cluster head will be high.

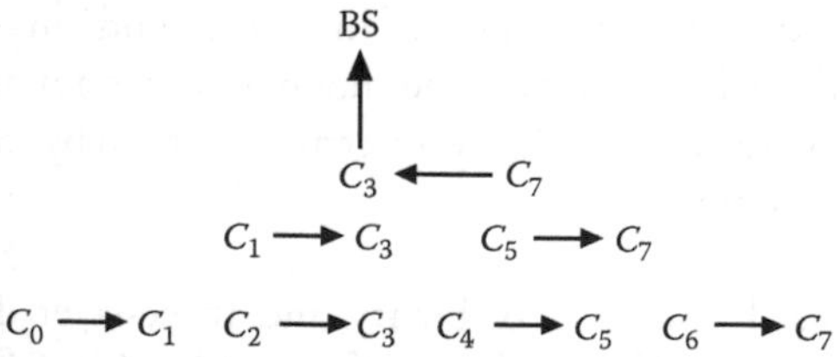

Figure 3.18 The layers of the PEGASIS algorithm.

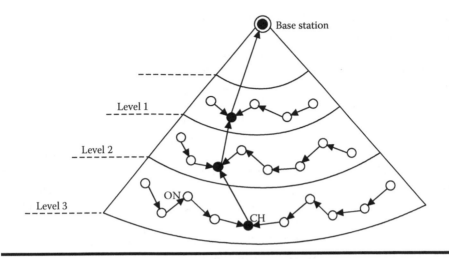

Figure 3.19 Hierarchical topology built by the CCS algorithm.

2. In cluster head election, the residual energy of the node isn't considered which leads to the uneven energy consumption.
3. In the protocol based on chains such as PEGASIS and CCS, nodes can communicate with their closest neighbors with low transmitting power. However, the longer the chain is, the larger the delay is.
4. The cluster head election is based on position information rather than the residual energy of the node, so that the energy of the cluster head will run out quickly, thereby causing an energy hole.

Wang et al. proposed a new method for building a chain in Reference [34]. In the improved algorithm, the first and second steps of building a chain are the same as in PEGASIS. The main idea is to put the next joining node between two adjacent nodes of the chain. The standard of chain building is that the energy consumption of data transmission is minimal this way. This method is known as the minimum-energy chain building method. The experiment result shows that the improved algorithm can reduce energy consumption by a third over the PEGASIS algorithm when 1% of nodes run out of energy in the middle density condition.

In Reference [35], Du et al. adopted a simulated annealing algorithm to form clusters based on the PEGASIS algorithm and selected the cluster head for each cycle by an energy factor.

The network model of the algorithm is that a certain number of sensor nodes with limited energy are distributed in the monitoring area. Assume that the nodes are static and can obtain the geographical positions of other nodes by a device. There exists one base station in the monitoring area, which is responsible for receiving data from the monitoring area and clustering the sensor nodes. Also, assume that energy is limitless.

In each cycle, the algorithm selects the node with the most residual energy as the cluster head, which needs to transmit the fused data to the base station. The node is regarded as dead when its residual energy is lower than or equal to 0. At this time, the other nodes will build a new chain and start a new communication on the new chain until all the nodes die. The square of the length in the simulating annealing algorithm is reduced by a half compared with the original Greedy algorithm, so that it can reduce the energy consumption of the overall network and push back the death time of the first node. The time until the death of the first node is about 1.8–3 times longer than in the original algorithm, and the death time of 20%, 50%, and 80% of the nodes is also longer than in the original algorithm, thereby improving the lifetime of the network.

Wang, Basagni, et al. used an improved genetic algorithm to replace the Greedy algorithm in Reference [36], considering that the energy consumed by transmitting is proportional to the square of the distance. It builds a chain with the minimum square of the distance rather than the minimum distance, which can ensure that the energy consumption is minimal.

Besides, in the process of cluster head election, PEGASIS only adopts the method of cycling. Although the operation is simple, it does not consider the factor of energy, which easily causes the premature death of the far apart nodes. Aiming at this drawback, the PEGASIS algorithm selects the node with maximum energy as the cluster head, which can balance the energy and reduce premature deaths. Adopting the genetic algorithm to improve the formation of the chain can reduce the distance of transmission. Since the energy consumed by transmitting data is proportional to the square of the transmission distance, it is better to form a chain with a minimum sum of the square of distance and to select the cluster head based on energy to balance energy consumption. The simulation result shows that the lifetime of the first dead node is 1.5 times that of the one in the PEGASIS algorithm. Almost half of the nodes are improved in the lifetime. Moreover, the energy consumption is more balanced, which improves performance, such as in the lifetime of the overall network.

The PEDAP algorithm [37] improves the PEGASIS algorithm further; its key idea is constructing all nodes in the sensor network into a small aggregation tree. The base station (BS) knows the geographical positions of all nodes and confirms the energy consumption of each cycle according to the energy model, so that BS can predetermine the residual energy of any node. After a certain number of cycles, BS recalculates the route information to delete the dead nodes; then nodes need to send the information (including the position, the residual energy, and the data slot) to each other. In this way, all nodes only need to receive the message from BS. PEDAP consumes less energy than PEGASIS in the setting stage. However, the base station cannot know that the node is dead; it also cannot delete it in time if it does not die from running out of energy.

MADG algorithm [38] sets the mobile area of the base station as a buffer area. Firstly, transmit the data to the buffer area along the shortest route; then collect data in the movement process of the base station and prove that it will cost minimum energy consumption when the buffer position is $0.707R$ away from the center.

Authors in Reference [39] proposed the EEPB algorithm aiming to solve the problem of uneven energy consumption caused by the long chain and first node selection in the PEGASIS algorithm. In order to avoid the long chain among the adjacent nodes, the improved algorithm sets a distance threshold in the process of forming the chain. The node that has more residual energy and is closer to other nodes will be set as the first node of the chain to balance energy consumption among the nodes and even among the whole network. Meanwhile, adopting the algorithm, which reduces the frequency of rebuilding the chain, can further decrease the energy consumption of the network. The simulation result shows that the improved algorithm has better performance in the aspects of complexity, balance of energy consumption, and prolonged lifetime.

The Energy efficient clustering protocol to enhance the lifetime of WSN (EECPL) is proposed in Reference [40]; it combines the advantages of LEACH-C and PEGASIS. The specific idea is as follows.

The base station confirms the number of clusters and determines which nodes can be cluster heads or cluster members according to the information received from the nodes. Then the base station broadcasts to all the nodes about their roles. After that, the cluster members in each cluster construct a chain using a method similar to PEGASIS and select the leader node of each chain. In the process of data transmission, the cluster head builds an intra-cluster TDMA scheduling table and informs every node in the chain. A node can send data to its neighbor only in its own slot. The neighbor node fuses the received data with its own data and transmits the fused data to the next node. Finally, the leader node sends all data to the base station. The topology structure built by the algorithm is shown in Figure 3.20. The theory and simulation can prove that the protocol can save a lot of energy and prolong the lifetime of the network compared with LEACH-C.

In Reference [41], a routing algorithm CCM is proposed based on cluster-chain; it combines the low energy consumption of PEGASIS and the small delay of LEACH. The network model of the algorithm is illustrated as Figure 3.21. The sensor nodes are arranged evenly in a linear array. In the first part, the node in each array will be selected as the first node in turn based on its geographical position for balancing energy consumption among the nodes, thereby avoiding the energy consumed by the selection of the first node. In the process of data transmission, the first node sends the token to the nodes at the sides by the method similar to the process of PEGASIS. A node only communicates with its closest neighbor. It fuses data from the former neighbor with its own data and transmits it to the next neighbor. Finally, the first node fuses the data of the chain. If the first nodes of each

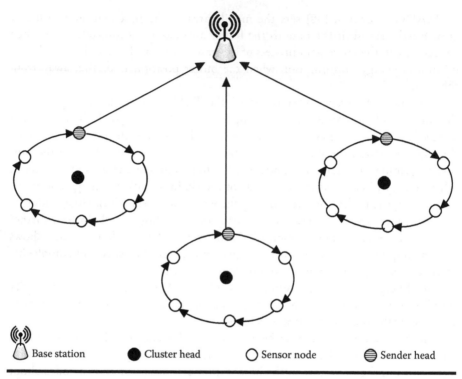

Base station   ● Cluster head   ○ Sensor node   ⊜ Sender head

Figure 3.20   **The cluster-chain topology built by EECPL.**

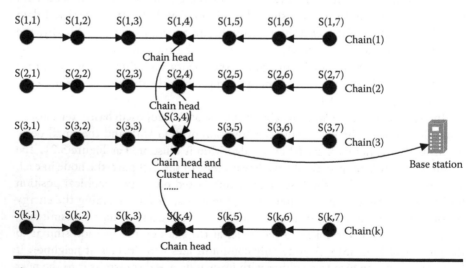

Figure 3.21   **The chain-cluster topology built by the CCM algorithm.**

chain send the data to the base station simultaneously, it will cause interference. In order to avoid interference in the second part, the first nodes constitute a chain. The cluster head is selected based on the residual energy of the first node. Thus the first node can transmit the aggregated data to the cluster head by multihop mode. The cluster will send the data to the base station directly without processing. Then, the algorithm ends.

Theoretical analysis and simulation result can prove that CCM algorithm has the advantage of low energy consumption in PEGASIS and small delay of LEACH. However, the network model used in the algorithm is too idealistic and is not suitable for real application.

3.2.4.5 Energy Heterogeneous Clustering Algorithms

The LEACH algorithm and many improved algorithms based on LEACH are the basis of the homogeneous network. In the real sensor network, however, a hetero-geneous situation is common. For example, the nodes with the same initial energy have different remaining energy for various reasons. Also, new nodes will join the network to maintain the regular work of the network when there are dead nodes in the operation, and the energy of the new nodes is generally higher than original nodes, which will cause heterogeneous energy. Therefore, designing a clustering algorithm for an energy-heterogeneous network is important.

The Stable Election Protocol (SEP) [42] is proposed by Smaragdakis et al. It aims for a two-level heterogeneous network, in which there are senior nodes with higher energy and regular nodes with lower energy. SEP adopts two different thresholds of cluster head elections with energy weight for the two kinds of sensor nodes according to different initial energy.

Assume that the total number of nodes in the network is n; the ratio of senior nodes against the total number of nodes is m; the ratio of the energy of the senior node against the energy of the regular node is α; then the total additional energy is $n - \alpha m$; the proportion of optimal cluster heads is p_{opt}. In SEP, the probability of cluster head election for the regular node is defined as

$$P_{nm} = \frac{P_{opt}}{1 + \alpha \cdot m}. \tag{3.16}$$

The probability of cluster head election for the senior node is defined as

$$P_{adv} = \frac{P_{opt}}{1 + \alpha \cdot m} \times (1 + \alpha). \tag{3.17}$$

Therefore, the regular node and the senior node have different periods of cluster head election. The election period of the regular node is $1/P_{nm}$, and the election period of the senior node is $1/P_{adv}$. The probability of the senior node being the cluster head is $1+\alpha$ times that of the regular node. The election threshold of the corresponding regular node is

$$T(S_{nrm}) = \begin{cases} \dfrac{P_{nrm}}{1 - P_{nrm}\left(r \bmod \dfrac{1}{P_{nrm}}\right)}, & if \quad s \in G' \\ 0, & others \end{cases} \qquad (3.18)$$

The election threshold of the senior node is

$$T(S_{adv}) = \begin{cases} \dfrac{P_{adv}}{1 - P_{adv}\left(r \bmod \dfrac{1}{P_{adv}}\right)}, & if \quad s \in G'' \\ 0, & others \end{cases} \qquad (3.19)$$

in which, G' is the set of regular nodes selected as the cluster heads in the previous round; G'' is the set of the senior nodes selected as cluster heads in the previous round. $T(S_{nrm})$ can make sure that the election period of being the cluster head for the regular node is $\dfrac{1}{P_{opt}}(1 + \alpha \cdot m)$ round, and in each round, the average number of regular nodes becoming cluster heads is $n \cdot (1 - m) \times P_{nrm}$; $T(S_{adv})$ can make sure the election period of being the cluster head for the senior node is $n \cdot m \times P_{adv}$. Therefore, the average number of cluster heads in a heterogeneous network is

$$n \cdot (1 - m) \times P_{nrm} + n \cdot m \times P_{adv} = n \times P_{opt}. \qquad (3.20)$$

This is the same as the expected number of cluster heads. Figure 3.22 is the illustration of the election period when $m = 0.2$ and $\alpha = 3$.

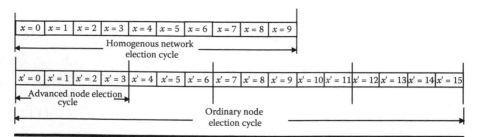

Figure 3.22 The illustration of the election period in the SEP network. (From Smaragdakis, G. et al., SEP: A stable election protocol for clustered heterogeneous wireless sensor networks, In: *Proceedings of the International Workshop on SANPA*, 2004.)

The SEP algorithm modifies the cluster head election mechanism. The probability of being the cluster head is related to initial energy, which is beneficial to balancing energy consumption in the network and prolongs the stable period of data transmission. Also, the SEP algorithm can improve the total number of packets transmitted in the network. Besides, the election of the SEP cluster head is based on the initial energy of the node. In the election of each cycle, SEP does not need to know the specific energy of all nodes and does not need to master the geographical location; thus, it is suitable for real networks.

The cycle of the senior node is less than that of the regular node in SEP, which gives the senior node more chance to be the cluster head. Therefore, the senior node will die at the same time as the regular node, which can make full use of and save energy. Moreover, synchronous deaths of the senior and regular nodes can save the time in the stable stage and prolong the stable time of the network.

In the multilevel heterogeneous network, initial energy is distributed at random in the closed interval $[E_0, E_0(\alpha_{max})]$, in which E_0 is the lower limit of energy and α_{max} decides the maximum initial energy. At the beginning of the operation, the initial energy of each node is set as $E_0(1+\alpha_i)$, in which α_i is a multiple of E_0 and greater than E_0. Therefore, the total initial energy of a multilevel heterogeneous network equals

$$E_{total} = \sum_{i=1}^{N} E_0(1+\alpha_i) = E_0\left(N + \sum_{i=1}^{N}\alpha_i\right). \quad (3.21)$$

Just like the two-level heterogeneous network, the clustering algorithm in a multilevel heterogeneous network should consider the difference in initial energy. It is easy to extend SEP into the situation of a multilevel heterogeneous network. Each node s_i has different weighted probability according to initial energy:

$$p(s_i) = \frac{p_{opt}N(1+\alpha_i)}{N + \sum_{i=1}^{N}\alpha_i}. \quad (3.22)$$

The probability threshold can be obtained by replacing p_{opt}. This kind of clustering algorithm in multilevel heterogeneous networks is still regarded as SEP.

The Distributed Energy-Efficient Clustering Algorithm (DEEC) is a distributed energy-efficient clustering solution for heterogeneous sensor networks; it is a modified algorithm based on SEP and proposed by Qingli. The cluster head election of the DEEC protocol is based on the ratio of the residual energy to the average energy. The node with higher initial energy and residual energy can have the priority as the cluster head, so that the election of the cluster head can adopt the change in energy and balance the energy consumption, thereby prolonging the stable period and improving the scalability of the network.

The algorithm includes three parts.

1. The cluster head election algorithm based on residual energy

   Set p_{opt} as the ratio of optimal cluster head; set n_i as the cluster head cycle period of the node s_i. We select the cluster head cycle period n_i based on the residual energy $E_i(r)$ of the node s_i in cycle r. Set p_i as the reciprocal of n_i, and it can be regarded as the average probability of node s_i being the cluster head in cycle n_i. When the node has the same energy in each election period, set $p_i = p_{opt}$ so that all the nodes can die at almost the same time. If the nodes have different residual energy, the average probability of the high-energy node is larger than that of the low-energy node, so that the energy can be consumed evenly and the lifetime of the network can be prolonged. Set $\overline{E}(r)$ as the average energy in cycle r, then it holds that

$$\overline{E}(r) = \frac{1}{N} \sum_{i=1}^{N} E_i(r). \tag{3.23}$$

In order to calculate $\overline{E}(r)$ by formula 3.23, each node needs to know the total energy of all nodes, which is difficult to achieve. The method of estimating the average energy $\overline{E}(r)$ will be introduced in a later section. Regard $\overline{E}(r)$ as the reference energy and compare the residual energy with the average energy $\overline{E}(r)$, so that it holds that

$$P_i = P_{opt} \left[1 - \frac{\overline{E}(r) - E_i(r)}{\overline{E}(r)} \right] = P_{opt} \frac{E_i(r)}{\overline{E}(r)}. \tag{3.24}$$

Formula 3.24 indicates that the average election probability p_i will be higher than p_{opt} when the residual energy is larger than the average energy; the average election probability will be decreased less corresponding value than p_{opt} when the residual energy is less than the average energy. Meanwhile, formula 3.25 can ensure that the average cluster head in each cycle is

$$\sum_{i=1}^{N} P_i = \sum_{i=1}^{N} P_{opt} \frac{E_i(r)}{E(r)} = P_{opt} \sum_{i=1}^{N} \frac{E_i(r)}{\overline{E}(r)} = NP_{opt}. \tag{3.25}$$

NP_{opt} is the number of optimal cluster heads in theory. In formulas 3.18 and 3.19, p_i replaces p_{opt}, so that the threshold at which each node s_i can be determined as cluster head by itself can be obtained as

$$
T(S_i) = \begin{cases} \dfrac{P_i}{1 - P_i\left(r \bmod \dfrac{1}{P_i}\right)}, & \textit{if } s \in G \\ \\ 0, & \textit{others} \end{cases} \tag{3.26}
$$

Note that the mode of $1/p_i$ in formula 3.26 is the period n_i of being the cluster head. The different periods n_i of being the cluster head are selected for the nodes s_i with different residual energy when p_i is decided by the residual energy:

$$
n_i = \frac{1}{p_i} = \frac{\overline{E}(r)}{p_{opt}E_i(r)} = n_{opt}\frac{\overline{E}(r)}{E_i(r)}, \tag{3.27}
$$

in which, $n_{opt} = 1/p_{opt}$ represents the reference of the period of being the cluster head. Formula 3.27 indicates that the period of being the cluster head will be decreased a corresponding proportion when the ratio of the residual energy to the average energy is larger and vice versa, so that the nodes with high energy will be more likely to be cluster heads. All nodes will run out of the energy at almost the same time.

2. The processing of the heterogeneous node

The average probability p_i decides the cluster head cycle period n_i and the threshold $T(s_i)$ of node s_i. As shown in formula 3.25, p_{opt} is the reference value of p_i, and p_i varies with p_{opt}. In the homogeneous network, all nodes have the same initial energy, so that the nodes use the same value p_{opt} as the reference of p_i and the reference value of the cluster cycle period of each node is $1/p_{opt}$. The node needs to use various reference values according to different initial energy. In the two-level heterogeneous network, choose the weighted probability given by formulas 3.16 and 3.17 as the reference value and replace the p_{opt} in formula 3.25; then it holds that

$$
p_i = \begin{cases} \dfrac{p_{opt}E_r(r)}{(1+\alpha\lambda)\overline{E}(r)}, & s_i \textit{ is the regular node} \\ \\ \dfrac{p_{opt}(1+\alpha)E_i(r)}{(1+\alpha\lambda)\overline{E}(r)}, & s_i \textit{ is the senior node} \end{cases} \tag{3.28}
$$

Combining formula 3.28 with formula 3.27, the probability threshold $T(s_i)$ for cluster head election can be obtained. Therefore, threshold $T(s_i)$ is directly related to the initial energy and the residual energy of the node.

It is easy to extend the model into the multilevel heterogeneous network. Use the weighted probability in formula 3.22 to replace p_{opt} in formula 3.24; then it holds that

$$P_i = \frac{p_{opt}N(1+\alpha_i)E_i(r)}{(N+\sum\limits_{i=1}^{N}\alpha_i)\overline{E}(r)}. \tag{3.29}$$

It can be known from formulas 3.22 and 3.29 that $I_i = \left(N+\sum\limits_{i=1}^{N}\alpha_i\right)/p_{opt}N(1+\alpha_i)$ represents the basic cycle period of s_i, which is regarded as the reference period. The corresponding I_i is different if the initial energy is different. Note that $n_i=1/p_i$. The cycle period n_i of each node fluctuates around its reference period I_i according to the change of the residual energy. $n_i < I_i$ if $E_i(r) > \overline{E}(r)$ and vice versa. This means that the node with high initial energy and residual energy will have a greater chance to be the cluster head, so that the energy will be well distributed in the process of the evolution.

3. The estimation of the average energy

As known in formula 3.24, the calculation of p_i needs each node to know the average energy $\overline{E}(r)$, which is difficult to achieve. Note that the average energy $\overline{E}(r)$ is just a reference value for the residual energy of the node, so using the estimated value will not affect the performance of the algorithm. If we know the lifetime of the network, the approximate estimated value of the average energy can be obtained:

$$R = \frac{E_{total}}{E_{round}}. \tag{3.30}$$

The process of transmitting L bit message through a distance d uses the same wireless circuit energy consumption model as LEACH.

Assume that N sensor nodes are well distributed in an $M \times M$ area. For simplicity, assume that the base station is located at the center of the area (where the base station is deployed will not make a great impact on the analytic results). Each cluster member sends an L bits message to the cluster head in each cycle. Then the sum of energy consumption in a cycle is

$$E_{round} = L\left(2NE_{elec} + NE_{DA} + k\varepsilon d_{toBS}^4 + N\varepsilon_{fs}d_{toCH}^2\right), \tag{3.31}$$

in which k is the number of cluster heads; E_{DA} is the cost of the cluster head for executing data fusion; d_{toBS} is the average distance of the cluster head and the base station; d_{toCH} is the average distance of the cluster member and the cluster head. Assume that the nodes are well distributed; then it holds that

$$d_{toCH} = \frac{M}{\sqrt{2\pi k}}, \quad d_{toBS} = 0.765\frac{M}{2}. \tag{3.32}$$

In formula 3.31, solve the partial derivative of E_{round} on k and let the partial derivative be 0. Then the number of the optimal cluster head is

$$k_{opt} = \frac{\sqrt{N}}{\sqrt{2\pi}} \sqrt{\frac{\varepsilon_{fs}}{\varepsilon_{mp}} \frac{M}{d_{toBS}^2}}. \qquad (3.33)$$

Combining formulas 3.32 and 3.33 with formula 3.31, then the sum of energy E_{round} of each cycle can be obtained. Note that the total energy E_{total} is known. Then the estimated value R of the lifetime can be calculated by formula 3.30.

Assume that each node consumes the energy evenly, that is, each node consumes equal energy in each cycle. Then the average energy of each node in cycle r is

$$\overline{E}(r) = \frac{1}{N} E_{total} \left(1 - \frac{r}{R}\right). \qquad (3.34)$$

At the beginning of the operation of the network, all nodes need to know the total energy and the lifetime of the network. In DEEC protocol, these two parameters are calculated in advanced by the base station through the algorithm mentioned earlier; then the base station broadcasts them to all nodes. When it comes to the new election period, the node uses the information to calculate the average probability p_i by formulas 3.34 and 3.29. Then bring p_i into formula 3.27 and obtain the probability threshold $T(s_i)$. The node can decide whether it becomes the cluster head.

The DEEC algorithm is a clustering routing algorithm based on residual energy. It selects the cluster head according to the residual energy. The node with more residual energy has larger probability of being the cluster head. Compared with the SEP algorithm, it can prolong the lifetime of the network effectively, especially the stable period.

Meanwhile, the DEEC algorithm adopts different probability reference values of cluster heads for the senior node and the regular node. The senior node applies a larger reference value; then it has more chance to be the cluster head, so that it can die at the same time with the regular node, and the stable period of the network is prolonged. However, the DEEC algorithm does not make a specific analysis for the senior node and the regular node; thus, the senior node and the regular node tend to die at the same time just from the trend compared to the SEP algorithm, and it cannot ensure this in reality. That means there is a time difference between the senior node and the regular node in the operation result of the DEEC algorithm.

Many existing clustering algorithms consider heterogeneous energy, but they are just utilized symbolically and tentatively without special analysis. However, SEP and DEEC make the classification for the node energy and process differently for the nodes with different energy. Also, they analyze the clustering algorithm of an energy-heterogeneous network in theory and extend the application fields of the clustering algorithm. Experiments prove that these two kinds of algorithms can balance the energy among the nodes and avoid the waste of energy.

3.2.4.6 Self-Adaptive Clustering Algorithms

The Algorithm for Cluster Establishment (ACE) [44] is an adaptive distributed clustering algorithm with a good feedback mechanism. In ACE algorithm, the cluster forming consists of the generation and movement of the cluster. Each node operates ACE algorithm based on the information feedback among the neighbors. Finally, the two logical parts form the cluster iteratively.

In ACE, the nodes in the network are usually divided into the following three states: unclustered state, clustered state, and the cluster head node. Nodes in the unclustered state are the nodes that have not joined any cluster, and nodes in the network are all in the unclustered state at the beginning stage. Nodes in the clustered state are cluster members of one or more clusters. When it comes to the iterative period, the node executes different iterative algorithms according to its state.

1. The generation of the cluster

   If A is out of the cluster currently, A will calculate the number of exclusive members in the cluster if it becomes the cluster head. Exclusive member means the cluster member only belongs to A. Then node A will calculate the value of $f_{\min}(t)$, which is a limiting function based on the clustering time and is calculated as follows:

   $$f_{\min}(t) = \left(e^{-k_1 \frac{1}{cI}} - k_2 \right) d, \qquad (3.35)$$

   in which, t is the operation time of the clustering algorithm; c is the times of iteration in the clustering algorithm; I is the time that one iteration needs; d is the average degree of the node (i.e., the average number of neighbors); k_1 and k_2 are the decreasing factors, and $k_1 = 2.3$, $k_2 = 0.1$ in ACE. If $L \geq f_{\min}(t)$, node A will decide to be the cluster head and select a random value as the cluster ID. It will broadcast RECRUIT message (i.e., request message of joining the cluster to its neighbors). The neighbors that receive the message will join the A cluster. A node can join multiple clusters at the same time and choose a cluster head as its final cluster head at the end of the protocol. $f_{min}(t)$ decreases with the improvement in operation time of the clustering algorithm, so that it is beneficial for the node with exclusive cluster members to be the cluster at the beginning stage, which can form a cluster with reasonable topology. Afterward, the threshold of clustering will be lower and lower. Since the threshold is low at the last cycle of iteration, the nodes that are not covered can easily form a cluster.

2. The movement of the cluster

   If A is the cluster head, A will try to find an optimal candidate cluster head (refers to the node with maximum exclusive members) in the whole cluster. Assume that B is the optimal candidate cluster head of A; then the exclusive member of B not only includes its neighbors out of the cluster, but also includes the exclusive members of A. If B is A itself, the iteration of this cycle ends and the structure of the cluster stays unchanged; if B is the other node in the cluster, the movement algorithm will be executed: A sends PROMOTE message to B; then B broadcasts RECRUIT message using id of A cluster after receiving the message; finally all the nodes that receive the RECRUIT message join the B cluster. A will broadcast ABDICATE message after receiving the RECRUIT message from B. In this way, the node will move to B cluster from A cluster if it belonged to A cluster and is a neighbor of B; if it is not a neighbor of B, it will quit the cluster. Until then, the movement from A to B is finished. When the next iteration begins, A will do nothing if it is a node in the cluster and waits for the next iteration period.

   When all nodes finish the iteration algorithm, a few nodes may not be covered. A "clean-up" iteration needs to be done at the end. In the process, the cluster movement will not be executed. All nodes that are not covered will become cluster heads or multihop cluster members of another cluster by their neighbors. The pseudocode of ACE algorithm is as follows [44].

```
procedure SCALE_ONE_ITERATION()
  if myTime > 3×EXPECTED ITERATION LENGTH then
    if myState=CLUSTER-HEAD then
      return DONE
    else if my State=CLUSTERED then
      wait for my cluster-heads to terminate, then pick one as my cluster-head
      return DONE
    else if myState=UNCLUSTERED then
```

```
            pick a random cluster node to act as my proxy after it terminates
            wait for it to terminate, then return DONE
      end if
         else if myState=UNCLUSTERED
         and numLoyalFollower() ≥ f_min(myTime) then
            myClusterID←generate_New_Random_ID()
            locally_broadcast(RECRUIT, myID, myClusterID)
         else if myState=CLUSTER-HEAD then
      bestLeader←myID        bestFollwerCount←numLoyalFollowers
         for all n where n is a potential new cluster-head do
            followerCount=Poll_For_Num_Loyal_Followers(n, myClusterID)
            if followerCount>bestFollowersCount then
               bestLeader←n
               bestFollwerCount←followerCount
            end if
         end for
         if bestLeader is not myID then
            send(bestLeader, PROMOTE, myClusterID)
            wait for bestLeader to broadcast its RECRUIT message
            locally_broadcast(ABDICATE, myID, myClusterID)
         end if
      end if
   end if
end procedure
```

The ACE algorithm has good robustness. It can respond to node failure and packet loss quickly. The generated cluster can reduce overlap and decrease the probability of communication interference, which is independent of convergence speed and network scale.

However, ACE has many drawbacks.

1. In the last cycle of iteration, the clustering threshold will be pretty low. Thus, the node out of a cluster with a few exclusive members will elect itself to be the cluster head in this cycle. The clusters formed by these cluster heads have a large overlapped area, which will increase the

communication collision caused by channel competition and increase the communication overhead of the node.

2. In ACE, there are still 2%–4% nodes out of the cluster in the network after the last cycle of iteration. These nodes will usually join the adjacent cluster and be the 2-hop cluster members. In general, if all cluster members are neighbors of the cluster head, the cluster head needs to send an instruction to all cluster members, which can be achieved by simple broadcasting. If there are 2-hop cluster members, the cluster members need to forward the broadcasting message, thus increasing the communication overhead and the probability of communication collision.

3. The cluster head election does not consider the important factor of energy, which means that the node with low energy may be selected as the cluster head and die prematurely.

4. When it satisfies the request of communication cost and energy consumption, it is difficult to determine how many iterations are needed in the construction stage of the cluster.

5. The message complexity of the algorithm is high, which increases the overhead.

Aiming for overcoming the drawbacks of ACE, Hu et al. proposed a modified algorithm [45], which contains two parts: the merge algorithm for the node out of the cluster and the merge algorithm for the redundant cluster.

3.2.4.6.1 The Merge of the Node out of the Cluster

Aiming for overcoming the second drawback of ACE, which is that there are still nodes out of the cluster after the last cycle of the iteration, these nodes will join the adjacent cluster as 2-hop cluster members. The merge mechanism for the nodes out of the cluster merges the nodes to reduce overlap and communication overhead.

After the last iteration of ACE, all nodes out of the cluster will set a timer and select a waiting time at random. When the timer is triggered (e.g., node D in Figure 3.23), node D will send a merge request, which includes the ID of node D, to the cluster head of the adjacent cluster. If cluster head B receives the merge request, B will broadcast candidate information to the cluster members and try to find an optimal candidate for cluster head. Candidate information includes the cluster member list of cluster B and ID of node D. The cluster member list consists of two fields: the ID of the cluster member and a signature that is used to identify whether the cluster member is the exclusive member.

All neighbors of B that can be optimal candidates for cluster head of B need to satisfy these conditions: the node is adjacent to all cluster members and adjacent to

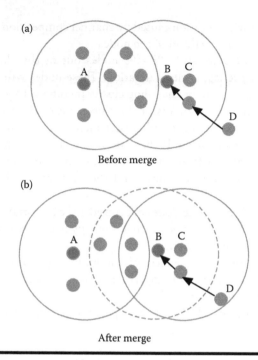

Figure 3.23 The merge for the node out of the cluster. (a). Before merge and (b) after merge.

node *D* as well; if the node becomes the cluster head, the number of its exclusive members is maximum. If node *B* finds this kind of candidate cluster heads, *B* will send a reply to node *D*, which includes the id of *B* and the id of the candidate cluster head.

Node *D* may receive reply messages from multiple cluster heads at the same time. Node *B* will select a cluster head randomly and send it the merge request. When the cluster head (assume it is still node *B*) receives the merge request from *D*, it will start the process of cluster movement, which is consistent with the cluster movement of ACE. Figure 3.23 (a and b) shows the whole merge process of the node out of the cluster. We can know from Figure 3.23b that the overlapped area among the cluster after the merge process is clearly lower than before. In the optimal algorithm, the merge algorithm for the node out of the cluster needs to be iterated twice. The first iteration is after the clustering of ACE. There exist some nodes out of the cluster in the network. The number of nodes out of the cluster can be reduced through the merge algorithm and be beneficial for the merge algorithm for the redundant cluster afterward. The merge algorithm for the redundant cluster may cause the occurrence of the node out of the cluster. Therefore, the second iteration of the merge algorithm for the node out of the cluster needs to be executed after the merge algorithm for the redundant cluster.

The partial pseudocode of the merge algorithm for the node out of the cluster is shown as follows [45].

```
Procedure unclustered_node_merge()
   if myState=UNCLUSTERED then
      send Merge Investigation to the cluster headers of neighboring clusters
      wait for replies
      choose a cluster header from replies
      send Merge-Request to the chosen cluster header
   end if
   if myState=CLUSTER-HEAD then
      wait for message
      if message is Merge investigation then
         send Candidate to its neighbors
         wait for replies
         check the replies and find a best candidate
         send a reply the unclustered node
      else if message is Merge-Request then
         migrate the cluster onto the new cluster head
      end if
   end if
   if myState=CLUSTERED then
      wait for Candidate message
      if it is a candidate for the new cluster
         send reply to the cluster header
      end if
   end if
end procedure
```

3.2.4.6.2 The Merge for Redundant Clusters

Aiming to solve the first drawback of ACE, some nodes out of the cluster along with a few exclusive members will elect themselves to be the cluster heads at the last cycle of iteration. The cluster formed by these cluster nodes has a large area that overlaps with its adjacent cluster. Therefore, removing the redundant cluster, reducing the number of clusters, and decreasing the overlapped area among the clusters can reduce the probability of communication collision and communication overhead.

When the timer of the cluster head (e.g., node B in Figure 3.24a) is triggered, cluster head B will execute the merge algorithm for the redundant cluster. The specific process of the algorithm is as follows. At first, B counts the number L of its exclusive members. B is an isolated cluster head if $L=0$, which means cluster head B does not have any exclusive members currently. Then node B will find whether there exist neighbor cluster heads. If there exist neighbor cluster heads, B will broadcast an ABDICATE message to all the cluster members and inform them to quit B cluster. Then node B will join the cluster of neighbor cluster heads as a cluster member.

If the number L of the exclusive members of B is greater than 0 and $L \leq L_{avg}$ (in which L_{avg} is the average number of the exclusive member of the cluster in the network; the selection of L_{avg} will be introduced in detail in a later section), that is, the number of exclusive members of B is lower than the average number, which explains that the overlapped area between cluster B and the adjacent cluster is large. Thus, B cluster needs to be merged.

Next, cluster head B will send a Merge Investigation message to its adjacent cluster head. The message includes the exclusive member list of B, whose structure

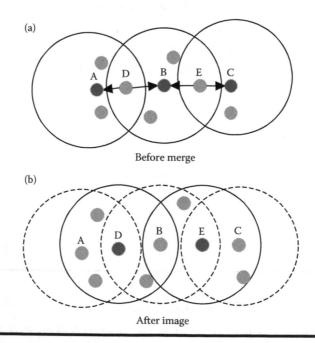

Figure 3.24 The merge of the redundant cluster. (a). Before merge and (b) after merge.

is consistent with the cluster member list. When the cluster head (node *A* or node *C* in Figure 3.24a) receives the message, node *A* will broadcast the Candidate message to its neighbors, which includes the cluster member list of *A* and the exclusive members of *B*. *A* finds an optimal candidate for cluster head among all its neighbors with this message.

When the neighbor of *A* (node *D* in Figure 3.24a) receives the Candidate message from *A*, node *D* will check its neighbor list. If the neighbor list of node *D* includes all the exclusive members of *A* and all or partial exclusive members of *B*, node *D* will reply with a message to node *A* that includes the exclusive members of *B* in the neighbor list of *D*. Then node *A* will find an optimal candidate node from the nodes that reply to the message. The optimal candidate node should satisfy these conditions: The neighbor list of this node contains all the exclusive members of A, and the exclusive members of B in the neighbor list is maximum. After selecting the optimal candidate node, node *A* will send a reply message to node *B*, which includes the id of the optimal candidate node and the exclusive members of *B* in the neighbor list of the candidate node.

After receiving the reply messages from all adjacent cluster heads, node *B* will judge whether its cluster can be merged by the adjacent cluster according to the reply messages. If *B* finds an optimal candidate node from the reply messages and the neighbor list of the candidate node includes all the exclusive members of *B*, the cluster of *B* can be merged with the cluster of the optimal candidate cluster head. If *B* cannot find an optimal candidate cluster head that satisfies the conditions above, *B* will try to find multiple candidate nodes from the reply messages. Although the neighbor list of these candidate nodes does not include all the exclusive members of *B*, the union set of the neighbor list of these candidate nodes includes all the exclusive members of *B*. Thus, the cluster of *B* can be merged with the clusters whose cluster heads are optimal candidate nodes.

For example, nodes *G* and *H* are two exclusive members of *B*, and *D* and *E* are the optimal candidate nodes for cluster *A* and cluster *C*, respectively. The neighbor list of *D* only includes node *G*, while the neighbor list of *E* only includes *H*. Since the neighbor list of *D* and *E* does not include both exclusive members *G* and *H* of *B*, *B* cluster cannot be merged with the cluster whose cluster head is *D* or *E*. However, the union set of exclusive members of *B* included in the neighbor lists of nodes *D* and *E* is {*G*, *H*}, which involves all the exclusive members of *B*. Therefore, if a new cluster is formed with the cluster head *D* or *E*, the exclusive members of *B* and *B* can join the cluster whose cluster head is *D* or *E*. When *B* finds one or multiple appropriate candidate nodes, *B* will send Merge request message to all the cluster heads of the candidate nodes and send ABDICATE message to all the cluster members, informing the cluster members to quit the cluster. When the cluster head receives the Merge request message, it will execute the cluster movement, the process of which is the same as ACE.

After ACE clustering, the number of exclusive members of some cluster is large (greater than the average number of exclusive members), and the overlapped area between this kind of cluster and its neighbor cluster is small. In general, this kind of cluster is unlikely to be merged by the neighbor cluster. Therefore, in the merge algorithm for redundant cluster, it will improve some unnecessary communication overhead and the probability of communication collision if each cluster head sends a Merge Investigation message to its neighbor cluster. Thus, the algorithm considers that only the cluster head with a small number of exclusive members will send a Merge Investigation message. Generally, the number of exclusive members of these cluster heads should satisfy $L \leq L_{avg}$.

In order to avoid the collision and the situation of isolated nodes in the merge process, the algorithm proposes a solution. Assume that each node has a unique id in the network (the unique id can be assigned before deployment), and the cluster head can generate a unique cluster id when the cluster is formed. The timer of the node can be set by the id of the node and the id of the cluster head. Let only one node broadcast message in a time slot, thereby reducing the probability of communication collision.

In the process of the merge between the node out of the cluster and the redundant cluster, the cluster head will broadcast a Candidate message to the cluster members when it receives the merge check information from the neighbor node. When the cluster member receives the Candidate message, the node will store the id of the sender and set a timer. It will delete the saved id after a period of time. If the node receives a Candidate message from another cluster head during the waiting time, the node will send a retry message to the cluster head and inform the cluster head that there is a collision currently. When the cluster head receives the retry message, it will reset the timer and rebroadcast the Candidate message after a period of time.

The partial pseudocode of merge for the redundant cluster is as follows [45].

```
Procedure cluster_merge()
  if myState= CLUSTER-HEAD then
    Count the number L of loyal members
    if L≤Lavg then
      if L=0 and there exists a neighboring cluster header then
      broadcast an ABDICATE message to its neighbors
      become a member of the neighboring cluster header
    else
      send a Merge Investigation to the header nodes of neighboring
      clusters
      wait for replies
      try to find one or several candidates based on the replies
```

```
            send Merge-Request to the cluster headers of the candidates
        end if
        else
            wait for Merge Investigation
            send a Candidate its neighbors
            wait for replies
            check the replies from its neighbors and find a best candidate
            send a reply to the cluster node that sends the investigation
        end if
    end if
    if myState=CLUSTERED then
        wait for candidate message
        if it is a candidate for the new cluster then
        send a reply to its cluster head
        end if
    end if
end procedure
```

The main idea of the algorithm is that after the clustering of the ACE, merge the nodes out of the cluster and the redundant clusters to reduce the overlapped area among the cluster, obtaining a more reasonable cluster topology. The algorithm also proposes some strategies on how to avoid the collision in the merge process. The simulation proves that the algorithm can reduce the number of redundant clusters efficiently in the network and greatly decrease the size of the overlapped area in the cluster.

3.2.4.7 Uneven Clustering Algorithms

The cluster head is responsible for collecting the data, processing, and forwarding it. Thus, the energy consumption of the cluster head is much more than that of the cluster members. That is, there is an unbalanced situation between the cluster head and the cluster members. In order to solve the problem, the clustering algorithm usually cycles the role of the cluster head. Algorithms such as LEACH cycle the cluster head periodically according to the predetermined time. This method can balance energy consumption, but there is yet another unbalanced energy consumption (i.e., the imbalance among the cluster heads). In the inter-cluster single-hop network, the cluster head that is far away from the base station needs to transmit a long distance and thus will consume much more energy than the cluster head closer to the base station, thereby causing premature death. In the inter-cluster multihop network, the cluster head near the base station needs to forward a great amount of data from other clusters; thus, the cluster head near the base station will consume much more energy and die prematurely. In the two networks, cluster heads that die prematurely will stay in a nonmanaged state for a long time, resulting in network partitioning. This is the "hot spot problem" [46].

Researchers endeavor to solve the problem with an uneven clustering idea. Many solutions are proposed on the basis of this idea. Three classic solutions are:

1. Divide the network into rings and design the clustering algorithm under the ring model to balance energy consumption.
2. Design a competition radius with a different size for the cluster head, thereby constructing the cluster structure with different sizes.
3. Design the communication cost function for nodes that are not the cluster heads that join a cluster, thereby constructing the clusters with different sizes.

Then we will explain the process of these three methods using specific clustering instances.

3.2.4.7.1 Ring Algorithm

The unequal clustering size (UCS) protocol [47] is the first uneven clustering protocol for the "hot spot" problem in the inter-cluster multihop clustering routing of sensor networks, proposed by Soro et al. Solving the "hot pot" problem by uneven clustering idea is first proposed in the protocol.

The protocol assumes that the network model is a two-layer concentric ring with the base station as the center. Since the cluster head in the inner ring is close to the base station, it must forward the data of the outer ring. Thus, it can reduce the energy consumption of the cluster head by decreasing the number of cluster members in the inner ring, thereby saving the energy of forwarding data. The specific strategy of the algorithm is as follows.

The first step: Divide the whole network into a two-layer concentric ring with the base station as the center. The inner ring (close to the base station) is set as the first layer, and the outer ring is set as the second layer. The radius of the first layer is R_1, which can control the size range of the first-layer ring. Once the cluster range of the first layer is determined, the rest of the monitoring area is the second layer. The radius of the second layer is noted as R_a. The number of the cluster in each ring is determined. Assume that there are m_1 clusters in the first layer and m_2 clusters in the second layer.

The second step: After the layer division, the cluster in each layer will be divided. Since the number of clusters is determined, UCS protocol divides each cluster by the angle division method. The division method in the first layer is that the whole ring is divided into m_1 equal parts. Each part is a cluster with angle of $2\pi/m_1$. The division method in the second layer is that first the second layer and the first layer are regarded as a big ring, and the big ring will be divided into m_2 equal parts with angle of $2\pi/m_2$; then the area of each part deletes the area of the first layer, and the rest of the parts are the clusters of the second layer. The cluster structure obtained by the angle division is shown in Figure 3.25.

The third step: After the division of all of the clusters, in order to consume the minimum energy, UCS finds a node at the center of each cluster to be the cluster head. The distance between each cluster and the base station is equal in the first layer, noted as d_{ch1}; the distance between each cluster head and the base station is also equal in the second layer, noted as d_{ch2}.

The fourth step: Calculate the approximate distance d_{ch21} between the cluster head in the second layer and the corresponding closest cluster head in the inner ring according to the distance of the cluster head in the first layer and the second layer to the base station. Based on the communication model, calculate the total energy consumption E_{ch1} of the cluster head in the second layer for collecting data, sending data, and forwarding the data, and calculate the energy consumption E_{ch2} of the cluster head in the first layer for collecting data and sending data. In order to balance the energy consumption among the cluster heads, UCS protocol assumes $E_{ch2} = E_{ch1}$, so that the radius R_1 of the first layer is obtained, which can balance the energy consumption of the cluster heads in two layers.

In a word, the main idea of UCS is to reduce the number of cluster members in the first layer by controlling the value of R_1, thereby decreasing the energy

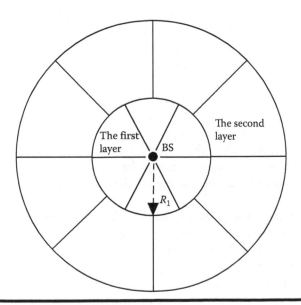

Figure 3.25 UCS clustering topology.

consumption of the cluster head in the first layer for dealing with intra-cluster data and saving the energy for forwarding inter-cluster data.

UCS protocol is the first uneven clustering protocol and first solves the hot spot problem caused by inter-cluster multiple hops. It proposes a new idea for the routing protocol of WSNs. However, the algorithm has many drawbacks.

The network model of the UCS algorithm is too idealistic. The distribution of the nodes in the ring area is predetermined, which is not suitable for the random deployment of WSNs. Also, it requests that the base station be located at the center of the monitoring area; then the idea of clustering by angle with the base station as the center in each layer ring can be achieved. Thus, this requires very strict position of the base station. In the practical application, the base station is not necessarily in the network center. In general, however, the base station is located far away from the monitoring area. Moreover, it is not easy to divide the monitoring area into rings in the real application, especially in a large-scale network. Also, it is not appropriate to divide the network into two-layer rings. The number of layers should change according to the real size of the network. This limitation of UCS makes it less expansibile.

When selecting the cluster head, although UCS considers selecting from the center of the cluster to reduce total energy consumption, the algorithm does not consider the energy of the cluster head, that is, a node with low energy may be selected as the cluster head. It is advisable to first consider the residual energy of the cluster head and then the position of the cluster head.

EECA [48] proposes a nonuniform clustering algorithm for energy-homogeneous inter-cluster WSNs, a static clustering algorithm based on an even ring model. That is, the network is divided into concentric rings with equal width and the base station as the center. The number of the clusters in different rings is equal, so that the scale of the cluster close to the base station is small, thereby balancing energy consumption among the cluster heads. Meanwhile, the algorithm proposes a continuously working mechanism of cluster heads to reduce the energy consumed by selecting the cluster head and constructing the cluster.

A dynamic clustering algorithm based on a nonuniform ring is proposed in Reference [49]. The cluster head adopts a single-hop mode to communicate with the sink. Therefore, the scale of the cluster far away from the sink is small, thereby balancing the energy consumption among the cluster heads. However, these two algorithms do not consider the balance of the energy consumption among the regular nodes.

The circular monitoring region is also divided into rings with equal width in Reference [50]. The authors believe that the network can avoid the energy hole problem if the density of the node in the ith ring is in proportion to $k-i+1$. k is the optimal number of equal-width rings. In the algorithm, the node close to the base station has a low data rate.

UVGCR [51] is a relatively complete nonuniform clustering algorithm. It calculates the optimal number of cluster heads in each ring under the equal-width concentric-ring topology. Each ring will be divided according to the number of cluster heads. In each cluster, the cluster head will be selected based on residual energy and intra-cluster communication cost. Then the cluster heads in each cluster establish an inter-cluster routing tree with the base station as the center. Finally, the location of the node will change with cluster reconstruction and so will the probability of being the cluster head, letting more nodes have a chance to be the cluster head to balance energy consumption.

We proposed a new clustering idea, CBMBC [52], based on the ring model. The algorithm analyzes the condition of balanced energy consumption in theory. The algorithm divides the network into the concentric rings with the base station as the center. The ring in each layer is divided into clusters of even size, so that the distance between the regular node and the cluster head is appropriately equal in each layer and the energy consumption of the regular node can be balanced. Meanwhile, the initial energy of the cluster head in different rings is different. The cluster head close to the base station in the ring has more initial energy to achieve balance among cluster heads. Besides, the initial energy of the cluster head is set according to the initial energy of the regular node. An equal lifetime for cluster heads and regular heads can avoid wasted energy and prolong the lifetime of the network.

The network model is as follows.

Divide the circular monitoring area into multiple rings of equal widths. In each ring, the area is divided into many clusters with equal size and equal scale. The location of the cluster and the required energy must be precalculated. Then put the cluster head at the corresponding location. Each cluster consists of the cluster head and the regular nodes around in the range of the surrounding clusters.

Assume that there exist N nodes and they are well distributed in a circular area with radius R. Each ring is divided into clusters of even size. The optimal initial energy of the cluster head and the optimal number of each ring can be calculated. Then the corresponding cluster head will be located at the corresponding position. The base station is located at the center of the circular area.

We simplify the network model by these reasonable assumptions.

1. Each node has a unique signature (id).
2. The ability of the cluster heads for fusing the data from the cluster member is equal. Since the data from the cluster head of other rings has little relativity with the data in the ring, it needs to be forwarded to the inner cluster head or to the base station instead of being fused.
3. Each regular node sends a packet with l length in each unit of time.
4. The lifetime of the network is defined as the time from network deployment to the time when the first node dies.

The symbols and the related definitions used in the algorithm are shown as Table 3.1.

We use the energy model same as in LEACH, which will not be explained again here.

Table 3.1 The Symbols and Definitions

Symbol	Definition
R	The radius of the monitoring area
N	The total number of nodes
id	Node identity
k	The symbol of the ring
W	The width of the ring
N_k	The node number of the k-layer ring
m_k	The cluster number of the k-layer ring
d_{chk}	The distance of the cluster head from the base station in the k-layer ring
d_{tochk}	The distance of the nodes ring from the cluster head in the k-layer ring
E_{non}	The unit energy consumption of the regular node
E_{iniNon}	The initial energy consumption of the regular node
E_{CHk}	The average energy consumption of the cluster head in k-layer ring
E_{iniCHK}	The initial energy consumption of the cluster head in k-layer ring
E_D	The unit energy consumption of the cluster head for processing the fused data

The specific descriptions of the algorithm and the related conclusion are as follows.

N nodes are well distributed in a circular area with radius R. The base station is located at the center of the circular area. Our solution is to divide the network into many concentric rings with the base station as the center and the ring signature as 1-layer ring, 2-layer ring… t-layer ring from the base station, in which 1-layer ring is a circle with the base station as the center and we regard it as a ring. The width of each ring is w. Design multiple clusters with even scale in all rings. Since the size of the cluster is appropriate, the energy consumption among the regular nodes can be balanced well. Additionally, set different amounts of initial energy for the cluster heads in different rings according to different distances from the base station, so that the energy of the inner cluster head is higher to allow it to forward the data from the cluster heads of the outer ring, while the cluster heads of the outer ring have low energy. However, the cluster heads within each ring are homogeneous. Therefore, the lifetime of the cluster head can be balanced. Set the energy of the cluster head according to the energy of the regular node and the ring location of the cluster head. Adjust the location of the cluster head based on the precalculated optimal number of clusters in each ring. Then divide the nodes in each ring into their corresponding clusters with the centrally located cluster head, so that the lifetime of the cluster head and the regular node can be balanced. Therefore, the lifetime of all the nodes in the whole network can be as synchronous as possible, thereby avoiding energy waste. Different from LEACH, CBMBC belongs to static clustering, which can avoid the periodical cycle and unnecessary energy consumption.

In the process of the data aggregation, the regular node transmits the collected data to the cluster head directly. The cluster head will forward the fused data to the cluster head of the inner ring. That is, the cluster head of $k+1$-layer ring sends the data to the cluster head of k-layer ring, then the cluster head forwards it to the cluster head of $k-1$-layer ring. This way, data will be forwarded to the base station. In order to highlight the advantages of the algorithm, since the data in different clusters has little relativity in real applications, we assume that the cluster head forwards data from one hop cluster head to the next hop cluster head instead of fusing other data with its own.

3.2.4.7.1.1 The Energy of the Cluster Head in Each Layer Ring

According to the previous analysis, the energy consumption of the cluster heads in different rings is different. In order to maintain the synchronization of death time of the cluster in different rings, we need to set different initial energy for the cluster head in different rings.

Theorem 3.1 E_{iniCH} and $E_{iniCH(k-1)}$ comprise the initial energy of the cluster heads in k-layer and $k-1$-layer, respectively, then $E_{iniCHk} < E_{iniCH(k-1)}$.

Proof: The sizes of the clusters in all of the rings are even, and the nodes are well distributed, which means the quantity of nodes in each cluster is appropriately equal. All the regular nodes only need to send the collected data to their cluster heads directly. Therefore, the energy consumption of the regular nodes in each cluster is appropriately equal. The difference in energy consumption is mainly the difference in the energy consumption of the cluster heads in different rings.

The average energy consumption of the cluster head in k-layer is

$$E_{CHk} = lE_{elec}\frac{N_k}{m_k} + lE_D\left(\frac{N_k}{m_k}+1\right) + l\left(E_{elec} + \varepsilon_{fs}w^2\right)$$

$$+ l\frac{\sum\limits_{i=k+1}^{t} m_i}{m_k}\left(2E_{elec} + \varepsilon_{fs}w^2\right). \tag{3.36}$$

The average energy consumption of the cluster head in $k-1$-layer is

$$E_{CH(k-1)} = lE_{elec}\frac{N_{k-1}}{m_{k-1}} + lE_D\left(\frac{N_{k-1}}{m_{k-1}}+1\right) + l\left(E_{elec} + \varepsilon_{fs}w^2\right)$$

$$+ l\frac{\sum_{i=k}^{t} m_i}{m_{k-1}}\left(2E_{elec} + \varepsilon_{fs}w^2\right). \tag{3.37}$$

According to formulas 3.36 and 3.37, $E_{CHk} < E_{CH(k-1)}$, which means that the average consumption of the cluster head in different rings is different. The closer to the base station it is, the higher the average energy consumption of the cluster head. Thus, in order to maintain the synchronization of lifetime of the cluster in different rings, $E_{iniCHk} < E_{iniCH(k-1)}$ correspondingly. That is, the closer to the base station it is, the higher the initial energy of the cluster head.

Theorem 3.2 If the initial energy of the cluster head in k-layer ring satisfies $E_{iniCHk} = E_{CHk}\dfrac{E_{iniNon}}{E_{nonCHk}}$, the lifetime of the cluster head in different rings can be synchronized.

Proof: Since the energy consumption of the regular nodes in each cluster is appropriately equal, the initial energy of each cluster head and the regular node in its cluster need to satisfy $\dfrac{E_{iniCHk}}{E_{CHk}} = \dfrac{E_{iniNon}}{E_{nonCHk}}$, that is, $E_{iniCHk} = E_{CHk}\dfrac{E_{iniNon}}{E_{nonCHk}}$, to balance the energy consumption between the cluster head and the regular node, that is, to keep consistent with the cluster and its regular nodes. Therefore, the initial energy of the cluster head, which keeps the synchronization of the cluster head, can be calculated according to the average energy consumption of the cluster head in each cluster.

3.2.4.7.1.2 The Optimal Number of the Cluster Heads in Each Ring In the process of the data aggregation, the regular node communicates only with its cluster head. The difference in energy consumption of the nodes in different rings is not large. Besides communicating with other cluster heads, the cluster head needs to forward data from the cluster head from the outer ring. Since the amount of data from different rings varies, the energy consumption among the cluster head in different rings is not balanced. Therefore, we calculate the optimal number of cluster heads in each ring from the view of minimizing energy consumption of the cluster in each ring.

Theorem 3.3 The relationship between the number of cluster heads in the first-layer m_1 and the number of the clusters in each layer m_k satisfies $m_k = \dfrac{2k-1}{2k-3}m_{k-1}$.

Proof: Divide the circular area into t rings, then the total number of nodes in k-layer ring N_k is

$$N_k = \frac{\pi(kw)^2 - \pi[(k-1)w]^2}{\pi R^2} N = \frac{2k-1}{t^2} N. \tag{3.38}$$

The total number of nodes in $k-1$-layer ring is

$$N_{k-1} = \frac{2k-3}{t^2} N. \tag{3.39}$$

Since $\dfrac{N_k}{m_k} = \dfrac{N_{k-1}}{m_{k-1}}$, it holds that

$$\frac{m_k}{m_{k-1}} = \frac{N_k}{N_{k-1}} = \frac{2k-1}{2k-3}. \tag{3.40}$$

Theorem 3.4 The optimal number of cluster heads in the first-layer ring is $m_{1-opt} = \dfrac{\sqrt{2N_1}}{2}$.

Proof: The optimal number of cluster heads can be obtained from the view of minimizing the total energy consumption of the node in the first-layer ring.

It is known that the number of nodes in the first-layer ring is $N_1 = \dfrac{N}{t^2}$. The average energy consumption of a cluster head is

$$E_{CHk} = lE_{elec} \frac{N_1}{m_1} + lE_D \left(\frac{N_1}{m_1} + 1 \right) + l \left(E_{elec} + \varepsilon_{fs} w^2 \right)$$

$$+ l \frac{\sum\limits_{k=2}^{t} m_k}{m_1} \left(2E_{elec} + \varepsilon_{fs} w^2 \right). \tag{3.41}$$

The average energy consumption of a node that is not a cluster head is

$$E_{nonCHk} = lE_{elec} + l\varepsilon_{fs} E[d_{toch1}^2], \tag{3.42}$$

in which, $E[d_{toch1}^2] = \displaystyle\int_0^{2\pi} \int_0^{\frac{w}{\sqrt{m_1}}} \frac{r^3}{\pi w^2} \, dr \, d\theta = \frac{w^2}{2m_1}$.

Thus, the average energy consumption of a node that is not a cluster head is

$$E_{nonCHk} = lE_{elec} + l\varepsilon_{fs} \frac{w^2}{2m_1}. \tag{3.43}$$

Therefore, the total energy consumption in a cluster is

$$E_{1-cluster} = E_{CH1} + \frac{N_1}{m_1} E_{nonCH1}. \tag{3.44}$$

Therefore, the total energy consumption of all clusters in the first-layer ring is

$$E_{1-total} = m_1 E_{1-cluster} = N_1 l(2E_{elec} + E_D) + m_1 l(E_D + E_{elec} + \varepsilon_{fs} w^2)$$

$$+ N_1 l \varepsilon_{fs} \frac{w^2}{2m_1} + l \sum_{k=2}^{t} m_k (2E_{elec} + \varepsilon_{fs} w^2). \tag{3.45}$$

In order to minimize total energy consumption in the first-layer ring, get the derivation of m_1; then the optimal number of the cluster heads in the first-layer can be written as $m_{1-opt} = \frac{\sqrt{2N_1}}{2}$.

Thus, we can infer that the optimal number of cluster heads in the first-layer ring is not affected by the number of cluster heads in outer rings.

From Theorems 3.3 and 3.4, we can calculate the optimal number of cluster heads in each ring.

3.2.4.7.1.3 Energy-Heterogeneous Efficiency of the Cluster Head

Aiming at the model the paper [52] proposed, assume that the cluster heads in each ring are energy homogeneous. We regard the assumed model as a cluster head energy-homogeneous model (CHEH).

Theorem 3.5 Compared with the CHEH protocol, the energy that the CBMBC protocol can save is $E_{waste} = \sum_{k=1}^{t} m_k E_{iniCH1} - \sum_{k=1}^{t} m_k E_{iniCHk}$.

Proof: In the CBMBC model mentioned in the paper, the total energy consumption is:

$$E_{CBMBC-total} = \sum_{k=1}^{t} m_k E_{iniCHk} + E_{nontotal}, \tag{3.46}$$

in which, the energy consumption of the cluster head in the first ring is the maximum, which is E_{iniCH1}. The initial energy of the cluster head in the first ring is also the maximum from the view of Theorem 3.1. If we let the lifetime of model CHEH be equal to the lifetime of the network model mentioned earlier, the minimum initial energy of the cluster heads in each ring is still E_{iniCH1}. Then the total energy consumption of nodes in CHEH is

$$E_{CHEH-total} = \sum_{k=1}^{t} m_k E_{iniCH1} + E_{nontotal}, \tag{3.47}$$

in which

$$E_{iniCH1} = E_{CH1} \frac{E_{iniNon}}{E_{nonCH1}}. \tag{3.48}$$

Therefore, from the view of formulas 3.46 through 3.48, compared with the assumed model CHEH, the saving energy of the network model proposed in the paper [52] is

$$E_{waste} = \sum_{k=1}^{t} m_k E_{iniCH1} - \sum_{k=1}^{t} m_k E_{iniCHk}. \tag{3.49}$$

Thus, it can be seen that the proposed algorithm model can make full use of the energy resource and avoid energy waste compared with the energy-homogeneous situation.

The simulation proves that compared with uneven clustering algorithms such as the Energy-Efficient Uneven Clustering (EEUC), the algorithm can use the energy of the node better and avoid energy waste based on idealistic clustering. However, since the algorithm is centralized, the scalability is not strong enough. Thus, it is suitable for medium and small networks.

3.2.4.7.2 Construct a Competitive Radius with Different Sizes

Li et al. proposed an EEUC algorithm [53]. Its main idea is that the cluster head communicates with the base station by the multihop mode to avoid large energy consumption caused by long-distance communication and save energy. In order to reduce the amount of energy the cluster head close to the base station consumes by forwarding data from other cluster heads, the competitive radius with different size is designed to establish uneven clusters. The competitive radius of the cluster close to the base station is small, forming a small cluster. The number of cluster members in the cluster is small, so that the energy consumed by processing data from the cluster members is small. Then the saving energy can be used to forward the data from other cluster heads. On the contrary, the cluster head far from the base station does not need to consume a lot of energy forwarding data. We can set a larger competitive radius for the cluster head, so that energy consumption among cluster heads can be balanced, thereby prolonging the lifetime of the network.

In the stage of deployment, when the sensor nodes are deployed randomly in the monitoring area, the base station broadcasts a signal to the whole network, which includes the transmitting power P_{tx}, wavelength, and the antenna gain of base station G_r. When the node receives the signal, it calculates the distance to the base station according to the free space equation. Since $P_{rx} = \dfrac{P_{tx}G_tG_r\lambda^2}{(4\pi)^2 d^2}$, it holds

that $d = \dfrac{\lambda}{4\pi}\sqrt{\dfrac{P_{tx}G_tG_r}{P_{rx}}}$, in which d refers to the distance between the base station and the node.

After this stage, the node can estimate the distance between itself and the base station, which is the necessary condition of constructing uneven clustering topology. The reason is that the node can adjust the transmitting power according to the distance to avoid the energy consumption caused by unique power; also, the node can calculate its competitive radius according to the estimated distance.

EEUC is a multihop uneven clustering routing protocol-based competition. The clustering algorithm can be divided into the stages of selecting the cluster head, forming the cluster, and data transmission.

3.2.4.7.2.1 The Stage of Selecting the Cluster Head

In the clustering network, the cluster head needs to be responsible for many tasks, not only receiving and processing data sent from the cluster members, but also sending data to the base station. Therefore, the selection of the cluster head affects the performance of the network extremely. The cluster head selection mechanism of the EEUC protocol is different from that of the LEACH and HEED protocols. LEACH is simple and without additional consumption, which selects the cluster head based on probability. However, the cluster head is not well distributed, and the node with low energy may be selected as the cluster head. The HEED protocol selects the cluster head by iteration. The cluster head can be well distributed, but the iteration will cause additional communication consumption. EEUC protocol combines the advantages of these two protocols. It selects the cluster head by distributed competition based on the residual energy of the node. The node that is selected as the cluster head has higher energy and consumes less additional energy. Besides, the energy consumption among the cluster heads can be balanced, and the cluster heads are well distributed.

The process of the cluster head selection is as follows: preset the probability of being the candidate cluster head as T; when the random value generated by a node is lower than T, the node becomes a candidate cluster head and participates in the election of the cluster head; nodes that do not participate in the election will switch to the sleeping state until the stage of cluster head election ends. Assume that an arbitrary node s_i is selected as the candidate cluster head; then the node calculates its competitive radius R_c according to the distance between itself and the base station. It will broadcast a COMPETE_HEAD_MSG message, which includes its id and residual energy, with R_c as the radius. The calculation formula is as follows:

$$R_c = \left[1 - \alpha \frac{d_{\max} - d(s_i, BS)}{d_{\max} - d_{\min}}\right] R_{\max}, \tag{3.50}$$

in which, $d_{\max}$ and $d_{\min}$ indicate the maximum and minimum distance between the node and the base station, respectively; $d(s_i, BS)$ is the distance between the node s_i and the base station; $R_{\max}$ is the maximum competitive radius; α is the random adjustment parameter in the interval $(0,1)$.

It can be seen from the formula that the farther a cluster head is from the base station, the larger the competitive radius R_c is. It follows that the closer the cluster is to the base station, the smaller the size of the cluster is. So, intra-cluster overhead can be saved for forwarding data from long-distance cluster heads. The scale of the cluster far from the base station is large, so that energy consumption among cluster heads can be balanced.

Meanwhile, s_i will receive the COMPETE_HEAD_MSG from its neighbors. Whenever s_i receives a COMPETE_HEAD_MSG, it will update its set of cluster head neighbors S_{CH}. If the residual energy of s_i is greater than the residual energy of all the nodes in S_{CH}, s_i will broadcast a FINAL_HEAD_MSG message to declare itself the cluster head. If s_i receives a FINAL_HEAD_MSG message from S_{CH}, it will broadcast a QUIT_ELECTION_MSG to declare it is quitting the cluster head election. All nodes that receive the QUIT_ELECTION_MSG message will delete s_i from their S_{CH}. Figure 3.26 is a figure of competitive area for the candidate cluster head. The nodes i, j, k, and s are four candidate cluster heads. Candidate cluster head j and candidate cluster head s are the neighbor candidate cluster heads. Since candidate cluster s is surrounded by candidate cluster head j, only one can be the cluster head, while candidate i and candidate k can be the cluster heads at the same time.

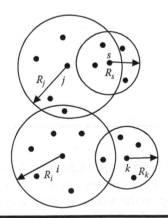

Figure 3.26 The figure of the competitive area for candidate cluster heads.

The pseudocode of the stage of cluster head election is as follows [53].

1: $\mu \leftarrow RAND(0,1)$

2: *if* $\mu < T$ *then*

3:    *beTentativeHead* $\leftarrow$ *TRUE*

4: *endif*

5: *if beTentativeHead* = *Truethen*

6:    *CompeteHeadMsg*(ID, R_{comp}, RE)

7: *else*

8:    *EXIT*

9: *end if*

10: *On receiving a COMPETE_HEAD_MSG form node* s_j

11: *if* $d(s_i, s_j) < s_j.R_{comp}$ *OR* $d(s_i, s_j) < s_i.R_{comp}$ *then*

12:    *Add* s_j *to* $s_i \cdot S_{CH}$

13: *end if*

14: *while beTentativeHead* = *TRUE do*

15:    *if* $s_i \cdot RE > s_j \cdot RE$, $\forall s_j \in s_i \cdot S_{CH}$ *then*

16:       *FinalHeadMsg*(ID) *and then EXIT*

17:    *end if*

18:    *On receiving a QUIT_ELECTION_MSG form node*

19:    *if* $s_j \in s_i \cdot S_{CH}$ *then*

20:       *QuitElectionMsg*(ID) *and then EXIT*

21:    *end if*

22:    *On receiving a QUIT_ELECYION_MSG form node* s_j

23:    *if* $s_j \in s_i \cdot S_{CH}$ *then*

24:       *Re move* s_j *from* $s_i \cdot S_{CH}$

25:    *end if*

26: *end while*

3.2.4.7.2.2 The Stage of Forming the Cluster

After the cluster head election, the regular node wakes up from the sleeping state. Each cluster node broadcasts a CH_ADV_MSG message to the whole network, and the radius of broadcast is the maximum competitive radius. If other cluster heads receive the message, they remain unhandled. If the regular node receives the message, it will calculate the distance to the cluster head; then it records the distance and the information of the cluster head. The regular node chooses a cluster head with the minimum communication cost (i.e., the closest cluster, according to received information of all cluster heads). Then it will send the message JOIN_CLUSTER_MSG to the cluster head. When the cluster head receives all of the joining messages, it will build a TDMA scheduling table according to these nodes and broadcast it to all the cluster members, which can ensure that all cluster members send data in their own slots to avoid collisions with others. When data is not present in the slot of a node, the node will switch to the sleeping state to save energy. The algorithm proves that there is only one cluster head in the range of competitive radius of arbitrary cluster head when the clustering topology is constructed.

3.2.4.7.2.3 The Stage of Data Transmission

The cluster head collects data from the cluster members and fuses it; then the cluster head sends the data to the relay cluster head or the base station. The relay cluster head only forwards data from other cluster heads; it does not fuse data.

At the beginning of the inter-cluster data transmission, each cluster head broadcasts a NODE_STATE_MSG message with the same power, which includes the id of the cluster head, the current residual energy, and its distance from the node. If cluster head i receives the NODE_STATE_MSG message from cluster head j, the appropriate distance d_{ij} between them can be calculated. We define the set of relay cluster heads of the cluster $R_{CH(i)}$ as

$$R_{CH}(i) = z\{d_i < d_j\}. \tag{3.51}$$

If $R_{CH(i)}$ is an empty set, node i can communicate with the base station directly.

When the cluster head selects the relay cluster head, it considers two factors: the energy overhead for transmitting to the relay cluster head and the residual energy of the relay cluster head. First, the cluster head finds the two cluster heads whose communication cost is minimum, then it chooses the cluster head with larger residual energy as the final relay cluster head. The calculation of E_{relay} is as follows.

$$E_{relay} = d_j^2 + d_{ij}^2, \quad j \in R_{CH}(i). \tag{3.52}$$

In order to reduce the workload of data forwarding by the cluster head nodes in the border district close to the base station, the algorithm introduces a threshold TD_MAX. If the distance between the cluster head and the base station is lower than the threshold, the cluster head will communicate with the base station directly; otherwise, its data needs to be forwarded to the base station through other cluster heads.

Figure 3.27 is the illustration of the routing mechanism of EEUC.

In the whole process, the message complexity of EEUC algorithm is O(N). The message overhead of the algorithm is small, and the energy consumption is efficient. Nonuniform clustering strategy can balance energy consumption among

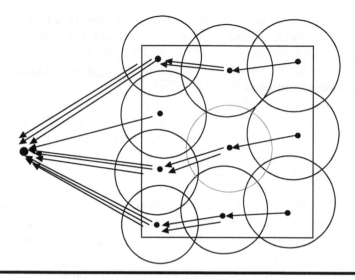

Figure 3.27 The illustration of routing mechanism of EEUC.

cluster heads efficiently. The simulation results show that the cluster heads generated by EEUC are well distributed, which can prolong the lifetime of the network efficiently compared with LEACH and HEED protocols.

However, EEUC still has some drawbacks.

1. EEUC algorithm only considers the situation of randomly uniform distribution and only solves the energy hole problem under the situation of uniform distribution. The nodes in the network are not evenly distributed. The uneven distribution of nodes will unbalance the energy consumption of nodes in the WSN, which is based on clustering. Besides, the method that constructs uneven clusters by uneven competitive radius is not suitable for this situation because there may be a lot of dense nodes in a cluster with a small competitive radius, while node distribution is sparse in a cluster with a large competitive radius.
2. In the design of a competitive radius of the cluster, EEUC only considers the distance from the cluster head to the base station, ignoring the energy of the node. In this situation, two cluster heads with different energy and the same competitive radius have the same distance to the base station. When the cluster with lower energy dies, the other cluster head may have part of its energy remaining. That partial energy will be wasted.

Aiming at solving the first drawback of EEUC, we proposed a new clustering routing protocol [54] based on multihop heterogeneous WSNs. The protocol consists of an energy-aware distributed clustering (EADC) algorithm and an energy-efficient inter-cluster multihop routing protocol. EADC adopts the residual energy as the parameter for electing the cluster head, thereby choosing the node with high energy as the cluster head. It also adopts the idea of competitive radius to get a good distribution of the cluster heads. That can achieve a balance of energy consumption among the cluster members. Surely, since the unbalance of energy consumption among cluster heads may occur in the method of uneven distribution, we proposed an energy-efficient inter-cluster multihop routing protocol. When the cluster head selects the next-hop neighbor cluster head, it will select the cluster head with relatively high energy and a few cluster members as the next hop. Let the cluster head with fewer cluster members be responsible for more tasks of forwarding the data, which can balance the energy consumption among the cluster heads. We will introduce the whole algorithm according to the two parts of the routing protocol (i.e., clustering algorithm EADC and inter-cluster multihop routing protocol).

1. EADC algorithm

    The whole process can be divided into three stages: obtaining the information with the time of T_1, cluster head election with the time of T_2, and forming the cluster with the time of T_3.

    Obtaining the information: In this stage, each node broadcasts the message Node_Msg with communication radius r, which includes the id of the node and the value of residual energy. Meanwhile, the node will receive the Node_Msg message from its neighbors. Each node that receives the Node_Msg message calculates the average residual energy E_a of its neighbors:

$$E_a = \frac{1}{d} \sum_{i=1}^{d} N_i \cdot E_r, \qquad (3.53)$$

in which, d is the number of the neighbors; $N_i (1 \leq i \leq d)$ represents all of the neighbor nodes; E_r indicates the residual energy of the ith neighbor of the node.

    When each node completes the calculation of the average residual energy E_a, it can obtain the time the Head_Msg message was sent to the cluster head with the following formula:

$$t = \begin{cases} \dfrac{E_a}{E_r} \cdot T_2 \cdot V_r & (E_r \geq E_a) \\ \\ T_2 \cdot V_r & (E_r < E_a) \end{cases}, \qquad (3.54)$$

in which V_r is a random value in [0.9,1]. We introduce V_r to reduce the probability that two nodes send Head_Msg at the same time.

The pseudocode of the stage of obtaining the information is as follows [55].

---

begin (information collection algorithm)

    state ← *Candidate*

    Broadcast *Node_Msg*

    while (T_1 has not expired) **do**

        Receive *Node_Msg*

        Update neighborhood table NT[]

    end while

    t_i ← broadcast delay time for competing to be a cluster head

end

Cluster head election: In this stage, if a node has not received Head_Msg message from any other nodes before time t, the node will broadcast a Head_Msg message to the network with R_c as the radius to declare itself the cluster head. Otherwise, the node quits the election.

The pseudocode of the stage of cluster head election is as follows.

---

begin (cluster head competition algorithm)

    while (T_2 has not expired) **do**

        if *CurrentTime* < t_i **do**

            if receive a *Head_Msg* from a neighbor NT[j] **do**

                stage ← *Plain*

            NT[j].*state* ← *Head*

            else

                Continue

            end if

        else if *state=Candidate* **do**

            state ← *Head*

            Broadcast *Head_Msg*

        end if

    end while

end

Forming the cluster: In this stage, the noncluster head nodes choose the closest cluster head and send Join_Msg messages so they can join the cluster as cluster members. The cluster head builds a scheduling list of intra-cluster nodes according to the received Join_Msg messages; then it sends the scheduling to the cluster members by broadcasting Schedule_Msg messages. Until then, the whole stage of cluster establishment ends. The nodes in the cluster form a cluster of Voronoi structure.

The pseudocode for the stage of forming the cluster is as follows [55].

```
begin (cluster formation algorithm)
    while (T₃ has not expired) do
        if state=Plain&& has not sent Join_Msg do
            Send Join_Msg to the nearest cluster head
        else if state=Head do
            Receive Join_Msg from its neighbor Plain node
        end if
    end while
    if state=Head do
        Broadcast Schedule_Msg
    end if
end
```

2. Inter-cluster multihop routing algorithm

In this stage, we will construct a routing tree based on the cluster head set of EADC. Multihop communication is adopted between the cluster head and the base station. In a large-scale network, the cluster is generally far away from the base station. Thus, multihop communication between the cluster head and the base station saves more energy.

In the last part, EADC selects a well-distributed set of cluster heads (we will prove the good distribution of the cluster heads in the next part), which means the overlapped area of the cluster is even. Since the nodes are distributed unevenly, the number of nodes in the cluster is not even. There are more cluster members in the place with dense nodes; the cluster has fewer cluster members in the place with sparse nodes. That will cause an imbalance of the energy consumption of fusing and transmitting the data among the cluster heads. In multihop WSNs, the cluster heads consume energy fusing and transmitting data in the cluster (we regard this as intra-cluster energy consumption) and forwarding data from other clusters (we regard this as inter-cluster energy). In order to achieve a balance of energy consumption among the cluster heads, we need to adjust the energy consumption for forwarding the data from other cluster heads. Let the cluster head in the place with sparse nodes do more tasks of forwarding, thereby relieving the imbalance of energy consumption among the cluster heads.

In all cluster heads, some nodes need to be child nodes of the base station, communicating with the base station directly. Therefore, the cluster head s_i needs to judge whether it can communicate with the base station directly based on its distance from the base station $d(s_i, BS)$. Here we introduce a threshold distance DIST_TH. If $d(s_i, BS)$ is lower than DIST_TH, it can communicate with the base station directly and set its next hop as the base station. Otherwise, it needs to communicate with the base station by the multihop routing mode.

At the beginning of the routing algorithm, all cluster heads broadcast a Route_Msg message with R_r as the power, which includes its id, residual energy, the number of cluster members, and the distance to the base station. Otherwise, continue to the next construction. Node s_i, whose $d(s_i, BS)$ is greater than DIST_TH, needs to choose its next hop according to the received Route_Msg. s_i needs to choose the node that satisfies the condition as follows as its next hop: the node has high residual energy and a small number of cluster members, and its distance to the base station is not greater than $d(s_i, BS)$. Here we give the formula of s_i selecting s_j as the next hop:

$$R(i, j) = \alpha * \frac{s_j \cdot E_r}{E_{\max}} + (1 - \alpha) \frac{1}{s_j \cdot Num_{mem}}, \qquad (3.55)$$

in which, $E_{\max}$ is the maximum energy of nodes in the network, and here we assume that $E_{\max}$ is known; $s_j \cdot Num_{mem}$ is the number of cluster members of cluster head s_j. α is a constant value in [0, 1]. The more residual energy and the fewer cluster members, the greater the value of R. Here, s_j chooses a node with large R as the next hop. When the values of R are equal, s_j will choose the cluster head with large $d(s_j, BS)$, thereby relieving the forwarding tasks of the cluster heads closer to the base station.

Then, the construction of inter-cluster routing ends. The stage is also completed in two stages: intra-cluster communication and inter-cluster communication. The process of intra-cluster communication is the same as in LEACH. For inter-cluster communication, the cluster head fuses the data of the cluster members then sends it to the next-hop node along the routing tree. If the cluster head receives data from other cluster heads, it will forward the data to its next-hop node directly without fusing it.

The pseudocode of clustering routing construction algorithm is as follows [55].

```
begin (cluster-based routing algorithm)
  Broadcast Route_Msg
  if disttoBS<DIST_TH do
    nexthop←BS
  else
    while (T₄ has not expired) do
```

Receive *Route_Msg*

Compute the value of R

Update cluster head neighborhood table $CHNT[]$

end while

if s_m has no cluster members

$nexthop \leftarrow s_m$

else if s_j has the max value of R in $CHNT[]$

Update $MR[]$

end if

if s_k has the max value of *disttoBS* in $MR[]$

$nexthop \leftarrow s_k$

end if

end if

end

Theoretical analysis proves that the cluster head set chosen by EADC can cover the whole network, that is, there are no isolated nodes in the network. There is no other cluster head in the range with R_c as the radius of arbitrary cluster. The control message complexity of the whole network is $O(N)$, and the time complexity is $O(1)$. The simulation results show that the number of cluster heads generated by EADC is basically the same regardless of whether the nodes are distributed evenly or unevenly. The number of cluster heads is not affected by the distribution of nodes. The even size of the cluster can ensure the balance of the energy consumption among cluster members. Compared with the LEACH protocol, EADC can generate a stable number of cluster heads. The simulation results also show that the overall performance of the algorithm is better and the lifetime of the network is longer in the situation where the nodes are distributed unevenly.

Aiming at the second drawback of EEUC, we proposed a new uneven clustering algorithm EADUC [55]. EADUC proposes that an effective clustering algorithm should have the following properties: (1) completely distributed algorithm, (2) well-distributed cluster heads as much as possible to achieve the workload balance of energy among the nodes, (3) small overhead of the clustering algorithm, (4) the ability to deal with the energy-heterogeneous problem. Considering the problem of energy balance among cluster heads, the paper [55] adds a property: (5) even energy among cluster heads. For example, generate clusters with different sizes to balance the energy among cluster heads in uneven clustering; this method has been proven to be able to prolong the lifetime of the network. (6) The cluster head set generated by the algorithm can cover all nodes in the network.

The algorithm is divided into the stages of forming the cluster and data transmission. The stage of forming the cluster is further divided into the stages of cluster head election and clustering, which will be introduced respectively as follows.

1. The stage of cluster head election

   As in the EEUC, in the stage of deployment, the base station needs to broadcast a signal to the network with a given transmitting power. When each sensor node receives the signal, it calculates the appropriate distance to the base station according to the strength of the received signal, which is necessary information for constructing clusters with uneven sizes.

   Since EADUC also aims at the heterogeneous network, assume that the maximum energy E_{max} of the node in the stage of deployment is known and used as a standard for measuring residual energy. This is also necessary information for constructing uneven clusters.

   In order to calculate the relative residual energy in the competitive range of the node, each node needs to store a neighbor list to maintain information on its neighbors. At the beginning of each round, the first stage begins, that is, obtaining the information on the neighbors. We set the time of the stage as T_1. Each node in the stage can broadcast a Node_Msg message with r as the communication radius, which includes the id of the node and its residual energy. Meanwhile, the node will receive the Node_Msg message from its neighbor. Each node that receives the Node_Msg message from neighbors updates its list of neighbor nodes. After updating, each node calculates the average residual energy of its neighbor nodes E_a according to its list of neighbors:

   $$E_a = \frac{1}{d} \sum_{i=1}^{d} N_i \cdot E_r, \tag{3.56}$$

   in which d is the number of neighbors of the node; $N_i (1 \le i \le d)$ represents all of the neighbors of the node; $N_i \cdot E_r$ indicates the residual energy of the ith neighbor of the node.

   For each node, after calculating the average residual energy E_a, the time at which the cluster header message Head_Msg is sent can be obtained with the following formula:

   $$t = \begin{cases} \dfrac{E_a}{E_r} \cdot T_2 \cdot V_r & (E_r \ge E_a) \\[2mm] T_2 \cdot V_r & (E_r < E_a) \end{cases}, \tag{3.57}$$

   in which, T_2 is the time of the next stage (i.e., the stage of cluster head selection). V_r is a random value in [0.9, 1], which is introduced to reduce the probability that two nodes send a Head_Msg at the same time.

After T_1 expires, it enters the cluster selection phase, which is a key part of the whole cluster establishment process, whose time is set as T_2.

In the stage, if a node has not received a Head_Msg message from any other node before time t, the node will broadcast Head_Msg message with R_c as the radius to declare itself the cluster head. Otherwise, the node quits the election and becomes a regular node.

In an energy-heterogeneous network, the energy of the node is different. The node with low initial energy will die first when energy consumption is equal, thereby affecting the lifetime of the network. Therefore, only reducing the workload of the node with low energy and prolonging its lifetime, the lifetime of the whole network can be prolonged. Combining the two factors (the distance to the base station and the residual energy of the node), EADUC proposes a new calculation formula of competitive radius:

$$R_C = \left[1 - \alpha \frac{d_{\max} - d(s_i, BS)}{d_{\max} - d_{\min}} - \beta \left(1 - \frac{E_r}{E_{\max}} \right) \right] R_{\max}, \qquad (3.58)$$

in which, $d(s_i, BS)$ is the distance between the node and the base station; α and β are the range of control parameters, which are in $0 \sim 1$. E_r is the current residual energy of the node; $R_{\max}$ is the maximum competitive radius of the cluster head. It can be seen in formula 3.58 that the competitive radius is affected by two factors (the distance to the base station and the residual energy of the node). Thus, the node that is further away from the base station and has more residual energy will have a larger competitive radius. Therefore, the scale of the cluster is large if it is far away from the base station and its cluster head has more residual energy; the scale of the cluster is small if it is close to the base station and its cluster head has less residual energy. Regarding the residual energy as a factor of the scale of the cluster will cause energy consumption not to achieve a strict balance. However, the cluster head with more residual energy covers a larger area, and the cluster head with less residual energy covers a smaller area, which can avoid the premature death of a node with less residual energy or the node close to the base station, thereby prolonging the lifetime of the network.

2. The stage of forming the cluster

   After the overtime of T_2, the last stage (forming the cluster) begins. The algorithm sets the time of the stage as T_3. In the stage of cluster head selection, each node that is not the cluster head may receive multiple Head_Msg messages from different cluster heads. In order to save energy of the noncluster head nodes, it will send a Join_Msg message to the closest cluster head and join the cluster. Then the whole stage of cluster construction ends and the nodes in the network form a cluster structure of Voronoi.

3. The stage of data transmission

   The stage is divided into intra-cluster communication and inter-cluster communication. Intra-cluster communication is the same as in LEACH. Inter-cluster communication adopts the inter-cluster routing mode of EEUC, which will not be introduced again.

EADUC has the following characteristics.

1. The algorithm chooses the node with smaller E_a/E_r as the cluster head, which ensures that the algorithm chooses the node with relatively higher energy in a certain range as the cluster head, instead of selecting only the node with the most residual energy as the cluster head. This method is more beneficial for balancing the energy of the nodes, thereby prolonging the lifetime of the whole network.

2. There are some nodes with residual energy lower than the average residual energy of the neighbor nodes, and they have not received any declaring message from any cluster heads. We regard these nodes as "gap" nodes. The second part of formula 3.57 can make sure that the "gap" node can be the cluster head before T_2, so that it can avoid the occurrence of the "isolated node," and the set of cluster heads can seamlessly cover all nodes in the network. Since there are a few "gap" nodes, EADUC can ensure that the node with high energy can be the cluster head.

3. The selection of the competitive radius in the algorithm considers two factors (the distance to the base station and the residual energy of the node). Clusters with different sizes are generated by the competitive radius, which can balance the energy among the cluster heads and prolong the lifetime of the network.

4. The cluster heads generated by the algorithm are evenly distributed. The time nodes wait to be the cluster head varies, which ensures that there is only one cluster in the range of R_c. Obviously, the cluster heads of EADUC are evenly distributed.

We can make a conclusion by theoretical proof: The control message complexity of the whole network in EADUC clustering algorithm is O(N), and the time complexity is O(1).

The simulation shows that the cluster heads generated by the algorithm are evenly distributed, and the number of the cluster heads is stable. Compared with LEACH, HEED, and EEUC, it can save energy efficiently and prolong the lifetime of the network.

In the real application of WSNs, since the nodes are deployed randomly, nodes are distributed unevenly, instead of being distributed as in the ideal situation. However, some existing algorithms are designed based on the network model under an even distribution situation. In order to be compatible for the unevenly distributed network, we proposed a new competitive radius [56] based on the analysis of EEUC and EADUC. The formula of this competitive radius is as follows:

$$R_C = \left[1 - \alpha \frac{d_{max} - d(s_i, BS)}{d_{max} - d_{min}} - \beta \left(1 - \frac{E_{ir}}{E_{max}} \right) - \gamma \left(\frac{n_i}{N - n_i} \right) \right] R_{max}, \quad (3.59)$$

in which, n_i is the number of the neighbor nodes in the range of communication radius of the cluster head. It can be seen from the formula above that the closer the node is to the cluster head, the less residual energy the node has; the more neighbor nodes exist, the smaller the competitive radius of the cluster head is. Similarly, it saves energy for forwarding inter-cluster data by reducing the energy consumption of processing intra-cluster data. Besides, the construction of the inter-cluster routing tree considers the number of cluster members in the range of competition. Cluster heads with large numbers of cluster members should avoid being selected as routing nodes. That is, when the cluster chooses the next-hop routing node, it will choose the cluster head with large $cost(s_i, s_j)$. The $cost(s_i, s_j)$ can be calculated as follows:

$$cost(s_i, s_j) = \omega \frac{E_{jr}}{E_{max}} + (1 - \omega) \left(1 - \frac{n_j}{N} \right). \quad (3.60)$$

Similar to the EELTC [57] and LEACH protocols, the reconstruction of the cluster is continuously conducted in the operation process. Each reconstruction of the cluster is regarded as a round. The network model is shown in Figure 3.28.

Each round is divided into two stages: forming the cluster and stable data transmission. The stage of forming the cluster is further divided into cluster head selection and cluster forming.

1. Network deployment

   First, the base station needs to broadcast a signal in the network with a given transmitting power, which includes the boundary d_i of each layer. When each

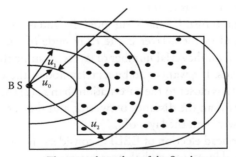

The upper boundary of the first layer

Figure 3.28   The network model of EELTC.

sensor node receives the signal, it can calculate the appropriate distance and decide on a layer according to the strength of the received signal.

2. Cluster head selection and cluster forming

In the establishment of the cluster, the base station broadcasts a message packet that includes the energy of each node and the information of the location. Based on the layer and energy of the node, each candidate cluster head sets a broadcast time to broadcast information for cluster head election by formula 3.61:

$$S_{i \cdot Twait}^{k} = \left(\omega_1 \frac{\max E_k - S_{i \cdot E}^{k}}{\max E_k} + \omega_2 \frac{k_{\max} - k}{k_{\max}} + \omega_3 \frac{d_{\max}^{k} - d}{d_{\max}^{k}} \right) \times t_0, \qquad (3.61)$$

in which, $\max E_k$ is the maximum energy of k-layer nodes; $S_{i \cdot E}^{k}$ is the residual energy of the ith node in k-layer; $k_{\max}$ is the total number of layers in the network; $d_{\max}^{k}$ is the distance between the center of k-layer and the base station; d is the distance between the node and the middle line of the layer.

The time for broadcasting the message of the cluster head election depends on formula 3.61. It also depends on the layer on which the node is located: The cluster head election of the next layer begins after the end of the cluster head election of this layer. For the cluster head selection of this layer, more residual energy and less distance to the center of the layer increases the probability of the node's being selected as the cluster head.

The competitive radius can be calculated according to formula 3.62. UB_k is the upper boundary of k-layer, and LB_k is the lower boundary of k-layer. Assume that node s_i will be the cluster head at the end. Then other nodes in the range of the competitive radius of node s_i will quit the election and become regular nodes:

$$S_{i \cdot R}^{k} = \frac{UB_k - LB_k}{2}, \quad k = 1 \dots n. \qquad (3.62)$$

3. The stage of data transmission

Multihop data transmission is adopted in inter-cluster communication. The cluster head in the k-layer is the relay node of the cluster head in the $k+1$-layer based on the serial number of layers. Assume that nodes s_i and s_j are two cluster heads. If s_j wants s_i to be its relay nodes, these conditions need to be satisfied: (1) s_i is closer to the base station than s_j, (2) the distance between s_i and s_j is smaller than the distance between s_j and the base station, and (3) the layer of s_i is lower than the layer of s_j.

The cluster head election of EELTC considers the energy of the node and the geographical location and balances energy among the nodes. In the stage of forming the cluster, even the hierarchical algorithm is adopted; in the data transmission, multihop data transmission protocol is adopted to balance the energy consumption among the cluster heads. However, the protocol does not give the optimal combination of the even hierarchy and multihop routing.

A distributed clustering routing protocol—distributed energy balanced unequal clustering (DEBUC)—for WSNs is proposed in Reference [58]. It combines energy-efficient balanced uneven clustering and inter-cluster multihop routing. The broadcast time of the protocol depends on the residual energy of the candidate cluster head and the residual energy of its neighbors. Meanwhile, the scale of the cluster closer to the base station is made smaller by controlling the competitive range of the cluster head at different positions, thereby balancing energy consumption among the nodes in the cluster and among the cluster heads. DEBUC adopts inter-cluster multihop routing. Each cluster head uses the Greedy algorithm in the set of neighbor cluster heads to select its relay nodes according to the residual energy of the node and the costs of intra-cluster and inter-cluster communication. DEBUC can save the energy of a single node efficiently, thereby balancing energy consumption and prolonging the lifetime of the network.

The uneven clustering algorithm LUCA [59], based on location information, is proposed by Lee et al. Similar to the EEUC, the idea is that the closer to the base station a cluster head is, the smaller its competitive radius is, thereby constructing a relatively small cluster structure. The authors specifically analyzed a single cluster, finally obtaining an accurate competitive

radius $r = \left[\dfrac{1}{r_0} \sqrt[3]{\dfrac{3D}{\lambda\pi}} \right]$. The competitive radius is related to the distance D between the node and the base station and the local node density λ. The closer to the base station a cluster is and the larger its local density, the larger its range, so it can save intra-cluster energy for inter-cluster data transmission.

3.2.4.7.3 The Communication Cost of Joining the Cluster

The method of building uneven clusters of the EEUC is to construct different competitive radii for different cluster structures. However, the energy-efficient clustering scheme (EECS) [60] proposes a new formula for communication cost. Regular nodes join the cluster according to their communication cost, thereby constructing clusters of different size. The EECS algorithm is executed by rounds. Each round is divided into three stages: cluster head election, forming the cluster, and data transmission.

In the stage of deployment, the base station broadcasts a Hello message to the whole network with a given power. The sensor nodes calculate their approximate distance from the base station according to the strength of the received signal, so that they can choose an appropriate transmitting power for communicating with the base station. In the process of forming the cluster, the message is used to balance the workload among the cluster heads.

1. The cluster head election

   The algorithm predetermines a threshold T in [0, 1] for the whole network to control the proportion of the nodes that participate in the cluster head election. Each node will generate a random value in [0, 1], denoted as μ. If $\mu < T$, the node becomes the candidate cluster head and broadcasts the election message COMPETE_HEAD with R as the radius, which includes its id and current residual energy. Only nodes in the range of radius R can receive the message. When the candidate node N_i receives the message from the candidate node N_j, N_i quits the election immediately and becomes a regular node if the residual energy of N_j is greater than the residual energy of N_i. Compare the id of the two nodes and choose the node with the lower id, if the residual energy is equal; N_i will continue to receive other broadcast messages if the residual energy of N_j is lower than the energy of N_i. After a period of time, the broadcast of the election information is finished and the stage ends. The candidate cluster that has not received messages from other cluster heads will be the final cluster head.

2. Forming the cluster

   The cluster head broadcasts the message HEAD_AD to all nodes in the network; this includes the id of the cluster head and the distance between itself and the base station. The regular nodes will choose the best cluster head to join in and send the message JPIN_REQ when it receives the message. The node joins a cluster that is close to itself and close to the base station. The algorithm makes numerical normalization for these two distances. The nodes calculate their weighted average for the communication cost of joining the cluster, then they choose the cluster with minimum cost. The formula of communication cost is as follows:

$$cost(j,i) = w \times f(d(P_j, CH_i)) + (1 - w) \times g(d(CH_i, BS)). \qquad (3.63)$$

The subfunctions of two distances are as follows:

$$f = \frac{d(P_j, CH_i)}{d_{f\_max}}, \quad g = \frac{d(CH_i, BS) - d_{g\_min}}{d_{g\_max} - d_{g\_min}}. \qquad (3.64)$$

In the formula, $cost(ji)$ is the cost for node N_j to join the cluster i; $d(P_j, CH_i)$ is the distance between the node and the cluster head; f subfunction makes sure to minimize the communication cost between the node and the cluster head; $d(CH_i, BS)$ is the distance between the cluster head i and the base station; the subfunction of g ensures the minimization of the communication cost between cluster head i and the base station; the set of weight w is a tradeoff between the energy of the cluster member and the energy consumption of the cluster head according to the specific application, whose goal is to maximize the lifetime of the network. Node N_j chooses cluster i with minimum $cost(j, i)$ to join; it chooses the cluster head close to the base station and far from itself. Therefore, in the cluster stage, these cluster head nodes will have more member nodes, thus ensuring the load balance of each cluster head.

3. Data transmission
   The process of this stage is same as in LEACH; thus, it will not be discussed again.

   The overhead of the control packet in the EECS protocol is lower than that for HEED. The elected cluster heads have high energy and are evenly distributed. Besides, the distribution of the number of cluster heads is more stable than in LEACH. EECS can distribute energy evenly among all nodes in the network, thereby improving the efficient utilization of the energy. The simulation proves that the lifetime is improved about 135% when compared to LEACH.

   The Energy Residual Aware clustering algorithm [61] is also an improvement on LEACH. It adopts the same cluster head election method but adds communication cost in the process of forming the cluster. The communication cost includes residual energy, the communication energy between the cluster head and the base station, and the communication energy between the cluster member and the cluster head. The communication cost can provide a "better" cluster head for a noncluster head node, which is the cluster head with minimum communication cost and the maximum residual energy.

   Uneven clustering algorithm MRPUC [62] combines the advantages of EEUC and EECS. It constructs the cluster with a different size by building the competitive radius of the cluster and the communication cost of joining the cluster for noncluster members. Each node collects related information from neighbors then selects the node with the highest residual energy as the cluster head. The closer to the base station, the smaller scale the cluster is. When the noncluster head nodes select the cluster head, the communication cost function includes the distance to the cluster head and the residual energy of the cluster head. Therefore, the node will choose the cluster head that is closer to itself and has more residual energy.

4. Other uneven clustering algorithms
   In addition to the three methods already described for constructing nonuniform clustering, there are algorithms based on the same idea but with different methods; they are briefly described as follows.

   Le et al. proposed an uneven clustering algorithm in Reference [63] that divides the network into uneven grids. The larger the distance between the grid and the base station, the larger the grid. The cluster head is selected based on the residual energy from the grid in each round. The node with highest residual energy will be the cluster head, and the nodes select the closest cluster to join. The cluster heads generated by the algorithm are evenly distributed. The farther away the base station, the more nodes participate in the cluster head rotation.

A clustering algorithm based on an optimal parameter is proposed in Reference [48]; it divides all nodes in the network into uneven static clusters. The scale of the cluster will be adjusted according to its distance from the base station, ensuring that cluster information far away from the base station can arrive at the base station accurately; the energy consumption of inter-cluster communication can be reduced by optimizing the related parameter for controlling the scale of the cluster. The cluster head acts as the local control center continuously, and the time of continuous work is obtained by optimizing the residual energy and location information, which can reduce the replacement frequency of the cluster head and the communication energy consumption in the cluster efficiently, thereby maximizing the lifetime without reducing the coverage and connectivity.

In Reference [64], the WSN is divided into some equal-sized regions, and then the nodes are divided into unequal clusters. The smaller the distance between the area and the base station, the more clusters there are in the area; thus, the number of nodes in each corresponding cluster is smaller. In the process of the cluster head election, the algorithm considers the residual energy of the node, the difference of the degree, and the related geographical location in the network. The algorithm divides the nodes closer to the base station into smaller clusters to reduce the intra-cluster energy consumption, thereby saving the energy for inter-cluster forwarding and solving the energy hole problem.

3.2.4.8 Energy-Driven Clustering Algorithms

In order to balance the energy consumption among the nodes in the cluster, each node in the network has a chance to be the cluster head in the cluster head rotation. The cluster head rotation strategy of existing clustering algorithms includes periodic rotation and energy threshold trigger rotation. Periodic rotation includes the algorithms mentioned previously, such as LEACH and HEED. These algorithms perform cluster head rotation and topology reconstruction in the presetting time, which can balance energy consumption in the network. However, each rotation needs to be executed in the range of the whole network, so that it will cause a lot of additional overhead and function interruption, and the period of rotation is difficult to determine. Therefore, some researchers propose a cycle mode based on energy threshold trigger. These algorithms trigger the process of the cluster head cycle based on dynamic calculation of the energy threshold. In this kind of algorithm, the cluster head cycle can be limited in a small range such as in the cluster or extending to the neighbor cluster, instead of cycling in the whole network. In order to avoid the overall cluster head cycle, this method is acceptable. In order to minimize the waste of energy and maximize the lifetime of the network, the algorithm needs to calculate and set an appropriate trigger energy threshold.

Recently, there was some progress on the energy threshold trigger rotation. In Reference [65], the authors analyzed the calculation of the energy threshold of EDAC [66], EDCR [67] and so on, and they gave the optimal solution under a certain condition. The energy threshold is calculated dynamically according to the residual energy $E_{th} = p \cdot E_{res}$, in which $p \in [0,1]$ is a predetermined value. In this method, the cluster head rotation will be more frequent along with the decline of residual energy. When the average energy is low, the residual energy is consumed mostly on frequent rotation instead of data transmission, that is, the efficiency η of the node energy decreases. In Reference [68], based on single cluster study, the paper [68] analyzed and proved that the energy-driven cluster head rotation strategy is better than the time-driven cluster head rotation strategy, and it gave the suboptimal solution under a single-cluster model. However, these two strategies are limited under a single-hop network model. They assume that the traffic of each cluster head is balanced, which is not suitable for the real situation in the large-scale WSN.

Huang et al. analyzed the energy consumption of a randomly distributed WSN based on cluster structure and proposed a calculation method for energy threshold trigger rotation. Meanwhile, they established a cross-layer clustering topology and the adaptive cluster rotation algorithm (ACRA) [69]. The algorithm combines the super-frame scheduling mechanism in media access control (MAC) layer, achieving the quick establishment of clustering topology and failure recovery. In the normal work stage, the cluster head chooses the back-up cluster head in the cluster according to residual energy. When the energy of the cluster head is up to the threshold or the cluster head becomes invalid, the back-up cluster head will replace the former cluster head, become the new cluster head, and then take over the most former cluster members. The nodes that cannot join the new cluster will join the neighbor cluster, thereby completing the reconstruction of the topology. The algorithm analyzes energy consumption with the cluster as a unit, modifying the energy threshold of triggering the cluster head rotation as $E_{th} = \left| E_{cur} - (E_{CH})_i t_i \right|_{\max} = E_{cur} - \dfrac{(E_0 - (E_{CH})_i - E_{CM}\overline{T})}{1 - E_{CM}/(E_{CH})_i}$, in which E_{cur} is the current residual energy of the node; E_0 is initial energy of the node; E_{CH} is energy consumption of each round; E_{CM} is energy consumption of the cluster members in each round; T is the number of rounds the network can support. The algorithm compares its performance with that of existing algorithms such as LEACH and EDAC. The results show that ACRA algorithm can make the energy utilization more efficient and prolong the lifetime of the network on the basis of minimizing the number of cluster head rotations.

Based on the existing works, we proposed an energy-driven uneven clustering protocol (EDUC) [70] aiming to solve the disadvantages of the existing algorithms.

The algorithm combines the advantage of uneven clustering and the energy-driven clustering. We use EDUC as an example to give the reader an intuitive understanding of this kind of algorithm.

The network model adopted by the algorithm is shown as follows.

Assume that there exist N sensors that are distributed evenly in an $M \times M$ area, and the node has the following properties:

1. The node will not move after deployment.
2. The energy of the node is heterogeneous and uncharged.
3. The node cannot know its location information.
4. The transmitting power of the node can be controlled, that is, the node can adjust transmitting power according to the distance of the receiver.
5. A unique base station is deployed at a fixed location beyond the sensing area, and all the nodes in the network know the location information of the base station.
6. Each node has a globally unique id signature.

The energy model adopted by the algorithm is the same as that of the LEACH algorithm.

The details of the EDUC algorithm are as follows.

3.2.4.8.1 The Process of Forming the Cluster

In the stage of deployment, the base station will broadcast a signal with a given transmitting power. Each sensor node calculates the approximate distance to the base station according to the strength of the received signal. Then, the process of forming the cluster begins.

T_1 period after the beginning of the process of forming the cluster is called the stage of the cluster head competition, whose duration is T_1. At the beginning of the stage of the cluster head competition, all nodes calculate the time they have to wait t_w before being the cluster head according to their residual energy. For arbitrary node i, the calculation of its waiting time is

$$t_{wi} = \left(1 - \frac{E_{curi}}{E_{max}}\right) \cdot T_1 \cdot V_r, \tag{3.65}$$

in which, E_{curi} is the current energy of node i; E_{max} is the maximum residual energy of the node in the network. At the beginning of the process of forming the cluster, E_{max} can be the maximum initial energy of the node, which is regarded as a known value. V_r is a random value in [0.9, 1]. We introduce V_r to reduce the probability that two nodes send a Head_Msg at the same time.

In the time period of the cluster head competition, if node i has not received a Head_Msg message for any other nodes before time t_{wi}, the node will broadcast a Head_Msg message with R_{Ci} as the radius to declare itself the cluster head. In formula 3.65 mentioned earlier, we introduce V_r to reduce the probability that two nodes send a Head_Msg at the same time. Here, we control the transmitting radius of sending a Head_Msg message as R_C. In this case, the probability that several nodes send the Head_Msg message at the same time is low. Therefore, when the nodes send Head_Msg messages, the probability of collision is very low; thus, we neglect the probability.

If node i has received the Head_Msg message from node u before time t_{wi}, the node will restore the id of node u and the distance to node u, then quit the competition and become a noncluster head node. Surely, node i can still receive the Head_Msg message from other nodes after being the noncluster head node, to ensure that it can find an appropriate cluster head as its cluster head in the next stage of forming the cluster. We give the calculation formula of R_C below:

$$R_{Ci} = \left[1 - \alpha \frac{d_i - d_{min}}{d_{max} - d_{min}}\right] R_{max}, \tag{3.66}$$

in which, d_{max} and d_{min} represent the maximum distance and the minimum distance between the node and the base station, respectively; d_i is the distance between the node and the base station. α is the parameter of controlling the range of value, which is in $0 \sim 1$; R_{max} is the maximum value of the competitive radius of the cluster head. This formula shows that the competitive radius of the node is affected by the distance d_i. The larger the value of d_i, the lower the value of R_C and the smaller the scale of the cluster far from the base station. Now, the radius of the cluster controlled by i is

$$R_a = 2R_{Ci}. \tag{3.67}$$

When it is beyond the time T_1, the stage of forming the cluster begins; its time duration is T_2. The noncluster head nodes select the closest cluster head from their stored list of cluster heads and send Join_Msg messages. The Join_Msg message includes the id of the node and its residual energy. In this process, we need the CSMA mechanism to ensure the success of sending the message. When the cluster head receives the Join_Msg message from a noncluster head node, it will store the information of the cluster member, including the residual energy E_{curi} and the distance to the cluster head d_{toCH}, then count the number C of the cluster members.

When it is beyond the time T_2, the cluster head generates a time-division multiple address TDMA slot table according to the stored information of the cluster members, then encapsulates the TDMA slot into the Schedule_Msg message and broadcasts the message to its cluster members. The cluster members can obtain the TDMA slot table from the received Schedule_Msg message.

The flow figure of the process is shown in Figure 3.29.

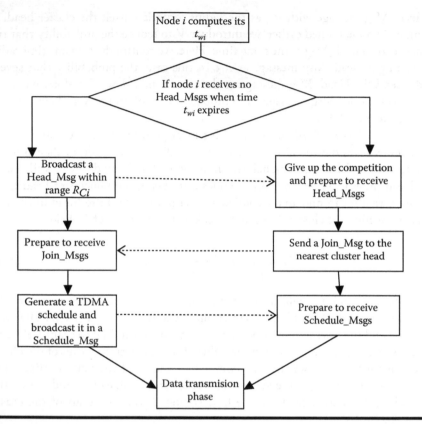

Figure 3.29 The flow figure of the process of forming the cluster in EDUC.

3.2.4.8.2 The Process of Self-Organized Data Transmission

In the stage of data transmission, the cluster member collects the data and sends it to the cluster head by the single-hop mode in its own slot according to the received TDMA scheduling table, so that it can avoid collisions with cluster members in the same cluster. When all cluster members in the TDMA scheduling table have transmitted data once, the cluster head fuses it and sends the fused data to the base station. In order to avoid collisions among the nodes in different clusters, we need to introduce a simple direct sequence spread spectrum (DSSS) model, and each cluster adopts a different code. Therefore, each cluster member only communicates with its own cluster head. If it receives the message from other clusters, it will shield automatically. The packet sent by the cluster head to the cluster members includes the current residual energy of the cluster member. The cluster head can update the energy list of the stored cluster members in time according to the received packet.

When the cluster head finds that its energy is lower than the threshold, it will calculate the priority value of the cluster members. The algorithm uses p_i to indicate the priority of node i. The cluster head chooses the first three nodes with the highest p value and transmits the triggered message, which includes the triggering time and the diameter R_a of the next cluster head. Here, choosing three nodes to transmit the triggering time is to ensure the smooth operation of the reconstruction of the cluster. In the time of t_a after receiving the triggered message, if the cluster member has not received the message from any other nodes in the cluster, it will become the next cluster head and broadcast the information in the cluster. The next process is the same as the process of forming the cluster.

The formula for node i to calculate its p_i is

$$p_i = \beta \frac{E_{curi}}{E_{max}} + (1-\beta)\left(1 - \frac{d_{toCHi}}{d_{toCH\,max}}\right), \tag{3.68}$$

in which, E_{max} and $d_{toCHmax}$ indicate the maximum residual energy and the maximum distance to the cluster head, respectively; E_{curi} and $d_{toCHmax}$ represent the current residual energy and the value of the distance to the cluster head, which is between 0.5 and 1, respectively.

For the triggering time of the three chosen nodes, the calculation is as follows:

$$t_{ai} = \frac{i}{10}T_1 \quad (i=1,2,3). \tag{3.69}$$

Then the derivation of the energy threshold will be analyzed specifically.

In an ideal situation, each node can become the cluster head once in the lifetime of the clustering network, which can consume the minimum energy of cluster head rotation.

We will analyze the energy consumption of each cluster. In the process of data collection, cluster members send the collected data to the cluster head according to the received TDMA schedule. When the last member in TDMA scheduling has completed the data transmission, the cluster head fuses the data and sends it to the base station. The process can be seen as a cycle of data collection. In each process of data collection, the energy consumption of all the cluster members can be represented as

$$E_{CM} = C\left(E_{elec} + E_{sen} + \varepsilon d_{toCH}^n\right)l, \tag{3.70}$$

in which, d_{toCH} obeys the uniform distribution on $[0, R_a]$, thus the expectation is $2R_a^n / (n+2)$. Combine it with formula 3.70 and then it holds that

$$E_{CM} = C\left(E_{elec} + E_{sen} + \varepsilon \frac{2R_a^n}{n+2}\right)l. \tag{3.71}$$

The energy consumption of the cluster head is

$$E_{CH} = CE_{elec}l + E_{sen}l + (C+1)E_{com}l + \left(E_{elec} + \varepsilon d_{toBS}^n\right)l$$
$$= \left[(C+1)E_{elec} + E_{sen} + (C+1)E_{com} + \varepsilon d_{toBS}^n\right]l. \quad (3.72)$$

Therefore, the total energy consumption of all the nodes in a cluster is

$$E_{total} = E_{CH} + E_{CM}$$
$$= \left[(2C+1)E_{elec} + (C+1)E_{com} + (C+1)E_{sen} + \varepsilon\left(d_{toBS}^n + \frac{2CR_a^n}{n+2}\right)\right]l. \quad (3.73)$$

The energy consumption described is called effective energy consumption. Besides, in each process of cluster construction, some energy needs to be consumed, which is additional energy consumption. The additional energy consumption is represented as E_{aCH}. In the process of being the cluster head, the node needs to broadcast a Head_Msg and a Schedule_Msg and send the Trigger_Msg to the three cluster members. Also, it needs to receive the Join_Msg message from its cluster members. Therefore, the additional energy consumption of the cluster head is

$$E_{aCH} = 5\left(E_{elec} + \varepsilon R_a^n\right)l + CE_{elec}l$$
$$= \left[(C+5)E_{elec} + 5\varepsilon R_a^n\right]l. \quad (3.74)$$

E_{aCM} represents the additional energy consumption of all cluster heads, since each node only sends a Join_Msg and receives the control message from the cluster head. There are C cluster members in the cluster head, thus

$$E_{aCM} = C\left(E_{elec} + \varepsilon\frac{2R_a^n}{n+2} + 3E_{elec}\right)l$$
$$= C\left(4E_{elec} + \varepsilon\frac{2R_a^n}{n+2}\right)l. \quad (3.75)$$

Therefore, in a cluster head rotation, the total additional energy of the cluster is

$$E_{acluster} = E_{aCH} + E_{aCM}$$
$$= \left[(5C+5)E_{elec} + \left(\frac{2C}{n+2}+5\right)\varepsilon R_a^n\right]l. \quad (3.76)$$

There are $C+1$ nodes in a cluster. Therefore, there are $C+1$ times of cluster head rotation at most. Then in the whole lifetime of the cluster head, the total additional energy consumption is

$$E_{atotal} = (C+1)E_{acluster}$$

$$= (C+1)\left[(5C+5)E_{elec} + \left(\frac{2C}{n+2}+5\right)\varepsilon R_a^n\right]l. \tag{3.77}$$

In the whole cluster, if T represents the number of rotations for data collecting, it holds that:

$$T = \frac{\displaystyle\sum_{i=1}^{n+1}(E_{0i}-E_{res})-E_{atotal}}{E_{total}}, \tag{3.78}$$

in which, E_a indicates the initial energy of node i.

Considering a single node i in the cluster, it can be the cluster head once at most and be the cluster member for C times. Thus, the additional energy consumption of being the cluster head is E_{aCHi}, and the additional energy consumption of being the cluster member is E_{aCMi}. The additional energy consumption E_{anodei} of the node is

$$E_{anodei} = E_{aCHi} + E_{aCMi} \tag{3.79}$$

$$E_{aCHi} = 5\left(E_{elec} + \varepsilon R_a^n\right)l + CE_{elec}l$$

$$= \left[(C+5)E_{elec} + 5\varepsilon R_a^n\right]l \tag{3.80}$$

$$E_{aCMi} = C\left(E_{elec} + \varepsilon\frac{2R_a^{\,n}}{n+2} + 3E_{elec}\right)l$$

$$= C\left(4E_{elec} + \varepsilon\frac{2R_a^{\,n}}{n+2}\right)l. \tag{3.81}$$

Assume that the rotation number of data transmission is t_i when node i is the cluster head and the residual energy is E_{res} when the network dies. Then this formula can be obtained:

$$E_{curi} - E_{res} = E_{anodei} + E_{CHi}t_i + (T-t_i)\sum_{j=1,\,j\neq i}^{n}E_{CMi}$$

$$= E_{anodei} + \left[E_{CHi} - E_{CMi}\right]t_i + TE_{CMi}, \tag{3.82}$$

in which, E_{CHi} and E_{CMi} represent the energy consumption of node i being the cluster head and being the cluster member in a round of data transmission, respectively:

$$E_{CMi} = \left(E_{elec} + E_{sen} + \varepsilon \frac{2R_a^{\,n}}{n+2} \right) l \qquad (3.83)$$

$$E_{CHi} = CE_{elec}l + E_{sen}l + (C+1)E_{com}l + \left(E_{elec} + \varepsilon d_{toBS}^{\,n} \right) l$$

$$= \left[(C+1)E_{elec} + E_{sen} + (C+1)E_{com} + \varepsilon d_{toBS}^{\,n} \right] l. \qquad (3.84)$$

t_i can be calculated by formula 3.82:

$$t_i = \frac{E_{curi} - E_{res} - E_{anodei} - TE_{CMi}}{E_{CHi} - E_{CMi}}. \qquad (3.85)$$

The energy threshold is

$$threshold = E_{curi} - E_{CHi}t_i. \qquad (3.86)$$

Analyze this process; then it can be obtained that EDUC clustering algorithm has the characteristics as follows:

1. In the process of the cluster head rotation, the cluster member with high residual energy will be the next cluster head; this can reduce the times of cluster head rotation and decrease the energy waste brought by the cluster head rotation.
2. Formula 3.65 ensures that the waiting time of all the nodes is lower than T_1. For an arbitrary node, if it has not received a Head_Msg message from its neighbor, it will be the cluster head before the overtime of T_1, so that the set of the cluster heads can achieve the seamless overlap of all nodes in the network. Since the waiting time of the node is different, two nodes will not become the cluster head at the same time in the same competitive range. Therefore, there is only one cluster head in the same competitive range.
3. Uneven clustering is achieved by the selection of competitive radius R_C, so that it can achieve the balance of energy consumption among the clusters.
4. The cluster uses a method of energy-driven cluster head rotation. Each node can be the cluster head for once at most, so that the times of cluster head rotation can be the minimum. Therefore, the additional energy consumption is minimized.

The energy efficiency η of EDUC will be analyzed in the following. In EDAC, η is defined as

$$\eta = E_e / E_t = E_e / (E_e + E_a), \qquad (3.87)$$

in which, E_e indicates the efficient energy consumption of data transmission; E_a refers to the additional energy consumption of maintaining the topology. In EDUC, each node can be the cluster head for once at most. Therefore, in the lifetime of the network, the additional energy consumption of the whole network is

$$E_a = NE_{anodei}. \tag{3.88}$$

Compared with the time-driven cluster head rotation algorithm, EDUC has lower additional energy consumption and can obtain higher energy efficiency. Besides, in the data-driven cluster head rotation algorithm, the cluster head rotation is operated locally, which can avoid the function interruption caused by overall cluster head rotation in the algorithm.

The parameters in the algorithm will be analyzed in the following. In formula 3.66, R_{max} decides the value of competitive radius R_{Ci}. The larger the value of R_{max}, the larger the radius of the cluster; on the contrary, the lower the numbers of clusters is. α decides the uneven degree of the cluster size. The larger the value of α, the more even the size of the cluster is. R_{max} and α affect the number of the clusters. From formula 3.66 we see that the node that is far away from the base station has a smaller competitive radius R_{Ci}, since the cluster heads that are far away from the base station need to transmit for a long distance. Their energy consumption of data transmission higher than the cluster head that is close to the base station. Therefore, the clusters have relatively small size to achieve the balance of energy consumption among the clusters.

In formula 3.68, the priority P_i of node i to be the next cluster head is affected by the current residual energy and the distance between the node and the cluster head, while β refers to the impact on P_i caused by the residual energy and the distance to the cluster head. Here, β selects the value in 0.5~1. It regards the residual energy as the main parameter and the distance between the node and the cluster head as the auxiliary parameter, based on which the cluster member with high residual energy will be selected as the next cluster head. Besides, the new cluster head will be out of the marginal area in the cluster as much as possible.

3.2.4.9 Grid Clustering Algorithms

The routing protocol Two-Tier Data Dissemination (TTDD) Model [71] is based on the layer structure in WSNs, proposed by Lu et al. It aims for data transmission in the situation where the base station moves frequently in WSNs, that is, the sensor nodes stay fixed, but the base station can move, so data can be transmitted from multiple source nodes to multiple mobile base stations to achieve effective data transmission with low energy consumption. The application is WSNs for detecting enemy tanks on the battlefield. Many sensor nodes are deployed in the battlefield to sense the location of enemy tanks. The sensor node that detects enemy tanks can send data to the device (i.e., the base station) in the hand of scouts via WSNs.

The process of the TTDD algorithm can be divided into three parts: forming the grid, querying the sender, and data transmission.

The stage of forming the grid is the key part of the TTDD protocol, which needs to construct the grid by dissemination nodes in the whole WSN. The dissemination node is similar to other cluster heads in the routing protocol based on layer structure, but the relationship between it and other nodes is not close like the relationship between the cluster head and the cluster member is. When a sensor node detects an enemy tank, the node becomes a source node (such as node A in Figure 3.30). The source node will broadcast a data announcement, and the transmitting process of the data announcement is the process of forming the grid. If there exist multiple tanks in the network, there are multiple source nodes. Each source node will launch to build a corresponding grid. The source node calculates the geographical location of all the dissemination points first according to its own geographical location. Assume that the geographical location of the source node is $L_s = (x, y)$, then the location of the dissemination point is $L_p = (x_i, Y_j)$, in which $\{x_i = x + i \cdot \alpha; y_j = y + j \cdot \alpha; j = \pm 0, \pm 1, \pm 2, ...\}$ and α are the parameters of the TTDD protocol, referring to the width and height of each cell. It can be seen from Figure 3.30 that the dissemination point is the cross point of the horizontal dotted line and the longitudinal dotted line. The dissemination point responsible for the routing function is the sensor node closest to the dissemination point.

In the process of forming the grid, the spread of the data announcement can use the simple Greedy algorithm. The node closest to the given dissemination point is the final end of data announcement, which is the search dissemination node.

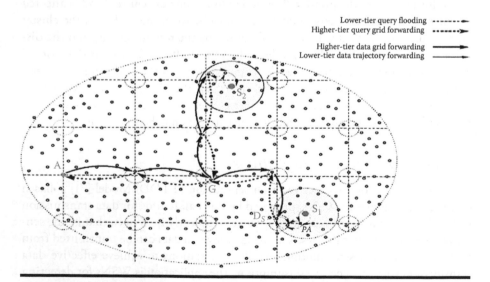

Figure 3.30 The instance of the TTDD algorithm. (From Luo, H. et al., TTDD: Two-tier data dissemination in large-scale wireless sensor networks, *Wireless Networks*, 2005.)

The source node sends the data announcement along four directions to four dissemination: up, down, left, right, respectively. The dissemination points use the same method to spread the data announcement along four directions after receiving it. With the spread of the data announcement, the virtual network made by the dissemination points will be formed (the black dots shown in Figure 3.30).

When the sink needs the data, it can broadcast a request querying the dissemination nodes in the range of a cell to find the closest dissemination node. The dissemination node closest to the sink is called an immediate dissemination node. Once the immediate dissemination node is found, the sink node can send the query request packet to the immediate dissemination node. The immediate dissemination node will forward the query request to an upstream dissemination node closer to the source node and so on until the query request arrives at the source node.

After receiving the query request packet, the source node sends the collected data back to the immediate dissemination node along the negative direction, and then forwards the data to the sink node. If the sink node has moved to a new location, the data can be forwarded by the primary agent and immediate agent. The agent mechanism can solve the mobility problem efficiently.

It is important to note that the TTDD protocol assumes that all nodes in the sensor network have an equal wireless communication distance. That means that the query request and data packet among adjacent nodes are forwarded by other nodes, instead of being transmitted directly.

The TTDD protocol can also support multiple sink nodes and data fusion. Figure 3.30 gives an instance of two sink nodes S_1 and S_2; they can send query request packets to the source node A by their dissemination nodes, respectively. The query request packet can be fused after arriving at node G, while the source node A can only reply with a data packet. The data packet will be sent back to the sink nodes S_1 and S_2 along the forwarding route after arriving at node G.

The TTDD protocol can solve the frequent mobility of sink node efficiently, which is the best advantage of the algorithm. However, in the case of the rapid movement of the monitoring target, the TTDD protocol will cause a large delay in the process of building the grid, query requests, and data packets; this will result in poor real-time data acquisition. Therefore, the TTDD protocol is not suitable for the application of monitoring goals with fast mobility and high real-time demand. Besides, although the TTDD protocol supports multiple data sources, constructing the grid is a little complicated and causes large overhead when there are many data sources, because each data source will launch to build a grid. Therefore, the TTDD protocol is not suitable for applications with multiple data sources.

Hierarchical geographic multicast routing (HGMR), proposed by Koutsonikola, is a multicast protocol based on geographical location. The protocol combines the key design idea of geographic multicast routing (GMR) [73] and hierarchical rendezvous point multicast (HRPM) [74] perfectly and optimizes these two protocols. HGMR has energy-efficient forwarding and scalability, so it can be used in large-scale WSNs.

In HRPM protocol, the whole network layer is divided into several units. Each unit has an access point (AP), which manages the location information of the destination in the corresponding unit. The source node forwards the data to the AP with the highest level. The AP with the highest level sends the data to the local AP with lower level until the packet arrives at the AP with the lowest level. These transmissions are replaced by GMR in HGMR. HGMR will not have the scalability problem, because only the destination of the management process is present in the radio unit (Figure 3.31).

The advantages of HGMR are as follows.

1. The management of the cluster members is simple and needs no additional cost because of the application of geographical hash algorithm.
2. According to the number of nodes acting in different roles, the data transmission in different layers of HGMR makes the routing energy efficient to some degree.
3. HGMR does not have the scalability problem because the destinations are stored in a unit, which is easy to manage.

However, HGMR has the following problems.

1. The size of a unit may be applied in GMR extensively, and there are extremely few destinations in the network. Some destinations cannot be divided in the network. Then the size of the unit equals the scale of the network.
2. All transmissions are focused on the APs. Although APs can change into other nodes by hash function, this is limited in the unit.

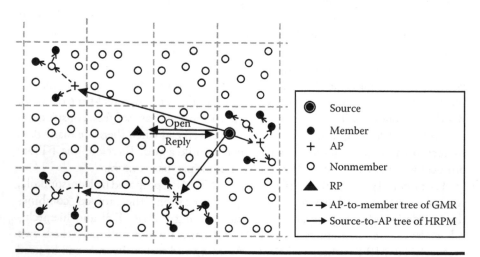

Figure 3.31   The instance of HRPM algorithm.

3. The packet has to be transmitted from the upper AP to the lower AP. That means the packet needs to be transmitted to the upper AP first, although the lower AP is closer to the source than the upper AP, which makes for low efficiency of the routing path.

3.2.4.10 Responsive Hybrid Clustering Algorithms

WSNS can be classified into proactive WSNs and reactive WSNs according to the different data transmission modes. Proactive WSNs monitor the surroundings continuously and transmit the monitoring data with a constant rate; reactive WSNs only transmit the monitoring data when the monitoring object changes. The Threshold Sensitive Energy Efficient Sensor Network (TEEN) protocol [75] is a WSN reactive hierarchical routing protocol. It is similar to LEACH, but it uses the strategy in the stage of data transmission, which is different from LEACH. TEEN sets two threshold parameters: hard parameter and soft parameter, using a filter method to reduce data traffic. TEEN, which can respond to an emergency quickly, is applied to monitor the change of some special events; thus, it is not suitable for WSNs that need to collect data continuously.

The network model used by TEEN is similar to that for LEACH. The model is briefly summarized as follows.

1. The base station is far away from the nodes in the WSN. All nodes can communicate with the base station. All nodes in the network are homogeneous, and the transmitting power of the node is adjustable.
2. The data is the center of the WSN. The cluster member sends collected data to its cluster head. The cluster head processes the data and sends it to the base station. In the process, assume that only one packet is transmitted at once.
3. The cluster head assigns TDMA slots for the cluster members and broadcasts the hard and soft parameters to the cluster members. Each node can only send the data in its specific slot, avoiding collisions with other nodes.

The operation of TEEN protocol is also executed by period. Each round is divided into the stages of forming the cluster and stable data transmission. In the stage of forming the cluster, the cluster head is selected and the cluster structure is formed. In the stage of data transmission, the data is transmitted. A new round will be executed when a round ends.

1. The selection of the cluster head: The specific process of cluster head selection is the same as for LEACH, so it will not be explained again.
2. The process of forming the cluster: When the cluster head broadcasts the message proclaiming itself the cluster head to other nodes, hard and soft thresholds are spread as well. The hard threshold is the threshold the monitoring data cannot exceed; soft threshold is the changeable range of the

monitoring data. The node can join the closest cluster according to the rule of minimum communication cost, and then send the joining message, which includes the id of the cluster head and the id of the node. The cluster head builds a TDMA scheduling table for each cluster member and assigns the transmitting slot according to the joining message. Afterwards, the stage of data transmission begins. The flow figure of the process is shown in Figure 3.32.

3. The stage of data transmission: The node senses surroundings continuously. It only transmits data to the cluster head when the monitoring data exceeds the hard threshold for the first time. At the same time, the monitoring data will be stored as sensor value (SV). Afterwards, when the node wants to send data to the cluster head again, the monitoring data has to show that the data value is larger than the hard threshold and that the difference of the data value and stored SV is not lower than soft threshold. Then the node will send and store the data as a new SV. When the data transmission of this round ends and the cluster head of the new round is determined, the cluster head will reset and broadcast these two parameters.

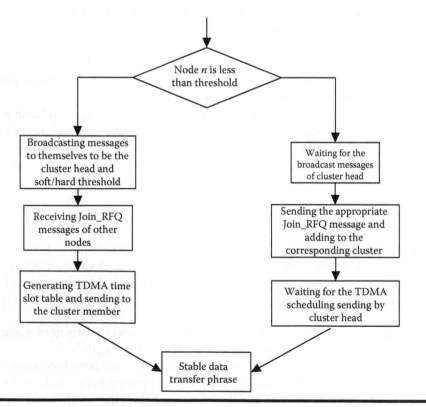

Figure 3.32 The process of TEEN algorithm.

TEEN protocol can be used for monitoring some emergent events and is suitable for the application environment, which needs real-time sensing. Besides, TEEN can reduce the times of data transmission greatly by setting hard threshold and soft threshold, thereby saving more energy. Along with the change of the cluster head, users can reset the value of two parameters, thereby controlling the times of data transmission.

However, TEEN has some drawbacks.

1. TEEN adopts the same clustering algorithm as LEACH, so the drawbacks in the process of forming the cluster in LEACH also exist in TEEN. For example, the cluster head election does not consider the energy factor and the uniformity of clustering.
2. The cluster head in TEEN also uses the single-hop mode. Although the communication is simple, TEEN is only suitable for the relatively small WSN with low scalability.
3. TEEN protocol is not suitable for the application environment, which needs to send data to the base station periodically. That is because the node will not send any data to the base station if the monitoring data is not up to the hard threshold; thus, the base station will not obtain the data and cannot know whether the node becomes invalid.
4. Once the monitoring data satisfies the request of the threshold, it will be sent immediately, which can cause interference easily. If TDMA mechanism is used in TEEN, it will lead to data delay, which doesn't meet the design idea of TEEN.

APTEEN protocol [76] is an extension of the TEEN algorithm and a combination of LEACH and TEEN. It is a hybrid data transmission mode with a proactive and reactive data transmission mode. APTEEN uses a multilayer clustering hierarchical structure as does TEEN. It can set the period and the related threshold of TEEN protocol according to the need of the users and the type of application, that is, it can collect the data periodically and make quick responses to emergency events.

The aspects for which APTEEN extends TEEN are as follows.

1. Along with the determination of the cluster head, the parameters the cluster head will broadcast are
   Property: used to represent a set of physical parameters that the user expects to obtain
   Threshold: consists of hard threshold and soft threshold
   Scheduling: adopts TDMA scheduling mode, assigning corresponding slots for each node
   Counting time: represents the maximum period for sending successful reports
2. The node operating the APTEEN protocol uses the same mechanism as TEEN for data transmission. In order to change what TEEN cannot apply in the periodic transmission system, the protocol stipulates that if the node has

not transmitted any data during the counting time, it will force the node to check and send data to the sink node.

3. In order to achieve a better application in hybrid network system, APTEEN adopts the TDMA scheduling method.

Based on the assumption that adjacent nodes may monitor the same object, in APTEEN the base station divides the nodes into sleeping-awake pairs. The awake node is responsible for responding to the query; the sleeping node switches to sleeping status to save energy. These two nodes switch roles when the cluster head rotates. APTEEN modifies the TDMA of LEACH (as shown in Figure 3.33). The slots of each pair of sleeping-awake nodes are separated in length by half of the TDMA frame. If there is emergent data, the sleeping-awake pair can occupy each other's slot to improve the response time.

4. APTEEN can support three different types of query: historical query, which can analyze the previous monitoring data; single query, which can obtain the current state of the network; and persistent query, which can monitor some event continuously in a period.

The simulation shows that on the index of energy consumption and lifetime of the network, TEEN and APTEEN outperform the LEACH protocol, and the performance of APTEEN lies between that of TEEN and LEACH. Since TEEN reduces the times of data transmission, it obtains the best performance index. The important drawback of TEEN and APTEEN is that constructing a multilayer clustering hierarchical structure that can support hard and soft threshold mechanisms is complicated and has high overhead.

3.2.4.11 Multilayer Clustering Algorithms

Clustering can be divided into single layer and multilayer. In single-layer clustering, the nodes in the network are divided into two layers: the cluster head is the high layer, and the cluster member is the low layer. Most clustering algorithms only have one layer of cluster heads. This kind of algorithm has some advantages: It is easy to achieve, and it has small control overhead. Multilayer clustering is based on

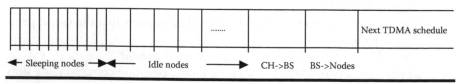

Figure 3.33 TDMA scheduling of APTEEN. (From Manjeshwar, A., Agrawal, D. P., APTEEN: A hybrid protocol for efficient routing and comprehensive information retrieval in wireless sensor networks, In: *Proceedings of the 2nd International Workshop on Parallel and Distributed Computing Issues in Wireless Networks and Mobile Computing*, Lauderdale, FL, USA, 195–202, 2002.)

single-layer clustering. It clusters the nodes in the network according to the layer requirement. In multilayer clustering, the cluster heads in the lower layer are cluster members of the cluster heads in the higher layer. Multilayer clustering can reduce energy consumption further and fuse the data. In the hierarchical clustering network, the nodes that share a cluster head are believed to belong to the same cluster.

In a cluster, the cluster head needs to compress the data from its attached node as the local intermediate processing center. If multiple cluster heads of a lower layer send compressed data to the same cluster head of the upper layer, we say that these clusters belong to the same layer. Generally, the process of multilayer clustering algorithm is divided into two types (i.e., top-down clustering mode and down-top clustering mode). The sequence of forming the cluster structure in these two methods is different.

The forming process of a k-layer clustering strategy by down-up mode is as follows: Set the first layer as the lowest layer; set the k-layer as the highest layer. All regular nodes judge whether they can be selected as the cluster head of the first layer according to a certain clustering rule. If a node can be selected as the cluster head, it will broadcast a message that it is the cluster head in its transmission range. When all clusters of the first layer are selected, the same clustering process will be executed in the cluster heads of the first layer. Then the second-layer cluster heads will be selected from these cluster heads by the same clustering rule. Similarly, the third layer, the fourth layer... the k-layer cluster structure will be formed.

It can be seen by the definition that the forming process of k-layer clustering strategy by top-down mode is as follows: Set the first layer as the highest layer; set the k-layer as the lowest layer. First, select the cluster heads of first layer; then select them for the second layer, and so on until the k-layer. The specific process is that each node in the sensor network becomes the cluster head in a certain proportion based on a certain strategy and broadcasts its decision to the nodes in its transmission range. Each node selects the cluster head to join in according to a certain rule. Then the regular node in each cluster of the first layer executes the same clustering process. Similarly, with the third layer, the fourth-layer... the k-layer cluster structure will be formed. Figure 3.34 shows the formation of a WSN clustering topology for the k-layer. In a multilayer clustering sensor network, the process of data transmission is the opposite of the process of forming. That means the sensor nodes in the lowest layer send collected data to the cluster heads in the first layer; the cluster heads in k-layer compress the received data and send it to the cluster head in $k-1$ layer; the cluster heads in $k-1$ layer send the data to the next highest layer in turn until the data arrives at the highest layer. Finally, the cluster head of the first layer sends the compressed data to the base station. The energy consumption of the whole network is the sum of the data transmission and the control message in each structure.

Estrin et al. proposed a new hierarchical routing algorithm for WSNs to achieve a multilayer clustering algorithm [77]. The main idea of the multilayer clustering algorithm is that all nodes in sensor networks are divided into different layers

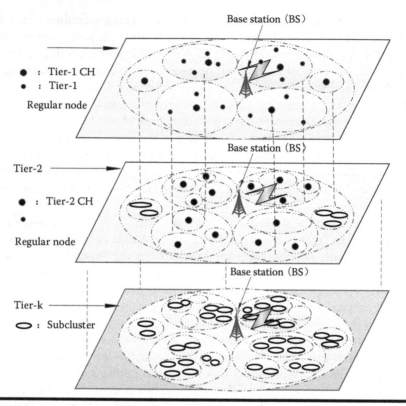

Figure 3.34   Multi-layer clustering structure.

according to a certain mechanism and strategy. The higher the layer is, the wider the transmission range of the node is. Conversely, the lower the layer is, the smaller the transmission range of the node is, that is, the coverage range is narrow. In the initial stage, all nodes are in the lowest layer, and they obtain the opportunity to enter the upper layer in some way. The specific process is that at the beginning of each round of the clustering algorithm, all nodes in the network broadcast their status information, which includes the residual energy, the layer they are in, and the id of their corresponding cluster heads. After broadcasting the message, the node switches to waiting status to obtain the information of its surroundings. The waiting time is inversely proportional to the layer in which the node is located. If there is no cluster head in the adjacent range of a node in the lowest layer, the node will enter competitive status after the waiting time. The node sets a timer that is inversely proportional to the residual energy and the number of received messages from other nodes in the same layer. A node that has more residual energy and is located in a dense area has a better chance to enter a higher structure. If the waiting time expires, the node goes to the higher layer, and it classifies the nodes that have already sent it messages as members of its own cluster. Then it will broadcast its status information to these nodes. The nodes that have already selected their cluster head will not execute the operation above; that is, they will not participate in the competition of the upper layer. After the establishment of the cluster structure in each round, a node in the higher layer decides whether it quits as cluster head according to its status information, which includes whether it has cluster members and whether it has enough residual energy. The multilayer clustering algorithm proposed by Estrin et al. has scalability. In their paper, Estrin et al. proved its effectiveness by applying the two-layer model.

Loscri et al. introduced TL-LEACH, which is a two-layer hierarchical LEACH protocol. The protocol is an extension of the LEACH protocol. It uses two methods to achieve energy and delay efficiency: the random, adaptive, and self-configuring cluster construction and local control of data senders. In TL-LEACH, the cluster head collects data as in LEACH, but it uses cluster heads between them and the base station as relays to forward the data instead of transmitting data to the cluster head directly.

TL-LEACH introduces two-layer hierarchical structure as shown in the figure: The cluster head in the high layer is regarded as the primary cluster head (CH_i), and the secondary cluster head is represented by CH_{ij}, and so on. The algorithm consists of four basic stages: broadcasting, forming the cluster, generating the scheduling, and data transmission. In the first stage, in each round, each node judges whether it can become a primary cluster head, a secondary cluster head, or the cluster head of other layers. If the node is selected as the primary cluster head, it has to broadcast to other nodes. The mechanism used in this stage is carrier sense multiple access (CSMA). Afterwards, the secondary cluster head continues to broadcast, and so on. In the second stage, each secondary cluster head judges which primary cluster head it belongs to then broadcasts the message to its primary cluster head. In the same way, the cluster head in the third layer judges which secondary cluster head it belongs to and broadcasts the message to the secondary cluster head. In the third stage, each primary cluster head builds a TDMA scheduling, assigning the transmitting slots to each node in the cluster. Each primary cluster head selects a CDMA code and informs all nodes in the second layer to use the code. In the same way, each secondary cluster head assigns the code and transmitting slots to its cluster members in the code and scheduling sent by the primary cluster head. In the last stage, all clusters are formed. Each node needs to transmit data to its cluster head in its corresponding TDMA slot (Figure 3.35).

The advantages of TL-LEACH are as follows.

1. Compared with LEACH, its two-layer mechanism can achieve a smaller average transmitting distance. A few nodes need to send the data to the base station for a long distance. Therefore, it can reduce energy consumption significantly.
2. TL-LEACH uses a paradigm with local coordination, which is highly scalable and robust.

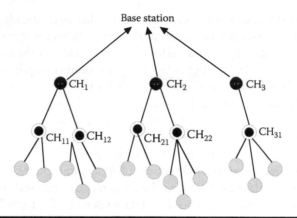

Figure 3.35 The clustering topology of TL-LEACH.

However, TL-LEACH has some disadvantages.

1. Although the average distance is reduced compared with LEACH, two-hop inter-cluster routing is still not suitable for a large-scale network. That is because data transmission only uses two hops from the source node to the base station. Long-distance communication leads to a great deal of energy consumption.

2. The protocol assumes an ideal homogeneous network. It does not consider energy in the process of cluster head election. The protocol cannot ensure the balance of workload under the situation where the initial energy is different.

Data aggregation-exact and approximate (DAEA) [79] is a three-layer clustering protocol. The clusters have the square areas and sizes, which are divided in advance and do not overlap each other. Based on this structure, in order to save the energy and fuse the data as much as possible, DAEA proposes selecting the cluster head for each cluster, that is, local aggregation (LA) and selects the upper cluster head from LA, that is, master aggregation (MA). The selection of LA is based on the energy of the node and the times it has been the cluster head. Select the optimal MA from the LA set. MA is responsible for forwarding data to the base station, thereby maximizing the lifetime of the network, which is an NP problem. DAEA adopts integer linear program (ILP) technology to solve the problem:

$$\alpha \times \sigma + \beta \times \rho, \tag{3.89}$$

in which, σ is the energy consumed by each LA; ρ is the number of selected MA; α and β are two balanced factors. Meanwhile, DAEA proposes nine constraining conditions, such as the maximum number limit of MA, the energy limit of MA for forwarding the data to the base station. The ILP algorithm is adopted to solve the problem. Besides, for selecting MA from LA, DAEA proposes three suboptimal solutions: genetic algorithm, k-means algorithm, and the Greedy algorithm.

The three-layer cluster head data fusion structure proposed by DAEA is a tradeoff between energy and delay. The addition of layers can save energy but increases the delay. DAEA is suitable for middle- and small-scale networks.

Bandopadhyay et al. [82] aim to minimize the energy consumption of the nodes in the network. They proposed an energy-efficient hierarchical clustering (EEHC) algorithm. It is a down-top clustering algorithm. It achieves optimal energy consumption by strictly limiting the layers in the cluster and the number of hops between the node and the corresponding cluster head. The algorithm is divided into two stages: initial and extensive.

In the initial stage (also called the single-layer clustering stage), each node has a probability p of becoming the cluster head (this kind of cluster head is regarded as a volunteer cluster head). If a node becomes the cluster head, it will broadcast an inviting message to its neighbor nodes. If the number of hops is lower than k, the node will make the hop number of the inviting message plus 1 and broadcast it by relays, like the nodes in the k-hop range that will receive the inviting message from the cluster head. Noncluster head nodes will choose the closest cluster head to join when they receive the inviting message. In the initial stage, there is another kind of cluster head: the passive cluster head. If a node is not a volunteer cluster head, and it has not received any messages from arbitrary volunteer cluster heads in time t, it will become a passive cluster head.

The extensive stage is a process of multilayer clustering. In the stage, the network is divided into a hierarchical structure with h layers: the clustering of the first layer is located at the lowest layer and the h-layer is the highest layer. In EEHC, the cluster head of the upper layer fuses the data from the lower layer then transmits the fused data to the upper layer. Finally, the cluster head of h-layer will send the fused data to the base station. The specific steps of multilayer clustering are as follows: in EEHC, multilayer clustering is executed down to top. That is, select the cluster head of the first layer; then select the cluster head of the second layer until the h-layer. The method of cluster head selection in each layer is the same as in the initial stage, but the probability p of each node and the radius k of the cluster in each layer are different in the specific operation.

The time complexity of EEHC algorithm is $O(k_1 + k_2 + \cdots + k_h)$, in which k_h is the cluster radius of h-layer. Therefore, EEHC can be adopted in a large-scale sensor network. Besides, since EEHC uses hierarchical structure to collect the data, EEHC can reduce the communication overhead effectively, thereby prolonging the lifetime of the network.

In the paper of Reference [81], the authors proposed a 2-layer hierarchical long-distance communication network, studying the distribution characteristics of the nodes in the network, such as the number of low-level nodes connected to high-level nodes and the total length of the connection between the lower node and the upper node in the hierarchical structure.

The paper from Reference [82] mainly proves by experiments that the energy consumption of WSN improves with the layer number of the clustering in the network, which is important. However, the results of these papers are based on a heuristic method. There is no comprehensive and theoretical basis and analysis for the relationship between the energy consumption of the network and the level of clustering in the clustering mechanism.

Lewis et al. [83] proposed a high energy-efficient multilayer structure for data compression in the sensor network. Their paper calculates the optimal number of cluster heads in each layer and proves by simulation that the multilayer structure can reduce energy consumption of the sensor node.

The paper referenced in [84] proposes an energy-efficient multilayer clustering algorithm (EEMC), which constructs multilayer clustering topology by a top-down mode. It calculates the optimal number of cluster heads and the optimal radius in each layer. Meanwhile, the algorithm proves that the EEMC algorithm will end in $O(\log\log N)$ iterations. The time complexity is $O(N)$ in the worst situation. But the algorithm assumes that the location of the node is known, which needs to configure a GPS for each node.

In Reference [85], a distributed algorithm is proposed to divide the sensor nodes into multiple layers and calculate the optimal number of cluster heads and the radius of the cluster, so that a node can send collected data to the base station through the cluster head and consume the minimum energy.

In Reference [86], a way to determine the number of clusters and layers is analyzed according to the number of nodes and the characteristics of the area. The simulation proves that energy consumption will be reduced along with increasing layer numbers. Besides, the energy consumption is obviously reduced when the layer number is increased from 1 to 2; energy consumption is reduced slowly when the layer number continues to be increased.

In the design of hierarchical clustering structure, the control message is an important energy consumer. Therefore, the energy model needs to be more comprehensive when we study the multilayer clustering algorithm in WSNs. In addition, the relationship between the energy consumption of the network and the level of clustering in the clustering mechanism requires a comprehensive and theoretical basis and analysis. Ying et al. studied the relationship between energy efficiency and clustering layer in clustering WSNs. They proposed a clustering scheme with optimal tiers and energy efficiency for WSNs COTE [87] by considering the energy consumption of communication and the energy consumption of the control message. The algorithm organizes the nodes in the network into an optimal hierarchical structure, thereby minimizing the energy consumption of the network. The complexity of the algorithm is low as well. The detailed process of the algorithm is as follows.

Network model: In order to establish the energy model for a multilayer WSN, in the paper [87], we study a network with a large sensing range, in which the base station is located at the center of the whole sensing area. All sensor nodes in the network are static. The cluster head has enough processing ability to fuse data from multiple nodes into a complete single message. Additionally, we make the following assumptions:

1. The sensor nodes are distributed randomly in the monitoring area.
2. The id of the node is unique.
3. The base station can be connected with the final user. It is located at the center of the whole sensing area. It has continuous power supply without limit. It can communicate with all nodes in the network and obtain the initial deployment situation.
4. The nodes in the WSN are homogeneous. All nodes have equal communication and processing ability. The energy consumption of transmitting a unit of data depends on the distance of the transmission. The energy of the node is limited and uncharged.
5. In the initial stage of each round, the unit length of the control message is m; in the transmission stage, the unit length of the data is 1.
6. The nodes in the sensor networks are distributed evenly. They can communicate with the corresponding cluster head directly.
7. Each sensor node can obtain its location information by GPS.
8. The communication environment is noncompetitive and error free, which means that data does not need to retransmit.

Energy model: When a node transmits a 1-bit message to another node with d distance, the consumed energy is

$$E_{pt} = l(e_t + e_2 \cdot d^2). \tag{3.90}$$

When a node receives a 1-bit message from another node with d distance, the consumed energy is

$$E_{pt} = l \cdot e_r. \tag{3.91}$$

In order to build the energy model, the algorithm sets $e_t = e_r = e_2$. The energy consumption for calculation is far lower than the energy consumption for communication; thus, it is ignored. The energy model is shown in Figure 3.36.

Before constructing the multilayer clustering structure, first, the algorithm analyzes the number of cluster heads in k-layer and the number of noncluster heads in the network model. It obtains the amount of control information in the process of building the j-layer cluster and then obtains the control information consumption for building the j-layer cluster. The algorithm analyzes the energy consumption of the single-layer clustering strategy as well. It obtains the optimal probability of being the cluster head in the first layer. On this basis, the algorithm analyzes the energy consumption of multilayer clustering strategy. It describes the solution of optimal layer in the high energy-efficient multilayer clustering algorithm as an

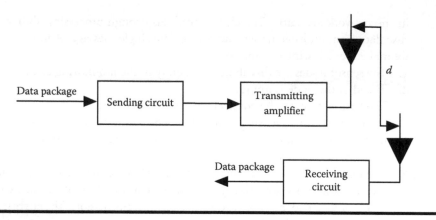

Figure 3.36   Energy model of COTE algorithm.

optimized model with the goal of minimizing the total energy consumption of the network. By solving this model, the optimal layer number and the optimal probability of being the cluster in WSNs multilayer clustering algorithm can be obtained. On the basis of this series of theoretical basic, the COTE algorithm can be divided into three parts: the establishment of the multicluster structure, the design of the routing algorithm based on the clustering structure, and the update of cluster structure and energy.

3.2.4.11.1 The Forming of Multilayer Cluster Structure with Optimal Layer

In the initial stage, the base station broadcasts the time synchronization message. All nodes will operate offset correction on the time domain of the synchronization message after receiving it. Then they set the corrected time as the local time. However, the node will wait for a random period of time instead of forwarding it immediately, so that it can avoid the collision caused by simultaneously forwarding the message of multiple nodes. The node judges whether the channel is idle after the random period of time according to the indicator of signal strength. If the channel is idle, the node will forward the corrected time. When all nodes have forwarded the time synchronization message once, the nodes in the network will keep time synchronization.

After the time synchronization, the node in the network will send its message (the id and the current energy) to the base station. Based on the information of the node, the base station uses the optimal layer number method in the section of theoretical analysis, thereby obtaining the current optimal clustering layer number k_{opt} and the optimal probability of being the cluster in each layer.

Before executing the clustering process, each regular node builds a list in advance. The list includes the id of neighbor nodes, the id of the cluster head, the energy of the cluster head, and the number of layers in the cluster. Each cluster head also builds a list to store the information of its neighbor nodes, which includes the ids of the neighbor nodes and cluster heads, the energy of the cluster heads and nodes, the corresponding cluster head in the upper cluster, and the layer number of the cluster.

After completing this work, the clustering process begins. The algorithm is executed by a top-down mode. First, the cluster head of the first layer is selected and the structure of the first layer is built; then the cluster head of the second layer is selected and the structure of the second layer is built; then this process is repeated for the third layer, fourth layer, and so on until the optimal layer. The time axis of the algorithm is similar to that of LEACH, but the operation adopted by each time slot is different. COTE is executed periodically to avoid the premature death of the node, especially the cluster head, because of over-consumption of energy. At the beginning of the initial stage, each node sends its information (including its current location and energy level) to the base station.

The process of forming the multilayer clustering structure of COTE consists of two stages: the initial stage and the forming of the cluster. Each round begins with the initialization and then executes the process of building the WSN topology structure (i.e., the forming of the multilayer cluster structure).

The cluster forming: The algorithm forms the multilayer clustering structure by the top-down mode. The specific forming process is to first construct the cluster structure of the first layer, and node in the network becomes a candidate cluster head with probability P_1; then each candidate cluster head sends a CANDIDATE message to its neighbor nodes to inform them of its decision, avoiding collisions in the process of exchanging messages with neighbor nodes; after time synchronization, each node is assigned a slot t, and it can only broadcast messages in its own slot with the order of signatures from small to large; each candidate node checks whether its neighbor has more energy. If there is no neighbor with more energy, the candidate node becomes the cluster head; otherwise, the candidate node quits the competition. The candidate node that becomes the cluster head will send a HEAD message to its neighbor nodes to inform them of its decision. The node in the network may receive the HEAD message from one or more cluster heads. The node judges the distance to the corresponding cluster head according to the size of the received message. The node will select the closest cluster head to join, which means the node will send a HEADMEMBER message to the cluster head to inform the cluster head of its decision. In this way, the cluster structure of the first layer is formed. Then the establishment of the cluster structure of the second layer begins. Afterwards, the process will be executed repeatedly until the cluster of optimal layers is established.

3.2.4.11.2 The Routing Algorithm Based on Clustering Structure

The whole routing design of COTE includes two parts: intra-cluster routing and inter-cluster routing.

The intra-cluster routing is similar to that of LEACH, so it will not be introduced here. For inter-cluster routing, the cluster head selects the next-hop cluster head according to the information recorded in the CH list. It also needs to notice the synchronized control problem of data transmission in the process of designing the routing algorithm. The cluster head needs to simultaneously transmit fused data to the cluster head in the upper layer, so that the cluster head in the upper layer can receive the collected data of the same period; that is, inter-cluster transmission needs to be controlled synchronously. The specific process is that the cluster head in the upper layer selects the longest frame as the uniform frame length for data transmission, according to data from the lower layer.

Afterwards, the data is transmitted from bottom to top. The cluster member in the lowest layer sends data to its cluster head; the cluster head sends the data to its cluster head in the upper layer; the cluster head in the final layer sends the data to the base station.

3.2.4.11.3 The Update of Cluster Structure and Energy

The status updates of COTE include those of cluster structure and energy.

The update of cluster structure is executed by rounds periodically. That means the optimal multilayer cluster structure will be built in the initial stage of each round.

For the update of energy, each cluster head sets an energy threshold, which corresponds to the maximum energy value of the cluster members of the cluster except the cluster head. In the process of network operation, once the energy of the cluster head is lower than the threshold, the update of energy begins. First, the cluster head sends its new energy value to its cluster members and its neighbor nodes. The node receives the energy update from its cluster head; it will modify the value in the NCH list if it is a regular node. If a neighbor is also a cluster member of the cluster head, the node will continue to broadcast its residual energy and the energy of its cluster head to its neighbor nodes. The regular node in the network sets another threshold, which is the minimum energy value needed for normal work. Once the residual energy of the regular node is lower than this threshold, the node will inform its neighbor nodes. Then the neighbor nodes will delete the node from the corresponding list and never send it messages.

At this point, the process of the COTE algorithm ends. The pseudocode of the algorithm is as follows.

1. **Initial phase**
   // Calculates the optimal layer $k_{optimal}$ for a given sensor network
   while $(i \geq 2)$
       Calculate the solution$(P_1,\ldots,P_i)$

$$\text{If}\left(\frac{1}{\sqrt{N_o P_1}} + \cdots + \frac{1}{\sqrt{N_o \prod_{j=1}^{i-1}(1-P_j)P_i}} = 1\right)$$

$k_{optimal} = i$

return $k_{optimal}$

else i=i++

end while

2. **Cluster formation phase**

    // Cluster head election

    for j=2 to $k_{optimal}$

        Set initial energy for s_i

        for i=1 to N_0

        if (s_i is eligible)

            If (s_i becomes a candidate node with a probability P_i)

                s_i broadcasts CANDIDATE to all its neighbors.

                if ($E_r(i)>E_r$(other candidate nodes))

                    Clusterhead(i)=1

                    s_i broadcasts a HEAD to all its neighbors

                end if

    //the routing forming

                else if (s_i receives HEAD_IMT)

                    s_i broadcasts its decision (HEAD_MEMBER) to its corresponding CH and registers it to CH's route table

                end if

            end if

        end for

    end for

3.2.4.12 Clustering Algorithms Based on Fuzzy Logic Control

In recent years, the fuzzy logic control method has been used to deal with the undetermined problem in WSNs. In the clustering algorithm, the cluster head is responsible for collecting and fusing data from cluster members and then it needs to transmit the data to the base station. In order to avoid the premature death of a node by consuming too much energy, the cluster head selection needs to consider not only the energy status of the node, but also factors that can affect the energy consumption of the node, such as its location and the topology information of local nodes. Therefore, in general, there are multiple standards for measuring and remarking on whether a node can become the cluster head, such as the energy of the node, communication costs, and quality of service. The cluster head selection needs to consider these relations, constraints, and even competing factors or goals. Therefore, cluster head selection is a multirule decision process. Fuzzy set and fuzzy set logic control theory are powerful tools for solving the multirule decision problem.

Every property of the node can be represented by a different measurement unit in mathematical terms. For example, set the residual energy of the node as 0.5 J and set the number of neighbor nodes as 20. However, it is difficult to give an accurate division standard if a certain rule is used to remark the properties. Usually, opposites without exact boundaries are adopted (e.g., "high and low" of residual energy, "remote and close" of the distance to the base station, "large and small" of the number of neighbor nodes, and "large and small" of the average cost of forming the cluster). These concepts all have a certain degree of ambiguity and so-called fuzzy concepts. Fuzzy set theory is generated by the fuzzy phenomenon of quantitative description.

In general, a fuzzy logic system consists of fuzzifier, rules, inference, and defuzzifier, as shown in Figure 3.37. Fuzzifier maps point x of discourse domain to the fuzzy set on discourse domain X; then the inference infers the fuzzy conclusion according to the fuzzy inference knowledge in the fuzzy rule library and the fuzzy set generated by fuzzifier; finally, defuzzifier defuzzifies it as an accurate y value on discourse domain Y. When a fuzzy logic system solves some special issues, the selection of fuzzifier, rules, inference, and defuzzifier can select the optimal fuzzy logic system by learning. The fuzzy logic system is composed of three parts: rules, which include a series of fuzzy rules; data library (or dictionary), which defines the membership function of a fuzzy set; and inference mechanism, which can execute the inference process and get a reasonable output conclusion according to rules and given truth. The common fuzzy inference models are the Mamdani inference model and the Sugeno fuzzy inference model.

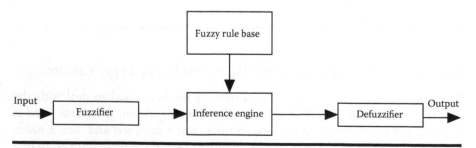

Figure 3.37   Fuzzy logic control system.

Many fuzzy logic control systems are applied extensively in cluster head selection. The basic steps of fuzzy logic control are fuzzier, inference, fuzzy rule library, and defuzzier. Although the input variables of these fuzzy logic control algorithms are different, the theories are similar. Their membership function is triangular or trapezoidal in general, because these two functions are suitable for real-time operation. Input variables are assigned to the membership degree of several layers. The fuzzy if-then rule can be used in the cluster head selection mechanism by these input variables. Fuzzy output sets also include many results and represent the probability of the cluster head selection. Afterwards, different defuzzy methods can be used to obtain an accurate value of output fuzzy sets from the membership function of fuzzy output. The fuzzy logic control algorithm is suitable for a middle-scale network. The experiment result shows that the fuzzy logic control algorithm can prolong the lifetime of the network effectively.

In the following, we will briefly introduce the process of cluster head selection based on fuzzy logic [88].

3.2.4.12.1 The Cluster Head Election Model of Fuzzy Multirule Decisions

Clustering algorithm defines many lingual variables according to many properties of the node, such as residual energy, the communication cost of transmitting to the base station, the average cost of forming the cluster, the number of neighbor nodes, the centroid distance of the cluster, the density of the node, and the centrality degree of the node. These properties are regarded as performance criteria. For example, the evaluation of the energy status of multiple nodes can be described as "higher residual energy" and "lower residual energy"; the evaluation of the status of neighbor nodes can be described as "many neighbor nodes" and "a few neighbor nodes."

According to this performance criteria, the cluster head election model can be built based on multirule. For example, if the residual energy of the node, the communication cost of the node and the base station, the average cost of forming the cluster, and the number of neighbor nodes are chosen as the accordance of the properties of the node in the algorithm, the cluster head election model based on multirule is shown in Figure 3.38.

According to the election model, the cluster head election of multirule decision can be explained as a fuzzy if-then rule:

If there exists a node
with high residual energy AND
with low cost of the communication with the base station AND
with low average cost of forming the cluster AND
with large number of neighbor nodes,
THEN the node is an ideal cluster head.

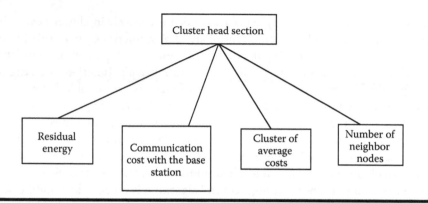

Figure 3.38 The cluster head election model based on multirule decision.

3.2.4.12.2 The Selection of Membership Function

For a fuzzy set, the determining methods of its membership function are various. In the fuzzy decision, there are five experimental methods of determining membership function: horizontal method, vertical method, inference method, parameter estimation, and fuzzy clustering method. The choice of method is related to the specific situation. From the view of practicality, there are five common types of membership function: linear membership function, slotted linear membership function, exponential membership function, hyperbolical membership function, and inverse hyperbolical membership. The types of membership function can be divided into two classifications: linear and nonlinear. Linear membership function assumes that the rate is a constant, which is the change rate of the decision-maker satisfaction level with the solution. Hersh and Caramazza proved that s-shape nonlinear membership function is used usually when the membership function can be explained as an effective function.

3.2.4.12.3 The Combination of Fuzzy Multiple Rules

Assume that there exist N sensor nodes. The properties of the nodes are noted as $U_k = \{u_k^1, u_k^2, \ldots, u_k^N\}$, in which $k \in [1, 4]$ is the number of properties; $u_k^i (1 \leq i \leq N)$ indicates the value of k-property. According to the theory of fuzzy set, it can be known that each property of the node can be regarded as a discourse domain, and the property set can be mapped to the fuzzy set by fuzzy membership function, thus the evaluation of the node can be described quantitatively by fuzzy membership degree. Therefore, four fuzzy sets $A_k, k \in [1, 4]$ can be explained as "high residual energy," "low cost of communication with the base station," "low average cost of forming the cluster," and "large number of neighbor nodes." Four fuzzy sets are defined as follows:

$$A_k = \{(u_k^i, u_{A_k}(u_k^i)) \,|\, u_k^i \in U_k\}, \tag{3.92}$$

in which, u_{A_k} is the membership function of A_k; $u_{A_k}(u_k^i)$ is the membership degree of u_k^i to A_k, indicating the degree of the property value belonging to the corresponding fuzzy subset. For simplicity, the specific instance is as follows.

Assume that the residual energy of node i is 1.5 J, and the number of neighbor nodes is 10, then $u_1^i = 1.5$, $u_3^i = 10$. Assume that by membership function u_{A1} and u_{A2}, the value of residual energy and the number of neighbor nodes, can be mapped as 0.7 and 0.3, respectively. That means the membership degree of the residual energy to "high residual energy" $A1$ in fuzzy set is 0.7; the membership degree of the number of neighbor nodes to "large number of neighbor nodes" $A2$ in fuzzy set is 0.3. That is, the evaluation of the energy status of node i and the number of neighbor nodes can be quantitatively described in the interval [0, 1].

For simplicity, denote $u_{A_k}(u_k^i)$ as u_k^i, then the fuzzy if-then rule of multirule decision cluster head election can be combined by S-ordered weighted averaging fuzzy subset as

$$u\left(u_1^i, u_2^i, u_3^i, u_4^i\right) = (1 - \beta)\frac{1}{4}\sum_{k=1}^{4} u_k^i + \beta \min\{u_k^i\}, \qquad (3.93)$$

in which u is the result of the combination, indicating the membership degree of overall evaluation of node i. In the cluster head election, the node participates in the competition based on this value.

Gupta et al. believe that fuzzy logic can reduce the overhead of cluster head election greatly. The cluster-head election using fuzzy logic (CEFL) algorithm [90] adopts the Mamdani fuzzy logic method to select the cluster head. The inputs of CEFL are energy, density degree, and centrality. Density degree of the node refers to the density of the surrounding nodes at its location. Centrality refers to the degree of closeness to the center of the cluster, which is measured by the sum of the distance square between the node and other nodes in the cluster. These three fuzzy variables are used to optimize the cluster head election, thereby prolonging the lifetime of the network. The energy and density degree can be assigned the membership degrees in three levels: high, medium, and low; the centrality can be assigned the membership degrees in three levels: close, adequate, and far; the fuzzy output set includes seven results: very small, small, rather small, medium, rather large, large, and very large, which indicates the probability of being the cluster head. According to the fuzzy rule, output variables can be obtained by input variables in a series of fuzzy logic methods such as the combination rule. Finally, CEFL defuzzifies the decision by the center of gravity. It finds an accurate value from the fuzzy output membership function, which can represent fuzzy sets best, that is, it finds an optimal clustering node from the fuzzy membership function.

The algorithm is also executed by round, and each round includes the stage of forming the cluster and the stage of data transmission. In the stage of forming the cluster, the base station collects the energy and location information of all sensor nodes; then it uses the if-then rule to select the cluster head according to the collected fuzzy variables; then it broadcasts the cluster head message and forms the cluster. The stage of data transmission is similar to that of LEACH. The experiment results show that the cluster selection algorithm can better prolong the lifetime of the network than LEACH can. However, the algorithm also has some drawbacks. For example, (1) it does not avoid the drawback of centralized algorithm, which means it can only be suitable for the middle-size network with low scalability; (2) the centrality of the input variable nodes in the CEFL does not do a good job of indicating the deployment location of the nodes, which is shown in Figure 3.39.

Assume that the radius of the cluster is R. Four nodes, 1, 2, 3, and 4, are distributed randomly on the radius of small circle r, which communicates with the large circle R. These four nodes are exactly four vertices of a square. Thus, all centrality calculations of the four nodes are the same:

$$d_{12}^2 + d_{13}^2 + d_{14}^2 \qquad (3.94)$$

in which, $d_{12}=d_{13}=d_{24}=d_{34}$; $d_{14}=d_{23}$. The centrality of four nodes is equal, which means the quality of clustering of these four nodes cannot be distinguished by centrality, but only by residual energy or density degree. It is common for the centrality of nodes to be equal. Therefore, it cannot identify the quality of the deployment location.

Algorithm CRPEL [91] is a cluster head election algorithm based on fuzzy logic, aiming to modify the drawbacks of CEFL. The basic idea of the algorithm is that at the beginning of forming the cluster in each round, the input invariables are the current residual energy and the number of adjacent nodes. According to the division rule of fuzzy lingual variables, the residual energy can be divided into four levels and the number of adjacent nodes can be divided into three levels. Combining the division of residual energy and the number of adjacent nodes, 12 fuzzy rules can be defined. Then execute the aggregation operation for the output result of fuzzy inference and form the single fuzzy output set; finally, the accurate output variable can be obtained by centroid defuzzifying, which is the probability of forming the cluster. The node with the highest probability will be selected as the cluster head.

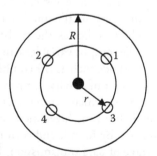

Figure 3.39   The instance of equal centrality of CEFL.

As the classical instance of this kind of algorithm, we will give a detailed introduction for the CRPEL algorithm.

The whole lifetime of the CRPEL protocol is operated periodically by round. Each round includes the stages of forming the cluster and data transmission. In the stage of forming the cluster, each node uses fuzzy logic inference rules to calculate the probability of being the cluster head according to the residual energy and the number of adjacent nodes. Then it broadcasts messages that include the id and the probability of being the cluster head. If the node receives the broadcast message from its neighbor nodes, it compares its probability with the received probability. It will become the cluster head and broadcast this if its probability is greater than other received probabilities; nodes that do not become the cluster head will receive the broadcast message from the cluster head and reply to the message to join in according to the proximity principle. In the stage of data transmission, the cluster head assigns TDMA slots to cluster members. Each cluster head transmits data to the base station according to the slots. The stage of data transmission is similar to that of LEACH and will not be described again.

The pseudocode of the stage of forming the cluster is as follows.

```
1.   initial
2.   for r=0:1:max
3.       S.pro=getp(S.energy, S.number);
4.       if S.pro > S.threshold;
5.           Broadcast Candidate_Msg(ID, S.pro);
6.           while Receiving Candidate_Msg from Si
7.               if S.pro < S.pro
8.                   S.type='N',
9.                   S.pro=Si.pro;
10.              end if
11.          end while
12.          if S.type!='N'
13.              S.type='C';
14.              Broadcast(ID,Head);
15.          end if
16.      else
17.          receive Broadcast(ID, Head);
18.          send(ID, Join_Msg) to ClosestHead
19.      end if
20.  end for
```

r is the current round; S.pro is the probability of forming the cluster; S.energy is the residual energy; S.number is the number of adjacent nodes; function getp () is the cluster head process based on fuzzy logic; S.threshold is the threshold, which is decided by the scale of the node, and a node can become the cluster head if its probability is higher than a certain threshold; S.type is the signature of status. The first line is the initial part; lines 3–5 use fuzzy logic to calculate the probability of being the cluster head for each node, and a node will be selected as the cluster head and broadcast an announcement, which includes id and probability S.pro, if its probability is higher than a certain threshold; in lines 6–11, the node receives the message of the candidate cluster head and joins in the cluster if its probability is lower than the received probabilities; in lines 12–15, the selected node is marked as the cluster head and broadcasts the message of being the cluster head; in lines 17–18, the node receives the broadcast message and joins the closest cluster head.

In the following, we will introduce the kernel of the algorithm (i.e., the cluster head selection based on fuzzy logic). The method is divided into several parts.

3.2.4.12.3.1 Fuzzify   There are two input variables in the fuzzy logic cluster head selection algorithm:

1. Residual energy: the residual energy of the node in each round. When the residual energy of the node is lower than 10%, the membership function of residual energy will be reduced rapidly. The changeable range of residual energy value E is [0, 1], which is just the standard unit and the unit of energy is Joule. For example, when the initial energy is 2 J, the value range multiplies a corresponding coefficient and changes to [0, 1]. Considering the level of fuzzy lingual variables and the scale of the rule table, the set of residual energy variables can be divided into four levels: very low, low, middle, and high. Residual energy is the most important factor in cluster head selection. The subtle change corresponds with different lingual variables.

$$E = \{e = VeryLow, e = Low, e = Middle, e = High\} \qquad (3.95)$$

2. The number of adjacent nodes: the number of adjacent nodes in the range of r_{opt}. r_{opt} is the minimum radium of ideal cluster, and its value is:

$$r_{opt} = \sqrt{\frac{M}{\pi * \pi}}, \qquad (3.96)$$

in which, M is the deployment area; k is the number of clustering nodes. The changeable range of the number of adjacent nodes is [0, 1]. Combining the level of fuzzy lingual variables and the scale of the rule table, the lingual variable set of the number of adjacent nodes can be divided into three levels: Few, Medium, Many. The number of adjacent nodes is also an important factor for cluster head selection. The division also needs to ensure that the change of the number of adjacent nodes corresponds with different lingual variables.

$$N = \{n = Few, n = Medium, n = Many\}. \qquad (3.97)$$

The output variables of fuzzy logic cluster head selection algorithm comprise the clustering probability. The changeable range of clustering probability P is [0, 1], which indicates the probability for becoming the cluster head. Combining the level of fuzzy lingual variables and the scale of the rule table, the lingual variable set of clustering probability can be divided into seven levels: very low, low, little low, medium, little high, high, and very high.

$$P = \{p = VeryLow, p = Low, p = LittleLow, p = Medium,$$
$$p = LittleHigh, p = High, p = VeryHigh\} \qquad (3.98)$$

3.2.4.12.3.2 Fuzzy Logic Rule Table   The fuzzy logic inference rule of the cluster head election adopts the Mamdani-style inference rule. In fuzzy logic inference, the fuzzy inference rule is obtained by refining the experience of skilled operators. The general form of the inference rule for fuzzy logic cluster head election is as follows:

Rule i : if $n = N_i$ and $e = E_i$, then $p = P_i$,

in which, N_i is the set of lingual variables of the number of adjacent nodes {Few, Medium, and Many}; E_i is the lingual variable of residual energy {Very Low, Low, Middle, or High}; P_i is the lingual set of the probability of being the cluster head {Very Low, Low, Little Low, Medium, Little High, High, or Very High}, I= 1, 2, 3,…,12.

Two input lingual variables of fuzzy logic cluster head election are the number of adjacent nodes and residual energy. The set of lingual variables of the number of adjacent nodes can be divided into three levels; the set of lingual variables of residual energy can be divided into four levels, so that the fuzzy inference has $3 \times 4 = 12$ rules. The inference rules are shown in Table 3.2.

Table 3.2   Inference Rules

	Very Low	Low	Middle	High
Few	Very low	Low	Little low	Medium
Medium	Low	Little low	Little high	High
Many	Little low	Medium	High	Very high

The table of fuzzy inference rules combines the membership functions of residual energy, the number of adjacent nodes, and the probability of forming the cluster; the 12 inference rules of the Mamdani-style mode are shown in Figure 3.40. The first rule in Figure 3.40 corresponds to the location (very low) of the first line and the first row of Table 3.2. The explanation is as follows: When the number of adjacent nodes is small and the residual energy is very low, the probability of forming the cluster is very low. Other rules are similar to the first rule.

3.2.4.12.3.3 Defuzzification

The fuzzy set of the probability of output variables forming a cluster can be obtained by adopting Min as T normal form to do the combining operation of the fuzzy set. The accurate probability of forming a cluster can be obtained by defuzzifying by centroid method. For example, when NodeNumber = 0.6 and RemainingEnergy = 0.9, the calculation result of probability = 0.826.

3.2.4.12.3.4 The Election of the Optimal Cluster

In the stage of forming the cluster, each node calculates the probability of being the cluster head based on its residual energy and number of adjacent nodes. The higher the value is, the higher the probability of being the cluster is. In the stage of data transmission, the cluster head needs to manage the cluster members, collect the fused data, and then send the data to the base station. Fuzzy logic calculation of the probability of forming the cluster is obtained by function getp(). The pseudocode of calculating the forming cluster probability is shown in Figure 3.41, in which the energy and

---

1. If(NodeNumber is Few) and (RemainingEnergy is VeryLow) then (probability is VeryLow)

2. If(NodeNumber is Few) and (RemainingEnergy is Low) then (probability is Low)

3. If(NodeNumber is Few) and (RemainingEnergy is Middle) then (probability is LittleLow)

4. If(NodeNumber is Few) and (RemainingEnergy is High) then (probability is Medium)

5. If (NodeNumber is Node_Number) and (RemainingEnergy is VeryLow) then (probability is Low)

6. If (NodeNumber is Node_Number) and (RemainingEnergy is Low) then (probability is LittleLow)

7. If (NodeNumber is Node_Number) and (RemainingEnergy is Middle) then (probability is LittleHigh)

8. If(NodeNumber isNode_Number) and (RemainingEnergy is High) then (probability is High)

9. If(NodeNumber is Many) and (RemainingEnergy is VeryLow) then (probability is LittleLow)

10. If (NodeNumber is Many) and (RemainingEnergy is Low) then (probability is Medium)

11. If(NodeNumber is Many) and (RemainingEnergy is Middle) then (probability is High)

12. If (NodeNumber is Many) and (RemainingEnergy is High) then (probability is VeryHigh)

Figure 3.40   The inference rule of Mamdani-style mode.

```
1.   function p=getp(energy, number)

2.   if energy belong to a particular region

3.      determine the fuction curve of remaining energy

4.   end if

5.   if number belong to a particular region

6.      determine the fuction curve of node number

7.   end if

8.   if (few~=0)

9.      if (verylow~=0)

10.        value of row one=min(energy, number)

11.     end if

12.  end if

13.  if (medium~=0)

14.     if (verylow~=0)

15.        value of row two=min(energy, number)

16.     end if

17.  end if

18.  if (many~=0)

19.     if(verylow~=0)

20.        value of row three=min(energy, number)

21.     end if

22.  end if

23.  p=veryhigh*((0.8+3/20*(veryhigh+16/3))/4+1/2)+0.8*high+
     0.65*littlehigh+0.5*medium+0.35*littlelow+0.2*low+verylo
     w*((0.2 -3/20*(verylow -4/3))/4);

24.  end function
```

Figure 3.41   The algorithm of forming cluster probability.

the number are the input variables of fuzzy logic; p is the probability of forming the cluster. Lines 3–5 are the definition of membership function of residual energy; lines 7–9 are the definition of membership function of the number of adjacent nodes, and the residual energy and the number of adjacent nodes correspond to the lingual variables; lines 10–28 define the fuzzy inference rule table, according to which the fuzzy inference output set can be obtained; lines 30–32 use the merge rule to combine the output fuzzy sets and utilize centroid to defuzzify.

The algorithm in Reference [92] proposes the CHEF algorithm on the basis of the algorithm in Reference [90]. CHEF is a distributed algorithm. Each node uses the if-then rule to calculate the probability of being the cluster head according to two fuzzy variables: residual energy and local distance. The algorithm applies the Mamdani method and COG to calculate the probability. Besides, it limits the number of candidate cluster heads based on the formula $P_{opt}=\alpha\times P$, in which P is the expectation of the cluster head; α is a constant value for defining the probability of being the candidate cluster head. Once a node becomes a candidate cluster head, it will broadcast its candidate probability. When a node receives all of the probabilities, a node will elect itself as the cluster head and broadcast the message of being the cluster head if its probability is higher than all the probabilities. When each noncluster head node receives many messages from the cluster heads, it will choose the closest cluster head and join the cluster. Since CHEF is a distributed algorithm, compared to CEFL, it reduces the energy consumption of sending the message to the base station, thereby prolonging the lifetime of the network.

The algorithms in References [93] and [94] are similar to CHEF. The cluster head selection algorithms adopt three fuzzy variables as the input of fuzzy logic controller, which are residual energy, the distance of centroid, and the data traffic of the network. The output lingual variable is the election probability of the cluster head. These two algorithms utilize the Mamdani method, which can obtain a better performance of the cluster head.

The hierarchical analysis method (AHP) [95] is a centralized cluster head selection mechanism. It uses the multirule decision method to select appropriate cluster heads. Residual energy, mobility, and centroid distance are believed to be three factors that can affect the lifetime of the network. The sink node collects related information from all nodes, then makes a decision according to the multirule decision method based on AHP. The cluster reconstruction is operated self-adaptively according to the mobility and residual energy. The simulation result shows that the hierarchical analysis method can greatly improve the lifetime of the network.

In order to improve the performance of the network as much as possible, especially for energy efficiency and QoS property, FHAP [96] proposes a multirule decision clustering algorithm based on the fuzzy hierarchical analysis method and hierarchical fuzzy integration. The new algorithm combines three aspects and their six properties. Three aspects are energy level, QoS status, and the location of the node, respectively. Each aspect includes two properties. Energy level consists of residual energy and the cost of communication between the node and its neighbors. QoS status consists of the quality of links and the times of reboot; the location of the node includes the number of neighbor nodes and the degree of closeness to the boundary. Each node executes the clustering algorithm in a distributed way. The simulation result shows that the multirule decision clustering algorithm based on the fuzzy hierarchical analysis method and hierarchical fuzzy integration can prolong the lifetime of the network efficiently (Figure 3.42).

Two online routing algorithms proposed in Reference [97] based on fuzzy logic theory: the FML algorithm and the FMO algorithm. The FML and FMO algorithms use fuzzy membership function and the aggregation operator to design weighted cost function, thereby optimizing different routing goals. The paper [97] defines two fuzzy lingual variables: residual energy and required energy. It also designs two membership functions to map these two lingual variables to two fuzzy sets: "high vitality" and "low energy consumption." The value of fuzzy membership degree describes the value of residual energy and the value of communication cost among the nodes, and then the value of membership degree can be used to calculate the weight of cost function.

3.2.4.13 Other Clustering Algorithms

In addition to the classical clustering algorithms we have described up to this point, there are a number of other excellent clustering algorithms that cannot be classified into these categories. Now we will introduce them.

3.2.4.13.1 Deterministic Cluster-Head Selection

Deterministic cluster-head selection (DCHS) algorithm [98] is similar to the LEACH algorithm in general. It also executes periodically by round. The algorithm

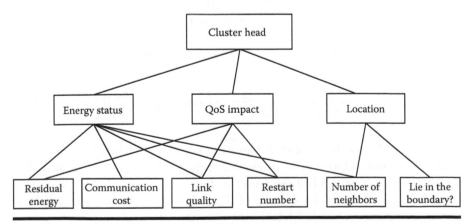

Figure 3.42   Three aspects and six properties of FHAP.

is relatively classical, and it modifies the LEACH clustering algorithm by adjusting the election threshold of the cluster head. Each period also includes the stages of forming the cluster and stable data transmission. In the stage of forming the cluster, each node executes a cluster election method obtained by modifying LEACH and judges whether it can become the cluster head. In the stage of stable data transmission, the cluster member sends data to the cluster head. Then the cluster head fuses the data and transmits it to the base station directly. The stage of forming the cluster of the next round will begin when this stage ends.

An analysis of LEACH reveals that the threshold $T(n)$ does not consider the residual energy of the node in the stage of forming the cluster. Therefore, each node has a chance to be the cluster head even if it has small residual energy. The energy consumption of the cluster head is very large, thus the energy of the node will run out quickly. Once the function of the cluster head interrupts, the whole cluster it manages will stay in a nonmanagement state for a long time. This monitoring area will appear as monitoring data omission, missing, or delay. Therefore, aiming at the drawback in the calculation formula of $T(n)$ in LEACH, DCHS considers the residual energy and modifies $T(n)$. The calculation of $T(n)$ is as follows.

$$T(n)_{new} = \frac{P}{1 - P[r \bmod(1/p)]} \frac{E_{n\_current}}{E_{n\_max}}, \tag{3.99}$$

in which, $E_{n\_current}$ indicates the current residual energy; E_{n_max} indicates the initial energy of the node. It can be known by an analysis of formula 3.99 that the modification of the formula can make the node with lower proportion of current residual energy and initial energy become the cluster head (i.e., the node with lower energy consumption ratio). The experiment results show that the cluster election algorithm can improve the lifetime 20%~30% compared with the LEACH algorithm.

Formula 3.99 considers the residual energy of the node, but the threshold has one drawback. That is, when the network is operated for a while, the current energy $E_{n\_current}$ of all nodes will be very low. Now the threshold $T(n)$ will become low, thereby leading to an imbalance of energy consumption and shortening the lifetime. Therefore, DCHS modifies $T(n)$ again to try to resolve this drawback:

$$T(n)_{new} = \frac{P}{1 - P[r \bmod(1/p)]} \left[\frac{E_{n\_current}}{E_{n\_max}} + \left(r_s div \frac{1}{p} \right) \left(1 - \frac{E_{n\_current}}{E_{n\_max}} \right) \right], \tag{3.100}$$

in which r_s indicates the number of rounds in which a node becomes the cluster head continuously. Once a node is selected as the cluster head, r_s is set as 0. The modification of formula 3.100 can solve the drawback of formula 3.99 effectively. It considers the influence of the energy of the node and the size of the threshold in cluster head selection, which can make the algorithm more reasonable.

3.2.4.13.2 EADEEG

Liu et al. proposed an energy-aware data gathering protocol for WSNs (EADEEG) [99]. It adopts a new parameter of cluster head competition, which can better solve the energy heterogeneous problem. EADEEG also adopts a simple and effective scheduling algorithm for intra-cluster nodes, which can control the density of active nodes and guarantee the coverage requirement by shutting down redundant nodes without increasing additional overhead. Therefore, the algorithm can greatly prolong the lifetime of the network.

The algorithm consists of three parts: forming the cluster, the selection of intra-cluster active nodes, and forming the routing tree.

3.2.4.13.2.1 Forming the Cluster

In the EADEEG protocol, each node needs a neighbor list to store the related information of its neighbor nodes. Each node is identified by a unique integer value, that is, the id is used to indicate the unique identity of the node. At the beginning of each round, each node broadcasts an E_Msg message with r as the radius, which includes the id of the node and the value of the residual energy. All nodes in the range of radius r of node v_i are regarded as the neighbors of the node. Each node updates its neighbor list according to E_Msg from all the neighbors. After updating the neighbor list, each node calculates the average residual energy of all neighbor nodes. E_a represents the average residual energy in the radius of node v_i; v_j is the neighbor of v_i within radius r; m indicates the number of neighbor nodes. Then E_a is

$$E_a = \frac{\sum_{j=1}^{m} V_j \cdot E_{residual}}{m}. \tag{3.101}$$

After obtaining E_a, each node can obtain the time of sending the declaring message, Head_Msg, according to this formula.

$$t = k \times T \times \frac{E_a}{E_{residual}}, \tag{3.102}$$

where k is a real value that is randomly distributed evenly between [0.9,1]; T is the predetermined value of continuous time for the cluster head selection algorithm; $E_{residual}$ represents the residual energy of the node.

If a node has not received Head_Msg message from any neighbor nodes before time t, the node will broadcast a Head_Msg message to its neighbors. If a node has received Head_Msg message before time t, it will quit the cluster head competition. In fact, if a neighbor broadcasts Head_Msg in $(t - \Delta t, t + \Delta t)$, there may exist multiple cluster heads in the same cluster. Slot Δt refers to the time of receiving the HEAD_Msg message in the worst situation. Since the cluster head declaring message Head_Msg is small and has a limited broadcast range, slot Δt is very small. So the probability that multiple nodes broadcast cluster head declaring message in the same cluster is small. The preceding description shows that the control overhead of EADEEG is very small because only a few nodes send a Head_Msg message in the process of cluster head competition. When the process of cluster head selection ends, in order to achieve maximum reduction of energy consumption, a regular node will send a Join_Msg message to the closest cluster head and join the cluster.

3.2.4.13.2.2 The Selection of an Intra-Cluster Active Node

In real application, the number of cluster members will be increased with the improvement of node density, which can increase not only the length of the scheduling packet, but also the energy of broadcasting and receiving the scheduling packet, thereby increasing the time of setting stage and causing additional delays. In fact, when the coverage density is large, there is redundancy in the detection message of sensor nodes, which means that multiple adjacent sensor nodes may collect the same event information. In order to save the energy of the node, it is necessary to remove these redundant messages. Therefore, the algorithm introduces the idea of intracluster coverage. The main idea is that each cluster head approximately calculates the minimum number k of active nodes that satisfy the expectation η for quantity of service; then according to the residual energy state of its neighbor list, it selects $k-1$ nodes with maximum energy as the active nodes in this round. These active nodes are responsible for monitoring tasks, and other nodes will switch to the sleeping state. Since the node is deployed randomly and the energy of the node changes in each round, the node with maximum energy can also be regarded as distributed randomly around the cluster head. It means that selecting active nodes by the maximum energy principle will not affect the overlap ratio η but can prolong the lifetime of a node with low energy.

$$k = \left\lceil \frac{\log(1-\eta)}{\log\left(\dfrac{|A| + 4\sqrt{|A|}\,r_s}{|A| + 4\sqrt{|A|}\,r_s + \pi r_s^2}\right)} \right\rceil, \qquad (3.103)$$

in which η indicates the required coverage ratio (the ratio of the area covered by all active nodes to the whole monitoring area A); k indicates the minimum number of active nodes; r_s is the sensing radius of the node.

3.2.4.13.2.3 Routing Tree Construction

After forming the cluster, the set of cluster head needs to select a cluster head as the unique node CH_b to communicate with the base station, thereby improving the energy efficiency. Since

CH_b only communicates with the sink node, the subgraph formed by all cluster heads needs to be connected. The inter-cluster communication radius is set as $2r_c$ in the algorithm so that it can ensure the connective of the subgraph formed by all cluster heads.

When the cluster head begins to compete to be CH_b, the probability that each cluster head broadcasts Comp_Root_Msg message is defined as:

$$P_b = \rho \times \frac{D(RS_{str}) \times E_a}{D(RS_{max}) \times E_{max}}, \tag{3.104}$$

in which, RS_{str} indicates the signal strength of receiving the "ok" message; RS_{max} indicates the signal strength of sink node broadcasting the "ok" message; D represents the estimation function of the distance; ρ is the coefficient affected by the size of network scale; E_{max} is the initial energy of the node. In a word, in order to reduce the number of the cluster head that completes CH_b, coefficient ρ is used to control the size of the set of candidate clusters. The algorithm sets $\rho = 1$. The paper [99] does not give a detailed explanation for how to obtain the optimal value of ρ according to the network scale.

It is easy to find from formula 3.104 that a cluster head will have more chance to be if it satisfies these conditions: (1) The cluster head is close to the base station; (2) the cluster head has enough energy in its area. The energy consumption of communication for CH_b depends on the distance between itself and the sink node. Obviously, the smaller the distance between CH_b and the base station, the more energy overhead there is for communication. Therefore, the algorithm uses $D(RS_{str})$ as a parameter of electing CH_b. For a cluster head, the larger the value of E_a, the more the residual energy its neighbor has. It can be known by the previous communication model that the energy consumption of communicating with the sink node is far more than with other nodes. In order to prolong the lifetime of the sensor network, CH_b needs to locate at the area with abundant energy. Therefore, the algorithm uses E_a as the second parameter for electing CH_b. High E_a means the energy of the area is abundant.

In Figure 3.43a, graph G is formed by seven cluster heads, and node 1 is the unique candidate cluster head for CH_b. At the beginning of forming the aggregating tree, node 1 sends the message Comp_Root_Msg (1, 1, 0.4) to its neighbor cluster heads (i.e., node 2 and node 3). When node 2 and node 3 receive the message (1, 1, 0.4), they modify the id of the forwarding node in the message and broadcast the new message to their neighbor cluster heads, (1, 2, 0.4) and (1, 3, 0.4), respectively. Note that node 5 is the shared neighbor cluster head of node 2 and node 3. The algorithm assumes that node 5 receives (1, 2, 0.4) first, then node 5 sends the modified message (1, 5, 0.4) to the neighbor cluster head and discards the message (1, 3, 0.4) from node 3. According to this process, each cluster head can know its father on the aggregating tree, so that it is easy to build an aggregating tree. Figure 3.43b describes the process of forming the aggregating

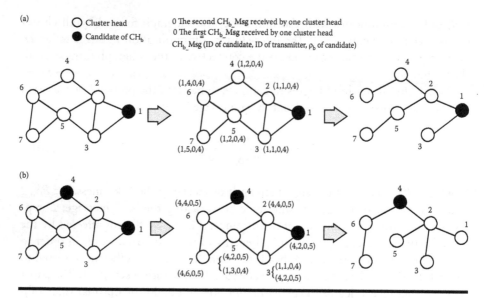

Figure 3.43 Inter-cluster routing tree construction in EADEEG.

tree by multiple candidate cluster heads in graph G. The algorithm specifies that the candidate cluster head with high P_b will become CH_b successfully. Since each cluster head can send two messages at most, the control overhead is small.

The advantages of EADEEG are as follows.

1. It proposes a cluster head competition mechanism, which has lower control overhead than other protocols, such as LEACH and HEED. It can ensure the even distribution of the cluster head.
2. EADEEG can solve the energy heterogeneous problem effectively by introducing a new parameter for the cluster head competition, thereby prolonging the lifetime of the network.
3. EADEEG protocol has a good scheduling function without additional control overhead, avoiding the communication overhead caused by node redundancy.
4. The paper [99] specifically analyzes the number of cluster heads, the optimal radius of the cluster, the complexity of the protocol, and storage overhead. It also proves the great performance of EADEEG with a lot of simulations.

However, EADEEG has some drawbacks.

1. The clustering algorithm of the EADEEG protocol will generate some seams areas in the monitoring area under some situations.
2. In the clustering algorithm of the EADEEG protocol, in order to ensure that the subgraph is connected, the inter-cluster communication radius is set as

$2r_c$, but the assumption cannot ensure that the set of cluster heads generated by the distributed algorithm is connected.

3. Similar to the reason in (2), the low boundary of the number of cluster heads generated by the EADEEG clustering algorithm has to be re-estimated as well.

3.2.4.13.3 BPEC

Aiming to solve the drawbacks of EADEEG, Zhou et al. proposed a new energy-aware distributed clustering algorithm (BPEC) [100], which uses the ratio of the average residual energy of the neighbor nodes against the residual energy of the node as the primary parameter and uses the degree of the node as the second parameter. The paper [100] defines three types of status for the sensor nodes: candidate, cluster head, and cluster member, which are represented by white, black, and gray, respectively. The process of the algorithm is as follows.

First, the stage of obtaining neighbor information starts at the beginning of clustering in each round. The time length is predetermined as TND. Then the key period begins, which is the stage of determining the cluster head, and the time length is THD. Finally, the stage of node ascription is when the noncluster head node chooses a cluster to join, and the time length is predetermined as TNA. Each node in the network first performs time synchronization, then launches the algorithm and completes the algorithm at the same time.

Step 1: A node broadcasts the Sensor_Msg packet with r_c as the communication radius, which includes the id of the node and the value of the residual energy E_r. Then, the node receives the Sensor_Msg from all neighbor nodes. It needs to calculate and update the value of average residual energy E_a and degree of the node d in the local information data structure NLI. Assume an arbitrary node v_i, whose neighbor is v_j. Calculate the value of E_a first: $E_a = \dfrac{1}{d} \sum\limits_{j=1}^{d} E_r$.

Here, E_r is used to represent the residual energy of node v_j. Then calculate the time t of sending the declaring message according to the following formula:

Scenario 1. When the node satisfies the condition $E_r > E_a$, it holds that

$$t_1 = \frac{E_a}{E_r} \times \frac{1}{d+1} \times T_{HD} \times \rho. \tag{3.105}$$

Scenario 2. When the node satisfies the condition $E_r \leq E_a$, it holds that

$$t_2 = \frac{T_{HD}}{2} + \left(1 - \frac{E_r}{E}\right) \times \frac{T_{HD}}{2} \times \rho. \tag{3.106}$$

Here, E in formula 3.106 is the initial energy of the node, and it is a random integer, uniformly distributed in [0.9, 1]. The function of E is reducing the probability that two nodes select the same t value.

Step 2: The stage of cluster head competition begins with time of THD (from 0 to THD) when the TND is beyond the time. If a node has not received the Head_Msg packet from any neighbor nodes before time t, it will broadcast the Head_Msg packet to its neighbors and declare itself the cluster head; otherwise, it will quit the cluster head competition and become a noncluster head node. Once the node determines its role, it modifies the state in the local information data structure NLE. If it is the cluster head, the state is changed from white to black; if it is a noncluster head node, the state is changed from white to gray.

Step 3: After the stage of determining the cluster head, the stage of node ascription begins with time length of TNA. The noncluster head node may have received the Head_Msg packet from several different cluster heads. In order to join the cluster, the node will send a Join_Msg packet to the cluster head with maximum residual energy by checking its neighbor list NT[]. The node whose state is gray needs to update its parent further, making the indicator refer to the id of its cluster head. The cluster head receives the Join_Msg packet from all cluster members and deletes the node that does not belong to its cluster from its neighbor list NT[]. Meanwhile, it updates the d value of local information NLI. Now the process of clustering ends.

BPEC has the following characteristics.

1. The BPEC clustering algorithm is a fully distributed parallel algorithm with good scalability; it is suitable for the large-scale WSN.
2. The cluster head selection solution of the BPEC clustering algorithm can ensure that the node with relatively more energy is selected as the cluster head, which can make each node consume the energy in balance, thereby prolonging the lifetime of the whole network.
3. BPEC can avoid making the boundary node the cluster head, thus avoiding isolated nodes.

3.2.4.13.4 Distributed Weight-Based Clustering Algorithm

Distributed Weight-based Clustering algorithm (DWBCA) [101] is a distributed clustering algorithm based on weight. This kind of clustering algorithm based on weight and the cluster head selection based on the fuzzy set have the same idea but different methods. Compared with this kind of algorithm, the cluster head selection method based on the fuzzy set has better accuracy. DWBCA calculates the weight of being the cluster head according to four parameters: the residual energy, the sum of the distance between the node and all noncluster head neighbor nodes, the degree of the node, and the distance between the node and the base station.

In DWBCA, the node in the network has three types of status: ready status, cluster head, and cluster member. At the beginning of the algorithm, the node stays in ready status. When the node self-elects to be the cluster head, the status switches from ready to cluster head. When the node decides to join a cluster, its status is changed to cluster member.

The DWBCA clustering algorithm includes five steps.

Step 1: The base station broadcasts a BS_INFO message to the whole network. After receiving the message, a node can estimate its distance from the base station according to the strength of the received signal.

Step 2: This stage is that of finding neighbors. Each node broadcasts NBRD (the neighbor finding message), which includes the id of the sender, residual energy, and the distance to the base station. After receiving the NBRD message, the neighbor node will update its neighbor list and estimate the distance between itself and the sender according to the strength of the received signal.

Step 3: After receiving the NBRDs of all neighbor nodes, the node will calculate its weight W. The calculation formula of W is

$$W = (w_1 + E_r) + (w_2 \times |D_n - \delta|) + \left(w_3 \times \frac{D_s}{N} \right) + \left(w_4 \times \frac{D_B}{D} \right), \qquad (3.107)$$

in which D_s is the distance between the node and all noncluster head neighbor nodes; D_n is the distance between the node and the base station; N is the degree of the node; D is the communication range of the sensor node; w_1, w_2, w_3, and w_4 are the weight coefficients; δ is the number of intra-cluster cluster members.

Step 4: The node will broadcast its weight to neighbor nodes. If the weight of the node is lower than that of the neighbor nodes, the node will become the cluster head.

Step 5: If the number of intra-cluster members is too large, a new cluster head needs to be selected to avoid excessive workload. After completing the cluster head selection, the noncluster head node will choose the closest cluster head to join.

EHPE [102], EESH [103] and MWBC [104] proposed distributed clustering algorithms to improve the performance of the network and prolong the lifetime of the network. In these algorithms, cluster head selection depends on several properties, such as the ideal degree of the node, current energy, the number of surviving neighbors, transmitting power, the quality of links, and the relative location of the node. Without considering the relation among the properties, the properties generate a combined value by the weighted sum method; then the cluster head will be selected by the probability or density method. The simulation result shows that all of these algorithms can prolong the lifetime of the network. As we introduced earlier, however, deciding the weight of each property by a cut and dry method lacks theoretical accuracy compared with the cluster head election method based on the fuzzy set.

3.2.4.13.5 EATCP

An Efficient Aggregation Timing Control Protocol (EATCP) [105] is an efficient aggregation timing control protocol. It builds the network topology into a cluster-tree construction and proposes an efficient aggregation timing control protocol based on the tradeoff between data effectiveness and energy. The timing control protocol adjusts the period of aggregation dynamically according to the quality of data aggregation, so that the most reasonable data aggregation period can be obtained, thereby improving the efficiency of data collection.

The topology of data aggregation protocol is built into the cluster-tree structure. The cluster-tree network means that the nodes in WSNs form different clusters at first, and the cluster head forms the reverse multicast tree with the sink node. The protocol determines the equal number C of nodes for each cluster. Meanwhile, it assumes that only cluster members can monitor the data, while the cluster head is only responsible for processing the data and delivering the data from the cluster member, instead of monitoring the data.

EATCP can be divided into the stages of forming and data aggregation. These stages are executed periodically. Assume that N_{rec} is the set number of received monitoring data; N_{opt} is the set number of ideal monitoring data; T_n is the length of the current data aggregation period; T_{n+1} is the length of the next data aggregation period.

3.2.4.13.5.1 Stage of Forming

Step 1: The sink node broadcasts "tree request information" in the whole network.

Step 2: After receiving the request information, the leaf nodes reply to the sink node. This step can selectively execute three data aggregation technologies: (1) full aggregation technology (i.e., multiple-entry-single-out aggregation technology). Each cluster head only sends one packet after the data aggregation operation; (2) layer-by-layer aggregation technology. In a cluster, if the hop number between each cluster member and the cluster head is different, which means that distances between some nodes and the cluster head are one hop while the distances between other nodes and the cluster head are two hops, the cluster head will execute the aggregation operation twice according to the hop number and generates two packets to send to the upper node. (3) no data aggregation operation.

Step 3: The sink node will set the ideal number (N_{opt}) of monitoring packets according to the depth of the aggregation tree, maximum delay, and the real application. Then it calculates the length of the next data aggregation period

(T_{n+1}) and broadcasts it in the whole network. After these three steps, all cluster heads and the sink node know the length of T_{n+1}.

3.2.4.13.5.2 The Stage of Data Aggregation

Step 1: The sink node multicasts "data request information" to the cluster heads; it includes the maximum data aggregation period (T) determined by the real application.

Step 2: The cluster head forwards "data request information" to each node in the cluster.

Step 3: The nodes in the cluster turn back to monitor the data immediately upon receiving the "data request information." After the predetermined time T_{n+1}, the cluster head executes data aggregation operation and sends the aggregated data to the sink node. The packet after aggregating includes the number of packets that participate in the aggregation. The sink node will use the number to calculate the appropriate T_{n+1} for next request task.

Step 4: Repeat steps 1–3 until the next query begins. In the next request, the sink node calculates the maximum aggregation period (T) according to the packet number received in the last request. The rule is that if the number of reply is small, increase T; if the number of reply is large, decrease T. EATCP only needs low control overhead to build the topology into the cluster-tree structure. Meanwhile, it can greatly improve the efficiency of data aggregation by adjusting the time needed. However, it does not consider the differentiated service for the data.

3.2.4.13.6 CLUBS

In Reference [106], Nagpal and Coore proposed a new distributed clustering algorithm CLUBS. The algorithm makes full use of local broadcasts to the cluster. The convergence time of the algorithm is related to the local node density.

CLUBS clustering algorithm's characteristics are as follows:

1. Each node in the network has to belong to a cluster head.
2. The maximum radius of all the clusters has to be consistent.
3. The cluster needs to support intra-cluster communication, that is, the cluster members can exchange information conveniently.

In the algorithm, the maximum distance between the cluster head and its cluster members is two hops. The specific process of clustering is as follows: In the stage of self-election, each node in the network generates a random integer value in a certain range; then the node executes decrement operation for the random integer gradually. If the node has not been interfered from its neighbors in the process that the integer is decreased to 0, it will declare itself the cluster head and broadcast RECRUIT message to nodes within two hops. When a neighbor node receives the message, the node stops the decrement operation for the random value immediately and accepts the request to join the cluster. If a node has joined a cluster, the node will be regarded as a "follower." Since CLUBS allows a certain overlap area among the clusters, a "follower" node can join other clusters if it receives a RECRUIT message from other cluster heads. If a node detects communication conflict in the process of decreasing progressively of random integer, it can be explained that multiple cluster heads launch a request to the node. Therefore, the node will stop the decrement operation and become a follower; it will find the appropriate cluster to join in after the communication conflict.

CLUBS is easy to achieve. It can be applied in an asynchronous network with great success. However, CLUBS has drawbacks: If adjacent cluster heads become neighbor nodes of each other, the cluster tends to be crushed because of communication conflict, and cluster heads need to be selected again.

3.2.4.13.7 MOCA

MOCA [107] is a random distributed multihop overlapped clustering algorithm. In the algorithm, Youssef et al. believe that there should be a certain overlapped area among the adjacent clusters, thereby achieving inter-cluster communication, topology discovery, positioning, and recovery after failure. After completing the clustering of the MOCA algorithm, the node in the network becomes a cluster head or a cluster member. Besides, the distance (unit: hop) between the node and its adjacent cluster head is no greater than k, which is regarded as the radius of the cluster in general.

The specific clustering process of the algorithm is as follows: At the beginning of the algorithm, each node in the network has a probability p to be the cluster head. When node A self-elects as the cluster head, it will broadcast its id to its neighbor nodes within its transmission range. Neighbor nodes will check the number of the hop that the packet passes after receiving the message. If the hop number is lower than k, node B will add 1 to the hop number and continue to broadcast the packet. Therefore, all nodes within k hops of cluster head A will receive the broadcast message from cluster head A. Besides, a node may receive the broadcast messages from multiple cluster heads at the same time. Afterwards, all the nodes that have received the message will send a joining message to cluster head A, which includes the ids of the cluster heads it knows. Therefore, after cluster head A receives the joining message from the node, it can judge whether the sending node is the boundary node by the number of cluster heads in the message. If the number of the cluster heads is greater than 1, the node is a boundary node, which means the node is located at the area overlapped by multiple clusters.

In MOCA, the number of clusters and the size of overlap area among the clusters are controlled by p. Therefore, the algorithm has great scalability. Moreover, since there exists a certain overlapped area among the clusters, the algorithm has great tolerance as well.

3.2.4.13.8 HCC

In the Hierarchical Control Clustering (HCC) [108] algorithm, each node in the network has a chance to launch a clustering request. If multiple nodes launch the clustering request at the same time, the node with the minimum id has the priority, and the other nodes need to stop the request.

The clustering process of HCC consists of two stages: forming the tree and forming the cluster. The stage of forming the tree is an establishment process of distributed breadth first search with the node that launches the clustering request as the root. In the network, node A broadcasts a message to its neighbor nodes every p unit times, which includes the minimum distance r between the node and the root with hop as the unit. The neighbor node B of A will check its routing distance to the root after receiving the message. If node B has no path to the root or the distance between node B and the root through node A is shorter than the other path, node B selects node A as its father and updates the path to the root and path hops. Afterwards, node B will broadcast the message in the network, which includes its id, id of its father, id of the root, and the size of the subtree. When the father node receives the broadcasting message, it will check whether the size of the subtree has changed. If it has changed, the father will update its subtree size correspondingly.

In the stage of forming the cluster, if the subtree size of a node is beyond the parameter k, the node will begin the clustering process based on its subtree. The parameter k controls the final result of clustering by controlling the subtree size. If the subtree size is lower than $2k$, the whole subtree will form a single cluster and the node will become the cluster head. Otherwise, the nodes in the cluster will form multiple clusters.

The clustering algorithm can adjust changeable situations of the network, such as in the situation of mobile nodes.

3.2.4.13.9 FLOC

Fast Local Clustering Service (FLOC) [109] is a distributed clustering algorithm. It divides the network into clusters of uniform size, and the overlap between clusters is very small. In FLOC, the regular nodes can be divided into i-band node and o-band node according to the distances among the nodes. The i-band node is close to the cluster head. Thus, it can suffer little interference and generally cannot lose packets. The o-band node is the opposite. Since it is far from the cluster head, it is easy for it to suffer interference and lose packets. The i-band node has better communication ability; thus, it is the main reference factor of the clustering protocol in FLOC.

The specific process of FLOC is as follows.

In the initial stage, node A waits a while. If the node receives the candidate message from B during this period of time and it does not belong to any cluster, the node will become an i-band cluster member of B. If the node has been the i-band cluster member of other candidate cluster heads, it will become an o-band cluster head of *B*; if node *A* has not received any informing messages in the waiting time, node *A* will elect itself as the candidate cluster head and broadcast the candidate message to its neighbors.

If there exist no o-band cluster members around a candidate cluster head, it will send inviting messages to its neighbors. The node will become the normal cluster head after i-band cluster members join the cluster.

If a node cannot join any cluster as an i-band cluster member, it will choose a close cluster head and join the cluster as an o-band cluster member. Afterwards, the node will quit the original cluster and join the new cluster as an i-band cluster member if it receives the candidate message from other candidate cluster heads.

FLOC has great convergence time, which is O(1). Therefore, FLOC is suitable for a large-scale sensor network. Besides, since an o-band cluster member can switch to an i-band cluster member of other clusters, FLOC possesses good tolerance and recovery.

3.2.4.13.10 Passive Clustering

In the clustering algorithms previously explained, the node participating in clustering needs to broadcast information to its neighbor nodes repeatedly. However, it causes large overhead to collect the information of neighbor nodes in WSNs. Besides, almost all clustering solutions require an initial clustering stage before data transmission in the network layer. The passive clustering strategy [110] uses the information of users' packets by listening to clusters without sending control messages periodically; it does not need an initial clustering process before the stage of data transmission; periodical mobility will not cause clustering again, which means that it does not need to cluster again; it can operate clustering without the overall information of neighbor nodes. The strategy can be used in various on-demand routing algorithms combining on-demand routing protocols.

The passive clustering strategy utilizes the information with data tasks, so that it can solve the logic separation and the broken chainage problem better. Clustering stability and convergence time are two advantages of the passive clustering strategy. In order to improve the clustering stability and accelerate the clustering convergence, the algorithm adopts a new cluster head selection method (i.e., the First DeclarationWins (FDW) principle), used in initial clustering and clustering maintenance.

The FDW principle has the node that first sends the packet become the cluster head; it is responsible for managing other nodes in its wireless overlap area. The new cluster head selection principle does not require clustering again and maintaining the weighted rule. Besides, FDW can solve the separation problem this way: If the cluster has not obtained a gateway for a period, the cluster head declares it will quit as cluster head, then other nodes in the cluster can obtain the identity of cluster head by competing.

The process of passive cluster and cluster maintaining are as follows.

Passive clustering utilizes the source D of the MAC packet to collect the information of neighbor nodes and broadcasts the clustering status of its neighbor nodes. The node has four clustering types of status and one middle status: (1) initial status, (2) cluster head, (3) ordinal node, (4) gateway, (5) cluster head ready.

The algorithm is described as follows.

1. The clustering sublayer adds two pieces of clustering status information in each MAC packet to be sent. If the current status of the node is cluster head ready, its status will switch to the cluster head status before labeling its status information. For the received packet, the clustering sublayer takes down and obtains the status information of the sender, then it executes the passive clustering algorithm and hands over the packet to the MAC layer.

2. The node stays in initial status after booting up. The status stays unchanged before the node receives the MAC packet. If the status of the sender is not the cluster head, the status of the node will be changed to cluster head ready. If a node sends a packet successfully before receiving any packet from other cluster heads, the node will become the cluster head; otherwise, it will become a regular node.

3. Except for the cluster head, all nodes in other statuses need to maintain their lists of neighbor cluster heads. Once the node receives the packets from other cluster heads, it needs to update its cluster head list and check the number of active cluster heads as well. When the cluster head list of noncluster head nodes is empty, the node will switch to the initial status. If a node in cluster head status receives the packet form other cluster heads, it will switch to ordinal node status.

4. In the process of clustering, each node needs to collect the information of neighbor nodes and store the information, such as adjacent node D, status, and idle time. If the idle time of the neighbor node is beyond the threshold, it will be deleted.

5. When the clustering sublayer boots up, the node will check the freshness of its list (cluster head list and neighbor node list) without an accurate timer when it sends or receives MAC packets. The information of clustering status is in the MAC packet, which is the additional overhead in the passive clustering algorithm. Passive clustering does not need special and explicit control packets or signals. The algorithm does not need the initial clustering stage before data transmission and communication. The algorithm can be executed without overall information of neighbor nodes. However, the clustering structure built by the algorithm may not be reasonable, and it is not easily controlled.

3.2.4.13.11 TCCA

In Reference [111], Selvakennedy and Sinnappan proposed the Time Controlled Clustering Algorithm (TCCA). TCCA controls the generation of the cluster by time stamping messages and time of lifetime (TTL).

The clustering process of TCCA is executed by round. Each round is divided into the stages of forming the cluster and stable status. The stage of forming the cluster is the process of cluster head selection and forming the cluster. The stage of stable status is the process of periodic data dissemination. The data dissemination includes data collection, fusion, and sending the data to the sink node.

In the stage of forming the cluster, each node i generates a random number R in [0, 1]. If R is lower than threshold $T(i)$, the node i will become the cluster head. The calculation of $T(i)$ is as follows:

$$T(i) = \max\left(\frac{P}{1 - P\left(r \bmod \frac{1}{P}\right)} \times \frac{E_{residual}}{E_{max}}, T_{min} \right), \quad \forall i \in G, \qquad (3.108)$$

in which p is the percent of the number of cluster heads against the total number of the node; r is the current round; G is the set of nodes that have not become the cluster head in the recent $1/p$ round; $E_{residual}$ is the residual energy of the node; E_{max} is the maximum energy; T_{min} is the minimum threshold.

After node A elects itself as the cluster head, it will send ADV message to its neighbors, which includes the id of the node, TTL, residual energy, and the time stamp. When a neighbor node receives the ADV message from A, the neighbor node will forward the message until TTL turns to 1. The radius of the cluster can be controlled by controlling the TTL of ADV. All noncluster head nodes that receive the ADV message from node A will check the TTL of the message. If node B has not received any ADV messages from any cluster head, node B will join the cluster of A and store the TTL of the ADV message. If node B has received ADV messages from other cluster heads, it will compare the TTL. If the TTL of current ADV message is lower than the one of the ADV before, it means node A is closer to node B. Therefore, node B will join A cluster and replace the stored value by TTL of the ADV message from node A. Once node B decides to join A cluster, node B will send a requiring message to node A, which includes the id of node B, the id of cluster head A, the stamp of ADV, and TTL. The time stamp can help the cluster head know the approximate distance between itself and its cluster members. The cluster head can obtain the hops between itself and its cluster members by TTL of the requiring message.

TCCA rotates the cluster head periodically, which can reduce the energy of data forwarding effectively. Besides, the radius of the cluster can be controlled by the TTL of the ADV message in TCCA. Therefore, TCCA has great scalability, which is suitable for large-scale WSNs.

3.2.4.13.12 DBC

Different from the general clustering protocol, DBC divides the cluster first and then selects the cluster head based on density. In DBC, each node calculates its average value L of the link length and variance first and then broadcasts the variance. When the node receives the variances of all the neighbors, each node calculates the average variance and then decides to join a cluster according to the following formula.

$$\begin{cases} \textit{join the cluster}, & \textit{if } l_j < (L - \mu) \\ \textit{leave the cluster}, & \textit{if } l_j \geq (L - \mu)' \end{cases}$$

in which l_j is the length of each link of the node. After forming the cluster, DBC will select the cluster head according to the residual energy and the number of neighbor nodes. The process is as follows.

1. Each node broadcasts a neighbor discovery message to collect the information of its neighbors.
2. Each node calculates the number of its neighbors according to the exchanged messages.
3. Each node multicasts a control message to other nodes in the cluster, which includes the residual energy and the number of neighbors.
4. The node that has the most neighbors and minimum residual energy still beyond the threshold will be selected as the cluster head.

DBC can establish an effective hierarchical routing to the base station. The simulation result proves that it can be applied in a large-scale WSN.

3.2.4.13.13 Public Problems

The clustering algorithm has various advantages as a hierarchical topology control method. Therefore, it has gained a lot of attention and research recently. Many good clustering algorithms are proposed, and the clustering mechanism is increasingly mature and improved. On the basis of the works of the pioneers, we found some aspects that need attention and research, and we summarize those as follows.

1. In the WSN, the lifetime of the network does not end when a few nodes die. How should one keep connectivity and overlap in the network when there are dead nodes, to allow the network to operate? This requires further study.
2. At present, the wireless channel model and energy model used in the research of clustering algorithm of WSNs are relatively simple and ideal, and there is a gap between the real network and the actual network, such as the physical interference and factors of severe environments. Some specific situation must be investigated, and the model needs to promise a certain degree of accuracy after theoretical study.
3. The study of the algorithms in wireless networks, especially the clustering algorithm, is usually based on the two-dimensional network model. In real

network application, however, nodes are deployed in a three-dimensional space. Therefore, achieving the extension of three-dimensional space for studying the algorithm is one challenge we face.

4. At present, the network model based on clustering algorithm usually assumes that node power is controllable, and the symmetric links between the nodes can be bidirectional for communication. Considering the use of the directional antenna, the clustering algorithm based on single-direction network and the weighted network deserves to be studied.

5. The research of some aspects such as the delay and coverage problems in the clustering network are few, which are also the focus point for further study. Since the clustering mechanism has many advantages, other problems based on the clustering mechanism can be objects for future research.

Bibliography

1. C. H. R. Lin, M. Gerla. *A Distributed Architecture for Multimedia in Dynamic Wireless Networks*. Global Telecommunications Conference, 1995. GLOBECOM'95. IEEE. IEEE, 2002, vol. 2:1468–1472.
2. M. Gerla, J.T.C. Tsai. Multicluster, mobile, multimedia radio network. *Wireless Networks*, 1995, 1: 255–265.
3. P. Basu, N. Khan, T. D. C Little. A mobility based metric for clustering in mobile ad hoc networks. In: *Proceedings of IEEE ICDCSW' 01*.Washington, DC: IEEE Computer Society, 2001, 413–418.
4. S. Basagni. Distributed clustering for ad hoc networks. International Symposium on Parallel Architectures, Algorithms and Networks, 1999, 310–315.
5. M. Chatterjee, S. K. Das, D. Turgut. WCA: A weighted clustering algorithm for mobile ad hoc networks. *Journal of Clustering Computing IEEE*, 2002, 5(2): 193–204.
6. S. Hedetniemi, A. Liestman. A survey of gossiping and broadcasting in communication networks. *Networks*, 1998, 18(4): 319–349.
7. Z. J. Haas, J. Y. Halpern, L. Li. Gossip-based ad hoc routing. In: *Proceedings of the IEEE INFOCOM*. New York: IEEE Communications Society, 2002, 1707–1716.
8. J. Kulik, W. R. Heinzelman, H. Balakrishnan. Negotiation based protocols for disseminating information in wireless sensor networks. *Wireless Networks*, 2002, 12(8): 169–185.
9. C. Intanagonwiwat, R. Govindan, D. Estrin, J. Heidemann. Directed diffusion for wireless sensor networking. *IEEE/ACM Transaction on Networking*, 2003, 11(1): 2–16.
10. D. Braginsky and D. Estrin. Rumor routing algorithm for sensor networks. In: *Proceedings of the First ACM International Workshop on Wireless Sensor Networks and Applications (WSNA)*, Atlanta, GA, USA, 2002, 9: 22–31.
11. B. Karp and H. Kung. GPSR: Greedy perimeter stateless routing for wireless networks. In: *Proceedings of the Sixth Annual International Conference on Mobile Computing and Networking (MOBICOM)*, Boston, MA, USA, 2000, 8: 243–254.
12. D. Niculescu and B. Nath. Trajectory based forwarding and its applications. In: *Proceedings of the Ninth Annual International Conference on Mobile Computing and Networking (MOBICOM)*, San Diego, CA, USA, 2003, 260–272.

13. R. C. Shah and J. M. Rabaey. Energy aware routing for low energy ad hoc sensor networks. In: *Proceedings of the Wireless Communications and Networking Conference (WCNC)*, Orlando, FL, USA, 2002, 350–355.
14. C. Schurgers and M.B. Srivastava. Energy efficient routing in wireless sensor networks. In: *Proceedings of Military Communications Conference on Communications for Network-Centric Operations: Creating the Information Force*, McLean, VA, USA, 2001, 357–361.
15. K. Sohrabi, J. Gao, V. Ailawadhi et al. Protocols for self-organization of a wireless sensor network. *IEEE Personal Communications*, 2000, 7(5): 16–27.
16. X. Liu. A survey on clustering routing protocols in wireless sensor networks. *Sensors*, 2012, 12: 11113–11153.
17. W. Heinzelman, A. Chandrakasan, H. Balakrishnan et al. Energy-efficient communication protocol for wireless microsensor networks. In: *Proceedings of the 33rd Annual Hawaii International Conference on System Sciences*, Hawaii, 2000, 10–18.
18. W. B. Heinzelman, A. P. Chandrakasan, H. Balakrishnan. An application-specific protocol architecture for wireless microsensor networks. *IEEE Transaction on Wireless Communication* 2002, 1: 660–670.
19. P. Tillapart, T. Thumthawatworn, P. Pakdeepinit, T. Yeophantong, S. Charoenvikrom, J. Daengdej. Method for cluster heads selection in wireless sensor networks. In: *Proceedings of the 2004 IEEE Aerospace Conference*. Chiang Mai: IEEE Press, 2004, 3615–3623.
20. S. Muruganathan, D. Ma, R. Bhasin et al. A centralized energy-efficient routing protocol for wireless sensor networks. *IEEE Communications Magazine*, 2005, 43(3): 8–13.
21. S. Ghiasi, A. Srivastava, X. Yang et al. Optimal energy aware clustering in sensor networks. *Sensors*, 2002, 2(7): 258–269.
22. F. Bajaber, I. Awan. Dynamic/static clustering protocol for wireless sensor network. In: *Proceedings of the 2nd European Symposium on Computer Modeling and Simulation*, IEEE Computer Society, 2008, 524–529.
23. LEACH-CCB: S. H. Manjula, E. B. Reddy, K. Shaila, L. Nalini, K. R. Venugopal, L. M. Patnaik. Base-station controlled clustering scheme in wireless sensor networks. The 1st IPIP Wireless Days, 2008, 1–5.
24. Y. Yin, J. Shi, Y. Li, P. Zhang. Cluster head selection using analytical hierarchy process for wireless sensor networks. In: *Proceedings of IEEE 17th International Symposium PIMRC*, Helsinki, Finland, 2006, 1–5.
25. P. Tillapart, S. Thammarojsakul, T. Thumthawatworn et al. An approach to hybrid clustering and routing in wireless sensor networks. In: *Proceedings of IEEE Aerospace Conference*, Montana, 2005, 1–8.
26. N. Jae-hwan, L. Byeong-jik, H. Nam-koo et al. Routing protocols based on super cluster header in wireless sensor network. In: Lorenz P and Dini P, eds *Networking ICN 2005*, Springer, Heidelberg, Germany, 2005, 731–739.
27. M. Younis, M. Youssef, K. Arisha. Energy-aware routing in cluster-based sensor networks. In: *Proceedings of the 10th IEEE International Symposium on Modeling, Analysis and Simulation of Computer and Telecommunications Systems*, Fort Worth, TX, USA: IEEE Computer Society, 2002, 129–136.
28. O. Younis, S. Fahmy. HEED: A hybrid, energy-efficient, distributed clustering approach for ad hoc sensor networks. *IEEE Transaction on Mobile Computing*, 2004, 3(4): 660–669.

29. P. Ding, J. Holliday, A. Celik. Distributed energy efficient hierarchical clustering for wireless sensor networks. In: *Proceedings of the 8th IEEE International Conference on Distributed Computing in Sensor Systems (DCOSS)*, Marina Del Rey, CA, USA, June, 8–10 2005, 322–339.

30. Y. Qi, J. Yu, N. Wang. Energy-efficient distributed clustering algorithm for wireless sensor network. *Computer Engineering*. 2011, 37(3): 83–86. (in Chinese).

31. S. Lindsey, C. Raghavendra, K. M. Sivalingam. Data gathering algorithms in sensor networks using energy metrics. *IEEE Transaction on Parallel and Distributed Systems*, 2002, 13: 924–935.

32. S. Lindsey, C. S. Raghavendra, K. Sivalingam. Data gathering in sensor networks using the energy*delay metric. In: *Proceedings of the IPDPS Workshop on Issues in Wireless Networks and Mobile Computing*. San Francisco: IEEE Computer Society, 2001, 2001–2008.

33. S. Jung, Y. Han, T. Chung. The concentric clustering scheme for efficient energy consumption in the PEGASIS. In: *Proceedings of the 9th International Conference on Advanced Communication Technology*, Gangwon-Do, Korea, February, 12–14 2007, 260–265.

34. W. Wang. *Research on Low Energy Hierarchy Routing Protocol in Wireless Sensor Networks*. The School of Information of ZheJiang University, ZheJiang, 2006. (in Chinese).

35. K. Du, J. Wu, D. Zhou. Chain-based protocols for data broadcasting and gathering in the sensor networks. In: *Proceedings of Workshop on Parallel and Distributed Scientific Engineering Computing with Applications*. 2003, 1926–1933.

36. Z. M. Wang, S. Basagni, E. Melachrinoudis, C. Petrioli. Exploiting sink mobility for maximizing sensor networks lifetime. In: Sprague RH, ed *Proceedings of the 38th Hawaii International Conference on System Sciences*, IEEE Computer Society, Washington, DC, 2005, 287–295.

37. Z. M. Wang, S. Basagni, E. Melachrinoudis, C. Petrioli. Exploiting sink mobility for maximizing sensor networks lifetime. In: Sprague RH, ed *Proceedings of the 38th Hawaii International Conference on System Sciences*, IEEE Computer Society, Washington, DC, 2005, 287–295.

38. G. Shi, M. Liao. Movement-assited data gathering scheme with load-balancing for sensor networks. *Journal of Software*, 2007, 18(9): 2235–2244. (in Chinese).

39. Y. Yu, G. Wei. An improved PEGASIS algorithm in wireless sensor network. *Acta Electronica Sinica*. 2008, 36(7): 1309–1313. (in Chinese).

40. F. Bajaber, I. Awan. Energy efficient clustering protocol to enhance lifetime of wireless sensor network. *Journal of Ambient Intelligence and Humanized Computing*, 2010, 1: 239–248.

41. F. Tang, I. You, S. Guo, M. Guo, Y. Ma. A chain-cluster based routing algorithm for wireless sensor networks. *Journal of Intelligent Manufacturing*, 2012, 23(4): 1305–1313.

42. G. Smaragdakis, I. Matta, A. Bestavros. SEP: A stable election protocol for clustered heterogeneous wireless sensor networks. In: *Proceedings of the International Workshop on SANPA*, 2004.

43. L. Qing, Q. Zhu, M. Wang. A distributed energy-efficient clustering algorithm for heterogeneous wireless sensor networks. *Journal of Software*, 2006, 17(3): 481–489. (in Chinese).

44. H. Chan, A. Perrig. ACE: An emergent algorithm for highly uniform cluster formation. *Lecture Notes in Computer Science*, 2004, 29(2): 154–171.

45. Q. Hu, Q. Li, X. Wang et al. An optimal algorithm for minimizing cluster overlap of ACE. In: *Proceedings of International Conference on Wireless Algorithms, Systems and Applications*, Dallas, 2008, 397–408.
46. C. Li, G. Chen, M. Ye, J. Wu. An uneven cluster based routing protocol for wireless sensor networks. *Chinese Journal of Computers*. 2007, 30(1): 27–36. (in Chinese).
47. S. Soro, W. B. Heinzelman. Prolonging the lifetime of wireless sensor networks via unequal clustering. In: *Proceedings of the 19th IEEE International Parallel and Distributed Processing Symposium*, 2005, Denver: IEEE Computer Society Press, 2005. 236–244. [doi: 10.1109/IPDPS.2005.365].
48. M. Xiang, W. R. Shi, C. J. Jiang, Y. Zhang. Energy efficient clustering algorithm for maximizing lifetime of wireless sensor networks. *International Journal of Electronics and Communications (AUE)*, 2010, 64(4): 289–298. [doi: 10.1016/j.aeue.2009.01.004].
49. Y. Huiyong, W. Zhihe, L. Yongyi. Clustering algorithm of wireless sensor networks based on uneven cirque model. *Information and Control*, 2008, 7(4): 509–512. (in Chinese).
50. S. Olariu and I. Stojmenovic. Data-centric protocols for wireless sensor networks. In: Stojmenovic I, ed *Handbook of Sensor Networks: Algorithms and Architectures*, John Wiley & Sons, Inc., 2005: 417–456.
51. H. Li, X. Shunjie, W. Guoqiang et al. Uneven virtual grid-based clustering routing protocol for wireless sensor networks. In: *2009 IEEE International Conference on Information and Automation*, Zhuhai/Macau, China, 2009.
52. J. Yu, X. Gu. A corona-based multi-hop balanced clustering protocol for wireless sensor network. (manuscript).
53. C. Li, M. Ye, G. Chen, J. Wu. An energy-efficient unequal clustering mechanism for wireless sensor networks[C]. *IEEE International Conference on Mobile Ad hoc and Sensor Systems Conference*. IEEE, 2005, 8: 604.
54. J. Yu, Y. Qi, G. Wang, X. Gu. A cluster-based routing protocol for wireless sensor networks with nonuniform node distribution. *International Journal of Electronics and Communications (AEU)*, 2012, 66: 54–61.
55. J. Yu, Y. Qi, Q. Guo and X. Gu. EADUC: An energy-aware distributed unequal clustering protocol for wireless sensor networks. *International Journal of Distributed Sensor Networks*, 2011, 2011: 8, Article ID 202145. [doi: 10.1155/2011/202145].
56. C. Chen, X. Gu, J. Yu, D. Yu. IDUC: An improved distributed unequal clustering protocol for wireless sensor networks. *WASA 2014 Proceedings of the 9th International Conference on Wireless Algorithms, Systems, and Applications*, vol. 8491, pp. 682–693.
57. F. Tashtarian, A. T. Haghighat, M. T. Honary, H. Shokrzadeh. A new energy-efficient clustering algorithm for wireless sensor networks. *Microcomputer Information*, 2007, 23(25):1–6.
58. C. Jiang, W. Shi, X. Tang, P. Wang, M. Xiang. Energy-balanced unequal clustering routing protocol for wireless sensor networks. *Journal of Software*, 2012, 23(5): 1222–1232. (in Chinese).
59. S. Lee, H. Choe, B. Park, Y. Song, C. -k. Kim. LUCA: An energy-efficient unequal clustering algorithm using location information for wireless sensor networks. *Wireless Personal Communications*, 2011, 56: 715–731.
60. M. Ye, C. F. Li, G. H. Chen, J. Wu. An energy efficient clustering scheme in wireless sensor networks. *Journal of Frontiers of Computer Science & Technology*, 2007, 3(2-3): 99–119.

61. H. Chen, C. S. Wu, Y. S. Chu, C. C. Cheng, L. K. Tsai. Energy residue aware (ERA) clustering algorithm for leach-based wireless sensor networks. *In: 2nd International Conference ICSNC,* Cap Esterel, French Riviera, France, 2007.

62. B. Gong, L. Li, S. Wang, X. Zhou. Multihop routing protocol with unequal clustering for wireless sensor networks international colloquium on computing, communication, control, and management, (ISECS2008), 2008, 552–556.

63. J. Yue, W. Zhang, W. Xiao, D. Tang, J. Tang. A clustering data fusion algorithm based on unequal division for wireless sensor networks. *Journal of Computer Research and Development.* 2011, 48(Suppl): 247–254. (in Chinese).

64. Y. Wang, T. L. X. Yang, D. Zhang. An energy efficient and balance hierarchical unequal clustering algorithm for large scale sensor network. *Information Technology Journal,* 2009, 8(1): 28–38.

65. S. Gamwarige and C. Kulasekere. Optimization of cluster head rotation in energy constrained wireless sensor networks. In: *IFIP International Conference on Wireless and Optical Communications Networks, WOCN'07,* Singapore, 2007: 1–5.

66. Y. Wang, Q. Zhao, and D. Zheng. Energy-driven adaptive clustering data collection protocol in wireless sensor networks. In: *International Conference on Intelligent Mechatronics and Automation,* Chengdu, 2004: 599–604.

67. S. Gamwarige and E. Kulasekere. An algorithm for energy driven cluster head rotation in a distributed wireless sensor network. In: *Proceedings of the International Conference on Information and Automation (ICIA2005),* Hong Kong, 2005: 354–359.

68. Y. Wu, Z. Chen, and Q. Jing et al. LENO: LEast rotation near-optimal cluster head rotation strategy in wireless sensor networks. In: *21st International Conference on Advanced Networking and Applications (AINA'07),* Canada, 2007: 195–201.

69. H. Heqing, S. Jie, Y. Daoyuan, M. Kui, L. Haitao. An energy-driven adaptive cluster head rotation algorithm for wireless sensor networks. *Journal of Electronics & Information Technology,* 2009, 31(5): 1040–1044. (in Chinese).

70. J. Yu, Y. Qi, G. Wang. An energy-driven unequal clustering protocol for heterogeneous wireless sensor networks. *Journal of Control Theory and Application,* 2011, 9(1): 133–139.

71. H. Luo, F. Ye, J. Cheng, S. Lu, L. Zhang. TTDD: Two-tier data dissemination in large-scale wireless sensor networks. *Wireless Networks,* 2005, [doi: 10.1007/s11276-004-4753-x].

72. D. Koutsonikola, S. Das, H. Y. Charlie, I. Stojmenovic. Hierarchical geographic multicast routing for wireless sensor networks. *Wireless Networks,* 2010, 16: 449–466.

73. J. A. Sanchez, P. M. Ruiz, I. Stojmenovic. GMR: Geographic multicast routing for wireless sensor networks. In: *Proceedings of 3rd Annual IEEE Communication Society Conference on Sensor and Ad Hoc Communications and Networks,* Reston, VA, USA, September 25–28, 2006, 20–29.

74. S. M. Das, H. Pucha, Y. C. Hu. Distributed hashing for scalable multicast in wireless ad hoc networks. *IEEE Transactions on Parallel Distributed Systems,* 2008, 19: 347–362.

75. A. Manjeshwar, D. P. Agrawal. TEEN: A routing protocol for enhanced efficiency in wireless sensor networks. In: *Proceedings of the 15th International Parallel and Distributed Processing Symposium (IPDPS),* San Francisco, CA, USA, 2001, 2009–2015.

76. A. Manjeshwar, D. P. Agrawal. APTEEN: A hybrid protocol for efficient routing and comprehensive information retrieval in wireless sensor networks. In: *Proceedings of the 2nd International Workshop on Parallel and Distributed Computing Issues in Wireless Networks and Mobile Computing*, Lauderdale, FL, USA, 2002, 195–202.
77. R. Govindan, E. Kohler, D. Estrin et.al. Tenet: An architecture for tiered embedded networks. In: *CENS Technical Report#56*, November 10, 2005.
78. V. Loscri, G. Morabito, S. Marano. A two-level hierarchy for low-energy adaptive clustering hierarchy. In: *Proceedings of the 2nd IEEE Semiannual Vehicular Technology Conference*, Dallas, TX, USA, 2005, 1809–1813.
79. J. N. Al-Karaki, R. Ul-Mustafa, A. E. Kamal. Data aggregation in wireless sensor networks—Exact and approximate algorithms. In: *Proceedings of the IEEE Workshop on High Performance Switching and Routing*. Phoenix, AZ, USA: IEEE Communications Society, 2004, 241–245.
80. P. Ding, J. Holliday, A. Celik. Distributed energy-efficient hierarchical clustering for wireless sensor networks. In: *Proceeding of the IEEE International Conference on Distributed Computing in Sensor Systems*, Marina Del Rey, CA, USA, July 1, 2005, 3560: 322–339.
81. S. G. Foss, S. A. Zuyev. On a voronoi aggregative process related to a bivariate poisson process. *Advance in Applied Probability*, 1996, 28(4): 965–981.
82. S. Bandopadhyay, E. J. Coyle. An energy-efficient hierarchical clustering algorithm for wireless sensor networks. In: *Proceeding of IEEE INFOCOM 2003*, San Francisco, CA, USA, 2003, 3: 1713–1723.
83. F. L. Lewis. Wireless sensor networks. In Cook DJ, Das SK, eds *Smart Environments: Technologies, Protocol, and Applications*, John Wiley & Sons, New York, 2004.
84. Y. Jin, L. Wang, Y. Kim, X. Z. Yang. EEMC: An energy-efficient multi-level clustering algorithm for large-scale wireless sensor networks. *Computer Networks*, 2008, 52: 542–562.
85. S. Bandyopadhyay, E. J. Coyle. Minimizing communication costs in hierarchically-clustered networks of wireless sensors. *Computer Networks*, 2004, 44(1): 1–16.
86. L. Li, W. Xiangming. Energy efficient optimization of clustering algorithm in wireless sensor network. *Journal of Electronics & Information Technology*. 2008, 30(4): 966–969. (in Chinese).
87. Y. Ying, L. Tan and W. Liu. COTE: A clustering scheme with optimal tiers and energy efficiency in wireless sensor networks. *IEEE Transaction on Vehicular Technology*.
88. Z. Sun. Research on energy-efficient routing protocols in wireless sensor networks. Dalian Maritime University.
89. R. Li. *Fuzzy MCDM Theory and Application*. Science Press, Beijing, 2002. (in Chinese).
90. I. Gupta, D. Riordan, S. Sampalli. Cluster-head election using fuzzy logic for wireless sensor networks. In: *Proceedings of the 3rd Annual Communication Networks and Services Research Conference*, Halifax: IEEE Computer Society, 2005. 255–260.
91. H. Yu, S. Xiaorui, K. Zhenhua. Energy-efficient cluster head selection in clustering routing for wireless sensor networks. In: *The 5th International Conference on Wireless Communications, Networking and Mobile Computing*, Beijing, China, 2009, 1–4.
92. J. M. Kim, S. H. Park, Y. J. Han, T. M. Chung. CHEF: Cluster head election mechanism using fuzzy logic in wireless sensor networks. In: *10th International Conference on Advanced Communication Technology, ICACT2008*, Taipei, Taiwan, 2008, 1: 654–659.

93. J. Anno, L. Barolli, A. Durresi, F. Xhafa, A. Koyama. Performance evaluation of two fuzzy-based cluster head selection systems for wireless sensor networks. *Mobile Information Systems*, 2008, 4: 297–312.

94. J. Annoa, L. Barolli, F. Xhafa, A. Durresi. A cluster head selection method for wireless sensor networks based on fuzzy logic. In: *IEEE Region 10 Annual International Conference, TENCON*, 2007, 833–836.

95. Y. Y. Yin, J. W. Shi, Y. N. Li, P. Zhang. Cluster head selection using analytical hierarchy process for wireless sensor networks. In: *IEEE International Symposium on Personal, Indoor and Mobile Radio Communications, PIMRC2006*, Helsinki, Finland, 2006, 11–14.

96. T. Gao, R. C. Jin, J. Y. Song, T. B. Xu, L. D. Wang. Energy-efficient cluster head selection scheme based on multiple criteria decision making for wireless sensor networks, *Wireless Personal Communication*, 2012, 63(4): 871–894.

97. M. R. Minhas, S. Gopalakrishnan, V. C. M. Leung. Fuzzy algorithm for maximum lifetime routing in wireless sensor networks. In: *Proceeding of IEEE Global Telecommunications Conference GLOBECOM'08*, New Orleans, LA, USA, 2008, 1–6.

98. M. J. Handy, M. Haase, D. Timmermann. Low energy adaptive clustering hierarchy with deterministic cluster-head selection. In: *Proceedings of the 4th IEEE Conference on Mobile and Wireless Communications Networks*, 2002, 368–372. [doi: 10.1109/MWCN.2002.1045790].

99. M. Liu, J. Cao, G. Chen. EADEEG: An energy-aware data gathering protocol for wireless sensor networks. *Journal of Software*, 2007, 18(5): 1092–1109.

100. X. Zhou, M. Wu, J. Xu, BPEC: An energy-aware distributed clustering algorithm in WSNs. *Journal of Computer Research and Development*, 2009, 46(5): 723–730.

101. Z. Fan, H. Zhou. A distributed weight-based clustering algorithm for WSNs. In: *Proceedings of International Conference on Wireless Communications, Networking and Mobile Computing*, Wuhan, 2006, 1–5.

102. W. Zhou, H. M. Chen, X. F. Zhang. An energy efficient strong head clustering algorithm for wireless sensor networks. In: *2007 International Conference on Wireless Communications, Networking and Mobile Computing, WiCOM*, 2007, 2584–2587.

103. H. S. Lee, K. T. Kim, H. Y. Youn. A new cluster head selection scheme for long lifetime of wireless sensor networks. *Lecture Notes in Computer Science*, 2006, 3983: 519–528.

104. H. Huang, D. Y. Yao, J. Shen, K. Ma, H. Liu. A multi-weight based clustering algorithm for wireless sensor networks. *Journal of Electronic & Information Technology*, 2008, 30(6): 1489–1492. (in Chinese).

105. F. Hu, X. Cao, C. May, Optimized scheduling for data aggregation in wireless sensor networks. *IEEE International Conference on ITCC*, Las Vegas, NV, USA, 2005, (2): 557–566.

106. R. Nagpal, D. Coore. An algorithm for group formation in an amorphous computer. In: *Proceedings of the 10th International Conference on Parallel and Distributed Systems, PDCS98*, Las Vegas, NV, USA, 1998.

107. A. Youssef, M. Younis, M. Youssef, and A. Agrawala. Distributed formation of overlapping multi-hop clusters in wireless sensor networks. In: *Proceedings of the 49th Annual IEEE Global Communication Conference Globecom06*, San Francisco, CA, USA, 2006.

108. S. Banerjee, S. Khuller. A clustering scheme for hierarchical control in multi-hop wireless networks. In: *Proceedings of 20th Joint Conference of the IEEE Computer and Communications Societies, INFOCOMŠ 01*, Anchorage, AK, USA, 2001.
109. M. Demirbas, A. Arora, V. Mittal, Floc: A fast local clustering service for wireless sensor networks. In: *Workshop on Dependability Issues in Wireless Ad Hoc Networks and Sensor Networks, DIWANS/DSN*, 2004: 700–709.
110. P. Santi. Silence is golden with high probability: Maintaining a connected backbone in wireless sensor networks. In: *1st European workshop on Wireless Sensor Networks*, Berlin, 2004.
111. S. Selvakennedy, S. Sinnappan. An adaptive data dissemination strategy for wireless sensor networks. *International Journal of Distributed Sensor Networks*, 2007, 3(1): AQ3.
112. M. O. Rahman, B. G. Choi, M. M. Monowar, C. S. Hong. A density based clustering for node management in wireless sensor networks. In: *10th Asia-Pacific Network Operations and management Symposium, APNOMS 2007*, Sapporo, Japan, October 10–12, 2007, 527–530.
113. Y. Wang, Q. Zhao, D. Zheng. Energy-driven adaptive clustering data collection protocol in wireless sensor networks. In: *Proceedings of the International Conference on Intelligent Mechatronics and Automation*, Chengdu, 2004, 599–604.

Chapter 4

Dominating Set Theory and Algorithms

4.1 Basic Concept and Models of the Dominating Set

4.1.1 Basic Concept

In graph theory, for a graph $G = (V, E)$, the dominating set is a subset $D \subseteq V$, so that each node $v \in V$ satisfies $v \in D$, or at least one neighbor is within D. Dominating number $\gamma(G)$ is the number of the vertex of the minimum dominating set (MDS) in G. The dominating set problem is to prove whether $\gamma(G) \leq K$ exists for $K \leq |V|$ in G. Garey and Johnson have proven that the dominating set problem is an NP complete problem [1]. If the subgraph introduced from D is connected, D can be regarded as a connected dominating set (CDS). The researchers model the wireless network as the graph $G = (V, E)$, where V is the set of the sensor nodes and E is the set of communication edges among the nodes. Figure 4.1 is a simple instance of the dominating set. The black nodes in the graph form the initial dominating set.

4.1.2 Network Model

If there exists an edge between the arbitrary nodes u and v within their communication range, the network can be modeled as an undirected graph. If there exists an edge $e(u, v)$ between the arbitrary nodes u and v, and node v is within the communication range of node u, but node u is not within the communication range of node v, the network will be modeled as a directed graph. The most original and most common network model is UDG. In this model, all nodes have the same communication range (which is generally 1), and two nodes can communicate with each other only if they are within communication range. In a wireless network, unit

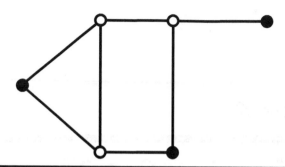

Figure 4.1   The instance of dominating set.

disk graph (UDG) is the most important graph model. Also, the model assumes that all nodes are in the unified plane.

4.1.2.1 Unit Disk Graph

The UDG model is made up of the intersection graphs with same scale disk in the plane. The model assumes that all the nodes have the unified communication range R. For arbitrary $u, v \in V$, e exists (u, v) if and only if $|uv| \le R$, in which $R=1$, generally. The dominating set problem and connected dominating problem based on UDG are also NP-complete problems [2]. Many other classical graph theory problems based on UDG are still NP-complete problems, such as coloring, independent sets, and the Hamiltonian cycle. Three UDG types can model the wireless network.

1. Adjacent model: The vertex in the graph refers to the node in the network. There is an edge between two nodes if and only if their Euclidean distance is the certain boundary value d.
2. Intersection model: The vertex in the graph refers to the node in the network. For two arbitrary nodes, if two disks intersect with two nodes as the center and the maximum communication range as the radius, there is an edge between two nodes. They still intersect if the two disks are tangent.
3. Inclusion model: The vertex in the graph refers to the node in the network. For two arbitrary nodes, if one disk includes the other one with two nodes as the center and the maximum communication range as the radius, there is an edge between two nodes.

Figure 4.2 is the instance of the UDG with weight.

4.1.2.2 Quasi Unit Disk Graph

Given a deterministic α, $0 < \alpha \le 1$. Graph G is a quasi-unit disk graph (QUDG), for two arbitrary nodes $u, v \in V$, if $|uv| \le \alpha$, $\{u, v\} \in E$ and if $|uv| > 1$, $\{u, v\} \notin E$.

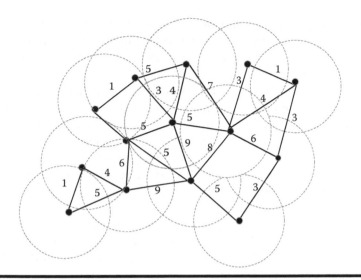

Figure 4.2   UDG model with weight.

If $\alpha = 1$, G is a UDG. Barrière et al. first proposed a communication model based on QUDG [3]. Since it cannot ensure that QUDG can obtain a plane and connected spanning subtree, there are not so many topology control protocols on QUDG.

4.1.2.3 Unit Ball Graph

For graph $G=(V, E)$, if there exists a mapping $\Phi : V \mapsto R^d$, which satisfies that if and only if $\|\Phi(u) - \Phi(v)\|_2 \leq 1$, $\{u,v\} \in E$ holds, so that graph G is regarded as a d-dimensional unit ball graph. When $d=2$, G is a UDG; when $d=3$, G is a unit ball graph. The unit ball graph can simulate the real network better than the UDG. Since the UDG can be regarded as a subclass of the unit ball graph and all nodes are limited in the same plane, all the passive complexity results about the UDG are suitable for the unit ball graph. Specifically, we have known that identifying the UDG is an NP-hard problem. Besides, the MDS, minimum CDS, maximum independent set, and minimum vertex covering problem are also NP-hard [4].

4.2 The Function of the Dominating Set

The energy of all nodes in wireless networks comes from the battery. The energy is limited and cannot be recharged. A node can only communicate with the nodes in its limited communication range (in general, assume that the communication range of each node is the same). If the Euclidean distance of two nodes is beyond the communication range, the two nodes can only communicate by forwarding through other sensor nodes instead of communicating directly. Therefore, the communication among the nodes may be single hop or multihop. Wireless networks are applied extensively in fields such as environment monitoring and disaster detection. The sensor nodes can sense the surrounding information then deal with the data and transmit it to the base station. All data will be aggregated at the base station. We deal with the data at the base station and obtain the information we need. Since the communication range is limited, most nodes cannot communicate with the base station directly; thus, they need adjacent nodes to forward. Besides, the communication power fades as a logarithmic ratio along with the increment of the distance, and the success rate of data transmission is reduced. If the distance between the source and destination is relatively large, communicating through the relay nodes can save more energy than communicating directly, thereby obtaining a higher success rate of data transmission.

When we use a dominating set, only the nodes in the dominating set need to stay active or they have higher energy while other nodes can stay in the energy-saving mode. Nondominating nodes will forward information to their dominating node after receiving information. Then the dominating node aggregates the information and forwards it to the base station. In general, we construct the CDS as the virtual backbone for routing. The dominating node will send data to the base station along with the virtual backbone network. In the wireless network with a dominating set, the lifetime of the network depends on the normal work time of the dominating set. Therefore, in the design of dominating set protocol in wireless networks, it needs to try to ensure that the nondominating nodes are even, which can avoid fast energy consumption of the dominating node caused by a heavy workload, thereby reducing the lifetime of the dominating set and the whole network. Meanwhile, in order to prolong the lifetime of the dominating set, we can find disjointed dominating sets in the network as much as possible and make them work in rotation [5]. The problem of finding the maximum disjointed dominating sets is regarded as domatic partition (DP), and the maximum number of disjointed dominating sets is the number of DPs. Moscibroda et al. proposed a scheduling solution for dominating set rotation in Reference [6], which can ensure that the current active dominating set works normally for a certain period, thereby prolonging the lifetime of the dominating set. In the wireless network, maximizing the lifetime of the dominating set leads to the research for the DP problem.

4.3 The Classification of Dominating Set Algorithms

4.3.1 The Maximal Independent Set Algorithm

The problem of the maximal independent set (MIS) has an extraordinary effect in various wireless networks, receiving extensive attention from the research fields of wireless networks. Given a graph $G=(V, E)$, the independent $I \subseteq V$ satisfies that $e(u,v) \notin E$ for $\forall u,v \in V$, that is, two arbitrary nodes in the independent set are not adjacent. When there is no superset in the independent set I, it is called the MIS. Since the MIS is a dominating set and it is easy to construct, many algorithms construct an MIS first when constructing the CDS. In this way, the approximate ratio of the algorithm depends on two factors. First, compared with the minimum CDS, how large is the MIS? Second, how many vertices are needed to connect an MIS? The paper [7] has proven that in each UDG G, $mis(G) \leq 4 \cdot cds(G) + 1$, where $mis(G)$ is the scale of the MIS; $cds(G)$ is the scale of the minimum CDS. In Reference [8], the authors modify the performance ratio of the algorithm and prove that $mis(G) \leq 3.8 \cdot cds(G) + 1.2$.

4.3.1.1 Related Works of MIS

Assume that each node has a unique signature in the network; then the distributed MIS algorithm is ordinary. In this model, each node will become a member of an MIS if it has the minimum signature among its neighbors and not all of its neighbors have joined in the MIS. Once a node knows its accurate location and that of its neighbors, it is very easy to construct MIS by deterministic algorithms. If the nodes do not need any location information, they can sense the distance between themselves and their neighbors, and the time the deterministic algorithm needs for calculating MIS is $O(\log^* n)$ [9]. It is essential for the research of wireless networks that the nodes do not need to know the location information in advance. Under the situation where the nodes do not need to know any information of location and distance, the time of deterministic algorithm for calculating MIS is $O(\log \Delta \log^* n)$, where Δ is the maximum degree of the node in the graph. In this model, the only useful information of the node is that it is connected with all of its neighbors.

Along with the in-depth research of the MIS problem, the design of the MIS algorithm has been ripe. MIS technology is applied extensively in the design of wireless network protocol, especially in the aspects of the CDS and coloring. In Reference [10], Kuhn et al. proposed an MIS deterministic construction algorithm in a bounded growth graph with time complexity as $O(\log \Delta \cdot \log^* n)$, where Δ is the maximum degree of the node in the graph; n is the total number of nodes in the graph. The bounded growth graph includes the common network model graph such as the well-known UDG. If all r-neighbors of an arbitrary node have a limited number of independent nodes, the graph is regarded as a bounded growth graph. The algorithm assumes that it does not need any information of location and distance, but only needs connection information for the node and its neighbors. This kind of assumption is also suitable for other regular graphs.

Marathe et al. [15] point out that in the UDG, an MIS can provide an MDS approximation method that can obtain the approximate factor 5. Alzoubi et al. [16] and Wan et al. [26] utilize a similar MIS method to obtain a connected dominating construction algorithm with the approximate ratio 8. Cardei et al. [37] also use a connected MIS to obtain a CDS with the approximate ratio 8.

In Reference [27], the algorithm assumes that each node knows its one-hop neighbors and two-hop neighbors, and it assigns a leader at the same time. The process of CDS construction is divided into two stages: the stage of MIS construction and the stage of MIS connection. In the first stage, the algorithm begins from the leader. The leader becomes the dominator and identifies its two-hop independent neighbor nodes. The selection of two-hop independent neighbor nodes is based on the maximum degree of heuristic information. Then the selected two-hop independent neighbors become the dominating nodes and begin the same construction process in their neighbor area. When all nodes are within the dominating range of the current dominators, the first stage of the algorithm ends. The second stage uses the Steiner tree to connect all of the nodes of the MIS that have been obtained in the first stage. The Steiner tree is a modified distributed depth first searching tree. The leader searches its neighbors in a greedy way and searches for the neighbor that connects the maximum number of neighbors. When all neighbors of the leader have been searched, all nodes in the MIS are connected; then the search ends. We analyze the approximate ratio of the algorithm in the paper [27] briefly. The scale of the MIS obtained in the first stage is denoted $|MIS|$. The essential factor of approximate analysis of the CDS scale is the number of connected sets. Each connected set can be connected with at least three dominators in the MIS. Therefore, the number of connected sets is $|MIS| - 2$. The size of the CDS is the sum of the MIS scale and the connected set scale: $|CDS| = \{2 * |MIS| - 2\}$. Given $|MIS| = 4opt + 1$ and combining the formula, it can be obtained that $|CDS| = 8opt$, where opt is an arbitrary optimal CDS scale.

Afterwards, Li et al. improved the performance ratio to $5.8 + \ln 4$ and $4.8 + \ln 5$ successfully. The distributed computing MIS is also used in the research of the virtual backbone network [16, 17]. Besides, the research of the independent set in the broadcasting network model is important as well.

4.3.1.2 Classical MIS Algorithm

The earliest MIS construction algorithm is random. The deterministic MIS construction algorithm was obtained after in-depth research. The earliest well-known sequential algorithm of constructing MIS can be outlined as follows: Initialize I as an empty set; for $\forall v = 1, \ldots, n$, if vertex v has no neighbor in I, add v into I. Valiant [11] and Cook [12] point out that there exists no fast parallel algorithm for the MIS problem; even though this kind of algorithm exists, the design mode of the fast parallel algorithm is different from the sequential algorithm. To our surprise, however, Karp and Wigderson [13] designed a fast parallel algorithm later, which can construct MIS quickly. They proposed a random algorithm with time complexity as $O((\log n)^4)$, algorithm complexity as $O(n^2)$, a deterministic algorithm with time complexity as $O((\log n)^4)$, and algorithm complexity as $O[n^3/(\log n)^3]$. The significant breakthrough is the simple MIS parallel algorithm proposed by Luby [14].

The first algorithm in the paper [14] is a Monte Carlo algorithm with a local property. The local property makes a useful protocol design tool in distributed computing environments and artificial intelligence.

4.3.1.2.1 Classical Distributed MIS Algorithm

In this section, we will introduce the simple MIS parallel algorithm proposed by Luby [14]. The algorithm is a landmark in the research field of distributed MIS algorithms. The important contribution of the author is the key technology that can change the Monte Carlo algorithm into a deterministic algorithm. It has laid a solid foundation for later MIS algorithms. Next, we will introduce in detail the proposed MIS construction algorithms. Input an undirected graph $G=(V, E)$ and a maximum independent set $I \subseteq V$ after executing the MIS algorithm. For $W \subseteq V$, it holds that $N(W) = \{w \in V : \exists v \in W, (v, w) \in E\}$. Let $d(v)$ be the degree of node v in graph G. The algorithm can be described as follows [14].

Begin
   $I \leftarrow \varnothing$
   $G' = (V', E') \leftarrow G = (V, E)$
   while $V' \neq \varnothing$ do
   begin
      $X \leftarrow \varnothing$
      In parallel, for all $v \in V'$,
         randomly choose to add v to X with probability $\dfrac{1}{2 \cdot d(v)}$ (*)
         {If $d(v) = 0$ then always add v to X}
      $I' \leftarrow X$
      In parallel, for all $v \in X, w \in X$,
          If $(v, w) \in E'$ then
             If $d(v) \leq d(w)$ then $I' \leftarrow I' - \{v\}$
             else $I' \leftarrow I' - \{w\}$
             {Note that I' is an independent set in G' } X
             $I \leftarrow I \cup I'$
             $Y \leftarrow I' \cup N(I')$
             $G' = (V', E')$ is the induced subgraph on $V' - Y$.
   end
   end

The algorithm will continue to execute the "while" cycle if $V' \neq \emptyset$. First, add node v into X with the probability $1/2 \cdot d(v)$ if the degree of the node is zero. In the cycle process, assign the value of X to the temporary independent set I'. For $\forall v, w \in X$, if there is an edge between v and w, delete the node with the lower degree from I', which is executed for the nodes in the X parallel. Finally, obtain the union set of set I' and set I. If V' is not empty, continue to execute the "while" cycle. This simple Monte Carlo algorithm can obtain the MIS I with $O((\log n)^2)$ as the time complexity.

4.3.1.2.2 Algorithm Analysis

Let m_1 be the edge number of G' before executing the "while" cycle; let m_2 be the random variable, which refers to the edge number of G' after executing the "while" cycle; let m_3 be the deleted edge number from G' when the "while" cycle is executed. Therefore, $m_2 = m_1 - m_3$. Theorem 4.1 can prove that $E[m_3] \geq \dfrac{1}{8} m_1$. Therefore, $E[m_2] \leq \dfrac{7}{8} m_1$. For all $v \in V$, let E_v be the events selected in step (*) of the algorithm; the events are independent of each other. Let $p_v = \Pr[E_v] = 1/2 \cdot d(v)$ and $sum_v = \displaystyle\sum_{w \in adj(v)} p_w$, in which $adj(v)$ is neighbor set of v.

Lemma 4.1: $\Pr[v \in N(I')] \geq \dfrac{1}{4} \cdot \min(sum_v, 1)$.

Proof: Without losing generality, assume that $\{1, \ldots, d(v)\}$ are the vertices in $adj(v)$. Let E' be the event E_1. For $2 \leq i \leq d(v)$, let $E_i' = \left(\displaystyle\bigcap_{j=1}^{i-1} \neg E_j \right) \cap E_i$ and $A_i = \displaystyle\bigcap_{\substack{x \in adj(v) \\ d(x) \geq d(i)}} \neg E_x$, then it holds that $\Pr[v \in N(I')] \geq \displaystyle\sum_{i-1}^{d(v)} \Pr[E_i'] \cdot \Pr[A_i \mid E_i']$.

Therefore, $\Pr[A_i \mid E_i'] \geq \Pr[A_i] \geq 1 - \displaystyle\sum_{\substack{x \in adj(i) \\ d(x) \geq d(i)}} p_x \geq \dfrac{1}{2}$. □

Lemma 4.2: $\displaystyle\sum_{i=1}^{d(v)} \Pr[E_i'] \geq \Pr\left[\displaystyle\bigcup_{i=1}^{d(v)} E_i \right] \geq \dfrac{1}{2} \cdot \min(sum_v, 1)$. The formula is established even though the events in $\{E_w\}$ are mutually independent. Therefore, $ET(W) = \{(v, w) \in E \mid v \in W, \text{or}, w \in W\}$.

Theorem 4.1: $E[m_3] \geq \dfrac{1}{8} \cdot m_1.$

Proof: For all $W \subseteq V$, the set of edges connected with W is $ET(W) = \{(v, w) \in E \mid v \in W, \text{ or, } w \in W\}.$

The edge $ET[I' \cup N(I')]$ is deleted when executing the "while" cycle for the first time. Each edge (v, w) belongs to $ET[I' \cup N(I')]$ because $v \in I' \cup N(I')$ or because $w \in I' \cup N(I')$. Therefore, it holds that

$$E[m_3] \geq \frac{1}{2} \cdot \sum_{v \in V} d(v) \cdot \Pr[v \in I' \cup N(I')] \geq \frac{1}{2} \cdot \sum_{v \in V} d(v) \cdot \Pr[v \in N(I')].$$

It can be known by Lemma 4.1 that $\Pr[v \in N(I')] \geq \dfrac{1}{4} \cdot \min(sum_v, 1)$. Therefore,

$$E[m_3] \geq \frac{1}{8} \left[\sum_{\substack{v \in V' \\ sum_m \leq 1}} d(v) \cdot sum_v + \sum_{\substack{v \in V' \\ sum_v \succ 1}} d(v) \right]$$

$$\geq \frac{1}{8} \cdot \left[\sum_{\substack{v \in V' \\ sum_v \leq 1}} \sum_{w \in adj(v)} \frac{d(v)}{2 \cdot d(w)} + \sum_{\substack{v \in V' \\ sum_v \succ 1}} \sum_{w \in adj(v)} 1 \right]$$

$$\geq \frac{1}{8} \cdot \sum_{\substack{(v,w) \in E' \\ sum_v \leq 1 \\ \wedge sum_w \leq 1}} \frac{1}{2} \left[\frac{d(v)}{d(w)} + \frac{d(w)}{d(v)} \right] + \frac{1}{8} \cdot \sum_{\substack{(v,w) \in E' \\ sum_v \leq 1 \\ \wedge sum_w \succ 1}} \left[\frac{d(v)}{2 \cdot d(w)} + 1 \right] + \frac{1}{8} \sum_{\substack{(v,w) \in E' \\ sum_v \succ 1 \\ \wedge sum_w \succ 1}} 2 \geq \frac{1}{8} \cdot |E'|$$

$$= \frac{1}{8} \cdot m_1$$

□

We assume that the events in $\{E_w\}$ are mutually independent. Next, we assume the events in $\{E_w\}$ are pairwise independent. Then we will prove that the expectation value of the "while" cycle iteration times is still $O(\log n)$ even in this weak assumption. Thus, we can obtain the deterministic execution solution of Algorithm 4.1. In the following, we prove Lemma 4.3. Many results in the paper need the support of Lemma 4.3.

Lemma 4.3: Assume there are n events $E_1, \ldots, E_n$. For $1 \leq i \leq n$, there is $\Pr[E_i] = p_i$; for $1 \leq i \neq j \leq n$, $\Pr[E_i \cap E_j] = p_i \cdot p_j$. Let $sum = \sum_i p_i$, then $\Pr\left[\bigcup_i E_i\right] \geq \frac{1}{2} \cdot \min(sum, 1)$.

Proof: Without losing generation, assume $p_1 \geq p_2 \geq \cdots p_n$; $E'_k = \bigcup_{i=1}^{k} E_i$; $\alpha_k = \sum_{i=1}^{k} p_i$. Then, for all $1 \leq k \leq n$, $\Pr[E'_n] \geq \Pr[E'_k]$. Since the events are pairwise independent, it holds that

$$\Pr[E'_k] \geq \alpha_k - \sum_{1 \leq i \prec j \leq k} p_i \cdot p_j \geq \alpha \left[1 - \frac{\alpha_k(k-1)}{2k}\right].$$

The last condition for establishing the inequality is when the left $p_i = \alpha_k / k$ obtains the minimum value. If $\alpha_n \leq 1$, $\Pr[E'_n] \geq \frac{\alpha_n}{2} = \frac{sum}{2}$; if $\alpha_n \succ 1$, let $l = \min\{k : \alpha_k \geq 1\}$. If $l = 1$, $\Pr[E'_1] \geq 1$; if $l \geq 2$, $\alpha_{l-1} \prec 1 \leq \alpha_l \leq \frac{1}{l-1}$. In summary, we can obtain that $\Pr[E'_l] \geq \alpha_l \cdot \left[1 - \frac{\alpha_l(l-1)}{2l}\right] \geq \frac{1}{2}$. ☐

Following this, we can obtain the conclusion: The average running time of the first MIS algorithm proposed in this paper [14] is very small, regardless of whether the set of events is mutually or pairwise independent. In the fifth section, the authors discuss how to build this kind of probability distribution: satisfy pairwise independent and ensure the node number of sample space is $O(n^2)$, so that the nodes can be sampled in parallel.

4.3.1.2.3 Deterministic MIS Construction Algorithm

Combining the conclusion of the former section, the authors obtain the deterministic MIS construction algorithm with low runtime. The algorithm overcomes the difficulty that E_v events have different probabilities in new and old sample spaces. Specifically, in the original probability space, $\Pr[E_v] = 1/2d(v)$ while in the new probability space, $\Pr[E_v] = p'_v = \frac{\lfloor p_v \cdot q \rfloor}{q} = \frac{\left\lfloor \frac{q}{2d(v)} \right\rfloor}{q}$, in which, q is the prime number between n and $2n$. The difficulty can be overcome by the modification as follows. If there exists a vertex $v \in V$, which satisfies $d(v) \geq \frac{n}{16}$, add v into the independent set I and delete $\{v\} \cup N(\{v\})$ from the graph. In this way, at least 1/16 vertices will be deleted from the graph. If there exists no such vertex, it holds that degree $d(v) \prec \dfrac{n}{16}$ for all $v \in V$, which means $\dfrac{q}{2d(v)} \geq \dfrac{n}{2d(v)} \succ 8$, so that $p_v' \geq \dfrac{8}{q}$. Therefore, $\dfrac{\lfloor p_v \cdot q \rfloor}{8} \geq 1$. Because $\dfrac{\lfloor p_v \cdot q \rfloor + 1}{q} \geq p_v$, it can be known that $\dfrac{8}{9} p_v \leq p_v' \leq p_v$. The algorithm is simple and fast, and it has a few processors and storage; thus, it has high practicality. In the following, the specific details will be introduced [14].

```
begin
  I ← ∅
  G' = (V', E') ← G = (V, E)
  While V' ≠ ∅ do
  begin
    In parallel, for all v ∈ V', compute d(v)
    In parallel, for all v ∈ V'
      If d(v) = 0 then add v to I and delete v from V'.
    compute n' = |V'|
    find v ∈ V' such that d(v) is maximum
    if d(v) ≥ n'/16 then add v to I and let G' be the graph
              induced on the vertices V' − ({V} ∪ N({v}))
    else (for all v ∈ V', d(v) ≺ n'/16)
    begin
      compute a prime q such that n' ≤ q ≤ 2n'
      randomly choose x and y such that 0 ≤ x, y ≤ q − 1 (*)
      X ← ∅
      In parallel, for all v ∈ V',
      begin
        compute n(v) = ⌊ q / 2d(v) ⌋
        compute l(v) = (x + vy) mod q
        if l(v) ≤ n(v) then add v to X
      end
```

$I' \leftarrow X$

In parallel, for all $v \in X, w \in X$,

    if $(v,w) \in E'$

        if $d(v) \le d(w)$ then $I' \leftarrow I' - \{v\}$

        else $I' \leftarrow I' - \{w\}$

$I \leftarrow I \cup I'$

$Y \leftarrow I' \cup N(I')$

$G' = (V', E')$ is the induced subgraph on $V' - Y$.

    end

  end

end

Each step of the algorithm is determined without the constraint of random probability. When the degree of each node in V' is lower than $n'/16$, calculate the prime number q, where $n' \le q \le 2n'$. The algorithm selects the values of x and y randomly, in which $0 \le x, y \le q - 1$. There are q^2 pairs of the value x and y. Whether v should be added into X by calculating $n(v)$ and $l(v)$ can be determined. X is the temporary independent set in the current cycle. The paper [14] has proven that the time complexity is $O((\log n)^2)$ and computing complexity is $O(mn^2)$.

4.3.2 Minimum Connected Dominating Set

In the graph, the CDS with the minimum scale is regarded as the minimum CDS. As we introduced, the dominating set and the CDS problem are both NP-complete problems, even in the UDG. Similarly, the minimum CDS problem is also an NP-complete problem, even in the UDG [15].

4.3.2.1 Related Works of the Minimum Connected Dominating Set

Guha and Khuller [18] first proposed the CDS algorithm. They proposed three approximate algorithms, two of which are based on the spanning tree and the other of which is composed of a forest. All the performance ratios of the three algorithms are $O(\log n)$. Then, Das and Bharghavan [19] modified the nonlocal algorithms proposed by Guha and proposed operating the Minimum Connected Dominating Set (MCDS) construction algorithm in the distributed network model. The algorithm gives the shortest path for network routing. The nodes can update the routing path quickly after moving. Meanwhile, the authors gave the modified version of MCDS algorithm in a bounded graph and obtained the smallest possible virtual backbone network, utilizing MCDS as the virtual backbone network of the wireless network.

Besides Reference [19], Das et al. proposed a series of routing algorithms for wireless networks [20–22], for which the main idea is constructing a minimum CDS. Each node stores a routing table, which records the topology structure information of the whole network. The node in the CDS is regarded as the backbone node. Although the topology structure changes, it will not affect the nodes in the CDS, thus it does not need to recalculate the routing table. Papers [19–22] use the approximate algorithms proposed by Guha and Khuller, because the approximate algorithm has two main advantages. First, each node only needs the information of two-hop neighbors instead of the topology structure of the whole network. Second, the algorithm executes $O(\gamma)$ rounds with time complexity as $O(\gamma\Delta^2 + v)$ and message complexity as $O(\Delta v\gamma + m + v\log v)$, where γ is the number of the nodes in the dominating set; m is the number of edges; v is the total number of nodes in the network; Δ is the maximum node degree. In these four papers, the differences of the algorithms are the mode of constructing the routing table and the way in which the routing table is delivered to the uncontrolled central node. Since MCDS is not guaranteed to include the middle nodes on the shortest path, the routing process cannot be completely limited to MCDS nodes. In other words, each MCDS node needs to know the topology of the whole network for calculating a routing table.

Wu and Li [23] propose a simple and efficient distributed CDS construction algorithm. The algorithm assumes that the connectivity among the nodes depends on their geographical distance from each other. The algorithm can obtain a CDS quickly in a given connected graph. Compared with the classical algorithms of Das et al., the algorithm has relative advantage in performance and CDS scale. Meanwhile, the authors study how to update and recalculate the dominating set when the graph structure changes, as well as how to use the obtained MCDS to find the routing information. The wireless network is self-organized. The difference from the algorithms of Das et al. is that the algorithm constructs a CDS first; then it removes the redundant nodes from the CDS. The initial obtained CDS is denoted as S, which includes at least two nonadjacent nodes. If node u in S has a neighbor in S with a higher id and the neighbor can dominate all the neighbors of u, or node u in S has two neighbors in S with higher ids that can dominate all neighbors of u, then u is the local redundant node. Remove all nodes like this from S. The algorithm is only suitable for UDG not the general graph of wireless ad hoc networks.

Wu and Li extend these algorithms in Reference [24]. The selection of the dominating node in the whole CDS relies on two factors: the degree of each node and its residual energy. The authors give a detailed introduction for routing rule and some instances of the rule based on energy value. The final goal of the authors is to ensure the balance of overall energy consumption and construct a relatively small CDS at the same time. In simulations, the authors compare the lifetime of the network under a different selection solution. The simulation results show that algorithms based on the rule of energy value can better prolong the lifetime of the network.

By assigning the priority to the node with large degree, Stojmenovic et al. [25] modified the distributed algorithm proposed by Wu et al. The significant contribution of their paper is the reliable broadcasting algorithm based on inside nodes. The algorithm includes the neighbor elimination mechanism, the maximum degree priority mechanism for inside node selection and the recommunication mechanism after acknowledged failure. If all the nodes use Global Positioning System (GPS) or another positioning method, the maintenance of the inside node is included in the positioning update process among the neighbor nodes. GPS can provide the location information (latitude and longitude, height) of the node in the network by communicating with the satellite. Besides, the node can measure the length of a received signal by exchanging signal strength information with its neighbors, thereby determining the location of the neighbor. In the execution process, the node only needs the location information of its neighbors or the neighbor list of each neighbor; thus, the algorithm is localized. The algorithm has the property independent of the node degree from the two aspects. First, the algorithm does not use any parameter set according to the average degree of the network, and the performance of the algorithm is not affected by the change in average node degree. However, the paper fails to give the minimum boundary value of the scale of the CDS. Constructing a smaller CDS problem remains to be solved.

In Reference [26], Wan et al. reanalyze the three algorithms proposed by Das and Bharghavan [19], Wu and Li [23], and Stojmenovic et al. [25]. The algorithm proposed by Das and Bharghavan [19] has logarithmic approximate factor, while the other two algorithms have linear approximate factors. However, the message complexity and the time complexity of the three algorithms are all high. The approximate factor of the distributed Das algorithm is between $\dfrac{\log \Delta}{2} - \dfrac{1}{2}$ and $3H(\Delta)$, where Δ is the maximum node degree; H is the harmonic function whose message complexity and time complexity both are $O(n^2)$. The approximate factor of the distributed algorithm proposed by Wu et al. is $n/2$ with the message complexity $\Theta(m)$ and time complexity $O(\Delta^3)$. The approximate factor of the distributed algorithm proposed by Stojmenovic et al. is $n/2$ or n with message complexity $O(n^2)$ and time complexity $\Omega(n)$. After the study of these classical algorithms, Wan et al. propose a distributed algorithm with better performance for each aspect. The algorithm includes two stages: constructing the MIS and constructing the dominating tree.

4.3.2.2 MCDS Distributed Algorithms with Good Performance

In this section, we will introduce the algorithms of Reference [26] proposed by Wan et al. in detail. The algorithm first adopts a series of distributed operations. Each node calculates its rank and the number of neighbors that have lower rank. All nodes are initialized as white. Then the nodes are colored according to the results of ranking. Finally, all the nodes become gray or black. Each node has a list of black neighbors, recording the id of the black neighbor. The specific coloring process is no longer introduced in detail. At the end, all the black nodes constitute an MIS. The distance of any two complementary subsets of black node sets is exactly 2 hops.

4.3.2.2.1 Stage 1: The Constructing Process of the MIS

By definition, the distance of any pair of nodes in an MIS is at least two hops. However, the distance of any two complementary subsets may be up to three hops. In this section, the constructing process makes sure that the distance of any two complementary subsets is exactly two hops. The constructing process will use the concept of "rank." The rank is generated by a spanning tree T with an arbitrary node as the root. Given a spanning tree T, the layer of the node is the hop number between the node and the root of T (the layer of the root is 0). The rank of the node consists of the layer of the node and the ID. According to the rank, all nodes can be sorted in lexicographic order. In the following, we will introduce the calculation of rank and the number of neighbors with low rank.

Each node has two measurement variables: x_1 and x_2. Variable x_1 calculates the number of neighbors that have not determined their layer and initializes the number of the neighbors'. Variable x_2 calculates the number of the child that has not completed the construction process and initializes the number of child nodes. Each node has a *levelList* to record its layer of the neighbor that is initialized as empty. There exists a local variable y to record the number of neighbors with low rank. After finishing the construction of the spanning tree T, the root node broadcasts a LEVEL message to declare that its layer is 0. After receiving the LEVEL message, the node adds the ID and the layer value of the sender into its levelList then subtracts the value of x_1 with 1. The node will set its layer value as the layer of the sender plus 1, if the sender is its father node in T. Then it broadcasts a LEVEL message to declare its layer value. If $x_1 = 0$, y is assigned the number of the neighbor with a lower rank, which can be calculated from the levelList. If a node is the leaf node in T and its layer is determined, it will send a LEVEL-COMPLETE message to its father node. When the node receives a LEVEL-COMPLETE message, it will subtract the value of x_2 with 1; if the value of x_2 is 0 after the update, the node is not the root node; then it will forward the LEVEL-COMPLETE message to its father node and reset x_2 as the number of the child node. When the value of x_2 is 0, the root node resets the value of x_2 as the number of the child node. Until now, each node knows its rank and that of all of its neighbors. The root node will construct the MIS by a coloring process.

All nodes will be initialized as white and will be marked gray or, finally, black. Each node has a blacklist value to record the ID of the black neighbor. Note that the blacklist can only record a maximum of five black nodes. The root node marks itself as black at first, then broadcasts a BLACK message. The node adds the ID of the sender onto the blacklist once it receives the BLACK message. If the node is white, it will change to gray and broadcast a GRAY message, which includes its layer value. After receiving the GRAY message, the white node will subtract from its y value with 1 if the rank of the sender is lower than its rank; if $y = 0$ after the update, the node will mark itself as black and broadcast the BLACK message. When a leaf node is marked as gray or black, it will send a MARK-COMPLETE message to its father. Once the node receives a MARK-COMPLETE message, it will subtract 1 from the value of x_2 the destination. If $x_2 = 0$ after the update and the node is not the root node, it will send a MARK-COMPLETE message to its father. Now, all the nodes have been marked as gray or black when the local variable x_2 of the root node equals 0. Then the root node continues to execute the construction process of the CDS.

In the following, we will introduce the properties of the black nodes after coloring. The next step of CDS construction relies on these properties.

Theorem 4.2: All black nodes consist of MIS, and the distance of any two complementary subsets of the black node set is exactly 2 hops.

The process of proof can refer to the process for Theorem 4.3.

4.3.2.2.2 Stage 2: The Construction Process of the Dominating Tree

The second stage constructs a dominating tree T^*. All nodes in T^* form the CDS. Each node initializes variable z as zero. After the end of the second stage, the value of variable z is 1, which means the node joins in the dominating tree T^*. Each node has the local variable *parent* and *childrenList* at the same time. *Parent* stores the father id of the node in T^*, which is initialized as empty; the *childrenList* stores the child id of the node in T^*, which is initialized as empty. The root node of T^* is a gray neighbor of the root node in T, which has the maximum number of black neighbors. In order to select the root node of T^*, it has a variable root and a variable degree (which are initialized as 0).

First, the root node of T assigns the value of local variable x_1 as the number of its neighbors; then it broadcasts a QUERY message. Once the node receives a QUERY message, if it is a gray node it will send a REPORT message to the sender, which includes the number of its black neighbors. If the destination node receives the REPORT message, the root node of T will subtract 1 from the value of x_1. If the number of black neighbors of the sender of the REPORT message is greater than the degree, the root node will reset the value of the degree as the number of black neighbors of the sender and set the value of the variable root as the ID of the sender as well. If a node receives the ROOT message, it will become the root node of T^*. Then it sets $z = 1$ and broadcasts an INVITE2 message. Other nodes will join in T^* according to the rules as follows.

1. After receiving INVITE2 information, set $z = 1$ for the black node whose z equals 0; set parent as the ID of the sender. It sends a JOIN message to the sender. Then it broadcasts INVITE1 information.
2. After receiving INVITE1 information, set $z = 1$ for the gray node whose z equals 0; set parent as the ID of the sender. It sends a JOIN message to the sender. Then it broadcasts INVITE2 information.
3. After receiving JOIN information, if the destination node is exact itself, the node will add the ID of the sender to its childrenList.

Theorem 4.2 guarantees that whenever a black node is not in the current T^*, at least one black node will join. Therefore, all black nodes will join T^* by the end. Thus all gray nodes will join T^* and become the middle nodes of T^*.

4.3.2.2.3 Performance Analysis

First, we analyze the message complexity and time complexity. After constructing the spanning tree T, the MIS construction process of the first stage uses the additional linear information, which costs only linear time. The construction process of the dominating tree T^* also uses linear information, which only costs linear time. Therefore, our algorithm needs $O(n)$ messages and $O(n)$ time besides the construction process of the spanning tree T. We construct spanning tree T with the algorithm, in which the message complexity and the time complexity are $O(n \log n)$ and $O(n)$, respectively. Note that the message complexity of our algorithm is controlled by the construction process of the spanning tree.

In the following, we analyze the CDS scale obtained by the algorithm (i.e., the number of the intermediate nodes in dominating tree T^*). Let OPT be an arbitrary minimum CDS and $|OPT|$ be its scale. First, we analyze the property of the independent set.

Lemma 4.4: In the UDG $G = (V, E)$, the scale of an arbitrary independent set is $4|OPT| + 1$ at most.

Proof: Let U be the independent set of V and T' the spanning tree of OPT. The preorder traverse of T' is given: $v_1, v_2, ..., v_{|opt|}$. Let U_1 be the set of adjacent nodes of node v_1 in U. For arbitrary $2 \leq i \leq |OPT|$, let U_i be the set of the nodes adjacent to node v_i in U except $v_1, v_2, ..., v_{i-1}$. Then, $U_1, U_2, ..., U_{|OPT|}$ forms a partition of U. Therefore, v_1 can be adjacent to 5 independent nodes at most (i.e., $U_1 \leq 5$). For arbitrary $2 \leq i \leq |OPT|$, at least one node is adjacent to node v_i in $v_1, v_2, ..., v_{i-1}$. Therefore, maximum U_i is located in the sector area with 240 degrees in the coverage range of node v_i, which satisfies that $|U_i| \leq 4$. Therefore,

$$|U| = \sum_{i=1}^{|OPT|} |U_i| \leq 5 + 4(|OPT| - 1) = 4|OPT| + 1 \qquad \square$$

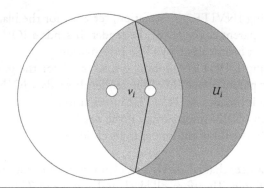

Figure 4.3 **Maximum U_i is located in the sector area with 240° in the coverage range of node v_i.**

Lemma 4.4 and its proof consist of the upper boundary of scale of CDS constructed by the algorithm.

Lemma 4.5: The number of intermediate nodes in T^* is $8|OPT| - 2$ at most.

Proof: If there is a black node in OPT, the total number of black nodes is $1 + 4(|OPT| - 1) = 4|OPT| - 3$ at most, according to the proof for Lemma 4.4.

Since each intermediate gray node has at least one black child node, the total number of gray intermediate nodes in T^* will not exceed the number of black nodes. Therefore, the total number of intermediate nodes in T^* is $2(4|OPT| - 3) = 8|OPT| - 6$ at most.

Now assume that there is no black node in OPT. Let k be the number of black nodes adjacent to the root node of T^*, then $k \leq 5$. According to the proof for Lemma 4.4, the total number of black nodes is $k + 4(|OPT| - 1)$ at most. Note that the root node of T^* has exactly k black children and that any intermediate gray node has one black node at least. Therefore, the total number of intermediate gray nodes is $4(OPT - 1)$ at most, except the root node T^*. Thus, the number of intermediate nodes is:

$$4(|OPT| - 1) + k + 1 + 4(|OPT| - 1) = 8|OPT| - 7 + k \leq 8|OPT| - 7 + 5 = 8|OPT| - 2$$

at most.

4.3.3 Weakly Connected Dominating Sets

In graph $G = (V, E)$, given a subset $S \subseteq V$, $N[S]$ is the set of nodes in subset of S and all of its one-hop neighbors. The weak subset exported by S is $\langle S \rangle_w = (N[S], E \cap (N[S] \times S))$. The vertex of $\langle S \rangle_w$ is S and all of its one-hop neighbors. $\langle S \rangle_w$ includes all edges that involve at least one vertex of graph G.

If S is a dominating set and $\langle S \rangle_w$ is connected, S is a weakly connected dominating set (WCDS).

4.3.3.1 The Related Works of Weakly Connected Dominating Sets

The concept of WCDS is proposed by Grossman [27]. The concept is derived from a long-term conjecture for a special Euler tour problem in a plane triangular partition. Dunbar et al. regulate the definition of WCDS further in Reference [28] and prove that the WCDS problem is NP-complete problem. Even in the simple binary graph, this conclusion holds. The authors studied the scale of WCDS and obtained the boundary value. In Reference [29] Chen and Liestman give a series of methods for searching minimum WCDSs in the given graphs. The main contribution of the paper is proposing a fully distributed searching WCDS algorithm. The performance of the algorithm is approximated to the centralized algorithm. Chen and Liestman [30] propose a regional distributed algorithm for maintaining WCDS when the structure of the network changes. The algorithm is a local algorithm when the region is small; the algorithm tends to be global when the region is large. Meanwhile, the WCDS scale is closely related to region size. When the region is large, the WCDS returned by the algorithm is relatively small. In the situation where the connectivity is not affected, the algorithm can ensure that the WCDS size matches its initial size.

WCDS construction plays a vital role in the clustering algorithm and the design process of the connected dominating set (CDS) construction algorithm. In general, the algorithm begins with constructing a WCDS. Guha and Khuller propose the second algorithm in Reference [18], which is used to construct a CDS by WCDS. The first WCDS construction algorithm selects the neighbor with the minimum id as the dominating node [31]. Later, many researchers downsize WCDS as much as possible by different technologies, thereby improving the stability of the dominating node in the set. In Reference [32], the node with the maximum node degree is selected as the dominating node, thereby obtaining relatively small WCDSs. Although the WCDS can be downsized in this way, selecting a dominating node by the maximum node degree improves the instability of the WCDS if the node is mobile, because the node degree will change along with the movement of the node. By contrast, selecting the dominating node by ID can improve the stability of the WCDS, because the ID will not change with the movement of the node.

Han and Jia [35] propose a distributed WCDS construction algorithm based on the region. The algorithm has a constant approximate ratio, linear time, and message complexity. The region algorithm divides the node into multiple regions then calculates the WCDS in each region and adds additional nodes to the WCDS to modify the boundary of each region. The greatest contribution of the algorithm is the region concept, ensuring weak connectivity by selecting the dominating node in each region. The approximate ratio of each region is decreased from 122.5 to 5. Meanwhile, the final scale of WCDS is reduced greatly. Dubhashi et al. [36] propose constructing a distributed algorithm within multiple logarithmic time, whose scale is at most $O(\log \Delta)$ times the minimum WCDS scale. Δ is the given maximum node degree. The authors also discuss how to construct a "low elasticity" dominating set. Low elasticity means that for any two adjacent nodes, the distance among their dominators is $O(\log n)$ at most.

4.3.3.2 The Distributed WCDS Algorithm

Alzoubi et al. propose two distributed algorithms in Reference [33], which can construct WCDS in $O(n)$ time. For the first algorithm, the approximate ratio is 5 and the message complexity is $O(n \log n)$. For the second algorithm, the approximate ratio is 122.5, which is larger than the first one, but its time complexity is only $O(n)$. The authors construct WCDS by MIS, modify the MIS algorithm in Reference [16], and obtain a new MIS construction algorithm by deeply analyzing various properties of MIS. The algorithm proposes a new sort method. The rank of the node is the unique signature, and all nodes will be sorted in ascending or descending order. In some situations, MIS needs to maintain the certain predefined properties. Therefore, some strict conditions will be attached when selecting the node of the MIS. The most basic principle is assigning the unique label for the node according to rank. In the construction process, sorting is obviously important when it needs to break the symmetry constraint.

Sorting is divided into two types: static and dynamic. Static sort means that the rank of the node will not be changed in the process of construction, such as the ID of the node. Dynamic sort means that the rank of the node may be changed in the process of construction, such as an ordered pair (degree, ID) or (degree, coordinate). In the construction process of the MIS algorithm, the ID and the coordinate of the node are used as the second rule for breaking symmetry. In the following, we will study the MIS algorithms proposed by Alzoubi et al.

4.3.3.2.1 Algorithm 4.1

Each node is sorted according to the ordered pair (layer, ID). In order to assign the layer for each node, we first construct a spanning tree T with node v as the root. After generating T, each node can determine its layer according to the distance to the root. The nodes are sorted in lexicographic order. Root node v is located at zero layer with the minimum rank. The rank of node 10 is (1, 10). Similarly, the rank of node 7 is (3, 7). This kind of rank is regarded as rank based on layer, whose goal is constructing the MIS with the following independent property: The shortest path between any two complementary subsets is exactly two hops. The MIS with this property is the WCDS. Note MIS as U, and initialize it as empty. The MIS construction algorithm is as follows.

$U = \emptyset$

While $(V \neq \emptyset)$

Let w be the node in V with the lowest rank

Add w to U

Mark w black, and all its neighbors gray

Remove w and all its neighbors from V

The MIS obtained by this algorithm can prove that the distance of any arbitrary two complementary subsets is exactly two hops; this is proven in Theorem 4.3.

Theorem 4.3: For the MIS U constructed by the MIS algorithm, the distance of any two complementary subsets is exactly 2.

Proof: Let $U = \{u_i : 1 \leq i \leq k\}$, where u_i is the ith node colored as black. For arbitrary $1 \leq j \leq k$, let H_j refer to the graph with $\{u_i : 1 \leq i \leq j\}$ as the vertex set. In the following, H_j will be proven as connected by induction. Since H_1 only includes one vertex, it is connected. Assume that H_{j-1}, $j \geq 2$ is connected. When node u_j is marked as black, its neighbor cannot be colored black, and its father in T has to already be colored gray. Therefore, there are adjacent black nodes u_i and u_j in $T, 1 \leq i \prec j$. Therefore, the distance between u_i and u_j is two hops, and (u_i, u_j) is the edge of H_j. Since H_{j-1} is connected, H_j is connected. Therefore, for arbitrary $1 \leq j \leq k$, graph H_j is connected. The connectivity of H_k proves that the distance between any two arbitrary complementary subsets is exactly two hops.

In the following, Theorem 4.4 proves that MIS is a WCDS, which is obtained by rank assignment based on the hierarchical method.

Theorem 4.4: The MIS obtained by rank assignment based on the hierarchical method is a WCDS.

Proof: In order to prove that S is a WCDS, we need to prove that S is a dominating set and that all edges relating to at least one node in S form a connected subgraph. Since S is the MIS, it is also a dominating set according to the definition. We color the edges adjacent to MIS black and other edges white. Therefore, weakly guiding subgraph G' includes all the black edges. We can prove G' is connected by contradiction. Assume that G' is unconnected, then at least two complementary subsets are separated by at least one white edge, and there is no black path among them. According to Theorem 4.3, the minimum hop between two arbitrary complementary subsets is exactly 2. Therefore, if there is an intermediate node that does not belong to the MIS of these two subsets, and the node is adjacent with at least one node in each subset of the MIS, these two edges need to be colored black. There is a black edge between two subsets, which contradicts the assumption. □

The first WCDS algorithm (Algorithm 4.1) proposed in the paper [33] makes full use of this theorem. The algorithm is divided into three stages: leader selection, hierarchical calculation, and coloring label. The stage of leader selection selects leader v and constructs the spanning tree with v as the root. The algorithm adopts the leader selection algorithm of Reference [34]. We can use ID or combine ID and degree to define the leader. After finishing the first stage, each node knows its father node and child node in T. In the stage of hierarchical calculation, each node marks its layer in T. From the root node, the layer of the root node is 0. Once a node receives the layer notice message, set its layer as the layer of its father plus 1; then inform its child node of its layer. At the same time, each node records the layer of its neighbors in the UDG. When the leaf node determines its layer, it will send a COMPLETE message to its father node. Each inside node will wait until it receives COMPLETE messages from all of its child nodes, then it will forward those messages to the root node. If the root node receives the COMPLETE messages from all child nodes, then the third stage begins. Now all nodes know their own layers and IDs, as well as those of their neighbors. This pair is the rank of each node. All the nodes are sorted in lexicographic order according to the rank. The leader has the minimum rank. In the stage of coloring label, all nodes are initialized as white. After finishing the stage, all the nodes will be colored black or gray. This stage will use two kinds of messages: the BLACK message and the GRAY message. A node will send a BLACK message after being colored as black; a node will send a GRAY message after being colored gray. These two message include the ID of the sender. In the beginning of the stage, the root node will mark itself black then broadcast a BLACK message to its neighbors. All of the other nodes execute the following steps:

1. Once a node receives a BLACK message for the first time, it will mark itself gray and broadcast a GRAY message.
2. A white node will mark itself black after receiving GRAY messages from neighbors of lower rank and broadcast a BLACK message.
3. All the edges connected to the black node will be colored black.

The time and message complexity of the algorithm depend on the complexity of the leader selection process, of which, the time complexity is $O(n)$, and the message complexity is $O(n \log n)$. Once the leader is selected, constant messages are needed only among the nodes. Lemma 4.6 proves that the WCDS scale obtained by this algorithm is at most five times the minimum WCDS scale.

Lemma 4.6: Assume *opt* is the optimal scale of MWCDS in UDG $G = (V, E)$. The WCDS scale generated by Algorithm 4.1 is $5 \cdot opt$ at most.

Proof: By the definition, each node in MIS belongs to MWCDS, or it is adjacent with at least one node in MWCDS; at most five neighbor nodes of each node in MWCDS belong to MIS. Therefore, the MIS scale is no greater than $5 \cdot opt$. Since the WCDS generated by Algorithm 4.1 is MIS, it holds that $|WCDS| \leq 5 \cdot opt$.

Lemma 4.7: For the dominating set S, if the minimum hop number of any two complementary subsets is two at most, S is a WCDS.

Proof: According to Theorem 4.4, if the minimum hop number of any two complementary subsets is two at most, S is a WCDS. When the minimum distance of any arbitrary two complementary subsets is one hop, the edges of two sets are black. Therefore, this weakly connected subgraph is connected, that is, S is a WCDS. □

4.3.3.2.2 Algorithm 4.2

In this section, we introduce Algorithm 4.2. WCDS obtained by this algorithm consists of two node sets: the MIS dominating node set and the additional-dominating node set. Lemma 4.7 has proven that a dominating set is a WCDS if the shortest path of any two complementary subsets in the dominating set is two hops at most. Algorithm 4.2 utilizes this conclusion to construct a WCDS by constructing a dominating set with the special property. The construction process is divided into three stages. The first stage constructs an arbitrary MIS, which proves that the shortest path of any two complementary subsets is two or three hops. In this way, it cannot ensure that the distance among arbitrary complementary subsets is exactly two hops. All the nodes in the MIS are regarded as MIS dominating nodes. The second stage modifies the MIS obtained in the first stage, making the distance between two arbitrary complementary subsets exactly two hops. Among arbitrary MIS dominators with exactly three-hop distances, select the intermediate nodes among three separate nodes as the additional-dominator. Finally, all the additional dominators and the MIS dominating nodes form the WCDS. In the third stage, any edge connected to a node in the WCDS will be colored black.

The specific content of Algorithm 4.2: Assume that each node has a unique ID and knows the IDs of all of its neighbors. Each node may have one of three colors: white, gray, or black. Each node is initialized as white, then it may be colored black or gray in the process of the algorithm. Each gray node has two lists: 1HopDomList and 2HopDomList. 1HopDomList includes the IDs of all dominators with one-hop distance from the gray node. Each item of 2HopDomList includes the ID of the two-hop dominator and the ID of the node that can arrive at the dominator and be adjacent to the gray node. Each MIS dominator has two lists: 2HopDomList and 3HopDomList. Each item of 3HopDomList includes the ID of the three-hop dominator and the IDs of two intermediate nodes that are passed by on the way to the dominator.

The specific steps of the algorithm are as follows:

1. If the ID of a node is lower than the IDs of all white neighbors, it will be colored black; it sends an MIS-DOMINATOR message to its neighbors to declare that it has become a dominator.
2. When a white node receives an MIS-DOMINATOR message for the first time, it will color itself gray and add the sender to the 1HopDomList. Then it will send a GRAY message.
3. Whenever a white node receives a GRAY message from a neighbor with a lower ID, it will color itself black and broadcast an MIS-DOMINATOR message to declare that it has become a dominator.
4. Once a gray node receives a GRAY or MIS-DOMINATOR message from all of its neighbors, the gray node will send a 1-HOP-DOMINATORS message, which includes its ID and those of its 1HopDomList.
5. When a gray node receives a 1-HOP-DOMINATORS message from a neighbor, it will add the ID of the dominator into its 2HopDomList list, which means the dominator is not within its 1HopDomList.
6. When the MIS dominator receives a 1-HOP-DOMINATORS message from a neighbor, it adds the ID of the dominator to the 2HopDomList, which means the dominator is not within its 2HopDomList except itself. If the ID of the dominator is within its 3HopDomList list, delete the dominator from the list.
7. When a gray node receives the 1-HOP-DOMINATORS message from each gray neighbor, it will send a 2-HOP-DOMINATORS message, which includes its ID and 2HopDomList.
8. When the MIS dominator u receives the 2-HOP-DOMINATORS message from neighbor v, for each entry (w, x) in the 2HopDomList of the message, the MIS dominator will add the entry (w, v, x) into its 3HopDomList if the dominator w is not within the 2HopDomList of u or within the 3HopDomList of u and the ID of u is lower than the ID of w. Then, w is a three-hop dominator and v and x are the intermediate nodes between w and u.
9. After receiving the SELECTION message with v as the destination, the node will mark itself black and broadcasts an ADDITIONAL-DOMINATOR message (which includes v, u, x, and w) to declare that it has become an additional-dominator.
10. Whenever the MIS dominator w receives the ADDITIONAL-DOMINATOR message, it adds the entry (u, x, v) to its 3HopDomList, where u is a three-hop dominator, and the nodes v and x are the intermediate nodes of w.

All MIS dominators and the additional-dominators form the WCDS U. Each edge adjacent at one or two nodes from U is colored black. The subgraph G', which contains all black edges, is the weakly induced subgraph. The WCDS is easy to maintain regardless of whether the node is mobile or has died. In the paper [33], the authors prove that they obtained the approximate ratio, time complexity, and message complexity of Algorithm 4.2. In the following, we will introduce the related theoretical proof of Algorithm 4.2. First, we introduce the proof related to the MIS properties.

Lemma 4.8: Let S be an arbitrary MIS in the UDG G and u an arbitrary node in S.

1. The number of the node that has a two-hop distance from node u in S is at most 23.
2. The number of the node that has a three-hop distance from node u in S is at most 47.

The detailed proof can be seen in Reference [33].

Theorem 4.5: Given a UDG $G = (V, E)$, for WCDS generated by Algorithm 4.2, the scale of U is $122.5opt$.

Proof: According to Lemma 4.8, in MIS, the total number of node pairs among which the distance is within three hops is at most $\dfrac{47|S|}{2}$. Since each pair like this will add at most one node into the additional-dominator set C, the number of the nodes in C is at most $\dfrac{47|S|}{2}$. According to Lemma 4.5, the total node number of U in WCDS is at most $\dfrac{47|S|}{2} + |S| = \dfrac{47 \cdot (5 \cdot opt)}{2} + 5 \cdot opt = 122.5 \cdot opt$. □

Theorem 4.6: Algorithm 4.2 for constructing a WCDS has $O(n)$ time complexity and $O(n)$ message complexity.

Proof: The worst time complexity for the MIS occurs when all nodes are arranged in either ascending or descending order and the maximum node degree is 2. In this case, each node has to wait for all other nodes with lower ids. Assume that we have a graph with n nodes $(v_1, v_2, ..., v_n)$; then each node v_i must wait for its neighbor node v_{i-1} to declare its state. Each node must wait one time unit more than the previous node had to. Node v_n has to wait the longest $(n-1)$ units. Also, each node sends only one message (either an MIS-DOMINATOR or a GRAY message). To find the additional-dominators, each gray node waits duration $O(\Delta)$ to build its 1HopDomList and 2HopDomList. An MIS-dominator node waits $O(\Delta)$ for 1-HOP-DOMINATORS and 2-HOP-DOMINATORS messages from all its neighbors before it selects an additional-dominator. The duration required to perform the rest of the procedures is constant. Since each node sends a constant number of messages, the total number of messages is $O(n)$. Thus, both the time complexity and the message complexity of the algorithm are $O(n)$. □

4.3.4 Extended Weakly Dominating Sets

In a given network, the dominating set is denoted as S. If each node belongs to S, one of its neighbors belongs to S, or k two-hop neighbors belong to S, S is regarded as an extended dominating set (EDS). When $k = 2$, the quasi-weak subgraph induced by S is $\langle S \rangle_{qw} = (N_2[S], E \cap (N_2[S] \times N[S]))$. $\langle S \rangle_{qw}$ includes the nodes in S and all the general neighbors and two-hop neighbors as the node set, where the edge set of graph G connected with at least one node of S or $N(S)$ is the edge set of $\langle S \rangle_{qw}$.

4.3.4.1 Classical Extended Dominating Set Algorithm

Wu et al. first proposed the concept of EDS based on cooperative communications in Reference [37]. The essence of cooperative communications is that each single-antenna node shares the antennas in the multiuser network environment, thereby constructing a multi-input multioutput system. The cooperative communication has several advantages as follows: (1) energy can be saved by multiple hops; (2) the antennas of mobile nodes provide spatial diversity for communication; (3) the cooperation among the nodes improves the data transmission rate. In cooperative communication, the same packet has multiple independent copies to be transmitted, which can improve diversity and resist the influence of signal fading. Under the condition without increasing the transmitting power, k copies of the same packet can arrive at the nodes beyond the normal communication range. In the mode of cooperative communication, if an arbitrary node u sends a packet in extended dominating set (EDS), and the packet is received completely at the end, EDS is strongly connected and called an ECDS. Only the node that receives the packet completely can forward the packet. If at least a special node satisfies the strong connectivity in EDS, EDS is weakly connected, called EWCDS. EDS, ECDS, and EWCDS are all NP-complete problems [38].

In Reference [38], a centralized Greedy algorithm is proposed to form the minimum EWCDS. The algorithm uses a "contribution" concept. Each forwarding node has contribution to all its neighbors as 1 and to all two-hop neighbors as $1/k$. Our goal is to find the minimum EWCDS, ensuring that non-ECDS nodes are reachable (i.e., the signal of each node is at least 1). The effective contribution of v to u refers to the contribution of v to u before the signal energy of node v reaches 1. The signal energy of each node is initialized as zero. Assume that the signal energy of node u is 0.5 and $k = 4$ before v forwards a message. If v, u are the mutual neighbors, the effective contribution of node v to u is 0.5; if v, u are the mutual two-hop neighbors, the effective contribution of node v to u is 0.25. When the node has the biggest effective contribution to all its neighbors and two-hop neighbors, it has the maximum effective contribution. In Algorithm 4.1, the node with the maximum effective contribution is selected as the root node, thereby constructing a tree. In each round, the algorithm selects the node with maximum effective contribution as the root node, until the signal energy of each node in the network reaches at least 1. For simplicity, assume $r' = 2 \times r$ and $k = 2$.

Extended MCDS algorithm is as follows:

---

1. Initialize the nodes: The node with the most significant contribution (as the root node) is grayed out; the other nodes are initialized to white.
2. Select the gray node with the maximum effective contribution to its white neighbors (regular neighbor and two-hop neighbor).
3. Update the signal energy value of each regular neighbor and two-hop neighbor of the selected gray node.
4. Color the selected gray node black and other white regular node gray. If the signal energy value of a white two-hop neighbor is at least 1, color the node gray.
5. Repeat steps 2, 3, and 4 until the signal energy value of each node is at least 1.

Algorithm 4.1 can obtain an EWCDS on a small scale. The high performance of the algorithm can be seen in the following simulation result, but the approximate ratio of the algorithm is not a constant. In order to obtain the EWCDS construction algorithm with a constant approximate ratio, we modify Algorithm 4.1 and adopt two kinds of black to label the nodes in EWCDS: black 1 and black 2. The extended rule of Algorithm 4.2 is as follows: When a gray node needs to be added into the EWCDS, if it has no black1 neighbor, it will be colored black1; if it has a black1 neighbor, it will be colored black 2; if it has black1 and black 2 neighbors at the same time, it cannot be added into the EWCDS. All white nodes can be covered by modifying the algorithm. Besides, the scale of EWCDS obtained by Algorithm 4.2 is 50 times the optimal scale of EWCDS, proved by the theorem. A node that executes Algorithm 4.1 can spread the obtained EWCDS to the whole network at the same time it collects global information.

The authors extend the AWF algorithm [9], which constructs CDS, and obtain the quasi-global algorithm of EWCDS. The AWF algorithm includes the methods of topology sorting, sequential clustering, and gateway assignment. In the extended AWF algorithm (E-AWF), the authors modify the gateway assignment method. They use the extended gateway assignment method and obtain an EWCDS. The approximate ratio of the E-AWF algorithm is a constant. The first two steps of the E-AWF algorithm are the same as those for the AWF algorithm. The third step is the extended gateway assignment method: Each nonroot black node assigns to its neighbor a minimum rank as the gateway only when it cannot reach the black node and the gateway node with a lower rank; otherwise, it assigns no gateway. Finally, the selected black node and the gateway form the EWCDS. The number of black nodes selected by the E-AWF equals that of the AWF algorithm. However, the number of gateway nodes selected by the E-AWF is equal to or lower than that of the AWF algorithm.

The authors also propose a quasi-local algorithm of the minimum unconnected EDS and extend it as a connected EDS algorithm. The so-called quasi-local algorithm means the algorithm can be completed with high probability within small constant rounds. The algorithm is based on a cooperative communication model, and each node executes the algorithm within the range of its two-hop neighbors. The specific details will not be introduced. Then the authors give the local algorithms for EDS and ECDS. The algorithms have two steps: (1) Use the labeling process [23] proposed by Wu and Li and the branching rule [39] proposed by Dai and Wu to construct the CDS; (2) under the guarantee of local coverage and connectivity, use the branching rule to delete nodes from the CDS. Theorem 4.7 proves that the scale of ECDS obtained by the algorithm is $O(1) \cdot |ECDS_{opt}|$, where $|ECDS_{opt}|$ is the optimal solution of the ECDS problem. The authors also discuss the application of ECDS/ESCDS under the communication-cooperation model. For example, as the virtual backbone network, it minimizes the energy consumption of sensing by controlling the active or sleeping state of the node, thereby prolonging the lifetime of the node. Constructing EWCDS is an effective method of clustering. Researchers can obtain many clustering algorithms with better performance by combining the dominating set problem and the clustering problem.

4.3.4.2 Three Novel EWCDS Algorithms

Yu et al. [40] studied EWCDS in depth and obtained three novel EWCDS algorithms.

The extended dominating ability of the node: In the network, each node is able to not only completely dominate itself and its one-hop neighbors; it also partly dominates its two-hop quasi-neighbors. In Figure 4.4, node u not only completely dominates u, w, and y; it also dominates x and z. The method extends the dominating ability of the node to its two-hop neighbor from its one-hop neighbor.

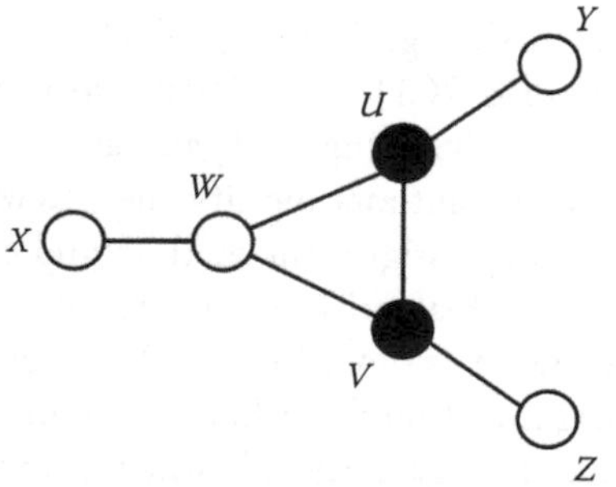

Figure 4.4 {*u, v*} is an EDS.

Figure 4.5 $d_u = 3$.

For simplicity, in the following algorithm description, the node rank will be the rule of the cluster head selection. At first, we redefine the concept of the degree of the node. The degree of node u refers to the sum of its regular neighbors and generic neighbors, as shown in Figure 4.5. The rank of node u is an ordered pair (d_u, id_u), where d_u is the node degree, and id_u is the ID of node u. If $d_u > d_v$ or $d_u = d_v$, and $id_u \prec id_v$, we consider that node u with rank (d_u, id_u) has a higher order than node v with rank (d_v, id_v).

4.3.4.2.1 An EWCDS Area Construction Algorithm Based on Extensive Area

The extended area algorithm EAA includes three stages: partition area, constructing the EWCDS in each area, and forming the EWCDS of the whole network. In the construction process of EDS, a node will be partitioned into an area naturally. Besides, in each area, the dominating node autonomously forms an EWCDS of the area, which is then used to form the EWCDS of the whole network. The execution process of the algorithm will be described in detail. For an arbitrary node $u \in V$, $v \in N_2(u) - N(u)$, v is a quasi-cluster head (dominating) neighbor if v is a cluster head (dominating node).

4.3.4.2.1.1 Partition the Area and Construct the EWCDS for Each Area

In this stage, the nodes in the network are partitioned into different areas, and each area is given a unique ID. Each node is also assigned an area ID to represent the area in which it belongs. Each node has one of the four states: unlabeled (UM), cluster head (CH), cluster member (CM), and half-dominating HD.

Algorithm description:

1. Initially, all the nodes stay in UM state;
2. Select the node u as the cluster head, which stays in the UM state and has the highest rank of its neighbors. Then broadcast a CH message to all neighbors. There has to be such a node initially.
3. When a node v receives a CH message,
   1. if v is the rule-neighbor of u and the current state of v is UM, v becomes a cluster member. If this is the first time it receives the CH message, v needs to broadcast a CM message.

2. if v is a quasi-neighbor of u and the current state of v is UM, which means that v receives the CH message for the first time, then it becomes an HD node, and the state is switched to HD.

   1. if v is a quasi-neighbor of u and the current state of v is HD, when v receives a different CH message for the second time, it becomes a cluster member and broadcasts a CM message.
   2. if v is a quasi-neighbor of u and the current state of v is HD, when v no longer receives a CH message, it becomes a cluster head and broadcasts a CH message.

4. The rest of the nodes execute the same process repeatedly until each node becomes a cluster head or a cluster member.

Based on this, a node u can become a cluster head if and only if:

1. node u has the highest rank among all its neighbors (rule-neighbor, quasi-neighbor),
2. node u has neighbors with higher rank, but these neighbors have become the cluster members of other clusters, or
3. node u only has one quasi-cluster head neighbor.

We call the cluster head satisfying Condition 1 the root cluster head and the cluster head satisfying Conditions 2 and 3 the nonroot cluster head. Obviously, the root cluster head affects the conditions, which can change a node into a noncluster head. In order to partition the graph, regard the ID of a root cluster head as the ID of the corresponding area with the cluster head as the center. We add areaID to the CH message to represent the area to which a cluster head belongs; it then holds that

1. When a UM rule-neighbor receives the CH message for the first time, it will become a cluster member of the area indicated in the CH message.
2. When a UM quasi-neighbor receives the CH message for the first time and it will no longer receive the other CH message, it becomes a cluster head and is located in the area indicated in the CH message.
3. When a UM quasi-neighbor receives a different CH message for the second time, it becomes a cluster member and is located in the area where the root cluster head has higher rank.

Each cluster member adds areaID to the CM message. Finally, the nodes with the same areaID form an area, then the graph is partitioned into different areas, and the cluster head in each area forms an EWCDS of the area.

4.3.4.2.1.2 Construct an EWCDS of the Whole Network

After partitioning the graph, in each area, either a root cluster head dominates the area or at least one noncluster head that has 2 hops distance to the root cluster head dominates the area along with the root cluster head. Therefore, the cluster head in each area forms an EWCDS for the spanner graph of the area.

Theorem 4.7: Combine the EWCDS of each area and then the EWCDS of the whole graph can be obtained.

Proof: In the area partition stage, we can see that when partitioning a UM quasi-neighbor, if the quasi-neighbor receives the CH messages from cluster heads of different areas, it will become a cluster member and the two areas are weakly connected. On the other hand, if the neighbor only receives one CH message from a root cluster head, it will become a cluster head, and the area of the root cluster head can be connected with other areas by the nonroot cluster head. Therefore, combining the EWCDS of each area can generate the EWCDS of the whole graph. Thus, we can conclude that, in EAA, the EWCDS of each area and EWCDS of the whole graph are formed simultaneously by the construction of EDS, that is, these three steps are completed in the same operation.

In order to explain the execution process of the whole algorithm, Figure 4.6 gives an instance of constructing EWCDS by the EAA algorithm. In the graph, the ID of a node is indicated around the node; the black node indicates the cluster head; the black node with a circle indicates the root cluster head; the white node indicates the cluster member.

The execution process is as follows:

1. Nodes 1, 2, and 3 declare that they will become cluster heads and broadcast the CH message because they have the highest rank among their UM neighbors (rule-neighbor, quasi-neighbor). In fact, they are the root cluster head.
2. When receiving the CH message, nodes 6, 7, 8, 9, 10, 12, 13, 14, and 15 declare that they will become cluster member and broadcast the CM message. They belong to the area of their root cluster head.

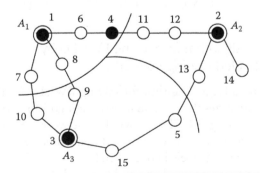

Figure 4.6   An instance of solving EWCDS by EAA algorithm.

3. When receiving a CH message for the first time, nodes 4, 5, and 11 declare that they will become the HD node. Since node 4 will no longer receive the other CH message, it becomes a cluster head and broadcasts a CH message. Besides, it locates in the area of node 1. Node 1 can receive the CH message again from node 4, thus node 11 becomes a cluster member and locates in the area of node 2. Node 5 can receive the CH message again from node 3, thus node 5 also becomes a cluster member. Since the rank of node 3 is larger than that of node 2, node 5 locates in the area of node 3.

4. The graph is partitioned into three areas A_1, A_2, A_3 with area signature 1, 2, and 3, respectively. According to the definition of EWCDS, the black node set {1, 2, 3, 4} forms an EWCDS of the whole graph.

4.3.4.2.1.3 Theoretical Performance Analysis   Theorem 4.7 proved the correctness of the EAA algorithm.

Theorem 4.8: The time complexity and message complexity of the EAA algorithm both are $O(n)$.

Proof: For selecting the root cluster head, the algorithm needs to compare the ranks of all nodes. When the nodes are sorted as a line of ascending or descending order, the worst situation is limited by duration $O(n)$. The rest of the algorithm can be completed in duration $O(1)$. Therefore, the time complexity of the extensive region algorithm is $O(n)$.

At the beginning, each node needs to send a HELLO message to its neighbors, so that it can obtain the rank of each node. Thus, it needs to send a HELLO message with $O(n)$ information at most. In the stage of comparing the size of rank, each node needs to exchange the message; thus, the total information is $O(n)$. Each root cluster head sends a CH message to its neighbors, thus it sends $O(n)$ information in the whole network at most. Similarity, each cluster member needs to send $O(n)$ information in a CM message.

Therefore, the time and message complexity of the EAA algorithm are both $O(n)$.

4.3.4.2.2 A Local Algorithm for Solving EWCDS by the Extended Cutting Rule EPA

This section will give a local algorithm for solving EWCDS by the extended cutting rule (EPA) and analyzes the performance of the algorithm. This is a novel local algorithm for constructing EWCDS in wireless networks. Here, a labeled node indicates a dominating node, and an unlabeled node indicates a dominated node.

Extended cutting rule: A labeled node u can become unlabeled if u has a labeled one-hop neighbor or k labeled two-hop neighbors and there is no node dominated only by u.

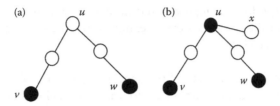

Figure 4.7 **(a) The graph with unlabeled *u* and (b) *u* cannot become unlabeled.**

As shown in Figure 4.7a, the labeled node *u* has two labeled neighbors *v* and *w*; thus, it can become unlabeled; as shown in Figure 4.7b, *u* cannot be unlabeled, because *x* is only dominated by *u*, although *u* has two labeled neighbors.

The EPA algorithm can be divided into two stages. First, select the node with the high rank as the cluster head of the one-hop neighbors. All the selected cluster heads form an unconnected dominating set of the whole graph. Then reduce the size of the dominating set by the extensive cutting rule and construct an EDS.

4.3.4.2.2.1 Find an Unconnected Dominating Set of a Graph

1. Select an unlabeled node with the highest rank of the one-hop neighbors as the cluster head and broadcast a CH message.
2. If a node *v* receives the CH message, *v* will become a cluster member if the current state is unlabeled. If *v* receives the CH message for the first time, *v* sends a CM message.
3. The rest of the nodes execute the same process repeatedly until each node has become a cluster head or a cluster member. After finishing this stage, each node in the network will become the cluster head or the cluster member finally. The cluster heads form a corresponding dominating set, because each cluster member has at least one cluster head neighbor, that is, all nodes can be dominated by the cluster heads. Obviously, the dominating set is unconnected since there may exist two cluster heads separated by 2 or more hops.

4.3.4.2.2.2 Construct EDS
After finishing the first stage of the algorithm, an unconnected dominating set of the graph can be obtained. In the following, the algorithm cuts the obtained dominating set by the extended cutting rule (i.e., two-hop neighbor information, thereby reducing the number of the cluster head and obtaining an EDS of a smaller scale).

According to the decreasing order of node ranks, check the dominating nodes obtained in stage 1 and check whether each dominating node has 2 neighbor dominating nodes.

1. If there are not 2 dominating nodes, the state of the dominating node stays unchanged, then check the next dominating node.

2. If there are 2 dominating nodes and no node only dominated by this dominating node (i.e., it satisfies the extended cutting rule), the dominating node becomes unlabeled.

The second stage reduces the scale of the dominating set. The obtained nodes form an EDS of the whole graph. That is because each node belongs to the dominating node set, one of its neighbors belongs to the set, or two neighbors belong to the set.

4.3.4.2.2.3 Construct EWCDS

Theorem 4.9: After finishing two stages, the obtained dominating node set is the EWCDS of the whole graph.

Proof: The dominating node set forms an unconnected dominating set of the whole graph in stage A, because two dominating nodes are separated by more than 1 hop, and the distances among the dominating nodes are at most 3 hops. The definition of EWCDS shows that the dominating set obtained in stage A is an EWCDS. Stage B does not destroy the connectivity, although it reduces the scale of the dominating node. Therefore, after stage B, the obtained dominating node set is an EWCDS of the whole graph with smaller scale. The theorem also proves the correctness of the algorithm.

To increase the understanding of the whole execution process of the algorithm, here we give an instance of the algorithm.

The black node in Figure 4.8a indicates the dominating node obtained after stage A; the black node in Figure 4.8b indicates the dominating node obtained after stage B (i.e., after the extended cutting rule). The specific execution process is as follows:

1. Nodes 1, 2, 3, 4, and 6 declare that they are cluster heads and broadcast the CH message, because they have the highest rank among their unlabeled one-hop neighbors.
2. After receiving the CH message, nodes 8, 9, 10, 11, 12, 7, 13, 14, 15, and 5 declare they are cluster members and broadcast the CM message.

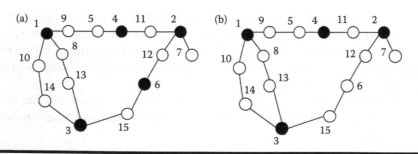

Figure 4.8 (a) {1, 2, 3, 4, 6} is an unconnected dominating set and (b) {1, 2, 3, 4} is an EWCDS.

3. After these two steps, the nodes in the whole graph become cluster heads or cluster members, as shown in Figure 4.8a.
4. Check whether nodes 1, 2, 3, 4, 6 satisfy the cutting rule in turn. Nodes 1, 3, and 4 are still the dominating nodes because they do not have 2 dominating quasi-neighbors. Node 2 is still a dominating node because node 7 is only dominated by node 2 although node 2 has two dominating quasi-neighbors 4 and 6. Node 6 has two dominating quasi-neighbors 2 and 3, which satisfies the cutting rule, thus node 6 becomes unlabeled. After step 4, the obtained node states are shown in Figure 4.8b. Combining wish theorem 3 shows that {1, 2, 3, 4} forms an EWCDS of the graph.

4.3.4.2.2.4 Theoretical Performance Analysis

Theorem 4.10: The time and message complexity of the EPA algorithm are both $O(n)$.

Proof: The algorithm needs to compare the node ranks of one-hop neighbors in the first stage. In the worst case (i.e., all nodes are sorted as a line by ascending or descending order of their ranks) the time complexity is limited by $O(n)$. In the second stage, judge the cutting condition of each black node obtained in the first stage and cut nodes by decreasing order of rank. The second stage only needs duration $O(1)$; thus, the time complexity of the whole algorithm is $O(n)$.

Next we analyze message complexity. In the first stage, each node sends information with a constant level; thus, the total number of messages in this stage is $O(n)$. In the second stage, only dominating nodes need to send the message for at most $O(n)$, which is twice the length of the first stage. Thus the message complexity of the whole algorithm is $O(n)$. Therefore, the time and the message complexity are both $O(n)$.

4.3.4.2.3 The EWCDS Constructing Algorithm Based on "Zone"—PA

In the centralized algorithm [30] for solving WCDS, Chen and Liestman use the term "zone" to indicate a special substructure (as shown in Figure 4.9) and use "improved value" of nonblack nodes as the rule for selecting black nodes. Based on the extension for dominating the ability of the node in the last section, here we redefine the terms "zone" and "improved value." A white zone indicates a white node; a black zone is a maximum set that includes a black node (the weakly spanning subgraph formed by the black node is connected) and all gray nodes (including rule-neighbor and quasi neighbor) that are adjacent to at least one black node in the zone. Figure 4.10 explains the definition. Node 4 is a white zone, and other nodes are n black zone, including black nodes 1, 2, and 3. The improved value of nonblack node u is the number of all the zones in $N_2[u]$; that is, the improved value of u is the zone number of the black zone after u is colored as black. As shown in

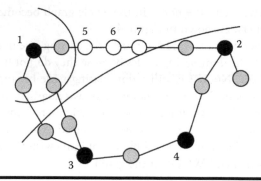

Figure 4.9   3 white zones and 2 black zones.

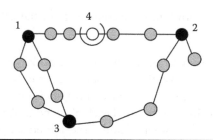

Figure 4.10   1 white zone and 1 black zone.

Figure 4.10, the improved value of node 4 is 2; that is, two zones are merged as a bigger black zone after node 4 is colored as black, thereby reducing the zone number in the graph.

4.3.4.2.3.1 Execute CPA in Centralized Mode

4.3.4.2.3.1.1 Algorithm Description   Given a graph $G = (V, E)$. Each node can have one color: white, gray, or black. All nodes are initialized as white; they change color during the execution of the algorithm. The specific process is as follows:

1. All nodes are initialized as white, which means there are n zones initially.
2. Select the node with the maximum improved value and color it black. All its white neighbors (rule-neighbor, quasi-neighbor) become gray. The black nodes are merged in a black zone with all of their gray neighbors, thereby reducing the zone numbers in the graph.
3. If there exist white nodes in the graph, repeat step 2 until there exists one black zone. Then the algorithm ends.

From the execution, we can see that the algorithm selects the node in a greedy way: reduce the zone number as much as possible until there exists one zone. In fact, the algorithm is an iteration of the process that colors the white or gray node black. Finally, all black nodes form the EWCDS.

Now, we give an instance of the centralized execution process of the CPA algorithm based on "zone," as shown in Figure 4.11.

The execution process of the algorithm is as follows:

1. Initially, there are 16 white zones in the graph. Node 1 is colored black since it has the maximum improved value: 7. Nodes 6, 7, 8, 9, 10, and 11 change to gray and are merged into a big black zone with node 1, thereby reducing 6 zone numbers in the graph, as shown in Figure 4.11a.
2. Color the node with the maximum improved value black among the white and gray nodes. Here, select node 2 with the maximum improved value 6, while nodes 12, 13, 14, 15, and 16 change to gray and are merged into a big black zone, thereby reducing to 5 the zones in the graph, as shown in Figure 4.11b.
3. In the third iteration, select node 3 with improved value 4 as black while 2 changes to gray and is merged into a bigger zone by combining two adjacent big zones, thereby reducing to 3 zones, as shown in Figure 4.11c.

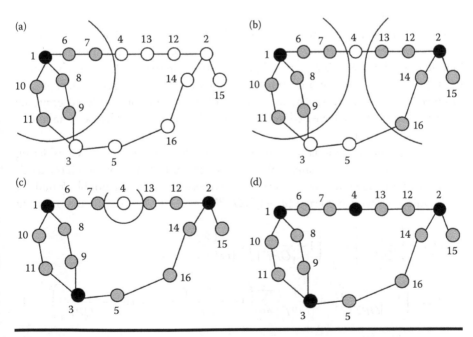

Figure 4.11 The process of construction EWCDS by the CPA algorithm and the DPA algorithm.

4. In the fourth iteration, select node 4 with the maximum improved value as black. After merging, the graph is a black zone; then the algorithm ends. The black node set {1, 2, 3, 4} forms the EWCDS of the graph, as shown in Figure 4.11d.

4.3.4.2.3.1.2 Theoretical Performance Analysis

Theorem 4.11: For a given graph G, let OPT indicate the minimum EWCDS of G; Δ indicates the maximum degree of G. Then the scale of EWCDS obtained by CPA algorithm is at most $(\ln \Delta + 1/2) * |OPT|$.

Proof: Let u be an arbitrary node in OPT; let the degree of u_1 (including the number of rule-neighbors and quasi-neighbors) be at most Δ, and u_1 can dominate at most $\Delta + 1$ different nodes (including u_1 itself). Since OPT is an EWCDS of G, there surely exists an element of OPT that has at most 4 hops to u_1. Assume u_2 is a node like that. There exists at least one node in the quasi-neighbors of u_2, which is also a quasi-neighbor of u_1, thus at most Δ new different nodes can be dominated by u_2. Also, since OPT is the EWCDS of G, there exists another element in OPT whose distance to u_1 or u_2 is at most 4. We assume the node is u_3, which can dominate Δ new different nodes. Then we can continue to discuss until including all $|OPT|$ elements in OPT. Therefore, G includes at most $n \leq (\Delta + 1) + \Delta * (|OPT| - 1)$ nodes; thus, $|OPT| \geq (n-1)/\Delta$.

In each iteration of the algorithm, we color a node black and add it to S. It can be seen that the improvement of any node is monotonically nonincreasing with iteration. At the beginning of the algorithm, the improved value of each node u is its degree plus 1. When a neighbor is colored black, u changes to gray, and its improved value is decreased by at least 2. When a neighbor is colored gray, the improved value of u is decreased by at least 1. When u is colored black, it no longer has an improved value.

Let a_i indicate the residual zone number of ith iteration and $a_0 = n$. Considering $(I+1)$th iteration, since the joining of nonblack node of OPT will merge all the residual a_i zones, thereby reducing $a_i - 1$ zones, there exists at least one nonblack node of OPT, which can reduce at least $\lceil (a_i - 1)/|OPT| \rceil$ zones. Here is the circular relation:

$$a_{i+1} \leq a_i - \left\lceil \frac{a_{i-1}}{|OPT|} \right\rceil \leq a_i * \left(1 - \frac{1}{|OPT|}\right) + \frac{1}{|OPT|}$$

$$\leq a_0 * \left(1 - \frac{1}{|OPT|}\right)^{i+1} + \frac{1}{|OPT|} \sum_{j=0}^{i}\left(1 - \frac{1}{|OPT|}\right)^{j} = (a_0 - 1)\left(1 - \frac{1}{|OPT|}\right)^{i+1} + 1$$

Let $i + 1 = |OPT| * \ln\left(\frac{a_0 - 1}{|OPT|}\right)$, then

$$a_{i+1} \le (a_0 - 1)\left(1 - \frac{1}{|OPT|}\right)^{i+1} + 1$$

$$= (a_0 - 1)\left(1 - \frac{1}{|OPT|}\right)^{|OPT| * \ln(\frac{a_0 - 1}{|OPT|})} + 1$$

$$\le (a_0 - 1)\left(\frac{1}{e}\right)^{\ln(\frac{a_0 - 1}{|OPT|})} + 1$$

$$= (a_0 - 1)\frac{|OPT|}{a_0 - 1} + 1 = |OPT| + 1$$

In other words, the residual zone number is at most $|OPT| + 1$ after $|OPT| * \ln(a_0 - 1)/|OPT|$ times of iteration. Each selected additional node can reduce at least 2 zones, thus the zone number will be reduced to 1 after selecting at most $\lceil |OPT|/2 \rceil$ additional nodes. Therefore, the total number of selected nodes is no greater than $|OPT| * \ln((a_0 - 1)/|OPT|) + \lceil |OPT|/2 \rceil$. Since $|OPT| \ge (n-1)/\Delta$, the solution that CPA algorithm can obtain is at most $(\ln \Delta + 1/2) * |OPT|$ nodes. □

Theorem 4.12: In the CPA algorithm, the message complexity is $O(n^3)$ and time complexity is $O(n \log n)$.

Proof: In the execution of CPA, each node in the network needs to know the improved value of its rule-neighbor and quasi-neighbor, and it has to know the improved value of other nodes in the network as well, thereby determining the node with the maximum improved value. Therefore, each node needs to broadcast HELLO message in the determining process, thereby determining the neighbor relation. It also needs to broadcast the neighbor information (including improved value). Therefore, the message account is $O(n^2)$ in the whole process. The algorithm iterates for n times at most; thus the total message complexity is $O(n^3)$.

Initially, each node in the network finds all its neighbors by broadcasting ID with time overhead $O(n)$. Then each node calculates its improved value and compares it with other nodes in the network with time overhead $O(n)$. The CPA algorithm selects the node with the maximum improved value and colors it black. The black node is merged into a black zone with its neighbors. The algorithm is executed iteratively until only one black zone is left in the whole network. The algorithm is executed at most $O(\log n)$ times; thus, the total time overhead is $O(n \log n)$.

It can be seen from this theoretical analysis that although the centralized algorithm can obtain the EWCDS with a small approximate factor, the message complexity and time complexity are too large; this is the drawback of most centralized algorithms and makes them unsuitable for the real network. In order to improve the feasibility of the algorithm in the real network, we will describe the distributed execution of the algorithm.

4.3.4.2.3.2 Distributed processing algorithm The Distributed Processing Algorithm (DPA) description:

1. Compare the one-hop rule-neighbor and quasi-neighbor and select the node with the largest improved value as the dominating node. Then send a CH message to its rule-neighbor and quasi-neighbor.
2. After receiving the CH message, the rule-neighbor and quasi-neighbor will color themselves gray and then send CM messages.
3. Execute the algorithm until there are no unlabeled nodes in the network.

After executing DPA, nodes 1, 2, 3, 4 become the dominating nodes, and other nodes become the dominated nodes, as shown in Figure 4.11d. Obviously, the time overhead of each execution is $O(1)$; thus, the total time overhead of the algorithm is $O(n)$. Besides, in the distributed execution, each node only needs to collect the improved value of its rule-neighbor and quasi-neighbor; thus, the message complexity is lower than the centralized execution, obviously. Therefore, Theorem 4.13 is established.

Theorem 4.13: The time complexity and message complexity of DPA algorithm are both $O(n)$.

4.3.5 The Edge Dominating Set

Assume a graph $G = (V, E)$ and a set $M \subseteq E$. For $\forall e \in E \setminus M$, e has common endpoints with all edges of M; thus, regard M as the edge dominating set of graph G. The edge dominating set has close relationship with the maximum minimum matching problem and the edge dominating set problem has been proven as NP-complete [1]. Yannakakis et al. proved further that the edge dominating set problem is an NP-complete problem even in the strict plane graph or the binary graph with a maximum degree of 3 in Reference [58].

4.3.5.1 Related Works of the Edge Dominating Set

Carr et al. [40] give an approximate algorithm for solving the edge dominating set in a weighted graph, of which the approximate ratio is $2\frac{1}{10}$. Afterwards, Fujito improves the approximate ratio of solving the edge dominating set in a weighted graph up to 2 in Reference [41]. Cardinal and Langerman propose a Greedy algorithm for a minimum edge dominating set in a weighted graph in Reference [42]. The edge weight is the sum of the degrees of two endpoints; the algorithm is executed iteratively. The approximate ratio is 2 when the edge with maximum degree is deleted each time. Randerath and Schiermeyer [52] designed the first EDS ordinary algorithm with $O(1.4423^{|E|})$ time complexity. Raman et al. [53] modify the runtime as $O(1.4423^n)$, where $n = |V|$ is the number set of the nodes. Fomin et al. [54] modify further the complexity results and obtain $O(1.4082^n)$ by the width of the graph. van Rooij and Bodlaender [55] utilize the Measure and Conquer algorithm to design a simple algorithm with $O(1.3323^n)$ time complexity. They limit the runtime within $O(1.3226^n)$ by checking the local structure. When the maximum node degree is limited to 3, the minimum duration needed by solving the edge dominating set is at least $O(1.2721^n)$ [56].

4.3.5.2 The Classical Edge Dominating Set Algorithm

Xiao et al. propose an algorithm with time complexity $O(1.3160^n)$, which can calculate an edge dominating set in a graph with n vertices. In the paper, Xiao et al. analyze the algorithm by the Measure and Conquer method and design a branching rule based on simple local structure, which is called "clique-producing vertices/cycles." The rule makes it easy to analyze the algorithm and its runtime.

4.3.5.2.1 Algorithm Description

We use a quintuple (G, C, I, U_1, U_2) to describe the algorithm, where G is a given network graph; $C \subseteq V$ satisfies a certain independent set $I \subseteq V - C$, $U_1 \subseteq V, U_2 \subseteq V$; each $G[U_1]$ is a group structure of $G[V \setminus (C \cup I)]$. Initialize $C = I = U_1 = \emptyset$, and $U_2 = V$. Regard the edge dominating set as M. If $C \subseteq V(M)$ and $I \cap V(M) = \emptyset$, M is noted as $(C, I) - eds$. The branching rule is used to remove the nodes in U_2. v is an arbitrary node in U_2. In the algorithm, the simplest branching process is to judge whether v is included in C or I; then branch it. When v is included in I, add all its neighbors into C. Once the new group is generated, remove all the nodes of the group structure from U_1. The other branching rule is "branching on a 4-cycle". Let $abcd$ be a 4-cycle. There exist edges ab, bc, cd, da in graph $G[U_2]$. The $\{a, c\}$ or $\{b, d\}$ will be added into C by this rule, thereby completing the branching on a 4-cycle. For a vertex $v \in U_2$ in graph $G[U_2]$, let $d(v)$ be the degree of v in $G[U_2]$. $N(v)$ is the set of all neighbors of v in $G[U_2]$, and $N[v] = N(v) \cup \{v\}$ is the set of vertices with a distance of at most 1 from v. $N_2(v)$ is the set of vertices with a distance of exactly 2 from v in $G[U_2]$, and $N_2[v] = N_2(v) \cup N[v]$. A vertex v is called a clique-producing vertex (cp-vertex for short) if at least one clique component will be generated by removing v from $G[U_2]$. A 4-cycle abcd is called a clique-producing cycle (cp-cycle for short) if removing {a, c} or {b, d} generates at least one clique component. The specific algorithm for the edge dominating set is as follows:

Input: A graph $G = (V, E)$ and partition of V into sets. Initially $C = I = U_1 = \varnothing$, and $U_2 = V$.

Output: A minimum $(C, I) - eds$

1. If {There is a clique component Q in $G[U_2]$}, move $V(Q)$ into U_1.
2. Else if {There are some cp-vertices in $G[U_2]$}, branch on an optimal cp-vertex by including it into either C or I.
3. Else if {There is a vertex v of degree ≥ 5 in $G[U_2]$}, branch on by including it into either C or I.
4. Else if {There are some degree-4 vertices in $G[U_2]$}, branch on an optimal degree-4 vertex by including it into either C or I.
5. Else if {There is a cp-cycle abcd in $G[U_2]$}, branch on it by including either {a,c} or {b,d} into C.
6. Else if {There are some degree-3 vertices in $G[U_2]$}, branch on an optimal degree-3 vertex by including it into either C or I.
7. Else if {$G[U_2]$ contains only components of cycles of length ≥ 5}, branch on any degree-2 vertex by including it into either C or I.
8. Else (Now $U_2 = \varnothing$ and $C \cup I \cup U_1 = V$ hold.) Compute the candidate $(C, I) - eds$ and return the smallest one.

The algorithm executes two kinds of branching rules, reducing time complexity by selecting the vertex or 4-cycle. When $G[U_2]$ contains a cp-vertex, we branch on an optimal cp-vertex, where a cp-vertex is optimal if removing the cp-vertex generates the largest total size of cliques. Otherwise, we will branch on a cp-cycle or a vertex of maximum degree. We branch on a cp-cycle when the maximum degree is lower than 3. For branching on a vertex of maximum degree d, we may choose an optimal d-degree vertex. A d-degree vertex $v \in U_2$ is called an optimal d-degree vertex if (1) the degree sequence $d(u_1) \leq d(u_2) \leq ... \leq d(u_d)$ of d neighbors $u_1, u_2, ..., u_d$ is the lexicographically minimum overall d-degree vertices; (2) $d(N[v])$ (the number of edges between $N[v]$ and $N_2(v)$) is maximized among such vertices satisfying the condition (1).

The authors use the Measure and Conquer method to analyze this algorithm, which was first proposed by Fomin et al. [59] and is a powerful method for analyzing the time complexity of branching algorithms. This method emphasizes the selection of measure method instead of using more and more branching and constraint rules to construct algorithms. The measurement coefficient used in the measure method is called weight in general. The runtime is minimized by determining the value of the coefficient. In order to obtain the optimal weight, generally, it needs to solve a quasi-convex function. Although the algorithm is simple, we obtain a great deal of constraining conditions of the quasi-convex function by considering multiple situations. In Reference [55], the authors utilize the Measure and Conquer method to obtain a simple algorithm by constructing an edge dominating set.

4.3.6 The Dominating Set Algorithm under the Mobile Model

Most wireless networks based on fundamental infrastructure are constructed by connecting one-hop wireless signals and wireless networks. The wireless ad hoc network is the noncenter network, which is constructed by self-organization. In general, the wireless network refers to the mobile ad hoc network (MANET). In MANET, the routing is different from the common wired network. Using the traditional routing protocol in a dynamic network is impossible, since the traditional routing protocol assigns the fussy computing task to mobile computers; however, the centralization of the mobile computers cannot meet the requirements of the dynamic network. For example, any routing mechanism has to consider the change of the network topology and the highly variable quality of the wireless link when the packet is routed in the dynamic environment of ad hoc networks. In a wired network, the failure of the link is not frequent because network frameworks are mostly static. Therefore, in order to ensure the same responsible level as the wired network, the routing in MANET needs more frequent computing than wired networks.

In an ad hoc network, topology control mainly includes the problems of processing the calculation and maintaining the connection among the nodes. Topology control covers the power control and hierarchical topology organization. Power control balances the connectivity of one-hop neighbors by adjusting the power of each node, thereby ensuring the connectivity of the network. The hierarchical topology control method refers to clustering in general. The mobility of the node leads to difficulty in the improvement of designing an effective protocol for ad hoc networks. In the past decade, researchers have done a great deal of work designing the network protocol based on mobility in MANET along with the tremendous development of wireless MANETs. Since the free mobility of the node in MANET, the change of topology is unpredictable. Besides, once a node is deployed, it is difficult to recharge it, which means the energy is limited. Currently, an effective method for solving this problem is constructing the virtual backbone network. The CDS is generally adopted in routing, unicast, broadcast, energy maintaining, topology control, and collision avoidance protocol in MANET as the virtual backbone network. Also, research shows that CDS is very effective in these applications. Thus, constructing a CDS and maintenance are hot topics of research in MANET.

4.3.6.1 The Introduction of a Mobile Model

In wireless networks, mobile hosts can move in many different modes. Generally, a mobile model is used to analyze the novel system or protocol in MANETs.

In ad hoc networks, the host moves according to different models. The simulation needs a practical model to evaluate the performance of the system and the protocol. The mobile model is an independent application. Besides, we predict that different mobile models will affect the performance of different network protocols in different ways. Generally, the simulation of the mobile system relies on the random mobile model. The characteristic of the model is that some nodes are randomly distributed within a given simulation area range U. According to some randomly distributed function, each node selects two or more parameters: a destination d in U, the movement rate v, an angle α, and the movement duration t. Then the node v moves to d as rate v or moves along the angle α for duration t. When the node arrives at d or moves for duration t, it may pause for a while and repeat the previous process; a different model makes different choices of U, d, v, α, and t. In wireless ad hoc mobile networks, the mobile model concentrates on the individual movement behavior in the mobile period, where the period means the minimum period for moving to a fixed direction with a fixed rate.

Currently, there are seven kinds of entity mobile models in ad hoc networks:

1. Random mobile model: a simple mobile model based on random direction and rate
2. Random point mobile model: a mobile model including pause times for changing destination and rate
3. Random direction mobile model: a mobile model that forces the node to move to the margin of the simulation area before changing the direction and rate
4. Mobile model with unbounded simulation area: a model that transfers the 2D rectangle simulation area onto a round plane simulation area
5. Gauss-Markov mobile model: a model that uses a tuning parameter to change the random degree in the mobile mode
6. Random mobile model with probability: a model that uses a set of probability to decide the next location of the mobile node
7. Mobile model in an urban area: the simulation area represents the residential district in a town

Zhao et al. propose an algorithm for solving the topology control problem in even mobile sensor networks [43]. They assume that the nodes move evenly on their own tracks. However, the model has the following drawbacks: (1) the whole algorithm is centralized, lacking practicability; (2) even a mobile model is too ideal, which greatly limits its application, because the node rarely has even movement all the time in real situations. Li et al. propose a topology control algorithm for the variable rate mobile networks [44]; it modifies the even mobile network model by considering the variable rate. The algorithm assumes that the node moves on a line segment with a determined starting position and ending position. It finds the one-hop neighbor first with the maximum distance among the nodes; then it deletes some nodes from the one-hop neighbor list by a quasi-XTC process, making energy more effective. However, this model also has some problems: (1) the mobile model has a large limit, that is, the node will not move only on a line segment in reality; (2) due to the mobility, there is a problem in the calculation method of one-hop neighbors: the node beyond the transmitting radius may not communicate with the node until it becomes a one-hop neighbor when it moves within the range of transmitting radius; (3) some one-hop neighbors may be deleted by mistake in the quasi-XTC process.

In ad hoc networks, most topology changes occur in a small area, that is, the change is localized. Therefore, the network structure can be abstracted as the local change, which can be achieved by the logic substructure called a cluster. The process of defining the substructure is regarded as clustering. In some situations, the special nodes called cluster heads are assigned to monitor the allocation of the information and information routing in the cluster. A routing algorithm operated on the cluster has relatively low overhead. Many heuristic methods of selecting the cluster head have been proposed. They obey two kinds of strategy: consulting or requesting. Consulting needs various gradual steps. Due to a lack of consensus on the nodes selected as cluster heads, it may lead to jitter during the election process.

A Heuristic Topology Control Algorithm of Cluster [45] algorithm combines the effects of communication overhead of the backbone network and residual energy for cluster head selection. The algorithm achieves a network topology with low global energy consumption and high robustness of the backbone network, thereby prolonging the lifetime of the network. The Topology-Aware Connected Domination Set [46] algorithm is a kind of topology-aware distributed minimum CDS approximate algorithm.

By comparison, the algorithm in Reference [65] can generate a smaller scale of the topology with higher stability and longer lifetime. Li et al. propose a clustering topology control algorithm [65] in MANETs, in which the node moves in an arbitrary direction with an arbitrary rate. The algorithm broadens the limit of the movement track. It has great scalability but does not achieve better energy efficiency.

Aiming to solve these problems, we propose a modified strategy in this chapter. The optimized operation is executed based on a widely applied model [63]: $p_i = Cr_i^\alpha$ and the concept of relay area [45] after constructing CDS [65], thereby saving more energy and improving energy efficiency further.

4.3.6.2 DETM-CDS

Han et al. execute the optimized operation based on a widely applied energy model: $p_i = Cr_i^\alpha$ and the concept of relay area after constructing CDS [65], thereby saving more energy and improving energy efficiency further.

4.3.6.2.1 The Network Model

In general, an ad hoc network is modeled as a graph $G = (V, E)$, where V is the set of network nodes and E is the set of links among the nodes. The existence of a link $(u, v) \in E$ also means $(v, u) \in E$, and nodes u and v are within packet-reception range of each other; u and v are one-hop neighbors of each other. The set of one-hop neighbors of a node i is denoted by N_i^1. Two nodes that are not connected but share at least one common one-hop neighbor are called two-hop neighbors. For simplicity, we assume that all the nodes have the equal transmitting radius R; the one-hop neighbor list of node v_i is defined as $L(i)$; node v_i can move freely in a given rectangle area; the energy consumption of node v_i is defined as p_i. We adopt an energy model that is adopted extensively [63]:

$$p_i = Cr_i^\alpha \tag{4.1}$$

Here, C is a constant within [2,4], which is the exponent of energy fading; r is the distance between the sender and receiver.

Now we give the concept of a relay area [64]: given node i, r and an arbitrary node x, if $p_{i \to x} > p_{i \to r} + p_{r \to x}$, the area where x is located is defined as the relay area related to r of node i, denoted as R_{ir}. Here, $p_{a \to b}$ represents the minimum power of direct communication from a to b.

4.3.6.2.2 The Construction of the Minimum Dominating Set

4.3.6.2.2.1 The Cluster Head Selection Method
In the paper [65], the new algorithm includes two parts: the cluster head selection process and connecting the MDS. The cluster head selection process is executed first. The algorithm adopts the function as the rule of cluster head selection, which is based on priority—mobile rate and energy. When the cluster head selection is finished, the construction of MDS is also finished. Because of the standard of cluster head selection—each noncluster leader is a one-hop neighbor of a cluster head—and the concept of a dominating set, it can be judged that we build a dominating set of the network when finishing cluster head selection. In the process of cluster head selection, the standard of selecting the cluster head is as follows:

1. The node has the highest priority among its one-hop neighbors.
2. The node has the highest priority among all one-hop neighbors of one of its neighbors.

Figure 4.12 shows the specific situations where node i becomes the cluster head. In Figure 4.12a, node i has the highest priority among its one-hop neighbors. In Figure 4.12b, node i has the highest priority among the one-hop neighbors of node b. The nearby number of each node represents the priority of the node at a

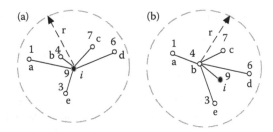

Figure 4.12   Two situations of node *i* being the cluster head.

certain time. In this chapter, we use the fraction in [0, 1] to represent the priority of the node. In the following part, we will discuss the calculation method of priority.

The components of the priority

1. The "will value" for the node—the function of mobility and energy level
2. The ID of the node (to avoid the collision when more than one node has the same will value, the node with the minimum ID has higher priority)

We use W_i to mark the will value of the node; $s_i \in (0, \infty)$ represents the rate of node *i*; $E_i \in [0,1)$ represents the residual energy of node *i*. $W_i = f(s_i, E_i)$ is defined as a function [43] by these rules:

1. In order to improve the living ability, each node needs to decide to become the cluster head according to its will value with a nonzero probability.
2. In order to keep the stability that will change in cluster head selection, the will value stays unchanged as long as the change of rate and energy level do not exceed a certain threshold.
3. In order to avoid the selection of cluster heads that quickly lose touch with their neighbors after selection, the will value is reduced greatly when the mobility of the node exceeds a given value.
4. In order to prolong the lifetime of the node, the W value of the node will be greatly reduced when the residual energy is decreased below a certain level.

Based on these standards, many functions may be used to calculate the will value of the node. Our method uses the formula in Reference [43]:

$$W_i = (c_1 \cdot E_i) = 2^{\log_2(c_1 \cdot E_i)\log_2(s_i + c_2)} \qquad (4.2)$$

where c_1 and c_2 are used to eliminate the boundary terms in their logarithm operation (details can be seen in Reference [43]).

Once the cluster head is selected, it will broadcast its state to its two-hop neighbors.

4.3.6.2.2.2 The Construction of a Connected Dominating Set

4.3.6.2.2.2.1 The Construction of Initial CDS The process of constructing a CDS can be divided into two steps: the selection process of the doorway node and the selection process of the gateway node.

> Step 1: In an MDS, if two cluster heads are separated by three hops without any other cluster heads in the middle, the node will be selected as the doorway, which has the highest priority on the shortest path between the two cluster heads. Besides, the node will be added into the backbone topology.
> Step 2: If two cluster heads or a cluster head and a doorway node are separated by two hops without any other cluster heads in the middle, the node with the higher priority among them will become a gateway to connect the cluster heads or the doorway node and the cluster head.

4.3.6.2.2.2.2 The Optimization of CDS The optimization process is executed in each cluster. According to the concept of the relay area, calculate whether there are two neighbors j and k in the one-hop neighbor list of the cluster head i, which satisfies $p_{i \to k} > p_{i \to j} + p_{j \to k}$. If there are these neighbors, k is within the relay area related to j of i. In this way, the energy consumed by sending a message to k from i will be more than the energy consumption of forwarding by relay node j; thus, we delete $L(i)$ of k in i. A situation may occur: Assume that for node i and its neighbors x, y, z, node y is in R_{ix} and node z is in R_{iy}. Obviously, we need to delete y and z from the one-hop neighbor list of i. But if we delete node y first, z will be kept. In order to avoid this situation, we propose a modified quasi-XTC method: Sort the nodes in a one-hop neighbor list as the lexiographic order and delete from the furthest node, so that this situation will not occur.

4.3.6.2.2.2.3 The Link in CDS The backbone topology is constructed by using links among the selected cluster heads, relay nodes, gateways, and doorways in the original network according to the following rules:

> Rule 1: All links between cluster heads are kept in the backbone topology.
> Rule 2: The one-hop links from doorways and gateways to the nodes in their respective sets are kept in the backbone topology (the first and the second processes of the initial CDS construction mentioned previously, respectively).

The links of the original network topology among gateways, among doorways, among relay nodes, or among regular nodes are not kept in the backbone topology. Doorways are always attached to cluster heads on one end and gateways on the other end. Gateways are always attached with cluster heads or doorways.

4.3.6.2.2.2.4 The Correctness Proof of the Algorithm

Lemma 4.9: The set of cluster heads generated by the algorithm is a dominating set.

Lemma 4.10: In a dominating set, the maximum distance to the next closest cluster head from any cluster head is 3.

Lemma 4.11: In CDS, two cluster heads within three hops of each other are connected by a path.

The proofs of these three lemmas are omitted but can be seen in Reference [65].

Theorem 4.14: The backbone topology generated by the algorithm is connected.

Proof: First, the cluster head set is a dominating set, which is generated by the first stage of the algorithm according to Lemma 4.9. Thus, all nodes in the network are either cluster heads or one-hop neighbors of cluster heads. That means all noncluster head nodes are connected with the cluster head. Second, we can construct a CDS according to Lemmas 4.10 and 4.11 before the last step in the second stage of the algorithm. Moreover, the algorithm shows that the clusters are connected by either the gateway or the gateway and the doorway. Finally, the operation of deleting the edge is executed in the cluster, which has no effect on the constructed connected topology. Therefore, the final backbone topology generated by our algorithm is connected.

Theorem 4.15: The backbone topology generated by our algorithm is energy efficient.

Proof: The time complexity for generating the cluster head is $O(n)$. Then the time complexity of finding the gateway and doorway depends on the maximum degree. We assume the maximum degree is d, thus the time complexity is $O(d^4)$. Besides, we can regard it as a small constant when the network scale is large. Finally, the time complexity of the deleting operation is $O(n)$. Therefore, the final time complexity of our algorithm is $O(n)$.

4.3.6.2.2.2.5 Simulation Results and Performance Analysis of the Algorithm
The stability and energy efficiency of the backbone topology are important goals of designing the protocols, which can be achieved by inheriting the idea of the DETM-CDS algorithm in Reference [65]. On this basis, the performance of the algorithm can be modified further by the relay area and quasi-XTC method. The corresponding simulation is as follows.

We use C++ to compare the performance of the DETM-CDS algorithm and the TMPO algorithm in Reference [65]. The simulation assumes that 100 nodes are distributed in a 1000×1000 m² area. All nodes have the same transmitting radius of 200 m in the simulation. All nodes move in a random direction with a random rate in the given area. The original topology is shown in Figure 4.13, where every node is a host and the network connectivity is very dense in some parts of the network, thereby increasing the overhead of network control functions. Now all nodes are regular nodes. Figure 4.14 shows the topology after selecting the cluster head in the DETM-CDS algorithm. Now it is not connected among the cluster heads. The regular node is connected with the corresponding cluster head of one-hop neighbors, and the black node represents the cluster head.

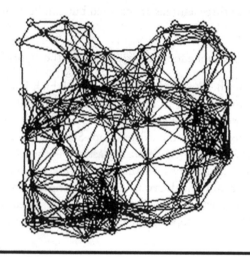

Figure 4.13 Initial topology.

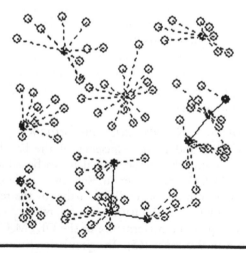

Figure 4.14 MDS.

Figure 4.15 illustrates the topology after the selection of doorway nodes and gateway nodes in the DETM-CDS algorithm. Now the backbone topology is connected. The black solid triangle refers to the doorway node; the hollow triangle refers to the gateway node. Figure 4.16 illustrates the network topology after completing the optimization operation of the DETM-CDS algorithm. Now the network topology is still connected and the hollow diamond refers to the relay node.

Figure 4.17 illustrates the average node degree of the cluster head obtained by the DETM-CDS algorithm and the TMPO algorithm. It can be seen that the average node degree of the cluster head obtained by the DETM-CDS algorithm

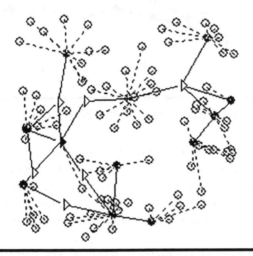

Figure 4.15   Add a doorway and a gateway node.

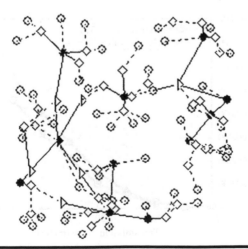

Figure 4.16   Final topology.

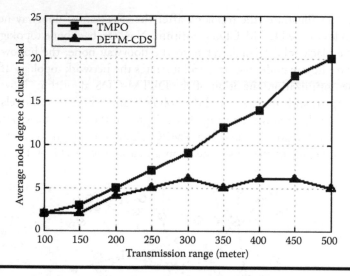

Figure 4.17 The average node degree of the cluster head.

is relatively small with a different transmitting radius. So, in the DETM-CDS algorithm, the communication workload of the cluster head can be reduced and the node degree of the cluster head is relatively stable. The node degree of the cluster head is kept around 5 when the transmitting radius keeps getting larger. Therefore, the topology is more stable and the workload of the node is more balanced.

Figure 4.18 shows the comparison result of the communication energy between the cluster head and the cluster members in the DETM-CDS algorithm

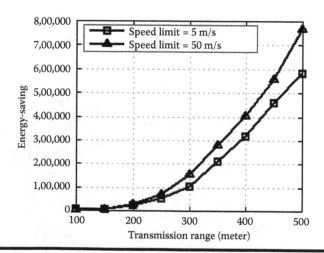

Figure 4.18 The energy saved by DETM-CDS compared with TMPO.

and the TMPO algorithm. The transverse axis represents the different transmitting radius and the longitudinal represents the energy savings of DETM-CDS in communication compared with TMPO. It can be seen that the larger the transmitting radius is, the more the energy is saved with DETM-CDS. We use ES to indicate energy savings. The calculation method of energy savings is that according to formula 4.1 and the idea of the quasi-XTC method, the message spread between node i and j is forwarded by relay node k, so the calculation formula of energy savings is $ES(e_i) = Cd(i,j)^\alpha - Cd(i,k)^\alpha - Cd(k,j)^\alpha$, where we ignore C for simplicity since it is a constant, and the value of α is 3. Because of the randomness of the topology, every time the transmitting radius changes, the simulation will adopt 50 experimental results and obtain the final result by evaluating the average for accuracy. The mobility scenarios are simulated; the rate is selected from [0, 5] in low-mobility scenarios and from [0, 50] in high-mobility scenarios. Nodes of different roles have different rates of energy consumption. Here, we ignore the energy consumed by local calculation and assume that the rate of energy consumption only depends on the role of the node. Once there is one node with energy 0, the simulation ends.

This simulation result illustrates that the algorithm ensures the connectivity of the network topology. Compared with the TMPO algorithm, this algorithm can save a lot of energy. Both the simulation results and the theoretical proof analysis show that the TMPO algorithm is energy efficient and extends the life cycle of the nodes, thus prolonging the network life cycle.

4.3.7 The Dominating Set Algorithm under the Interference Model

Interference may lead to retransmission or even multiple retransmissions because of transmission failure, which wastes the time and energy of nodes as well. We have a certain understanding of wireless networks: the energy of each node comes from the battery, which is not recharged. Therefore, it needs to reduce energy consumption as much as possible, prolong the lifetime of the network, and improve its practicality.

4.3.7.1 The Physical Interference Model

The model determines whether communication is successful by calculating Signal to Interference plus Noise Ratio (SINR) at the receiver of a link. The data can be received successfully if its SINR value is greater than the threshold. The formula is as follows:

$$\frac{P_v(u)}{N + \sum_{w \in S} P_v(w)} \geq \beta, \tag{4.3}$$

where $P_x(y)$ is the receiving power of the signal from y at x; N is the environment noise; S is a subset of $V \setminus \{u,v\}$, which includes the nodes in current communication; β is a constant value, which is related to the current required rate, scheduling solution, and so on.

Scheideler et al. [66] first proposed a distributed dominating set protocol based on the physical interference model in wireless sensor networks. The protocol considers the interference generated by all nodes in the network. The protocol is completely distributed and random, which can extensively adopt a physical carrier sensing to reduce message overhead. The protocol needs neither node signatures nor the given information of the system. The scale of information transmitted among the nodes is a constant bit.

4.3.7.2 The Protocol Interference Model

In this model, the communication between node v and node u is successful if and only if there are no other communication nodes in the region with node u as the center and a communication range as the radius, as shown in Figure 4.19. The model provides ideal conditions with no interference. However, it cannot reflect the superimposed interference of multiple signals in the wireless network.

4.3.7.2.1 The Edge Interference Model

4.3.7.2.1.1 The Maximum Edge Coverage Model   By definition, the interference value of a network is the existent maximum edge coverage value in the network. The edge coverage refers to the node number covered by an edge. Then coverage value $Cov(e)$ of edge $e = (u,v)$ is:

$$Cov(e) = \left| \left\{ w \in V, |v,w| \leq |u,v| \cup |u,w| \leq |u,v| \right\} \right| \tag{4.4}$$

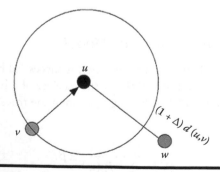

Figure 4.19   The graph of a protocol interference model.

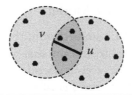

Figure 4.20 Edge coverage graph of edge *e* = (*u*, *v*).

The interference of graph $G = (V, E)$ is $\max_{e \in E} Cov(e) \cdot |u, v|$ is the distance between nodes u and v. As shown in Figure 4.20, all nodes in the range within the dotted line are covered by edge $e = (u, v)$.

LISE [109] is a common algorithm using the maximum edge coverage model. Actually, the algorithm constructs a t-spanner tree with the minimum possible maximum edge coverage value, where t is a constant value chosen at random. The algorithm greedily deletes the edge with maximum interference value from the edge set of candidate spanners until there is no edge satisfying the t-spanner property. Currently, much interference research is based on the LISE algorithm, such as [110].

4.3.7.2.1.2 The Maximum Edge Interference Load Model   Edge coverage considers the number of nodes that generate interference to an edge, while the model considers the effects of other active edges in the graph on the edge e. Thus, the inference load $I(e)$ is defined as the size of the set of the edge that generates the interference to edge e, that is:

$$I(e) = \left| \{(x, y) \in E \,|\, x, y \notin \{u, v\} \text{ and or } x \in D(u, R) \text{ or } \right. \tag{4.5}$$
$$\left. x \in D(v, R) \cup \{(x, y) \in E \,|\, x, y \notin \{u, v\} \text{ and } y \in D(u, R) \text{ or } y \in D(v, R)\} \right|,$$

where $D(u, R)$ represents the interference disk with center u and radius R. Thus, the maximum $I(e)$ of graph $G = (V, E)$ is $I(e)$.

The authors of Reference [111] utilize the maximum edge interference load model to improve the network performance based on the existing CDSs, which can make the backbone network more suitable for real application. The algorithm I-CDS proposed in the paper is based on Reference [112]. First, construct an MIS; the nodes in the MIS become the dominating nodes, and the nodes beyond the MIS become the dominated nodes. In the second stage, each dominated node identifies the dominating node within two hops at most; then it selects some relay nodes to connect with the dominating node. The algorithm calculates the interference value of each node by its edge interference load. Nodes are sorted according to interference value and identity.

4.3.7.2.2 The Node Interference Model

The two models just described are studied from the view of senders, which is the opposite of the real situation, which means that signal interference and message collision happen primarily at the receiver. Besides, according to the given definition, adding a node or an edge has obvious effect on the interference measurement [113]. In the network described in Figure 4.21, when adding the best node into a roughly evenly distributed cluster, it needs to construct a link that covers all nodes in the network. Therefore, the interference value is improved up to the total node number from a small constant. The situation shows that a large collision may occur, even if a node is added.

4.3.7.2.2.1 The Maximum Node Coverage Model The maximum edge coverage model proposes an interference definition with the receiver as the center, which defines the interference of the graph as the maximum interference value of an arbitrary node in the graph. The interference value of an arbitrary node u is

$$Cov(u) = \left| \{v \,|\, u, v \in V, |u, v| < v_r \} \right| \tag{4.6}$$

where v_r is the distance from node v to its furthest neighbor in graph G. Then the interference of graph $G = (V, E)$ is $\max_{v \in V} Cov(v)$. Figure 4.22 is the graphical presentation of the model and easy to understand.

In fact, if each node has a uniform transmitting range, the interference value of the node is the number of its one-hop neighbors. In Figure 4.23, the signature

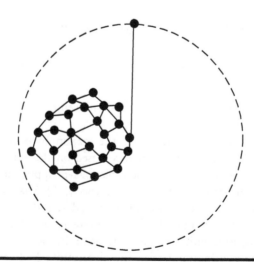

Figure 4.21   The change of network interference value after adding a node in the even network.

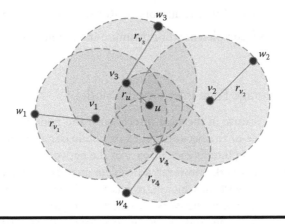

Figure 4.22 The illustration of node coverage of node *u*.

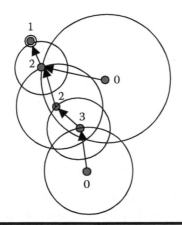

Figure 4.23 Maximum node coverage model.

around each node is its interference value. Therefore, the interference value of the graph is the maximum interference value among the nodes (i.e., 3).

4.3.7.2.2.2 The Maximum Node Interference Load Model Similarly, the model provides a new definition of node interference according to the drawbacks of the maximum edge interference load model. It considers the calculation of node interference load from the view of the edge, thus the interference load $I(v)$ of node v is

$$I(v) = \left|\{(u,w) \in E \, \middle| \, v \notin \{u,w\} \text{ and } v \in D(u,d(u,w)) \text{ or } v \in D(w,d(u,w))\}\right| \quad (4.7)$$

where $D(u,r)$ is a broadcast disk with radius r and center u; $d(u,w)$ refers to the Euclidean distance between node u and node w. Therefore, the interference load of graph $G = (V, E)$ is $\max\limits_{v \in V} I(v)$. The authors of Reference [114] utilize the model to prove that there is NP completeness of minimum interference in a plane geometric graph.

4.3.7.2.3 The Average Edge Interference Model

There is a common feature in the edge interference and node interference models: the global interference of the network relies on the maximum interference of the local network. Reducing interference in part of the network equals reducing interference in the whole network. However, a problem must be addressed: Interference is the same in one network in which part has high interference and the rest has low interference as in another network in which each part has high interference. Therefore, [115] extends the study in Reference [48] and proposes average edge interference, which uses the coverage value of each edge. Then the interference value of graph $G = (V, E)$ is

$$\textit{Average Edge Coverage}(G) = (\sum_{e \in E} Cov(e)) / |V|. \tag{4.8}$$

In the formula, $|V|$ represents the number of nodes in the graph. The change in the interference generated by this model is no greater than the change in the interference generated by the maximum edge coverage model, even if a tiny change occurs in the topology.

4.3.7.2.4 The Average Path Interference Model

Although the average edge interference model solves the drawbacks of the edge interference and node interference models, it does not consider the length of the path in the graph. That means the path can be extended without a limit, which has no effect on the calculation of interference. Therefore, this model defines the average path interference based on the path length. The formula of interference is as follows:

$$API(G) = TotIoptPI(G) / |V'|, \tag{4.9}$$

where $TotIoptPI(G) = \sum\limits_{u,v \in V} \sum\limits_{e \in IoptP_{uv}} Cov(e)$; $IoptP_{uv} = (e_1, e_2, \ldots, e_k)$ is the optimal path with minimum interference value between node u and node v; V' includes all node pairs. The authors consider the shortest path and provide a quasi-interference definition based on the same idea:

$$API(G) = TotSPI(G) / |V'|, \tag{4.10}$$

where $TotSPI(G) = \sum\limits_{u,v \in V} \sum\limits_{e \in SPuv} Cov(e)$, and SP_{uv} is the shortest path between node u and node v. The advantage of the interference model is that $G_2 = (V, E_2)$ can still generate low interference even if the average edge coverage of graph $G_1 = (V, E_1)$ is smaller.

4.3.7.2.5 The Interference Coefficient Model

Not all nodes generate interference to edge e in the network, thus the model divides nodes that may cause interference into three parts, as shown in Figure 4.24. Then the interference of the link can be redefined by the interference coefficient [117].

In the graph, edge $e_i = (u_i, v_i)$ divides the adjacent area into three parts: A, B, and C, where $B = B_1 \bigcup B_2$. Then:

1. If one endpoint of an arbitrary edge $e_j = (u_j, v_j)$ is within area A, the edge has an interference relation with edge e_i.
2. If the node u_j of edge $e_j = (u_j, v_j)$ is within area B, there is no interference relationship between the edge and edge e_i: if node u_j is within B_1 area, the edge has an interference relationship with edge e_j with a certain probability, no matter where in the B_1 or B_2 node v_j is located; if node u_j is within area B_2, edge e_j may interfere with edge e_i only when v_j is located in area A or B_1.
3. If u_j belongs to area C, edge e_j will not generate interference to edge e_i, no matter where node v_j is.

According to the definition of interference relationship between two edges, the calculation of the interference coefficient is

$$I_h(e_i) = \frac{q_h}{p_h}, \qquad (4.11)$$

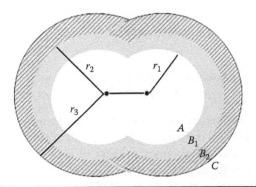

Figure 4.24 Three parts of the network: A, B, C. (From Feng, G. N. and Fan, P. Y., *Wireless Commun. Mobile Comput.*, 12(6), 529–544, 2010.)

where p_h is the number of the edge adjacent to node h; q_h is the number of the edge that has an interference relationship with edge e_i in these p_h edges.

Since the node in area B generates interference to edge e_i with good probability, the average area interference coefficient is introduced from the nodes in area B_1 and B_2:

$$k_l(e_i) = \frac{1}{|N_{B_l}(e_i)|} \sum_{h \in N_{B_l}(e_i)} I_h(e_i), \quad l = 1, 2. \tag{4.12}$$

Then the interference of edge e_i is defined as

$$I(e_i) := \sum_{h \in N_A(e_i)} I_h(e_i) + \sum_{h \in N_B(e_i)} I_h(e_i) = |N_A(e_i)| + k_1(e_i) \times |N_{B1}(e_i)| + k_2(e_i) \times |N_{B2}(e_i)|.$$

$$\tag{4.13}$$

The interference of the whole network $G = (V, E)$ is the maximal interference $I(e_j)$.

4.3.7.3 The Dominating Set Construction Algorithm Based on Interference

Currently, most research on dominating set ignores the interference problem, which believes that the lower the node degree is, the less interference there is. The author of Reference [47] assumes that a low node degree means low interference in a graph. However, Reference [48] indicates that there may be a high interference value in the solving process, even for a graph with the maximum degree as 2. In Reference [49], the interference model is based on the current flow in the network. But since the flow is limited by the specific application and the priori information of the network flow cannot be obtained, the static interference model based on node distribution is required. The research of interference for ad hoc networks derives from Reference [50]. The authors of Reference [51] classify the existing interference models and geometrize the models respectively.

4.3.7.3.1 Interference-Aware Topology Management Based on Priority Order

Guo et al. propose an interference-aware topology management based on priority order algorithm (I-TMPO) in Reference [61]. The algorithm considers the interference value of each node and assigns a priority to each node with rate factor. By the algorithm, each node can decide whether it is in the MDS according to its neighbor information. Then the node in MDS is connected as a CDS. In theory, the authors prove the correctness of the algorithm. The simulation result shows that the algorithm has better performance. The algorithm assumes that the mobile node in the wireless network has the same transmission range, and the interference radius equals the transmission radius. If two nodes are within transmission range of each other, there is a link between them. Each node has a unique identity, and time is synchronous in the network. Assume that each node has the newest information of its two-hop neighbors, which is obtained by the newest information of its one-hop neighbors. The interference model in the paper [61] is described as follows: In the model, $I(e)$ indicates the edge set that can generate interference to an arbitrary edge e. If u and v are two vertices of edge e_1, and x and y are two vertices of edge e_2, we define the interference disk $D(u, R)$ of node u as a disk with center u and radius R. If node u or v is covered by one of the interference disks of x and y, we say that edge e_1 interferes with edge e_2. According to this definition, we use $|I(e)|$ to represent the link interference value of each edge e. The interference value of node u is defined as the maximum interference value of all of its links, noted as I_u. Finally, define the interference value of the network as the maximum $|I(e)|$ in the CDS. Thus, the interference value $I(e)$ of edge $e=(u, v)$ can be indicated as $|I(e)| = |\{(x, y) \in E \| x, y \notin \{u, v\}$ and $x \in D(u, R)$ or $x \in D(v, R)\} \cup \{(x, y) \in E$ $|x, y \notin \{u, v\}$ and $y \in D(v, R)$ or $y \in D(v, R)\}|$. The interference value of node u is $I_u = \max|I(u, v)|$, where $(u, v) \in D(u, R)$. After completing the algorithm, the interference value of the network is $I(G) = \max|I(e)|$, where $e \in E'$ and E' is the edge set of the CDS.

I-TMPO algorithm includes two stages: the selection of MDS and CDS construction. The first stage is the MDS stage. The idea of the stage derives from the MDS construction method in Reference [65]: The selected cluster becomes the dominating node, and the cluster member becomes the dominated node. Besides, it has been proven that the scale of the MDS obtained by this method is smaller than that obtained by other methods. In order to achieve a workload balance, the reselection of the cluster head needs to be executed periodically with interval T. In the initialization of the network (i.e., $t=0$), we need to initialize the network: define a *workfor* property and type property for the node; then calculate the priority of each node, its one-hop and two-hop neighbors; then select the cluster head according to the following rules:

1. A node has the highest priority among its one-hop neighbors.
2. A node has the highest priority among the one-hop neighbors of one of its one-hop neighbors.

The cluster head selection uses the node priority, which is assigned based on the information of two-hop neighbors. The information of two-hop neighbors includes the identity i of the neighbor, the current time t, and the willing value W_i. W_i is a function represented by node interference value I_i and node mobile rate s_i:

$$W_i = 2^{-\log(c_1 + I_i)\log(c_1 + s_i)}, \tag{4.14}$$

where c_1 is a positive constant no lower than 2. c_1 makes the willing value of being the cluster head get larger when the interference and mobile rates of nodes are lower. As previously mentioned, there is an interval T of priority recalculation and the offset of the node in T is $i \cdot off$. Therefore, the time of recalculating the priority is $t = kT + i \cdot off$. The calculation formula of $i \cdot off$ is as follows:

$$i \cdot off = [Hash(i) \oplus T].\tag{4.15}$$

Then the priority calculation formula of node i is as follows:

$$i \cdot prio = [Hash(k \oplus i) \oplus W_i \oplus i].\tag{4.16}$$

Once a node calculates its priority, it is unchanged for the whole recalculation period. The priority changes only when a new recalculation period begins.

If a node is selected as the cluster head after this process, it needs to broadcast its property as the cluster head to all its two-hop neighbors.

After the stage of cluster head selection, the dominating nodes are obtained and the connection among one-hop cluster heads in the initial network is maintained. Now the network has multiple connected components. In order to achieve the goal, the next step is to combine these multiple connected components. Since the distance between a cluster head and its closest cluster head is at most 3 (see Reference [65]) and the original network is connected, the CDS can be obtained by adding some nodes (doorway and gateway) according to the two-neighbor information of each cluster head. If two cluster heads are three hops apart, store the middle node with the highest priority on its shortest path as a *doorway* and update the property *workfor* of the *doorway* as its cluster head. The selection of the *doorway* node reduces the distance between the two cluster heads by one hop, which extends the coverage of the cluster head. Second, if the distance between two cluster heads or between a *doorway* and a cluster head is two hops, select the intermediate node with the highest priority as the gateway node (located on the shortest path among multiple two-hop path, if it exists) of the two nodes. Moreover, update the property *workfor* of the gateway node as two endpoints of the path on which the node is located. The CDS is obtained by these two steps.

After the selection process, we indirectly give the connection of backbone topology: The connection among one-hop neighbor cluster heads in the original network, the one-hop connection between the *doorway* or gateway and the node in their property *workfor*. Generally, the *doorway* connects with the cluster head and the gateway; the gateway connects with the cluster head or *doorway*.

4.3.7.3.2 The Theoretical Analysis of the I-TMPO Algorithm

Lemma 4.12: After cluster head selection, the cluster head set obtained by the algorithm is a dominating set.

Lemma 4.13: The CDS obtained by the algorithm in Reference [65] has the same number of connected components as the original graph.

Theorem 4.16: I-TMPO obtains an interference-aware CDS.

Proof: After the first stage of the algorithm, the obtained cluster head set is a dominating set according to Lemma 4.12. Meanwhile, the network topology obtained in the first stage keeps its original connection. Since the second stage of the I-TMPO algorithm is the same as [65], it can be known that the I-TMPO algorithm obtains a CDS according to Lemma 4.13.

Each node competes to be cluster head based on the priority. The node priority considers interference value in the calculation. The node with lower interference value has higher priority; thus, the node has a large probability of becoming the cluster head. Therefore, after the first stage, the obtained MDS has less interference compared with the existing algorithms. In the second stage of the algorithm, the middle node is also selected based on priority. Similarly, it obtains a lower interference value. Finally, the interference value of the network is the minimum maximum interference of nodes in the CDS. Therefore, the CDS we construct can effectively reduce interference in real communication.

Theorem 4.17: In the I-TMPO algorithm, the message complexity is $O(n)$ and the time complexity is $O(n)$, where n is the node number of the network.

Proof: I-TMPO algorithm is localized. Each node needs to send the message for a constant number; therefore, the total message complexity of the algorithm is $O(n)$.

The algorithm is divided into two stages. In the first stage, the algorithm has two steps: node initialization and cluster head selection. Since the algorithm is distributed, the time complexity of the stage is $O(n)$. Assume the minimum cluster head number is D, thus the node number of the second stage is $M < n - D$ (i e., the time complexity of this stage is $O(M)$). Therefore, the total time complexity of I-TMPO algorithm is $O(n)$.

4.3.7.3.2 Simulation Analysis of the I-TMPO Algorithm

We use VC++ as the simulation platform; the setting of simulation parameters can be seen in Table 4.1. The I-TMPO algorithm and the algorithms in Reference [65] can be executed as in the table. The algorithms compare the performance in two aspects: MDS size and interference value. Here, the data is the average value under a different node density.

Figure 4.25a and b show the comparison results of the MDS sizes generated by two algorithms under low rate and high rate situations, respectively. As shown in

Table 4.1 The Setting of Simulation Parameters

Parameter	Value
Area size (m²)	650×450
Node number	100~250
Transmission radius (m)	100
Interference radius (m)	100
Low rate (m/s)	5
High rate (m/s)	50

the figure, regardless of high or low rate, the sizes of dominating sets obtained by the I-TMPO algorithm are both smaller than the original algorithm. Figure 4.26a and b are the comparison results of interference values generated by two algorithms under low and high rate situations. As shown in the figure, excluding the consideration of the mobile rate, the interference value after the interference-sensing algorithm is much lower than the value without the interference algorithm. Moreover, if the mobile rate is taken into consideration, it can be seen that using the I-TMPO algorithm in a low mobile rate has a better effectiveness of reducing the interference by comparing the two parts of Figure 4.26, which explains the vital importance of interference.

4.3.8 k-Dominating Set

4.3.8.1 k-Dominating Set and k-Connected Dominating Set

Assume a k-dominating set D, $D \subseteq V$. Each vertex v in graph G satisfies $v \in D$ or at least k neighbors of vertex v are within D. If the subgraph induced by D is connected, D is called a k-CDS. Currently, there is not much research on how to solve the k-dominating set problem. The classical algorithms are those proposed by Dai and Wu [68], Moscibroda and Wattenhofer [6], and Kuhn et al. [69], respectively. Dai and Wu propose three different algorithms in Reference [68]. The first is a random algorithm that constructs a k-connected k-dominating set with high probability. The second algorithm is another version of the algorithm proposed in Wu et al. [8]. This algorithm is deterministic and can obtain a k-connected k-dominating set all the time. In these two algorithms, all decisions are based on k-local information, which means each node only needs to know the nodes within its k-hop range. The third algorithm executes k-coloring for the network graph first and obtains k disjoint vertex sets. Then it uses the existing CDS algorithms for the disjoint vertex subsets of each color and obtains k CDS. The union of k CDSs is a k-CDS. The algorithm proposed by Moscibroda and Wattenhofer [6] is to find k disjoint dominating

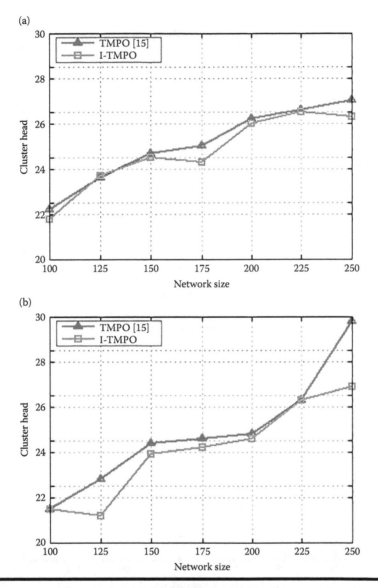

Figure 4.25 (a) **The number of the cluster heads in a low-rate situation and (b) the number of the cluster heads in a high-rate situation.**

sets, of which the union is a k-dominating set. The algorithm is based on coloring. Specifically, the algorithm tries to find the maximum k and find k disjoint dominating sets, instead of knowing the value of k. Kuhn et al. [69] propose two algorithms. The first one is about the regular graph and uses the distributed cycle method. The second one is about the UDG, which is divided into two stages. The first stage utilizes the algorithm of Gao et al. [70] to construct a 1-dominating set. In the second

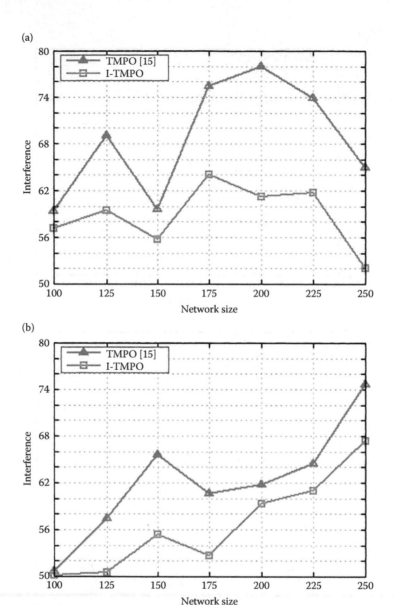

Figure 4.26 **(a) The interference value in a low-rate situation and (b) the interference value in a high-rate situation.**

stage, the 1-dominating set selects other dominators. The algorithm requires the nodes to know their geographical location, or they can modify their own communication range in the operation of the algorithm.

Couture et al. [71] propose a growth local algorithm to construct the k-dominating set. The algorithm does not require the node to master its geographical location or to dynamically change its communication range. Besides, the algorithm can construct the k-dominating set according to the j-dominating set ($j \leq k$). In the paper [71], the algorithm constructs a monotone increasing dominating set family, $D_1 \subseteq D_2 \cdots \subseteq D_i \cdots \subseteq D_k$, where D_i is an i-dominating set. In the UDG, the scale of each i-dominating set obtained by the algorithm is at most six times the scale of the optimal dominating set. The general idea is to construct an MIS to obtain the 1-dominating set; then construct a 2-dominating MIS, thereby obtaining a 2-dominating set. Repeat the process until the k-dominating set is obtained. The construction process of each dominating set is similar to the method in Reference [16].

4.3.8.2 The k-Connected m-Dominating Set

A graph G is k-node connected or k-connected if for any pair of nodes there is at least a k mutual independent path to connect them. In other words, graph G can keep connectivity if arbitrary $k-1$ vertices are deleted from graph G so that a vertex dominates itself and all its neighbors. An m-dominating set D_m is a subset of V. The arbitrary vertex in V/D_m can be dominated by at least m vertices in D_m.

k-connected m-dominating set (k-m-CDS): A CDS C is a k-m-CDS of graph G if spanning subgraph $G' = (C, E')$ of C is k-connected and C is also an m-dominating set of graph G.

4.3.8.2.1 The k-Connected m-Dominating Set Maintenance Algorithm

Most existing k-m-CDS construction algorithms need to reconstruct k-m-CDSs when the nodes move in the network. In Reference [67], the authors give a k-m-CDS maintenance algorithm under the mobile node situation in the wireless network. In the wireless network that uses the existing algorithm to construct the k-m-CDS backbone network, the maintenance algorithm divides the node mobile situations into three categories and proposes a local maintenance strategy for various mobile situations. The algorithm can greatly maintain the properties of k-m-CDS in the backbone network.

The paper [67] gives a k-m-CDS maintenance algorithm based on multiple relays. The algorithm can deal with mobile situations such as joining and leaving with great success. Assume that the whole network is k-connected; the maximum node degree is Δ and m; the dominating node can randomly detect the state of neighbor nodes within a two-hop range. Here we give some symbols used in the algorithm: Assume that V is the set of all nodes at time t; D indicates the existing k-m-CDS; D indicates the set of all marginal nodes. We have $V = D \cup B$, $D \cap B = \varnothing$.

$f_m(S)$ indicates the set of five nodes with the minimum ID in S; $N(p)$ indicates the set formed by all directed neighbors of node p. In the following, the mobility of the node is divided into three categories: the joining of new node, the leaving of the original node, and moving in the network; we discuss the execution process of the situations respectively.

4.3.8.2.1.1 The Analysis of the Mobile Situation of the Node in the Network In the wireless network, the mobility of the node mainly means that the node disconnects from its original neighbors and establishes connections with other nodes. Regardless of the dominating node or the marginal node, once the node leaves the original area, its neighbors execute the quitting algorithm immediately; when the node arrives at the new area, its new neighbors execute the joining algorithm after determining its stability.

The mobility process can be divided into three parts: start, move, and stop. The node creates action according to these three parts, and the description is as follows:

1. Start: When the node starts to move, the neighbor nodes execute the k-m-CDS maintenance algorithm corresponding to quitting if the neighbors detect the interruption of the link. It can be seen that the effect of start on the network is only limited to neighbor nodes around the mobile node.
2. Move: If the nearby nodes can detect the joining and quitting of the node simultaneously and judge that the node is moving, these nodes do not need to execute any maintenance work.
3. Stop: After a node moves to a location in the network and becomes static, the surrounding nodes judge that the node is new if they detect connections between themselves and it. Then the surrounding nodes will execute the k-m-CDS maintenance algorithm corresponding to joining. Similarly, the effect of stop on the network is only limited to the nodes around the mobile destination.

Algorithm analysis:

Since the maintenance algorithm for node moving in the network takes node joining and quitting algorithms as its major parts, the node mobility maintenance algorithm can be regarded as the superimposition of these two situations.

The algorithm is a completely distributed heuristic algorithm without state dependence: Whether for node joining, quitting, or moving, k-m-CDS maintenance does not need the node to determine its state. In the algorithm, surrounding nodes can judge the state of the corresponding node by detecting the information of its neighbors. Besides, they will adopt the corresponding algorithm to maintain k-m-CDS, in which the mobile nodes do not need to participate.

4.3.8.2.1.2 The Joining Situation of the New Node

4.3.8.2.1.2.1 Algorithm Description Assume that node p joins the network and that the network is connected. Now, we need the distribution of dominating nodes around p to discuss the maintenance strategy (the algorithm is completed by the dominating nodes).

After node p joins the network, $V' = V \cup \{p\}$, $B' = B \cup \{p\}$, $T = N(p) \cap D$.

1. If $|T| = l \geq m$, let $D_m = f_m(T)$, $D' = D$, and p joins in the D_m dominating domain.
2. If $|T| = l \prec mT' = N(p) / T$, $D_{m-l} = f_{m-1}(T')$, $D_{k-1} = f_{k-1}(T')$

When $N(p) \geq m$ let $D' = D \cap D_{m-l}$, $B' = B/D_{m-l}$, p joins in the dominating domain of $T \cup D_{m-l}$.

When $N(p) \prec m$, let $D' = D \cup D_{k-1} \cup \{p\}$, $B' = B/D_{k-1}$.

4.3.8.2.1.2.2 Performance Analysis

Lemma 4.14: If G is a k-connected graph, and G' is obtained by adding a node p into G in which p has at least k neighbors, we can say that G' is also k-connected.

The Lemma has been proven in Reference [9].

Theorem 4.18: If $k \leq m$, the algorithm ensures the obtaining of a k-m-CDS; when the number of added nodes is n_A, the effect of the maintenance algorithm on the approximate coefficient is $O(m \cdot n_A)$, it holds that the message complexity of the whole algorithm is $O(2\Delta)$ and the time complexity is $O(\Delta)$, where Δ is the maximum node degree.

Proof: In situation (1), k-m-CDS stays unchanged and ensures that the new joining nodes are m-dominated. In situation (2), a section of marginal nodes switches to the dominating nodes, and the final marginal nodes are certainly m-dominated. Meanwhile, according to Lemma 4.14, k-connectivity can also be ensured when $k \leq m$. Therefore, when $k \leq m$, the algorithm ensures the obtaining of a k-m-CDS.

In situation (1), k-m-CDS stays unchanged. In situation (2), under the worst situation, there exists no dominating node within a one-hop range of the new node; thus, it needs to add m new dominating nodes. If n_A indicates the number of joining nodes, the effect of the maintenance algorithm on the approximate coefficient is $O(m \cdot n_A)$.

When the new nodes join in, the dominating node needs to detect the new nodes and send them messages. The new nodes need to select a dominating node and join its dominating area. In situation (1), only the dominating node within a one-hop range can send the message. In the worst situation, all neighbors of P are dominating nodes. However, P needs to select just one dominating node and return an acknowledge message with message complexity $O(\Delta)$. In situation (2), the dominating node within a two-hop range of the new node needs to determine some new dominating nodes to dominate the new node. In the worst situation, all dominating nodes need to send the message to their marginal neighbors and all one-hop neighbors of P need to send the message to P. No matter what, P only needs to select maximum marginal nodes and return the message with time complexity $O(2\Delta)$. Therefore, the message complexity of the algorithm is $O(2\Delta)$.

Situation (1) has no iteration, of which the time complexity is $O(1)$; in situation (2), the dominating node needs to select marginal nodes to be the new dominating nodes, within $O(A)$ time. Therefore, the time complexity is $O(A)$.

4.3.8.2.1.3 The Leaving Situation of the Original Node

4.3.8.2.1.3.1 Algorithm Description Assume that the leaving of nodes has no effect on the k-connection of the whole network. When node P leaves the network, we have: $V' = V/\{p\}$. According to the property of p, the different discussions are as follows:

1. If $p \in B$, let $B' = B/\{p\}$, $D' = D$
2. If $p \in D$, let $D' = D/\{p\}$, $B_1 = N(p) \cap B$
    a. If the graph is connected and exported by B_1, utilize CDS-BD-D algorithm in B_1 to construct a CDS, D_1, $D'' = D' \cup D_1$;
    b. If the graph is not connected and exported by B_1, let $D'' = D' \cup B_1$

4.3.8.2.1.3.2 Performance Analysis

Theorem 4.19: The algorithm can ensure the obtaining of k-m-CDS; when the number of leaving nodes is n, the effect of the maintenance algorithm on the approximate coefficient is $O(nA)$; in the worst situation, the message complexity is $O(\Delta^2)$ and the time complexity is $O(Diam)$, where $Diam$ is the diameter of the connected component in the dominating area.

Proof: The m-dominating only needs to consider marginal nodes within the dominating area of p. When p leaves, nodes can be dominated by $m-1$ nodes of the original k-m-CDS. In (a), after constructing the CDS, the nodes outside the CDS are dominated by at least one node of the CDS. Thus, the marginal nodes are at least m-dominated after CDS joins in the original k-m-CDS. In (b), there surely exists a kth connected path among the $k-1$-connected nodes because the leaving of the node has no effect on the k-connectivity of the whole network. However, the kth path fails because of the leaving of node p; thus, it can be replaced by another path from the neighbor set of p. Therefore, k-connectivity can be ensured.

In the worst situation, all the marginal nodes in P dominating area join in k-m-CDS and assume that all n leaving nodes have no common marginal node. Now $n\Delta$ nodes are needed to join k-m-CDS. Therefore, the effect on the approximate coefficient is $O(n\Delta)$.

In situation (a), the CDS—BD—D algorithm is used to construct CDS. The message complexity is $O((\Delta+1)|V|)$ where $|V|$ depends on the marginal node number of all nodes leaving from the dominating area. In situation (b), each surrounding dominating node of B_1 needs to send a message to B_1 to determine its state, which needs $O(\Delta^2)$ messages. Therefore, the message complexity is $O(\Delta^2)$ in the worst situation.

Case (a) time complexity is $O(Diam)$; in case (b), B_1 needs time of $O(1)$ to join D directly. Therefore, the time complexity of the algorithm is $O(Diam)$.

4.3.9 Domatic Partition

In order to prolong the lifetime of the network, a sleeping scheduling mechanism is generally adopted. Each node has a chance to become the dominating node that consumed more energy, thereby balancing the energy consumption among the nodes in the network. The sleep scheduling problem can be abstracted as a DP problem. The essence of the DP problem is finding multiple disjoint dominating sets and executing sleeping schedules by cycling these dominating sets. Assume that $\Delta = \{D_1, D_2, ..., D_t\}$ is a DP of G; the sleep scheduling for each dominating set is that in a fixed period of T, the nodes in dominating set D_1 are activated while other nodes are sleeping; the algorithm executes in that way until each dominating set has been cycled once. After a sleep scheduling, the dominating node in each dominating set has duration T in the active state. The DP includes t dominating sets, thus the duration of cycling all the dominating sets once is tT. Obviously, increasing the number of DP t can prolong the duration of sleep scheduling, thereby prolonging the lifetime of the network.

4.3.9.1 The Research Meaning of Domatic Partition

DP has the function of balancing energy of the node and prolonging the lifetime of the network. Also, it can provide a certain support in some applications. DP can provide reliable support for different layers in the protocol stack of the sensor network. MAC protocol and the routing protocol belong to the protocols of different layers. In the construction process of these protocols, the message needs to be forwarded by topology control. If the same topology control is used to broadcast the message all the time, the node in the dominating set will die quickly by consuming too much energy. However, if different dominating sets are adopted in the DP to complete the construction of the protocols in different layers, the energy of the node can be consumed in balance.

DP has fault tolerance, which can make up for the effect of the node's failure. Since the node fails easily because of hardware trouble or energy depletion, the dominating set is required to have a certain fault tolerance. When a node of the dominating set fails, other dominating sets can replace it and continue to work (i.e., completing the collection, processing and transmitting of the information). The ability of fault tolerance depends on the number of dominating sets in the DP. The sensor network collects, processes, and transmits the sensing information. DP supports the sensor network in obtaining and effectively transmitting the sensing information of multiple types. Assume that the sensor network needs to broadcast a type of sensing information, which needs to be forwarded by a dominating set in the network. If there exist multiple types of sensing information, each type needs to occupy a dominating set. Assume that each node can provide the service for one type of sensing information at the same time, thus the maximum number of types of information the network can support equals the number of dominating sets. Therefore, the sensor network needs to find a DP with large partition number that can support multiple types of sensing information.

4.3.9.2 The Definition and Classification of the Domatic Partition Problem

According to the classification of the control set in domination partition, the DP problem can be divided into three types: DP, k-DP and connected DP (CDP).

4.3.9.2.1 Domatic Partition

In wireless sensor networks, the hierarchical structure is generally formed by searching the dominating sets in the network. Only the dominating nodes of the dominating set can transmit the data, which can greatly simplify the topology structure of the network, thereby reducing the transmission of redundant information.

Given a graph $G=(V, E)$, the dominating set D of G is a subset of vertex set V (i.e., $D \subseteq V$). Besides, each node $v \in V$ in G shows that it is in dominating set D or a neighbor of the node that is in dominating set D.

DP in graph G is the disjointed dominating set $\Delta = \{D_1, D_2, ..., D_t\}$, where each D_i is a dominating set of graph G and t is called the dominating number, which is the number of the disjointed dominating sets in the DP. The DP problem is to find a DP with a maximal partition number.

The lower boundary of the dominating number is 2. That is because as long as there is one dominating set, the other dominating sets consist of rest nodes under domination. The upper boundary of the dominating number is $\delta+1$, where δ is the minimum node degree. That is because if a node with the minimum degree can be dominated by δ nodes at most (assume that δ nodes belong to different dominating sets), no other node can dominate it (i.e., the upper boundary of DP is $\delta+1$).

4.3.9.2.2 k-Domatic Partition

Given a graph $G=(V, E)$; $d(u, v)$ refers to the hop number of the shortest u–v path between node u and node v. For the integer of $k \geq 1$, define that $N_k(v) = \{u : 0 \prec d(u,v) \leq k\}$, $N_k^+(v) = \{v \cup N_k(v)\}$. $N_k(v)$ is regarded as having a k-neighbor relationship of node v. Arbitrary node $u \in N_k(v)$ is regarded as a k-neighbor of node v. $D^{(k)}$ is a subset of vertex set V (i.e., $D^{(k)} \subseteq V$ in G, each node $v \in V$ is in k-dominating set $D^{(k)}$, or a k-neighbor of the node is in k-dominating set $D^{(k)}$.

A k-DP in graph G is a set of disjointed k-dominating sets $\Delta = \{D_1, D_2, ..., D_t\}$, where each D_i is a k-dominating set of G; t is the number of k-DPs, which is the maximal number of disjointed k-dominating sets in k-DP.

4.3.9.2.3 Connected Domatic Partition

The CDS is usually used in MAC, broadcasting, routing, etc. as a basic structure. CDS can be used in routing and domination as a virtual backbone network, which can limit routing on the nodes in CDS, thereby greatly reducing the message overhead for routing update and improving the efficiency of the broadcasting route. Besides, when the message is transmitted along a CDS, most redundant broadcasting will be deleted, thereby avoiding broadcasting storm.

Given a graph $G=(V, E)$, a CDS D in graph G is subset of vertex set V, that is, for $D \subseteq V$, D is a dominating set in graph G, and D is connected.

The DP of graph G is a set of the disjoint dominating sets $\Delta = \{D_1, D_2, ..., D_t\}$. If each dominating set D_i is a CDS, the DP is called a connected DP (CDP) of graph G. t is the number of CDPs, which is the maximal number of disjointed CDSs in the CDP. In the real application, it is relatively simple to extend a given dominating set to a CDS. However, it is more difficult to extend a given DP to a CDP.

4.3.9.3 Domatic Partition on the Special Graph in Graph Theory

4.3.9.3.1 Domatic Partition on the Interval Graph

This section will introduce the DP algorithm with linear time proposed in Reference [72]. First, we give the definition of the interval graph. In graph theory, interval graph is an intersected graph of multiple interval sets, in which each interval corresponds to a vertex in the graph. If two intervals are intersected, there is an edge between the two nodes, as shown in Figure 4.27.

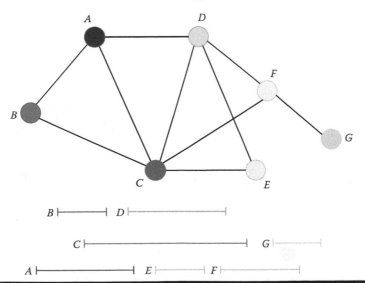

Figure 4.27 Interval graph.

In Reference [72], by using the properties of interval graph, a DP algorithm with $O(E)$ time complexity is proposed on the interval graph, where E represents the edge number. This algorithm improves $O(n^{2.5})$ time complexity of the algorithm up to a linear time in Reference [73], which explains that there are algorithms with linear time on the interval graph. The algorithm is divided into three steps:

1. Find node z with the minimum node degree in the graph. Let $v_1, v_2, \ldots, v_d$ be the neighbors of z:

$$DP = \{P_0, P_1, \ldots, P_d\}, \text{ where } P_0 = \{z\}, \; P_1 = \{v_1\}, \ldots, P_1 = \{v_d\}.$$

2. For $j = z - 1$ to 1,
     update the sets in DP so that every set in DP dominates $\{v_j, \ldots, v_z\}$.
3. For $j = z + 1$ to n,
     update the sets in DP so that every set in DP dominates $\{v_1, \ldots, v_j\}$.

4.3.9.3.2 Domatic Partition on the Circular Arc Graph

This section will introduce the DP algorithm on the circular arc graph proposed in Reference [74]. First, we give the definition of the circular arc graph. In graph theory, a graph is called a circular arc graph if there is one-to-one correspondence between the nodes of the graph. There exists an edge between two vertices if their circular arcs are intersected. The set of circular arc graphs is called a circular arc model, as shown in Figure 4.28.

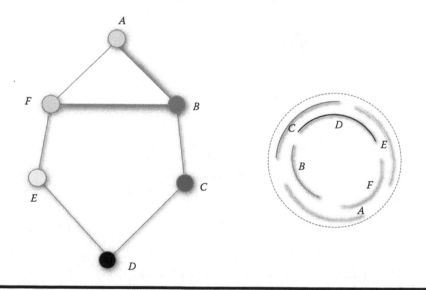

Figure 4.28   Circular arc graph.

Circular arc graphs are generalizations of interval graphs. If a circular arc has an endpoint that is not covered by other circular arcs, the circular arc can be cut off and extended as a straight line, which forms an interval graph. If a circular arc can be constrained as an interval graph, it can be solved with a linear time by the algorithm in Reference [73]. In Reference [74], the authors utilize this kind of constraint to propose a DP problem with $O(|V|+|E|)$ time complexity on the circular arc graph. The algorithm can be divided into two steps:

1. Calculate the minimum node degree δ in the graph.
2. If $\delta \le 7$, then find an MIS $V_1, V_2 = V - V_1$ in the graph, and output V_1, V_2 as DP.

Else

Constrain the circular arc graph as an interval graph G' and then use the algorithm in the last section to output the DP of graph G'.

End if

In the constrain process of the algorithm, the time complexity is $O(|V|)$. The DP on the circular arc graph can be found in duration $O(|V|+|E|)$.

4.3.9.3.3 Domatic Partition on a Strongly Chordal Graph

In this section, we will introduce the DP algorithm on the strongly chordal graph proposed in Reference [75], which is also a linear time algorithm and can obtain $\delta + 1$ disjointed dominating sets.

First, we give the definition of strongly chordal graph, a chordal graph with an odd chord in each even length circle whose length is at least 6. If there exists a chord in each circle whose length is at least 4, the graph is called a chordal graph, where the chord is the edge connecting the nonadjacent vertices in a circle. As shown in Figure 4.29, a circle (dotted line) has two chords A and B, and the graph is chordal. If you delete a chord, the graph will no longer be a chord graph, because there will be no chord in the circle with length 4.

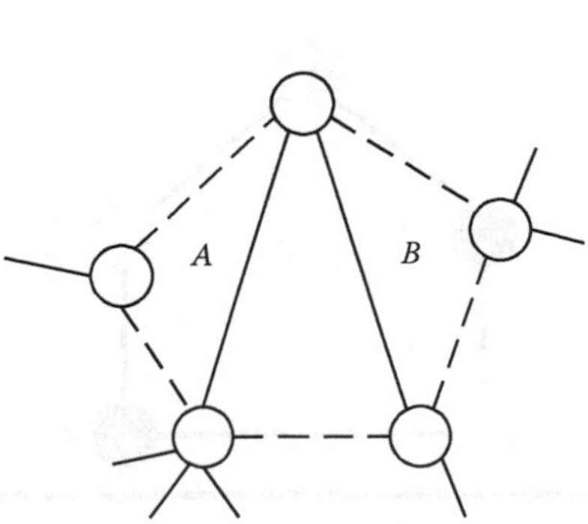

Figure 4.29 Strongly chordal graph.

If the number of DPs of graph G is $\delta+1$, where δ is the minimum degree of the node, graph G is fully controlled. Figure 4.30 is a hypercube with a minimum degree of $\delta=3$ and the number of DPs is $\delta+1=4$; thus, the graph is fully controlled; Figure 4.31 is a ring with a minimum degree of 2 and the number of DPs is $2 \neq \delta+1$; thus, the graph is not fully controlled.

There exists an eliminating order of the vertex in strongly chordal graphs, and the strongly chordal graph is completely dominated. The DP algorithm on strongly chordal graphs in Reference [75] can be divided into two steps:

1. Calculate the minimum degree δ of graph G.
2. Initialize $S_i = \{\Phi\}, 1 \leq i \leq \delta+1$

For $i = n$ to 1

Find the maximum k from the neighbor v_k of node v_i, which is not completely dominated.

If Found, then add node v_i into set S_i, $S_i = S_i \cup \{v_i\}$, where S_i represents a set of v_k which cannot be dominated.

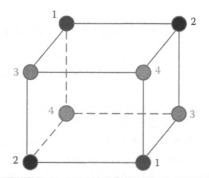

Figure 4.30 Hypercube.

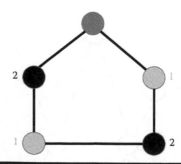

Figure 4.31 Ring.

If Not Found, then add v_i into an arbitrary set S_j, $S_j = S_j \cup \{v_i\}$, where S_j is a random set.

In the algorithm, each node v_i needs $O(d_i)$ time to determine v_k, where d_i is the degree of each node v_i. Then it needs $O(\delta + 1)$ time to determine the direction of v_i. Therefore, the time complexity of the algorithm is $O\left(\sum_{i=1}^{n} d_i + \delta + 1\right) = O(m + n)$.

The linear time DP algorithms on interval graphs, circular arc graphs, and strongly chord graphs have been given. In Reference [76], the authors also introduce a linear time DP algorithm on the total balanced hypergraph and prove that the DP problem on chord graphs and bipartite graphs is an NP-complete problem. In Reference [77], the authors give a linear time DP algorithm by utilizing the bipartite graph of BPF on the bipartite permutation graph.

The peer-to-peer network model is transformed to an interval graph in Reference [78]. The authors solve the distributed service problem with the DP algorithm on the interval graph. Therefore, a network model graph can be transformed to one of the previously shown special graphs and then the DP problem can be solved within the linear time. Interval graphs and circular arc graphs need to calculate the rank order of each node, which makes the model graph more complicated. However, the strongly chordal graph has the inherent node order, which is more suitable for the transformed model graph.

4.3.9.4 The Research Status of Domatic Partition Problem

In wireless sensor networks, DP algorithms can be solved by three methods. The first method is the Graph Coloring Heuristic Algorithm. The second method is linear programming. The goal of DP problem is maximizing the lifetime of the network, which can be changed into a linear programming model. The third method is even partition, which is suitable for UDG. The approximate ratio obtained on the UDG outperforms the former two methods. As shown in Figure 4.32, each solution will be introduced according to different classifications.

4.3.9.4.1 The Domatic Partition Algorithm Based on Coloring

In Reference [79], Feige et al. prove that every graph has a DP with $(1 - O(1))$ $(1 - O(1))(\delta + 1)/\ln \Delta$, and using a coloring heuristic, the algorithm can obtain a Polynomial-Time Centralized algorithm with the approximate ratio $\Omega(\delta/\ln \Delta)$, where Δ is the maximum node degree. The algorithm assumes the available coloring number is $\delta/(24 \log n)$, and the algorithm is divided into three stages. In the first stage, some given nodes are colored, and the nodes can be divided into two states: frozen and saved. With probability 1/2, the size of the maximum component of the subgraph induced by the saved node is $O(\Delta^6 \log n)$. In the second stage, the algorithm is executed in each connected component of the

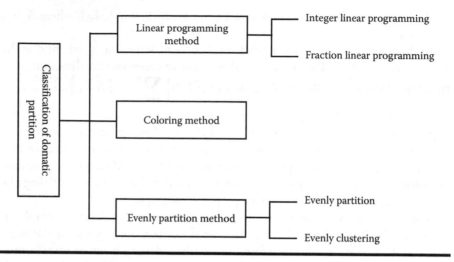

Figure 4.32 The classification of DP algorithms.

subgraph induced by saved nodes; frozen nodes will be colored, thereby generating a new saved node on each connected subgraph. With probability 1/4, the size of the connected component of the subgraph induced by the new saved node is $O(\Delta^6(\log\Delta + \log\log n))$. The third stage is divided into two situations: if $\Delta \succ \log\log n$, the obtained DP number is $O(\delta / (3\log\Delta))$; if $\Delta \leq \log\log n$, obtained DP number is $\Omega(\delta / \ln\Delta)$.

In Reference [80], Moscibroda et al. propose a distributed DP algorithm with approximate ratio $O(\log n)$ by utilizing the heuristic algorithm based on coloring. The algorithm is used to solve the maximization problem of network lifetime. Based on the centralized algorithm in Reference [79], the algorithm is achieved in a distributed way, which is more suitable for the wireless sensor network with large scale.

In Reference [81], Cardei et al. use a coloring heuristic algorithm to obtain a centralized algorithm for DP on the UDG. However, the authors fail to provide the theoretical proof related to the DP number. Besides, the algorithm is a centralized algorithm, which is not suitable for a wireless sensor network with a large scale. In Reference [82], Islam et al. also use a coloring heuristic algorithm to obtain a DP algorithm on the UDG. However, the theoretical proof related to the DP number is not provided in the paper. Besides, the algorithm needs global information, which is not suitable for wireless sensor networks.

In a graph, if a node set cannot completely dominate all nodes V of the graph, and at most $\varepsilon|V|$ nodes are not dominated, the node set is called a $(1-\varepsilon)$ dominating set. $(1-\varepsilon)$ indicates the coverage ratio of the dominating set against all nodes in the graph. The random geometric graph (RGG) refers to the model graph when nodes are distributed evenly on the UDG. References [83] and [84] study the $(1-\varepsilon)$ *DP* algorithm on RGG.

In Reference [83], Mahjoub et al. propose a $(1-\varepsilon)DP$ algorithm with a constant approximate ratio by the smallest last coloring algorithm and the local rules on the Gabriel graph (GG). The algorithm is divided into three stages. In the first stage, the SL coloring algorithm is used to color the graph, thereby generating k color classes. The nodes with the same color form an independent set S. In the second stage, each independent set S constructs a $2r$ subgraph. The $2r$ subgraph is a subgraph induced by independent set S. In the $2r$ subgraph, the edge between two nodes exists when the Euclid distance between two nodes is twice that of the fixed radius r (i.e., $2r$). In the third stage, a plane virtual backbone network is constructed on the $2r$ subgraph by GG rules. The centralized algorithm obtains a constant approximate ratio by some experiment data. Mahjoub et al. discuss the $(1-\varepsilon)DP$ further in Reference [84] and achieve the centralized algorithm in a distributed way. They also provide the analysis of the algorithm. Finally, the simulation shows that there are $\delta+1$ disjointed dominating sets with high probability, and each dominating set is almost the independent dominating set.

The $(1-\varepsilon)DP$ algorithm reduces the constraints of the DP problem, which cannot ensure seamless coverage, thereby leading to an energy hole; besides, the algorithm needs high node density, thereby causing high node redundancy. The experiment results of the algorithm show that the RGG can be completely dominated and the strongly chordal graph can also be completely dominated; thus, whether there exists some relationship between two graphs needs to be studied further.

In Reference [85], Mito et al. propose a CD algorithm on the directed path graph (DPG) with a single sink. The DPG is a model graph composed by the intersections of the directed path sets in the directed tree. The DPG with a single sink is a modularized directed tree with a sink node. The algorithm considers a CDP algorithm on an interval graph at first; then the CDP algorithm on the interval graph is extended to the DPG with a single sink. The basic idea of the CDP algorithm on the interval graph is scheduling the key nodes in the sink node set by a corresponding k-edge coloring problem.

4.3.9.4.2 The Domatic Partition Algorithm Based on Even Partition

In graph G, there is an edge if and only if the Euclid distance between two nodes is at most 1; otherwise, there exists no edge. In this way, the network graph is a UDG.

In graph G, if the k-neighbor relationship involves an independent set with at most $f(r)$ size, graph G is an f-limited growth graph, where $f(r)$ is a function on integer $r \geq 1$. In the r-neighbor relationship of the limited growth graph, the size of maximal independence relies on r, which is a constant number. That means that the size of maximal independence is limited as a constant. The UDG belongs to the limited growth graph.

According to the size of the allowed message account in each transmission, the message transmission model can be divided into two classical models: local and congest. In local mode, assume that each node can send a message with an arbitrary length to its neighbor in each round. However, the message amount exchanged among the nodes is limited. In the congest model, each node can limit the size of the message in each round. Generally, the size of the message is limited as $O(\log n)$ bits. Compared with a local model, congest model has more strict limits on the message amount.

In Reference [86], Pemmaraju et al. first propose three k-DP algorithms with constant approximate ratios in the UDG, where $k \geq 2$, and explain the algorithms can also be used in a limited growth graph. The first algorithm k-DP1 operates constant rounds under the situation where the information of the node's geographical location is known. The second algorithm k-DP2 operates $O(\log^* n)$ rounds under the situation where the information of the distance among the nodes is known. The third algorithm k-DP3 operates $O(\log \Delta \cdot \log^* n)$ rounds under the situation where the geometry information of the node is unknown but the connection information of the distance among the nodes is known. The algorithm first proposes the concept of even partition and then uses even partition to obtain a 2-DP algorithm; finally, it explains that the 2-DP algorithm can be extended to the k-DP algorithm.

In Reference [87], Pandit et al. first propose a DP approximate algorithm with a constant approximate ratio on the UDG, which will be introduced in detail in the later part.

In Reference [88], Misra et al. use DP to execute cycle scheduling of the cluster head. However, the algorithm fails to give effective theoretical proofs for the related partition number. The algorithm deals with the uncovered nodes by reconstructing the cluster, which exists as an infinite loop problem and may lead to an endless loop, thereby reducing the lifetime of the network. Afterwards, Misra et al. modify the algorithm in Reference [89]. They propose an effective cluster head cycle solution and prove that the DP number is a constant approximate ratio. The algorithm deals with uncovered nodes by the rank method instead of reconstructing the cluster. First, the node in the group partitions the rank according to its coordinate; then the node uncovered by the group can determine its rank according to the rank of the node that covers it.

Compared with the previous DP algorithm, the connected DP algorithm attracts less attention. The number of connected DPs is noted as $d_c(G)$. Reference [90] proves that $d_c(G) \leq K(G)$ in graph G (except complete graph) $d_c(G) \leq K(G)$, where $K(G)$ indicates the connection number of graph G. Reference [91] proves that in a plane graph, it holds $d_c \leq 4$ and the connected DP can be solved within linear time in some graphs, such as tree, ring, and complete bipartite graphs.

In Reference [92], Misra et al. propose a connected DP approximate algorithm with approximate ratio $\left\lfloor \dfrac{\delta+1}{\beta(c+1)} \right\rfloor - f$ on the UDG, where δ is the minimum degree of the node in the graph; $\beta \leq 2$; $c \leq 11$; the expected value of f is $\varepsilon \delta |V|$ with $\varepsilon \ll 1$ and $\delta \geq 48$. The algorithm assumes that it only needs to know the connection information among the nodes, instead of the information of geographical location and geometric distance. In Reference [93], Islam et al. propose a centralized algorithm, which can generate a family of CDS. The family of CDS can have intersections, which should occur as infrequently as possible.

4.3.9.4.3 The Domatic Partition Algorithm Based on Linear Programming

This section briefly introduces the solution for independent DP based on integer linear programming and fraction linear programming.

If all the dominating sets are independent sets in a DP, the DP is called an independent DP. The authors of Reference [94] study disjointed independent dominating sets in a graph and prove that there are independent DPs, including complete graphs, all the connected binary graphs, complete k-part graphs, $C_{2n}C_{3n}$ rings, and k-trees.

In Reference [95], Mahjoub provides an integer linear programming model corresponding to the independent DP and shows that a random geometrical graph can be dominated completely by combining coloring algorithms. Besides, there is an independent DP with high probability.

Reference [96] introduces a solution for DP by faction linear programming. The algorithm changes the sleeping scheduling problem based on DP into a faction linear programming model. Then the linear programming problem can be solved by a distributed G-K algorithm, thereby obtaining a fraction DP algorithm with logarithmic approximate ratio.

4.3.9.5 k-Domatic Partition

This section is about k-DP. First, we prove a transforming relationship between k-DP and an r-hop m-dominating set (r-m-DS); then we emphasize 2-DP. We propose a 2-DP approximate algorithm DP by Uniform Clustering (DPUC) with a constant approximate ratio $(\delta+1)/4$ based on even cluster partition in UDG, where δ is the minimum degree of the node. The DPUC algorithm can be executed in constant rounds and can be extended as a k-DP approximate algorithm. Meanwhile, the algorithm solves the public problem proposed in Reference [86], that is, in the situation where only the connected information is known, whether a k-DP approximate algorithm can be obtained in constant rounds. Finally, the simulation proves the correctness and feasibility of algorithm DPUC.

4.3.9.5.1 The Transforming Relationship between k-DP and r-m-DS

4.3.9.5.1.1 Related Research of r-m-DS   An r-m-DS of Graph $G=(V, E)$ shows that each node u beyond D has at least m dominating nodes in D within the r-hop range, where D is a subset of node set V; the hop number r is dominated by the distance; m is the dominating parameter and reflects the fault tolerance of the network. Connected r-m-CDS means that each node in $V\backslash D$ has at least m dominating nodes in D within the r-hop range, and subset D is connected.

In Reference [97], the authors propose two approximate algorithms of connected r-m-DS. The first algorithm uses a coloring heuristic algorithm to obtain a connected r-m-DS on the UDG. The second algorithm is a Greedy algorithm, which finds a connected r-m-DS on the general graph. In Reference [98], the authors also study the connected r-m-DS problem in wireless networks and propose two approximate algorithms. The fist algorithm constructs an m-dominating set on the power graph model of the original graph (i.e., an r-m-DS of the original graph) and then the dominating sets are connected as a connected r-m-DS. The second algorithm finds an r-m-DS on the original graph directly, and then the r-m-DS is connected as a connected r-m-DS. Given a graph $G=(V, E)$, a k-m-CDS means that each node in V\D has at least m dominating nodes in D, where D is a subset of node set V, and subset D is k-connected (i.e., there exist at least m disjointed paths in subset D).

In Reference [99], the authors propose four local construction protocols for m-connected m-dominating sets (m-CDSs). The first two protocols are m-Gossip and m-Grid, respectively. These two protocols extend the existing CDS algorithms, which are Gossip and Grid based on probability, to a random algorithm for finding the m-CDS. The third protocol extends an existing CDS algorithm, which uses the coverage condition, to a deterministic algorithm for finding m-CDS by the m-coverage condition; the fourth protocol extends many existing CDS algorithms to an m-CDS algorithm with a coloring heuristic algorithm. In Reference [100], the authors propose a centralized algorithm with an approximate ratio of 64 to construct a 2-connected virtual backbone network. A 2-connected backbone network is a special instance of a k-m-CDS when $k=2$, $m=1$. In Reference [101], a centralized algorithm is proposed. The algorithm is divided into three steps: The first step constructs a 1-connected m-dominating set; the second step constructs a k-connected m-dominating set; the third step constructs a k-connected k-dominating set, where $3 \le k \le m$. In Reference [102], Thai et al. propose a centralized algorithm, which is not easy to achieve. The algorithm constructs a 1-m-CDS at first; then the algorithm extends it to a k-m-CDS. In Reference [103], WuYiwei et al. propose a centralized CGA algorithm and a distributed DDA algorithm. However, the performance of the CGA algorithm cannot be ensured, and the DDA algorithm requires high message overhead. In Reference [104], WuYiwei et al. solve these two problems and propose a centralized ICGA algorithm and a distributed LDA algorithm. Compared with the CGA algorithm, the ICGA algorithm is a construction method with low message overhead and a fixed performance factor. In Reference [105], the authors propose a 3-m-CDS algorithm with a constant approximate ratio. Reference [116] proposes a minimal k-m-CDS algorithm with a constant approximate ratio of UDG, where $k \le 2$. Finally, the authors discuss how to construct a minimal k-m-CDS, where k is an arbitrary integer.

Given a graph $G=(V, E)$, a k-connected m-tuple dominating set means that each node in node set V has at least m dominating nodes in D, where D is a subset of node set V and subset D is k-connected. By definition, a k-connected m-tuple dominating set has a stronger constrain condition than a k-connected m-dominating set. In Reference [107], the authors propose a k-connected m-tuple dominating set problem and propose two approximate algorithms when dominating parameter $m=1$ and $m=2$, respectively.

In Reference [108], the authors provide an effective method for constructing a fault-tolerant virtual backbone network in the wireless network with different transmitting radii. In the paper, the fault-tolerant virtual backbone problem is abstracted as a problem that finds a k-strongly connected m-dominating set. The authors design the algorithms for solving 1-m-SCDAS and k-1-SCDAS. Finally, these two methods are combined to construct a k-m-SCDAS.

4.3.9.5.1.2 The Conversion between k-DP and r-m-DS

In this section, we use an r-m-DS to obtain a k-DP with partition number m, where $k=2r$. As shown in Figure 4.33, the black node indicates a 3-dominating set of the graph, that is, each white node can be dominated by three black nodes. According to a certain number strategy, the three black nodes are numbered and the numbers are mutually different; thus, black nodes with the same number can form a two-hop dominating set. The black node with number 1 can not only 1-dominate all white nodes, but also can 2-dominate black nodes with another number. Black nodes with numbers 2 and 3 form separate two-hop dominating sets. Therefore, there are 3 two-hop dominating sets, and they form a 2-DP.

Theorem 4.20: An r-m-DS of an arbitrary graph can be transformed to a k-DP with DP number m, where $k=2r$.

Proof: According to the definition of r-m-DS, the regular nodes outside the dominating set can be r-hop dominated by m nodes. The dominating nodes of each regular node are numbered from 1 to m, and the number of each node is different. Thus, the dominating node with the same number can form a 2r-hop dominating

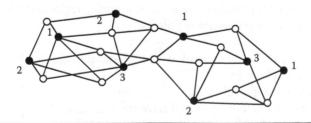

Figure 4.33   3-dominating set and 2-DP.

set (proven in the following). Since the node has m numbers, there exist m 2r-hop dominating sets, that is, a k-DP can be obtained, where $k=2r$ and the DP number is m. In the following, we prove that dominating nodes with the same number can form a 2r-hop dominating set of the graph.

First, a regular node can be r-hop dominated by dominating nodes with the same number, because each regular node can be r-hop dominated by m dominating nodes. Thus, a selected dominating node can also be r-hop dominated. Excluding regular nodes, dominating nodes with the same number can be two-hop dominated by dominating nodes with other numbers, because a dominating node can arrive at a regular node by r-hop and then arrive at another dominating node by another r-hop. Therefore, there are at most 2r-hops among the dominating nodes.

According to this theorem, if the nodes in the r-m-DS can be numbered by an appropriate number strategy, the existing r-m-DS can be extended to a k-DP algorithm.

4.3.9.5.2 Problem Description and Network Model

In Reference [40], some properties of k-DP number are provided by Zelinka et al. The first lemma proves that the k-DP number increases along with the improvement of the hop number k. In the wireless sensor networks, however, it is not improved with the larger value of hop number k. There exists a problem. Assume $D^{(2)}$ is a 2-dominating set in graph G. If a node $u \in V - D^{(2)}$ needs to send the message to the dominating node in $D^{(2)}$ but $D^{(2)}$ has no dominating node in its one-hop neighbor, how should node u send the message? One of the solutions for this problem is increasing the transmitting radius of node u so that a dominating node of $D^{(2)}$ is located in the transmitting range of node u. In this way, k-DP has more DP numbers, but this advantage may be offset because some nodes will consume more energy communicating with their adjacent dominating nodes by increasing the transmitting power. Therefore, in k-DP, the value of hop number k should be a small integer slightly larger than 1. Thus in this chapter, we emphasize 2-DP and explain that the 2-DP approximate algorithm can be extended to the k-DP approximate algorithm.

In the following, we give the network model adopted by the algorithm. The model is also suitable for the algorithms in the later part. Assume that N sensor nodes are distributed randomly in a square monitoring region with S area and that the sensor node has the properties as follows:

1. The network is a static network with high density, that is, the node will not move after deployment.
2. Each node has a globally unique id signature.
3. The nodes are homogeneous and have the same initial energy and the same transmission radius R.

4. A node cannot obtain the information of its geographical location and geometrical distance, and it only knows the connection information among the nodes.
5. The wireless transmitting power is manageable.

The first two properties are the regular configurations in general wireless sensor networks. The third property assumes that the node energy is homogeneous, which is the classical configuration of DP problems. This section studies the 2-DP on the UDG, thus we assume that the nodes have the same transmitting radius. The fourth property is beneficial for saving cost and energy consumptions of the node. There are three main methods for obtaining the geographical location information of the node: GPS, directional antenna, and a positioning algorithm. The location information of the node can be obtained by configuring additional hardware devices that will essentially increase the hardware cost and the corresponding energy overhead; the positioning algorithm needs to exchange a great deal of messages to calculate the location, which will cause large energy overhead as well. The fifth property considers the situation from the view of data transmission. For 2-DP, some nodes increase transmission power to communicate with their two-hop dominating nodes.

4.3.9.5.3 The 2-Domatic Partition Algorithm

Pemmaraju et al. propose a public problem in the conclusion of Reference [17]: In the situation where the geometric information of the node is unknown but the connected information among the nodes is known, can the runtime of k-DP3 be modified as a constant round? The key point of the problem is whether the geometric information plays a vital role in designing a fast-distributed k-DP approximate algorithm.

In this section, we propose a 2-DP approximate algorithm DPUC with a constant approximate ratio $(\delta+1)/4$ based on even cluster partition in UDG, where δ is the minimum degree of the node. The DPUC algorithm can be executed in constant rounds and can be extended as a k-DP approximate algorithm.

4.3.9.5.3.1 An Even Partition
Reference [86] gives the definition of an even partition. $\zeta = \{V_1, V_2, \ldots, V_t\}$ is a partition of vertex set V in graph G. ζ can be called an even partition when it satisfies two conditions:

1. The diameter of each subgraph induced by V_i is 2.
2. For each V_i, there is a constant C, letting $|V_i| \ge (\delta+1)/C|$, where δ is the minimum node degree.

Lemma 4.15 explains that a 2-DP can be obtained by an even partition.

Lemma 4.15: $\zeta = \{V_1,\ V_2,...,V_t\}$ is an even partition of graph G. Select an arbitrary different color from $\{1,\ 2,...,|V|\}$ and color each vertex V_i. D_r represents the vertex set colored r. For each integer r, D_r is a 2-dominating set of graph G when $1 \leq r \leq [(\delta+1)/C]$.

The proof is omitted but can be seen in Lemma 3 of Reference [86]. Lemma 4.12 showed that if an even partition is obtained in a graph, a 2-DP can be constructed by coloring the cluster members.

4.3.9.5.3.2 The Design of the DPUC Algorithm

The DPUC algorithm is divided into four stages: obtaining the information with duration T_1, cluster head competition with duration T_2, forming the cluster with duration T_3, and coloring with duration T_4.

In the stage of obtaining the information, each node broadcasts the Node_Msg message, which includes the id of the node. Meanwhile, the node will receive the Node_Msg message from its neighbors. Each node updates its neighbor list according to the received Node_Msg message. After updating, each node calculates the value of node degree d and then it calculates the time of sending the Head_Msg message according to formula 4.17:

$$
t = \begin{cases} \dfrac{D-1}{d} \times \dfrac{T_2}{2} \times \rho, d \geq D-1 \\[3ex] \dfrac{T_2}{2} + \left(1 - \dfrac{d}{D-1}\right) \times \dfrac{T_2}{2} \times \rho, d \prec D-1 \end{cases} \tag{4.17}
$$

ρ is a random value in interval [0.9, 1], whose function is to reduce the probability that different nodes select the same value t. D is the pre-estimated value of the node degree. According to the assumed network model, $D = N\pi R^2/S$. The duration of the stage of the cluster head competition is T_2, in which the first half duration $t_1 = \dfrac{D-1}{d} \times \dfrac{T_2}{2} \times \rho$ (from 0 to 2), determining most cluster heads with large node degree; the second half duration $t_2 = \dfrac{T_2}{2} + \left(1 - \dfrac{d}{D-1}\right) \times \dfrac{T_2}{2} \times \rho$ (from $T_2/2$ to T_2), selecting the cluster head from the uncovered area. It is easy to see that t_1 and t_2 satisfy $t_1 \prec \dfrac{T_2}{2} \prec t_2 \prec T_2$.

After T_1 ends, the stage of cluster head competition begins. In the stage, if a node has not received the Head_Msg message from any other node, it will broadcast a Head_Msg message to declare itself the cluster head. Otherwise, the node quits the competition and becomes a noncluster head. When the stage ends, all selected cluster heads form an MIS of the graph, for which the proof is given in

Theorem 4.4. Besides, the selected cluster head is distributed evenly, because the node will broadcast a Head_Msg message to its neighbors once it becomes the cluster head. The neighbors that receive the message will quit and become cluster members. Therefore, there are no other cluster heads in the coverage of a cluster head.

After T_2 ends, the stage of forming the cluster begins. In the stage, each non-cluster head may receive multiple Head_Msg messages from different cluster heads. The noncluster head node sends a Join_Msg message, which includes its id and the id of the cluster head, to its closest cluster head by adjacent sensing strategy [92]. Meanwhile, the cluster head assigns a coloring order number for each cluster member according to the sequence of the received Join_Msg message. Assume that the size of a cluster partition V_i is $|V_i|$, then each cluster member corresponds to the coloring order number from 1 to V_i.

Then, the first three stages of the DPUC algorithm are completed, which can be collectively called a clustering stage. Thus an even cluster partition is obtained, for which the proof can be seen in Theorem 4.22.

After T_3 ends, the stage of coloring begins. In this stage, each cluster head broadcasts the coloring message Color_Msg to its cluster members; it includes the id of the cluster members and the corresponding coloring order number. Meanwhile, when each cluster member receives the Color_Msg message, it will color itself with the corresponding order number r, where $1 \leq r \leq |V_i|$.

Then the DPUC algorithm ends, and all nodes with the same color form a 2-dominating set. By analyzing this process, it can be seen that the DPUC algorithm has the following properties:

1. The DPUC algorithm is a distributed algorithm, which is suitable for the wireless sensor network.
2. At first, the DPUC algorithm uses the first part t_1 of formula (1) and selects the cluster head with larger node degree in the first half of the duration, which is beneficial for gathering more nodes in a cluster.
3. The DPUC algorithm uses the second part t_2 of formula (1) and generates residual cluster heads in the second half of the duration. It still uses the node degree as the parameter factor for competing for the cluster head, which rejects the node with low node degree to become the cluster head objectively. Thereby it avoids "isolated" nodes and achieves seamless coverage for the nodes in the network.
4. The DPUC algorithm generates an even distribution of the cluster head in the cluster head selection stage. Since the duration of competing to become the cluster head varies, it can ensure that there is no other cluster head in the coverage area of a cluster head.
5. In the clustering and coloring stages, the DPUC algorithm only uses the connection information, instead of knowing the geometric information of the node.

4.3.9.5.3.3 Theoretical Analysis of the Algorithm   They analyze the correctness of the DPUC algorithm. First, it proves that the cluster is an even partition, which is generated by the DPUC algorithm in the clustering stage. According to the two conditions of even partition, it proves that the diameter of the subgraph induced by each cluster is 2. For each cluster, there is a constant C to make the node number of the cluster greater than $(\delta+1)/C$, where δ is the minimum node degree.

Lemma 4.16: In the clustering stage, the diameter of the subgraph induced by each cluster is 2.

Proof: After completing the clustering stage, the cluster head in each cluster dominates its cluster members by single hop. In the cluster, the distance from one cluster member to another is at most 2, because each cluster member can arrive at another cluster member through the cluster head. By definition of the diameter in the graph, the diameter of the subgraph induced by each cluster is 2.

Lemma 4.17: In the clustering stage, the minimum area of the cluster is $\dfrac{\sqrt{3}}{2}R^2$, the maximum area of the cluster is $\dfrac{\sqrt{3}}{2}R^2$, and the expected value of the cluster area is $\sqrt{3}R^2$.

Proof: In Reference [43], the cluster with the smallest area and the cluster with the largest area are proved, as shown in Figures 4.34 and 4.35. In Figure 4.34, the distance between cluster head A and the 6 neighbor cluster heads is $R+\varepsilon$ (in which, $\varepsilon \to 0$). When the distance between cluster head A and an arbitrary neighbor cluster

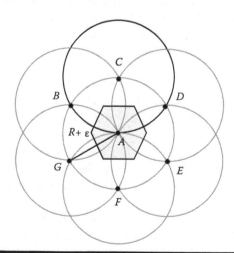

Figure 4.34   The cluster with minimum area.

head is no larger than R, cluster head A will be covered by 6 neighbor cluster heads. Thus, Figure 4.34 illustrates the situation of the minimum cluster area. The cluster head with the minimum area is explained by the gray part, which is a regular hexagon with length $\dfrac{\sqrt{3}}{3} R$. The area of the gray part equals $\dfrac{\sqrt{3}}{2} R^2$.

In Figure 4.35, the distance between cluster head A and the 6 neighbor cluster heads is $\sqrt{3}(R - \varepsilon)$, (in which, $\varepsilon \to 0$). When the distance between cluster head A and an arbitrary neighbor cluster head is larger than $\sqrt{3}R$, there is a blind seam area. Thus, Figure 4.35 illustrates the situation of the maximum cluster area. The cluster with the maximum area is called the gray part, which is a regular hexagon with length R. The area of the gray part equals $\dfrac{3\sqrt{3}}{2} R^2$.

Since the nodes are distributed randomly, the real area of the cluster is between the maximum area and the minimum area. Therefore, the expected value of the cluster is $\sqrt{3}R^2$.

Lemma 4.18: If the sensor nodes are distributed evenly with density ρ, for an arbitrary region with area S, the probability of the node number obeys Poisson distribution: $P(X = m) = \dfrac{(\rho \cdot S)^m \cdot e^{-\rho \cdot S}}{m!}$.

The proof is omitted but can be seen in Lemma 1 of Reference [44]. According to the property of Poisson distribution, the value of the Poisson distribution

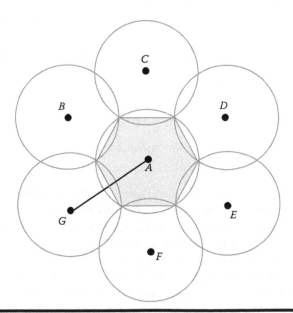

Figure 4.35 The cluster with maximum area.

ratio $P(m;\lambda) = \dfrac{(\lambda)^m \cdot e^{-\lambda}}{m!}$ $(\lambda = \rho S)$ changes along with the change of m. When $m = \lambda$, probability $P(m; \lambda)$ has a maximum value. Therefore, in a region with area S, the practical node number is in proportion to the area with high probability ρS.

Theorem 4.21: For the cluster generated in the clustering stage, there is a constant, which makes the node number of each cluster larger than $(\delta+1)/C$ with high probability, where the constant $C=4$.

Proof: According to Lemma 4.18, the minimum cluster has the minimum node number with high probability. According to Lemma 4.17, the area of the minimum cluster is greater than 1/4 of disk area πR^2. Thus, the node number of the minimum cluster is greater than $(\delta+1)/4$ with high probability. Therefore, the node number of each cluster is greater than $(\delta+1)/4$.

Theorem 4.22: In the DPUC algorithm, each cluster generated in the clustering stage is an even partition.

Proof: According to Lemma 4.16, the diameter of the subgraph induced by each cluster is 2, which satisfies the first condition of even partition; according to theorem 4.16, the node number of each cluster is greater than $(\delta+1)/4$ with high probability, which satisfies the second condition of even partition. Therefore, each generated cluster is an even partition.

Theorem 4.23 can be obtained directly by Lemma 4.15 and Theorem 4.22.

Theorem 4.23: For the integer $1 \le r \le [(\delta+1)/4]$, if D_r is the node set colored as r in the coloring stage, D_r is a 2-dominating set.

Theorem 4.24: The DPUC algorithm operates within constant rounds, and all generated cluster heads form an MIS.

Proof: The DPUC algorithm is a distributed algorithm, whose round number depends on the communication round number of a single node. However, the communication round number of a single node is a constant, which is independent of the scale of the whole network. Therefore, the DPUC algorithm can be completed within constant rounds and the time complexity is $O(1)$.

Here, we will prove that the generated cluster heads form an MIS. Since there is no other cluster head in the coverage area of a cluster head, all cluster heads form an independent set. Moreover, since each node in the network becomes the cluster head or a cluster member, the independence of the cluster head will be destroyed if an arbitrary cluster member joins the independent set formed by the cluster heads. Therefore, all generated cluster heads form an MIS.

Theorem 4.25 can be obtained directly by Theorem 4.23 and Theorem 4.24.

Theorem 4.25: In the situation where only connection information among the nodes is known, it can obtain a 2-DP algorithm with a constant approximate ratio within constant rounds on the UDG.

The 2-DP approximate algorithm proposed in this section can be extended as a k-DP approximate algorithm, where $k \geq 2$. For the extension method, in the clustering stage, temporarily enlarge the transmitting radius of each node as m times of the original radius; similarly, construct an even cluster partition with diameter $2m$ by the DPUC algorithm, thereby obtaining a k-DP, where $k = 2m$. However, it will consume more energy because the transmitting power is enlarged. Therefore, the tradeoff needs to be made further. Based on this analysis, Theorem 4.26 can be obtained.

Theorem 4.26: In the situation where only the connection information is known, it can obtain a k-DP approximate algorithm with a constant approximate ratio within constant rounds on the UDG, where $k \geq 2$.

4.3.9.5.3.4 Simulation analysis

Here, we compare the theoretical analysis value and the simulated experimental value of the DPUC algorithm. The experimental situations involves two situations: high and low density.

Situation 1 (low density): 100 nodes are evenly distributed in a square area with a 50×50 square unit.

Situation 2 (high density): 400 nodes are evenly distributed in a square area with a 50×50 square unit.

Figure 4.36 is the original network topology in situation 1 when the transmitting radius of the node is 16. Figure 4.37 is an even partition obtained in the clustering stage. In the figures, the black node indicates the cluster head, and the white node indicates the cluster member. Each cluster head dominates its cluster members by single hop. It can be seen from the figures that the generated cluster heads are distributed evenly and that they form an MIS.

Figure 4.38 is the distribution of dominating nodes in 2-DP obtained by the DPUC algorithm. The 2-DP includes 7 two-hop dominating sets. A different color signature indicates different dominating nodes in 2-DS. The nodes with

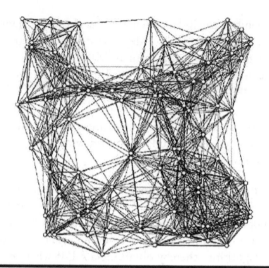

Figure 4.36 The network topology in situation 1.

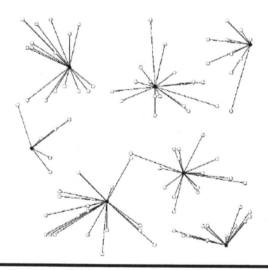

Figure 4.37 The topology of an even cluster partition.

the same color signature form a 2-DS. Figure 4.39 is the topology graph of 7 two-hop dominating sets in Figure 4.38. For clarity, we divide 7 2-DC into 3 figures. Figure 4.39a shows the 2-DS topology formed by colors 1, 2, and 3. Figure 4.39b shows the 2-DS topology formed by colors 4 and 5. Figure 4.39c shows the 2-DS topology formed by colors 6 and 7. In the topology, the solid line represents single-hop dominating for the nodes in the cluster, and the dotted line represents two-hop dominating for the nodes in the cluster.

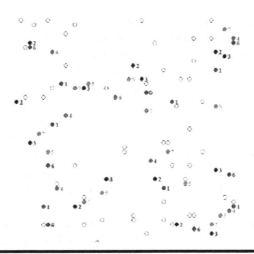

Figure 4.38 2-DP obtained by the algorithm.

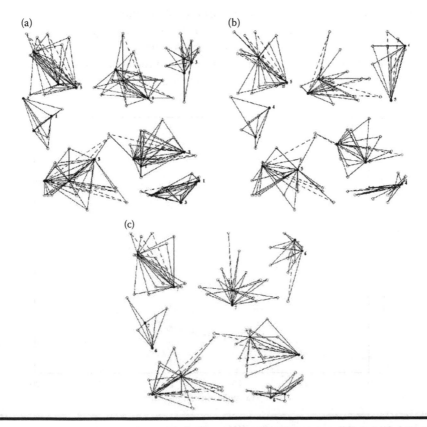

Figure 4.39 7 2-DS topology of 2-DP. (a) The first three 2-DS topology, (b) the fourth and fifth 2-DS topology, and (c) the last two 2-DS topologies.

Figure 4.40 explains that the curve of the 2-DP number varies along with the improvement of transmitting radius under the situation of low density and high density. It can be seen in the figure that the larger the density of the node in the monitoring area, the larger the 2-DP number is. The 2-DP number found by the algorithm is increased along with the improvement of the transmitting radius.

Figure 4.41 illustrates the comparison of the 2-DP number and the minimum node degree under the situation of low density and high density. It can be seen from the figure that the 2-DP number found by the DPUC algorithm is approximately the minimum degree of the node in the figure, which proves the correctness and superiority of the approximate ratio of the algorithm. The more the 2-domination partition number found by the algorithm is, the longer the sleeping scheduling duration of the two-hop dominating set is.

Figure 4.42 finds the average number of the node included in the two-hop dominating set under different density. It can be seen from the figure that the average number of the node included in 2-DS is reduced along with the improvement of the transmitting radius.

In summary, k-DP can play an important role in balancing the energy consumption. It can prolong the lifetime of the network by cycling the k-dominating set in k-DP. This chapter studies 2-DP, proposing a DPUC algorithm with constant-round runtime and constant approximate ratio based on even clustering. The algorithm extends the k-DP approximation algorithm. The main contribution

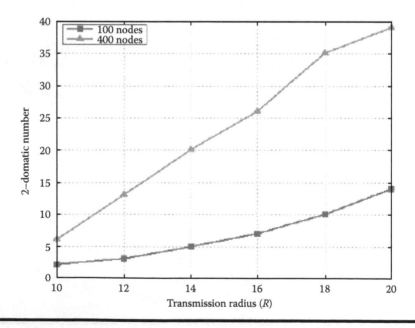

Figure 4.40   2-DP numbers under different situations.

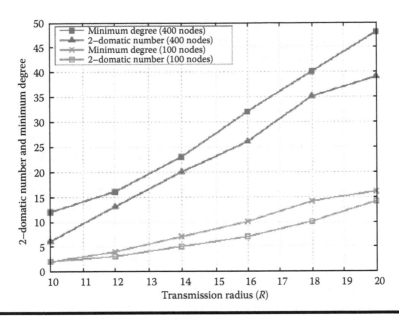

Figure 4.41   The comparison of 2-DP number and minimum node degree.

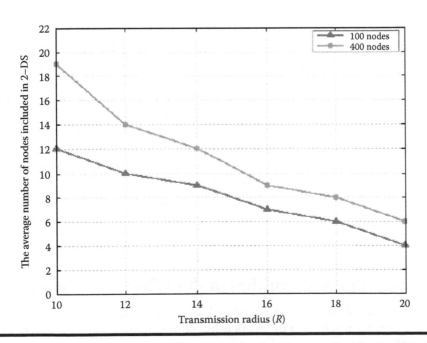

Figure 4.42   The average number of the node included in two-hop dominating set.

of the chapter is solving the public problems in Reference [86] and proposing the DPUC algorithm with the approximate ratio of $(\delta + 1)/4$, in which δ is the minimum degree of the node. Finally, the simulation further proves the correctness and superiority of the algorithm.

4.3.9.6 Public Problems

Since the DP problem plays a vital role in the wireless sensor network, DP is always a hot topic. Many researchers have done a lot of meaningful work. Research on the DP problem has obtained certain achievements. However, there are still many public problems to be solved along with the development of the sensor network and the extension of the application; these are mainly reflected in three aspects.

1. The public problem of k-DP

   The geometric information of the node includes the geometric information of the location and distance. The geometric information of the location is the coordinate information of the node; the geometric information of the distance is the distance among the nodes. In the situation where the connected information is known but the geometric information is unknown, whether the runtime of the k-DP algorithm can be improved to a constant is still a public problem.

2. The public problem of DP

   In order to obtain the geometric information of the node, additional hard devices are needed; this will increase the overhead of hardware cost and corresponding energy; a positioning algorithm needs to exchange a lot of messages to calculate its location, which will cause a great amount of energy overhead. In the situation where the connected information is known but the geometric information is unknown, finding a DP algorithm with a constant approximate ratio in the UDG is still a public problem. Overhead of hardware cost and corresponding energy could be saved by solving this problem.

3. The public problem of connected DP

   Compared with these two problems, the connected DP requires that each dominating set has to be a connected dominating set, which increases the difficulty of solving the problem. The existing DP algorithms are as difficult to extend as the connected DP algorithm. Extending a DP to a connected DP is still a public problem.

4.4 Distributed Algorithm in the Wireless Network

The distributed algorithm is an established tool for designing a sensor network. In this section, we will discuss the relationship of distributed computing theory and the application of sensor networks. Along this path, we propose several basic and provable distributed algorithms.

4.4.1 Introduction

Now, many computer and communication systems are distributed—consist of autonomic computing entities that can communicate with each other. The communication is achieved by transmitting the message in general. Recently, the distributed system has been applied extensively. The obvious distributed system is the Internet and a great many applications, such as the domain name system, P2P file sharing, and cloud computing. On the other hand, the distributed system exists on a small scale, such as a multicore processor or field programmable gate array. In fact, if we extend our vision beyond the computing system, the brain or society is a distributed system in some ways, in which nerves and humans are the roles of autonomic entity, respectively. Besides the obvious difference, the common point of all distributed systems is that many entities can work simultaneously in the system. These entities have some degree of freedom: they have their own hardware, their own data or code, and their own task. However, they share resources and information. In order to solve a problem involving all entities or entity subsets, coordination among the entities is necessary.

A sensor network is the totality of all nodes. Each node itself is a small computer, which can collect data by its sensors and communicate with other nodes via radio. Since power decreases with distance, generally, it is not feasible that all nodes communicate directly with each other (or with the base station). On the contrary, in order to communicate, the node has to become a relay node for other nodes. This situation can be modeled as a graph. A node set consists of sensor nodes (possibly including the base station) and the edge among two nodes infers that they can exchange messages directly by radio. Based on these reasons, a sensor network is a completely distributed system [119].

The distributed algorithm is the theoretical basis of the distributed system. We study how a node plans its communication and calculation to solve a given task effectively. Besides, we are interested in the impossible result and lower boundary, because they prove what cannot use a distributed algorithm. Overall, this field is called distributed computing.

In a large distributed system, the node cannot have global knowledge about the whole system at any time. However, each node can only know a local area of the system, and it has to make a decision based on local information. Many tasks can be solved locally. For example, a node can calculate the minimum measured temperature of its neighbors by communicating with its neighbors. In order to solve the global problem, some information has to run through the whole sensor network. Moreover, researchers want to know which task is local and which global in distributed computing. As we can see, many coordinated tasks related to the sensor network are neither local nor global. Actually, the task is between these two types.

There are many reasons the distributed algorithm is so attractive in designing sensor node protocol. First of all, we want to avoid the situation that a sensor node with limited memory has to store a great deal of information from long-distance nodes. In fact, it is an advantage if a node only needs to calculate a local part of a solution. More importantly, limiting the distance of information collection means (1) the algorithm is fast, and communication is the part that costs the most time and (2) the input or the topology change can be processed locally, that is, only some of the nodes need to recalculate their output. In other words, in a large system, fault or reconfiguring affects only a small part of the system. With good technology, the system will play the normal function from the global view even if some nodes break down, make a mistake, or even destroy the system on purpose. If a node breaks down, any part of the algorithm on the single node fails. In the worst situation, a node may use false information to attack the whole network. Last but not least, because the solution states as little as possible about the network. Moreover, the results of many distributed algorithms are simple and delicate. Although being delicate is not necessary for sensor networks, simplicity is necessary, especially for the limited computational power, memory, and energy of sensor nodes.

4.4.2 *The Distributed Algorithm*

For many years, researchers have regarded the study of distributed network algorithms as a pure research topic. These algorithms are too pure for hybrid distributed systems in the real world. Therefore, the field entered a dormant period in the 1990s. The coming of sensor networks (as well as something closely related such as ad hoc networks) drew the attention of researchers. Many corresponding applications arose suddenly. In order to better understand, we will do careful research on the standard models used by the distributed algorithm.

As described already, a distributed system is modeled as a graph $G = (V, E)$. Node set $V \cdot (|V| = n)$ is the calculation device; the edge set is defined as that in which the nodes can communicate with each other directly. In general, a distributed system focuses on a locality of a problem. In other words, the maximum distance (hop number) needed to receive the message is regarded as the function of node number n. In theory, the local synchronous message-transmitting model is generally studied in the purest form. To be more specific, the calculation is operated by rounds. In each round, all nodes exchange the message simultaneously. In other words, any synchronous distributed algorithm looks like the following form:

Algorithm 4.1: General Skeleton of a Distributed Algorithm

Each node v performs the following actions concurrently with all other nodes:

repeat

> send (possibly different) messages to neighbors
>
> receive neighbors' messages
>
> perform some local computations to prepare for the next round
>
> until termination;

For the research of distributed algorithms, we mainly focus on the runtime. The runtime of synchronous distributed algorithms is measured by the round number of synchronous communication, that is, how many rounds the communication calculation executes until all nodes finish.

4.4.2.1 The Classic Problem in the Distributed Computing- Maximal Independent Set Problem

Specifically, let us study an example, the so-called MIS problem, which we have introduced in detail. As we have discussed, in a distributed system, all the nodes can execute simultaneously. However, even though the task is localized in some ways, whatever the long-distance node is doing has little effect. Actually, the sensor network generally needs to avoid having two neighbors execute operations simultaneously. For example, if two neighbors try to transmit simultaneously, the packets may not both be received correctly because of wireless interference. On the other hand, we want to achieve parallelism. Especially, for each node, some neighbors are able to execute each operation.

The MIS problem is a basic symmetry-breaking problem, which is a fussy name for the centralized algorithm. Initially, assume the MIS is S and $S = \emptyset$. The algorithm just traverses the nodes one by one, instead of adding any neighbor of S into S. However, if the nodes can execute simultaneously, they can join S in the same round for a faster rate. We only need to ensure that no two adjacent nodes join S in the same round. Assume that the node has unique signature, so that the fussy sequential MIS solution is changed to a simple distributed algorithm. For simplicity, $N_v = \{w \in V \mid \{v,w\} \in E\}$ will indicate the neighbor of node $v \in V$ in the following.

When executing Algorithm 4.2, any active node with a locally maximum identity will join the independent set in the next round. Since it is impossible for two neighbors to both have the locally maximum identity, the collision will not occur. All neighbors of this kind of node will terminate in the next round, thereby ensuring no collision. Note that termination is safe for these nodes, because they have at least one neighbor in the MIS, which means they will be a part of any MIS that has involved their neighbors. The runtime is given by the maximum decreasing chain of identity, which is $D+1$ at most. D is the diameter of the graph, that is, the maximum length of the shortest path among the node pairs.

Unfortunately, D may be very large, which is depressing because a distributed solution is not better than a sequential solution in the worst case—it looks like a simple local definition problem, such as finding an MIS, needs a solution without global consequences.

Algorithm 4.2: Naive MIS

Input: each node $v \in V$ has a unique identifier $id(v)$

Output: each node v performs the following actions concurrently with all other nodes:

send $id(v)$ to neighbors

receive neighbors' identifiers

Memorize neighbors with higher priority as

$$A := \{w \in N_v \mid id(w) \succ id(v)\}$$

repeat

  if $A \neq \varnothing$ then

    send "join" to neighbors N_v

    join MIS and terminate

  if receive "join" message then

    send "not join" to neighbors N_v

  receive "not join" messages

$$A = A \setminus \{w \in N_v \mid received' \ not \ join' \ from \ w\}$$

until termination.

4.4.2.2 Finding a Fast Distributed Maximal Independent Set Algorithm

Clearly, up to this point no algorithm that is always fast has been created. Even if the algorithm does not consider the packet size, the runtime of the known fastest solution is $2^{O(\sqrt{\log n})}$ [120]. The diameter of an "interesting" graph is generally small. Although some algorithms are effective if the graph satisfies some properties, we hope to find a good solution for any network in the ideal situation. For a distributed algorithm, it is very difficult in many situations, because there always exists an awful instance for any fixed executing process. Besides, a node may take a lot of time to sense local information, because it can only sense a small part initially. Sometimes, a random mode can be used to overcome this obstacle or at least part of the obstacle. Random distributed algorithms obey the same rules as deterministic distributed algorithms. The only difference is that random algorithms may make decisions based on a "toss" mode. We will introduce another instance to explain this concept.

Algorithm 4.3 is a well-known version of the algorithm family and is essentially consistent with Algorithm 4.2. The difference is that the signature will be reselected randomly in each iteration. If a random value has a logarithmic size, the probability that two numbers are equal is negligible. By a simple fair argument, it can be proven that the edges connected with the expected final nodes are a constant part of the total number of residual edges. That is because it is established for any graph, especially a subgraph generated by the active nodes in each iteration; thus, the expected runtime is $O(\log n)$. We can prove that the algorithm can also end after $O(c \log n)$ rounds with a high probability, which means the probability is $1 - 1/n^c$. This is a powerful result because the algorithm will end after $O(c \log n)$ rounds, even though O is a moderate constant.

Algorithm 4.3: Randomized MIS [131]

Output: each node $v \in V$ knows whether it is in the MIS

Each node v performs the following actions concurrently with all other nodes:

repeat

    let $r(v)$ be a randomly chosen number

    send $r(v)$ to neighbors

    receive random numbers from all (nonterminated) neighbors N_v

    if $r(v) > r(w)$ for all $w \in N_v$ then

        send 'join' to N_v

        join MIS and terminate

    if receive 'join' message then

        send 'not join' to N_v

        do not join MIS and terminate

until termination.

4.4.2.3 Local Algorithms

The runtime of the algorithm is increased with the improvement of the input scale. For example, it takes much more time to order a hundred names than a thousand names. Only the most ordinary problem can be solved in constant time without considering the scale of input. However, an exception is that there exists a nontrivial distributed algorithm executing in a constant time. It operates well in the distributed system with large scale since it has high scalability and high fault tolerance. Although the model of the local algorithm is limited, researchers are optimistic.

4.4.2.3.1 Local Algorithms

The local algorithm is a distributed algorithm that can be operated in a constant synchronous communication round without considering the number of nodes in the network. In other words, in the local algorithm, the output of a node is obtained according to the effective input in the neighbor range of a constant radius.

Naor and Stockmeyer [121], Angluin [122], and Linial [123] proposed the study of the local algorithm. Angluin studied its limitation in the network without obvious feature. Linial proved seminal negative results if each node has a unique signature, and Naor and Stockmeyer proposed the first nonordinary result.

If the communication round of algorithm A is a constant, which is marked r, we call the algorithm a local algorithm. The constant value r may depend on the parameter of the problem family. For example, if we study a graph with a limited vertex degree, the value of r may depend on the parameter Δ. However, the value of r has nothing to do with the instance of the problem, especially for the vertex number of graph G.

The constant r is regarded as the local boundary. In the synchronous communication with r hops, the information needs to be transmitted for at least r hops. The output of node v may depend on local input i_u, $u \in B_G(v,r)$, and the distance of v is lower than all the nodes of r. It does not rely on the local input of any $u(u \notin B_G(v,r))$. The selection must be based on valid information within the local boundary.

4.4.2.3.2 Local Approximation

The ∂ approximation algorithm can generate feasible outputs, and the effectiveness of the output is within the ∂ factor of optimal effectiveness. In minimum and maximum problems, we believe $\partial \geq 1$. Therefore, for a minimum problem, the feasible solution generated by the ∂ approximation algorithm is $\partial \cdot OPT$ at most if OPT is the cost of the optimal solution; for a maximum problem, the feasible solution generated by the ∂ approximation algorithm is OPT / ∂ at least if OPT is the cost of the optimal solution.

The so-called ∂ local approximation algorithm is the ∂ approximation algorithm, and it is also a local algorithm. The local approximation algorithm is a local algorithm family. For the algorithm of this family, there exists a local $(1 - \varepsilon)$ approximation algorithm for an arbitrary $\varepsilon > 0$.

4.4.2.3.3 Fault Tolerance and Robustness

The local algorithm has high scalability, and it has high fault tolerance as well. The local algorithm has high recovery efficiency of faulty, topology change and input change. If vertex v changes the input, the effect only occurs in the range of $B_G(v,r)$.

Specifically, a local algorithm can keep the feasible solution in the dynastic graph with changeable edges and nodes. In a distributed problem with a certain scale, the local algorithm can support an arbitrary update within a certain time in each operation.

Naor and Stockmeyer indicated the relationship between a local algorithm and a self-stable algorithm [125,126] in Reference [127]. No matter what the initial status is, self-stable algorithms can achieve a legal stable status in a limited time. The research of self-stable algorithms shows that it is easy to change the deterministic distributed algorithm into the self-stable algorithm within a certain time. More relationships between local and self-stable algorithms can be seen in Reference [127] of Lenzen et al.

4.4.3 Conclusion

We believe that distributed algorithms can provide a lot of help to the designers of sensor networks. However, although the sensor network looks like a fully distributed system, in fact, there are a lot of difficulties between the abstract distributed algorithm and its implementation. We emphasize the main differences between the real sensor network and the ideal distributed system. We try to eliminate the gap between theory and practice by studying the drawbacks of distributed algorithms, successful instances, and public problems—or problems that are still experienced. We began our research with a simple introduction to abstract distributed algorithms. We will gradually study more real communication models. In this way, we will propose some basic technologies that explain how to execute the distributed computing and to find the perfect solution.

Bibliography

1. M. R. Garey, D. S. Johnson. *Computers and Intractability: A Guide to the Theory of NP-Completeness.* Freeman, San Francisco, CA, 1978.
2. B. N. Clark, C. J. Colbourn, D. S. Johnson. Unit disk graph. *Discrete Mathematics,* 1990, 86(1–3): 165–177.
3. L. Barrière, P. Fraigniaud, L. Narayanan. Robust position-based routing in wireless ad hoc networks withun stable transmission ranges. In: *Proceedings of the 5th International Workshop on Discrete Algorithms and Methods for Mobile Computing and Communications (DIALM'01),* ACM Press, New York, 2001, pp. 19–27.
4. S. Butenko, O. Ursulenko. On minimum connected dominating set problem in unit-ball graphs. Preprint Submitted to Elsevier Science, 2008.
5. M. Cardei, D. Z. Du. Improving wireless sensor network lifetime through power aware organization.*Wireless Networks,* 2005, 11(3): 333–340.
6. T. Moscibroda, R. Wattenhofer. Maximizing the lifetime of dominating sets. In: *IPDPS'05: Proceedings of the 19th IEEE International Parallel and Distributed Processing Symposium (IPDPS'05)—Workshop 12,* IEEE Computer Society, Washington, DC, 2005, 242.2.
7. P. J. Wan, K. M. Alzoubi, O. Frieder. Distributed construction of connected dominating set in wireless ad hoc networks. *Mobile Networks & Applications,* 2004, 9(2): 141–149.

8. W. Wu, H. Du, X. Jia, Y. Li, C. H. Huang. Minimum connected dominating sets and MISs in unit disk graphs. *Theoretical Computer Science*, 2006, 352(1): 1–7.

9. F. Kuhn, T. Moscibroda, R. Wattenhofer. On the locality of bounded growth. In: *Proceedings of the 24th annual ACM symposium on Principles of Distributed Computing, PODC'05*, ACM Press, Las Vegas, NV, 2005, 60–68.

10. F. Kuhn, T. Moscibroda, T. Nieberg, R. Wattenhofer. Fast deterministic distributed maximal independent set computation on growth-bounded graphs. In: *Proceedings of the 19th Int. Symposium on Distributed Computing (DISC)*, 2005.

11. L. G. Valiant. Parallel computation. In: *Proceedings of 7th IBM Symposium on Mathematical Foundations of Computer Science: Mathematical Theory of Computations*, May 24–26, 1982, Hakone Yama-no-Hotel, Japan.

12. S. A. Cook. A taxonomy of problems with fast parallel algorithms. *Information and Control*, 1985, 64(1–3): 2–22.

13. R. M. Karp, A. Wigderson. A fast parallel algorithm for the maximal independent set problem. *Journal of the ACM*, 1984, 32(32): 762–773.

14. M. Luby. A simple parallel algorithm for the maximal independent set problem. *SIAM Journal on Computing*, 1986, 15: 1036–1053.

15. M. Marathe, H. Breu, H. Ravi, D. Rosenkrantz. Simple heuristics for unit disk graphs. *Networks*, 1995, 25: 59–68.

16. K. Alzoubi, P. J. Wan, O. Frieder. Message-optimal connected dominating sets in mobile ad hoc networks. In: *Proceedings of the 3rd ACM International Symposium on Mobile Ad Hoc Networking and Computing (MOBIHOC)*, EPFL, Lausanne, Switzerland, 2002, 157–164.

17. R. Gandhi, S. Parthasarathy. Distributed algorithms for coloring and connected domination in wireless ad hoc networks. *Foundations of Software Technology & Theoretical Computer Science*, 2004, 1361–1365.

18. S. Guha, S. Khuller. Approximation algorithms for connected dominating sets. In: *Proceedings of the 4th Annual European Symposium on Algorithms (ESA'96)*, Springer, London, 1996, 179–193.

19. B. Das, V. Bharghavan. Routing in ad-hoc networks using minimum connected dominating sets. In: *IEEE International Conference on Communications, 1997. ICC '97 Montreal, Towards the Knowledge Millennium*. IEEE, 1997, 1: 376–380.

20. B. Das, E. Sivakumar, V. Bhargavan. Routing in ad hoc networks using a virtual backbone. In: *Proceedings of the 6th International Conference on Computer Communications and Networks (IC3N'97)*, 1997, 1–20.

21. B. Das, R. Sivakumar, V. Bhargavan. Routing in ad hoc networks using a spine. In: *International Conference on Computer Communications and Networks, 1997. Proceedings*. IEEE, 1997, 34–39.

22. R. Sivakumar, B. Das, V. Bharghavan. An improved spine-based infrastructure for routing in ad hoc networks. In: *Proceedings of the Internat. Symposium on Computers and Communications (ISCC'98)*, 1998.

23. J. Wu, H. Li. On calculating connected dominating set for efficient routing in ad hoc wireless networks. In: *DIALM'99: Proceedings of the 3rd International Workshop on Discrete Algorithms and Methods for Mobile Computing and Communications*, ACM Press, NewYork, 1999, 7–14.

24. J. Wu, M. Gao, I. Stojmenovic. On Calculating Power-Aware Connected Dominating Sets for Efficient Routing in Ad Hoc Wireless Networks. In: *International Conference on Parallel Processing*. IEEE Computer Society, 2001, 346–356.

25. I. Stojmenovic, M. Seddigh, J. Zunic. Dominating sets and neighbore limination-based broadcasting algorithms in wireless networks. *IEEE Transactions on Parallel and Distributed Systems*, 2002, 13(1): 14–25.
26. P. J. Wan, K. M. Alzoubi, O. Frieder. Distributed construction of connected dominating set in wireless ad hoc networks. *Mobile Networks and Applications*, 2004, 9(2): 141–149.
27. J. W. Grossman. Dominating sets whose closed stars form spanning trees. *Discrete Mathematics*, 1997, 169(1–3): 83–94.
28. J. E. Dunbar, J. W. Grossman, J. H. Hattingh, S. T. Hedetniemi, A. A. McRae. On weakly connected domination in graphs. *Discrete Mathematics*, 1997, 167/168: 261–269.
29. Y. Chen, A. Liestman. Approximating minimum size weakly-connected dominating sets for clustering mobile ad hoc networks. In: *International Symposium on Mobile Ad Hoc NETWORKING and Computing*, 2002, 165–172.
30. Y. Z. Chen, A. L. Liestman. Maintaining weakly-connected dominating sets for clustering ad hoc networks. *Ad Hoc Networks*, 2005, 3(5): 629–642.
31. A. Ephremides, J. Wieselthier, D. Baker. A design concept for reliable mobile radio networks with frequency hopping signaling. *Proceedings of the IEEE*, 1987, 75: 56–73.
32. M. Gerla, J. T.Tsai, Multicluster, mobile, multimedia, radio network. *ACM/Baltzer Journal on Wireless Networks*, 1995, 1: 255–265.
33. K. M. Alzoubi, P. J. Wan, O. Frieder. Weakly connected dominating sets and sparse spanners for wireless ad hoc networks. *International Conference on Distributed Computing Systems*. IEEE Computer Society, 2003, 96.
34. I. Cidon, O. Mokryn. Propagation and leader election in multihop broadcast environment. In: *12th International Symposium on Distributed Computing (DISC98)*, Greece, 1998, 104–119.
35. B. Han, W. Jia. Efficient construction of weakly-connected dominating set for clustering wireless ad hoc networks. In: *Global Telecommunications Conference, 2006. IEEE GLOBECOM '06*. IEEE, 2006.
36. D. Dubhashi, A. Mei, A. Panconesi, J. Radhakrishnan, A. Srinivasan. Fast distributed algorithms for (weakly) connected dominating sets and linear-size skeletons. In: *Proceedings of Symposium on Discrete Algorithms (SODA)*, 2003, pp. 717–724.
37. J. Wu, M. Cardei, F. Dai, S. H.Yang. Extended dominating set in ad hoc networks using cooperative communication. *Mobile and Wireless Communication Systems, Lecture Notes in Computer Science*, 2005, 3642: 1393–1396.
38. K. M. Alzoubi, P. J. Wan, O. Frieder. Distributed heuristics for connected dominating set in wireless ad hoc networks. *Journal of Communications and Networks*, 2002, 4: 22–29.
39. F. Dai, J. Wu. An extended localized algorithm for connected dominating set for mationin ad hoc wireless networks. *IEEE Transactionon Parallel and Distributed Systems*, 2004, 15(10): 908–920.
40. J. Yu, N. Wang, G. Wang. Constructing minimum extended weakly-connected dominating sets for clustering in ad hoc networks[J]. *Journal of Parallel & Distributed Computing*, 2012, 72(1): 35–47.
41. T. Fujito, H. Nagamochi. A 2-approximaiton algorithm for the minimum weight edge dominating set problem. *Discrete Applied Mathematics*, 2002, 118: 199–207.

42. J. Cardinal, S. Langerman, E. Levy. Improved approximation bounds for edge dominating set in dense graphs. *Theoretical Computer Science*, 2009, 410(8–10): 949–957.
43. L. Zhao, E. L. Lloyd, S. S. Ravi. Topology control for constant rate mobile networks. In: *Proceedings of IEEE GLOBECOM*, 2006.
44. J. Li, L. Huang, M. Xiao. Energy efficient topology control algorithms for variant rate mobile sensor networks. In: *International Conference on Mobile Ad-Hoc and Sensor Networks*. IEEE Computer Society, 2008, 23–30.
45. L. Lifeng, L. Ye. A heuristic cluster control algorithm of wireless sensor networks topology. *Journal of Computer Research and Development*, 2008, 45(7): 1099–1105 (in Chinese).
46. W. B. Xie, J. Li, M. Xian, Y. G. Chen. Distributed virtue backbone network algorithm based on topology characteristic. *Journal of Software*, 2010, 21(6): 1416–1425 (in Chinese).
47. Y. Wang, X. Li. Localized construction of bounded degree and planar spanner for wireless ad hoc networks. *Mobile Networks and Applications*, 2006, 11(2): 161–175.
48. J. Lee, B. Mans. Energy-efficient virtual backbones for reception-aware MANET. In: *Vehicular Technology Conference, 2006. Vtc 2006-Spring. IEEE*. IEEE, 2006, 1097–1101.
49. X. M. Zhang, Q. Liu, S. F. Dai, Y. Z. Liu.Traffic load-based interference-aware routing protocol for mobile ad hoc networks. *Journal of Software*, 2009, 20(10): 2721–2728.
50. P. Gupta, P. R. Kumar. The capacity of wireless networks. *IEEE Transactionson Information Theory*, 2000, 46(2): 388–404.
51. L. Yongzhen. Modeling and mitigating interference for wireless ad hoc networks. University of Science and Technology of China, 2009 (in Chinese).
52. B. Randerath, I. Schiermeyer. Exact algorithms for minimum dominating set. Technical Report zaik 2005-501, Universität zu Köln, Germany, 2005.
53. V. Raman, S. Saurabh, S. Sikdar. Efficient exact algorithms through enumerating maximal in dependent sets and other techniques. *Theory of Computing Systems*, 2007, 42(3): 563–587.
54. F. Fomin, S. Gaspers, S. Saurabh, A. Stepanov. On two techniques of combining branching and tree width, *Algorithmica*, 2009, 54(2): 181–207.
55. J. M. van Rooij, H. L. Bodlaender. Exact algorithms for edge domination. *Algorithmica*, 2012, 64(4): 535–563.
56. M. Xiao, H. Nagamochi. Exact algorithms for annotated edge dominating set in cubic graphs. TR2011-009, Kyoto University, 2011.
57. M. Xiao, H. Nagamochi. A refined exact algorithm for edge dominating set. In: *International Conference on Theory and Applications of MODELS of Computation*. Springer-Verlag, 2012, 360–372.
58. M. Yannakakis, F. Gavril. Edge dominating sets in graphs. *SIAM Journal of Applied Mathematics*, 1980, 38: 364–372.
59. F. V. Fomin, F. Grandoni, D. Kratsch. Measure and conquer: domination a case study. In: *International Colloquium on Automata, Languages, and Programming*. Springer, Berlin, Heidelberg, 2005, 191–203.
60. P. Krishna, N. H. Vaidya, M. Chatterjee, D. K. Pradhan. A cluster-based approach for routing in dynamic networks. *ACM SIGCOMM Computer Communication Review*, 1997, 27(2): 49–65.

61. G. Jing, Y. Jiguo, W. Guanghui. Interference-aware topology management in wireless ad hoc networks. *Computer Technology and Development*, 2012, 22(1): 133–136 (in Chinese).

62. H. Ping, Y. Jiguo, W. Guanghui. A distributed energy-efficient topology management algorithm in MANET. *Computer Technology and Development*. 2012, 22(1): 129–132 (in Chinese).

63. Q. Ling, Z. Tian. Impact of mobility on topology control of wireless sensor networks. In: *International Conference on Wireless Communications, NETWORKING and Mobile Computing*. IEEE, 2007, 2483–2486.

64. M. Zorzi, R. R. Rao. Geographic random forwarding (GeRaF) for ad hoc and sensor networks: energy and latency performance. *IEEE Transactions on Mobile Computing*, 2003, 2(4): 337–347.

65. L. Bao, J. J. Garcia-Luna-Aceves. Stable energy-aware topology management in ad hoc networks. *Ad Hoc Networks*, 2010, 8(3): 313–327.

66. C. Scheideler, A. Richa, P. Santi. An O(logn) dominating set protocol for wireless ad hoc networks under the physical interference model. In: *Proceedings of the 9th ACM international symposium on Mobile Ad Hoc Networking and Computing*, 2008, 91–100.

67. Q. Yunlong, Y. Jiguo, W. Kang. A maintaining algorithm for k-connected m-dominating sets in wireless mobile networks. *Computer Technology and Development*, 2010, 20(8) (in Chinese).

68. F. Dai, J. Wu. On constructing k-connected k-dominating set in wireless networks. In: *Parallel and Distributed Processing Symposium, 2005. Proceedings. IEEE International*. IEEE, 2005, 81: 1.

69. F. Kuhn, T. Moscibroda, R. Wattenhofer. Fault-tolerant clustering in ad hoc and sensor networks. In: *26th International Conference on Distributed Computing Systems (ICDCS)*, Lisbon, Portugal, 2006.

70. J. Gao, L. Guibas, J. Hershberger, L. Zhang, A. Zhu. Discrete mobile centers. In: SCG'01: In: *Proceedings of the 17th Annual Symposium on Computational Geometry*, ACM Press, New York, 2001, 188–196.

71. M. Couture, M. Barbeau, P. Bose, E. Kranakis. Incremental construction of k-dominating sets in wireless sensor networks, *Lecture Notes in Computer Science*, Springer Berlin, Heidelberg, 2006, 6(3): 202–214.

72. A. S. Rao, C. P. Rangan. A linear algorithm for domatic number of interval graphs. *Information Processing Letters*, 1989, 33: 29–33.

73. A. A. Bertossi. On the domatic number of interval graphs. *Information Processing Letters*, 1988, 28: 275–280.

74. M. V. Marathe, H. B. Hunt, S. S. Ravi. Efficient approximation algorithms for domatic partition and on-line coloring of circular arc graphs. *Discrete Applied Mathematics*, 1996, 64: 135–149.

75. S. L. Peng, M. S. Chang. A simple linear time algorithm for the domatic partition problem on strongly chordal graphs. *Information Processing Letters*, 1992, 43: 297–300.

76. H. Kaplan, R. Shanmir. The domatic number problem on some perfect graph families. *Information Processing Letters*, 1994, 49: 51–56.

77. K. W. Tsui, C. K. Yen, C. Y. Tang. On the domatic number of bipartite permutation graph. *National Computer Symposium (NCS)*, 2007, 12: 20–21.

78. J. Leblet, Z. Li, G. Simon. Domatic partition of a distributed service analysis of the interval completion approach. http://enstb.org/~gsimon/Resources/algotel-poster.pdf, 2009.
79. U. Feige, M. M. Halldorsson, G. Kortsarz, A. Srinivasan. Approximating the domatic number. *SIAM Journal of Computing*, 2003, 32(1): 172–195.
80. T. Moscibroda, R. Wattenhofer. Maximizing the lifetime of dominating sets. In: *Parallel and Distributed Processing Symposium.* IEEE, 2005, 4: 8–15.
81. M. Cardei, D. Maccallum, M. X. Cheng, M. Min, X. Jia, D. Li, D. Du. Wireless sensor networks with energy efficient organization. *Journal of Interconnection Networks*, 2002, 3(4): 213–229.
82. K. Islam, S. G. Akl, H. Meijer. Maximizing the lifetime of a sensor network through domatic partition. In: *Proceedings of IEEE Conference on Local Computer Networks (LCN'34)*, 2009.
83. D. Mahjoub, D. W. Matula. Employing $(1-\varepsilon)$ dominating set partitions as backbones in wireless sensor networks. In: *Meeting on Algorithm Engineering & Experiments. Society for Industrial and Applied Mathematics*, 2010, 98–112.
84. D. Mahjoub, D. W. Matula. Building $(1-\varepsilon)$ dominating sets partition as backbones in wireless sensor networks using distributed graph coloring. In: *IEEE International Conference on Distributed Computing in Sensor Systems.* Springer-Verlag, 2010, 144–157.
85. M. Mito, S. Fujita. Maximum connected domatic partition of directed path graphs with single junction. In: *International Conference on Computing and Combinatorics.* Springer-Verlag, 2008, 425–433.
86. S. V. Pemmaraju, I. A. Pirwani. Energy conservation via domatic partitions. In: *ACM International Symposium on Mobile Ad Hoc NETWORKING and Computing.* ACM, 2006, 143–154.
87. S. Pandit, S. V. Pemmaraju, K. Varadarajan. Approximation algorithms for domatic partitions of unit disk graphs. In: *International Workshop and, International Workshop on Approximation, Randomization, and Combinatorial Optimization. Algorithms and Techniques.* Springer-Verlag, 2009, 312–325.
88. R. Misra, C. Mandal. Cluster head rotation via domatic partition in self-organizing sensor networks. In: *International Conference on Communication Systems Software and Middleware, 2007. Comsware.* IEEE, 2007, 1–7.
89. R. Misra, C. Mandal. Efficient clusterhead rotation via domatic partition in self-organizing sensor networks. *Wireless Communications and Mobile Computing*, 2009, 9(8):1040–1058.
90. B. Zelinka. Connected domatic number of a graph. *Mathematica Slovaca*, 1986, 36(4): 387–392.
91. B. L. Hartnell, D. F. Rall. Connected domatic number in planar graphs. *Czechoslovak Mathematical Journal*, 2001, 51(1): 173–179.
92. R. Misra, C. Mandal. Rotation of CDS via connected domatic partition in ad hoc sensor networks. *IEEE Transactions on Mobile Computing*, 2009, 8(4): 488–499.
93. K. Islam, S.G. Akl, H. Meijer. Distributed generation of a family of connected dominating sets in wireless sensor networks. *IEEE International Conference on Distributed Computing in Sensor Systems.* Springer-Verlag, 2009, 343–355.
94. E. J. Cockayne, S. T. Hedetniemi. Disjoint independent dominating sets in graphs. *Discrete Mathematics*, 1976, 15: 213–222.

95. D. Mahjoub, A. Leskovskaya, D. W. Matula. Approximating the independent domatic partition problem in random geometric graphs—an experimental study. In: *Canadian Conference on Computational Geometry*, Winnipeg, Manitoba, Canada, August. DBLP, 2010, 195–198.

96. A. Schumacher, H. Haanpa. Distributed sleep scheduling in wireless sensor via fractional domatic partitioning. In: *Lecture Notes in Computer Science*. Springer, Berlin, Heidelberg, 2009, 5873: 640–654.

97. D. Y. Li, L. Liu, H. Q. Yang. Minimum connected r-hop k-dominating set in wireless networks. *Discrete Mathematics, Algorithms and Applications*, 2009, 1(1): 45–57.

98. Z. Zhang, Q. H. Liu, D. Y. Li. Two algorithms for connected r-hop k-dominating set. *Discrete Mathematics, Algorithms and Applications*, 2009, 1(4): 485–498.

99. F. Dai, J. Wu. On constructing k-connected k-dominating set in wireless network. In: *IEEE International Parallel & Distributed Processing Symposium*, 2005.

100. F. Wang, M. T. Thai, D. Z. Du. On the construction of 2-connected virtual backbone in wireless network. *IEEE Transactions on Wireless Communications*, 2009, 8(3): 1230–1237.

101. W. Shang, F. Yao, P. Wan, X. Hu. Algorithms for minimum m-connected k-dominating set problem. *COCOA*, 2007, 4616: 182–190.

102. M. T. Thai, N. Zhang, R. Tiwari, et al. On approximation algorithms of k-connected m-dominating sets in disk graphs. *Theoretical Computer Science*, 2007, 385(1–3): 49–59.

103. Y. Wu, F. Wang, M. Thai, et al. Constructing k-connected m-dominating sets in wireless sensor networks. In: *Military Communications Conference*. IEEE, Milcom, 2007, 1–7.

104. Y. Wu, Y. Li. Construction algorithms for k-connected m-dominating sets in wireless sensor networks. In: *ACM International Symposium on Mobile Ad Hoc NETWORKING and Computing*. ACM, 2008, 83–90.

105. D. Kim, W. Wang, X. Li, Z. Zhang, W. Wu. A new constant factor approximation for computing 3-connected m-dominating sets in homogeneous wireless networks. In: *Proceedings of INFOCOM*, 2010, 1–9.

106. W. P. Shang, F. Yao, P. J. Wan, X. D. Hu. On minimum m-connected k-dominating set problem in unit disk graphs. *Journal of Combinatorial Optimization*, 2008, 16(2): 99–106.

107. W. P. Shang, F. Yao, P. J. Wan, X. D. Hu. Algorithms for minimum m-connected k-tuple dominating set problem. *Theoretical Computer Science*, 2007, 381(3): 241–247.

108. R. Tiwari, T. Mishra, Y. Li, M. T. Thai. K-strongly connected m-dominating and absorbing set in wireless ad hoc networks with unidirectional links. In: *International Conference on Wireless Algorithms, Systems and Applications*. IEEE, 2008: 103–112.

109. P. Von Rickenbach, R. Wattenhofer, A. Zollinger. Algorithmic models of interference in wireless ad hoc and sensor networks. *IEEE/ACM Transactions on Networking*, 2009, 17(1): 172–185.

110. D. Mirela, J. Nagesh. Distributed construction of low-interference spanners. *Distributed Computing*, 2009, 22: 15–28.

111. Y. He, Y. Zeng. Topology control in wireless sensor networks with interference consideration. In: *Intelligent Control and Automation*. Springer, Berlin, Heidelberg, 2006, 202–206.

112. K. Alzoubi, P. J. Wan, O. Frieder. New distributed algorithm for connected dominating set in wireless ad hoc networks. In: *Hawaii International Conference on System Sciences*. IEEE, 2002, 3849–3855.

113. M. Fussen, R. Wattenhofer, A. Zollinger. Interference arises at the receiver. In: *International Conference on Wireless Networks, Communications and Mobile Computing*. IEEE, 2005, 1: 427–432.

114. T. N. Nguyen, D. T. Huynh. Minimum interference planar geometric topology in wireless sensor networks. In: *International Conference on Wireless Algorithms, Systems, and Applications*. Springer-Verlag, Berlin, Heidelberg, 2009, 149–158.

115. K. Moaveni-Nejad, X. Y. Li. Low-interference topology control for wireless ad hoc networks. *Ad Hoc & Sensor Wireless Networks*, 2005, 1: 41–64.

116. T. Johansson, L. Carr-Motyčková. Reducing interference in ad hoc networks through topology control. In: *Proceedings of DIALM-POMC'05*, 2005, 17–23.

117. G. N. Feng, P. Y. Fan. Interference minimum network topologies for ad hoc networks. *Wireless Communications and Mobile Computing*, 2010, 12(6): 529–544.

118. J. Zhang, C. Jia. Calculation of minimal dominating set in wireless sensor network with host switch-on/off. *Transactions of Tianjin University*, 2010, 16(4): 279–283.

119. D. Peleg. *Distributed Computing: A Locality-Sensitive Approach*. Philadelphia, PA: Society for Industrial and Applied Mathematics, 2000.

120. A. Panconesi, A. Srinivasan. On the complexity of distributed network decomposition. *Journal of Algorithms*, 1996, 20(2): 356–374.

121. J. R. Munkres. *Topology*, 2nd edition. Upper Saddle River, NJ: Prentice Hall, 2000.

122. D. Angluin. Local and global properties in networks of processors. In: *Proceedings of 12th annual ACM symposium on theory of computing (STOC, Los Angeles, CA, USA, April 1980)*, ACM Press, New York, 1980, 82–93.

123. C. Lenzen, R. Wattenhofer. Minimum dominating set approximation in graphs of bounded arboricity. In: *Proceedings of 24th international symposium on distributed computing (DISC, Cambridge, MA, USA, September 2010), Lecture Notes in Computer Science*, Springer, Berlin, Germany, 2010, 6343: 510–524.

124. M. Naor, L. Stockmeyer. What can be computed locally? *SIAM Journal on Computing*, 1995, 24(6): 1259–1277.

125. S. Dolev. *Self-stabilization*. Cambridge, MA: The MIT Press, 2000.

126. M. Schneider. Self-stabilization. *ACM Computing Surveys*, 1993, 25(1): 45–67.

127. C. Lenzen, J. Suomela, R. Wattenhofer. Local algorithms: self-stabilization on speed. In: *Proceedings of 11th international symposium on stabilization, safety, and security of distributed systems. Lecture Notes in Computer Science*, 2009, 5873: 17–34.

Chapter 5

Simulation and Example

5.1 Simulation

5.1.1 Computer Simulation Technology

In recent years, with the rapid development of wireless communication technology, wireless communication systems are increasingly complex, and solely relying on formula derivation to obtain system performance has been very difficult. With the rapid development of computer technology, the use of computer simulation of wireless communication systems becomes possible. Now, computer simulation in the performance evaluation of wireless communication systems becomes more and more important.

With the advancement of science and technology, especially the development of information technology and computer technology, the concept of "truth" has been developed and perfected, so it is very difficult to give a clear definition of simulation. But the basic meaning of a common system simulation is, to design a model of the actual system, to experiment with it in order to understand and evaluate the system's various operating strategies. Here, the model is generalized, including mathematical models, nonmathematical models, physical models, and so on.

5.1.2 Simulation Tools of Wireless Networks

The network structure and scale become more and more complex, with increasingly diversified network applications; solely relying on experience in network planning and design, network equipment development and network protocol development has not made adapting to the development of the network possible. Thus, a kind of scientific means is urgently needed to reflect and predict the performance of the network, and network simulation technology arises at a historic moment. It effectively improves the reliability and accuracy of network planning and design, significantly reduces the risk of network investment, and decreases unnecessary waste of investment.

To evaluate the performance of wireless network algorithms, more than experimentation is needed, especially for large-scale wireless networks containing large numbers of nodes. To simulate a wireless sensor network, researchers designed and developed many related platforms, including VC++, JAVA, PeerSim, OPNET, OMNET, MATLAB, NS2, and Atarraya.

PeerSim [1] is a simulation software of the peer-to-peer (P2P) overlay network to support structured and unstructured P2P network simulation. PeerSim has two simulation methods, cycle based and event driven. The event-driven model is relatively accurate. The cycle-based model lacks the simulation of the transport layer and cannot play the role of concurrency control, but occupying fewer resources is suitable for large-scale simulation. PeerSim itself does not take any specific protocol implementation but provides good scalability. Researchers have achieved bandwidth management protocol, a fault-tolerant FSM, Pastry, Chord, Peer sampling service, T-Man, and other agreements on the basis of PeerSim.

In 1987, OPNET released its first commercial network performance simulation mission, which provides a significant network performance optimization tool, making predictive network performance management and function of anti-earthquake possible [2].Network design and management are generally divided into three stages. The first stage is the design phase, including the network topology design, protocol design and configuration, and network equipment design and selection. The second stage is the release stage, designing the network with a certain performance, such as throughput, response time, etc. The third phase is fault diagnosis, troubleshooting, and the upgrading optimization in the actual operation. The entire product line of OPNET addresses different stages of network research and development, can be used for network design, and serves as the basis for the release of network performance. It can also be put into operation as network optimization and fault diagnosis tools.

OMNET [3] is an open source, nonprofit, academic, component-based modular network simulation platform developed by the Telecommunication Institute of the Budapest Polytechnic University. It has become a popular network simulation platform for science and industry. OMNET is an event-driven simulator for network system simulation of discrete events. It is often simulated for communication models, protocol emulation, hardware architecture validation, software system performance evaluation, and other discrete event-driven applications. As a discrete event simulator, OMNET has a powerful graphic interface and embedded simulation kernel, which can easily define the network topology, with the function of programming, debugging, and tracking.

The Network Simulator-Version2 [4] (NS2) is an object-oriented, event-driven network simulator written in C++ and OTcl, including Tcl/Tk, OTcl, NS, Tclcl, Nam, and other components. It implements TCP, UDP, and other network protocols; data transmission such as FTP and TELNET; and web simulation and routing queue management mechanisms such as Drop Tail, RED and CBQ, Dijkstr routing algorithms, and so on. NS2 can also be used for multicast and MAC layer protocol simulation. NS2 is a popular network simulation software; it can run on windows and UNIX, with open source code, good openness, and strong extensibility. It is an excellent simulation platform in the study of network topology and the analysis of network transmission data.

MATLAB is high-tech computing environment for scientific computing, visualization, and interactive programming released by the United States Mathworks Company. It integrates many powerful functions, such as numerical analysis, matrix calculation, visualization of scientific data, and modeling and simulation of nonlinear dynamic systems, into an easy-to-use Windows environment. It provides a comprehensive solution for scientific research, engineering design, and numerous scientific studies on effective numerical computation. It largely dispenses with the traditional editing mode of noninteractive programming languages (such as C and Fortran), representing an advanced level of international scientific computing software. MATLAB, Mathematics, and Maple are three examples of major mathematical software. MATLAB is the foremost application software of mathematics, science, and technology in numerical calculation. MATLAB can be used for matrix computing, drawing functions and data, implementing algorithms, creating user interfaces, and connecting to other programming languages. It is mainly used in engineering calculation, control design, signal processing and communication, image processing, signal detection, financial modeling, and design and analysis. Due to the powerful functions of MATLAB, many researchers use it as a simulation tool for wireless network algorithms.

The main purpose of Atarraya is to test the topology of the protocol A3 algorithm [6]. Atarraya is Spanish for fishing nets. The software is very compact and concise like the A3 protocol. However, due to the need to compare the performance of A3 with other well-known topology mechanisms, the design of the tool is not sufficient. A generic platform in which other topology algorithms can be embedded must be created to allow these algorithms to evaluate their simulators under the same conditions. Subsequently, topology control extensions include topology maintenance algorithms. Several topology maintenance algorithms are also included in the Atarraya simulator.

The final result of Atarraya is a generic, java-based, event-driven simulator for testing topology control algorithms in wireless sensor networks. Atarraya is still under development, but presently it is used not only for researching, developing, and testing new topology control algorithms, but also for teaching. Atarraya includes the necessary mechanisms to perform classical experiments related to wireless sensor networks, such as the giant component experiment [7], calculation of the critical transmission range, calculation of the minimum spanning tree of the graph, and other basic teaching concept examples.

The C++ language is an object-oriented programming language designed to encapsulate data and operating methods as objects [8]. The same types of objects are abstracted to form a common class. The class has an external relationship through a simple external interface. Objects communicate with each other through the message. The relationship between the programs is simple, with a good protection for the independence of the program module and data security. Moreover, the program has high reusability through inheritance and polymorphism.

Java [9] is a programming language that provides an environment for both application development and deployment. Java language is mainly located in network programming, making the program able to maximize the use of network resources.

5.2 Simulation Based on NS2 and Examples

5.2.1 Introduction to NS2

NS2 is a discrete, event-driven, object-oriented simulator for network environment simulation, mainly used for simulation proving of network research. NS2 simulates TCP and UDP in wired or wireless networks, as well as multiple routing protocols. NS2 uses the programming languages OTcl and C++. The bottom of the simulation platform of NS2 is written in C++, and the command and configuration interface is written in OTcl. All of the network elements simulated in NS2 are abstractions of the actual network.

NS2 can complete the following functions:

1. It can build a network topology. The network topology of NS2 is composed of nodes and links. The node is the simulation of equipment in the bottom three layers of the network, and the link is the simulation of a physical transmission link.
2. It can implement an agent of the Real-time Transport Protocol (RTP). This agent is a simulation of a network protocol. NS2 has achieved UDP, the TCP agent, and agents of some commonly used routing protocols.
3. The application data stream is loaded by application traffic. However, the RTP agent itself can generate data streams, so there is no need to load this application.

5.2.2 Characteristics and Structure of NS2

5.2.2.1 Characteristics of NS2

As an excellent simulation tool for studying the network topology and analyzing the nature of network transmission, the main features of NS2 are as follows:

1. Open source code: NS2 has become one of the most widely used network simulation platforms, because its development team provides free download, update, help, and use.
2. Discrete and event driven: The simulation is very efficient. "Event" refers to the state of the network changes. When the network is in a static state, it will

not perform any analog calculation; when the network state changes, the simulator will be triggered and start working so that simulation efficiency can be largely increased.

3. Object-oriented approach: The display of network modeling process is therefore easier, and scalability and reusability are ensured, improving the efficiency of program development. The process of configuring object properties is also simple. Some classes can also inherit from others; in order to meet user-specific requirements, new class components can be written in C++.

4. Combines with NAM image display software: Simulation results can be displayed in an animated way. xgraph tools can be used to describe the results of the simulation data in a more intuitive form of expression.

5. Uses two programming languages: C++ and OTcl, both efficient and flexible. Because the C++ program module has the characteristic of fast running speed, it is used to realize the concrete agreement. OTcl is suitable for simulation configuration. The TclcL module is used to associate and connect variables and objects in both languages.

6. Provides support for various business models and communication protocols such as FTP, CBR, ON/OFF, TCP, UDP, and static routing, dynamic routing, broadcast routing, multicast routing, hierarchical routing, and media access control (MAC) layer protocols.

5.2.2.2 The Hierarchical Structure of NS2

NS2 is an object-oriented network simulator, using C++ to write specific protocols; an OTcl interpreter is used in the front end to improve flexibility. The NS2 kernel defines a variety of classes; there is a hierarchy among various classes, known as the compiler class structure. The hierarchy is shown in Figure 5.1.

NS2 contains six main categories, described as follows:

1. Tcl class provides a method for the interpreter to access behavior, whose role is to obtain a reference of an instance. The OTcl process activates, reports the error state, stores, and searches the tcl object through the interpreter.

2. TclObject class is the typical base class in compiled and interpreted classes.

3. TclClass maps the class structures built in the interpreter of the NS2 compiler class structure and provides methods to instantiate new objects.

4. Tclcocommand class can create NS2 kernel output simple commands for the interpreter.

5. EmbeddedTcl class allows the user to compile or interpret code to extend the function of NS2.

6. Instvar class compares member variables of the compiled class structure to the corresponding member variables of the interpretation class structure for some methods and mechanisms sharing two types of variables.

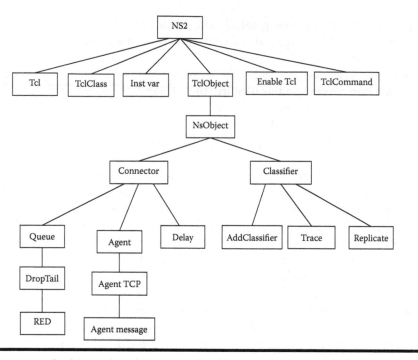

Figure 5.1   The hierarchy of the NS2 kernel.

5.2.3 The General Methods and Processes of NS2 Simulation

Before network simulation, we must analyze the level of simulation to be involved. NS simulation is divided into two levels: one based on OTcl programming level, the other on C++ and OTcl programming levels. At the first level, you can use the existing network elements of NS to achieve the simulation, without modifying the NS itself. However, if there is no network element required for simulation in NS, you need to add them to extend NS.

Assuming that the required network elements already exist in NS2, or if the user has completed the extension to NS, the remaining simulation steps are as follows:

1. Start writing OTcl scripts: First, simulate the configuration of the network topology, and identify basic characteristics of the link such as delay, load, and loss policies.
2. Establish the protocol agents such as protocol binding for end devices and traffic modeling.
3. Configure the parameters for the traffic model.
4. Set the trace object. NS2 can save the entire simulation process using the trace file. After the simulation, the user can obtain the desired result data by searching the trace file.

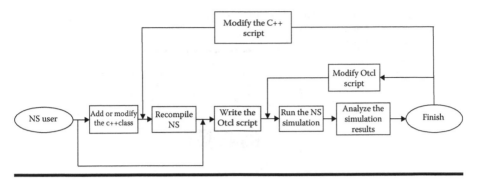

Figure 5.2   The general process of NS simulation.

5. Write other auxiliary processes, set the time required for the simulation. The OTcl script is now complete.
6. Interpret and execute the above-written OTcl script
7. Data can be obtained through the analysis of the results in the trace file.
8. Re-adjust the settings of the above configuration and conduct the simulation process again. Average the results of the repeated experiments for greater accuracy (Figure 5.2).

5.2.4 Installation of NS2

We improve the algorithm simulation experiment in the windows-based platform. Before the installation of NS2, we must install cygwin.

1. Installation of cygwin simulation software
   A user's folder will be generated in the home directory of cygwin at the first implementation. The environment parameter settings and related documents (such as .Bashrc, .Bashrc_profile, and .Inputrc) can be placed in the directory.
2. Installation of NS2
   Download the NS2.27 installation file then download the ns-allinone-2.27.tar.gz file on the home directory.
   1. Use the command tar xvfz ns-allinone-2.27.tar.gz to unzip the compressed folder.
   2. Put the patch file ns227-gcc34.patch in the Administrator directory, and execute the command: "patch -p0 < ns227-gcc34.patch"
   3. Use the cd command to point to the current path of ns-allinone-2.27, then implement command: "./install". During the installation, we ask the user whether or not to continue with the installation of diff, and we choose *y* to continue the installation.
      After the compilation of NS2, the relevant environmental parameters are set.

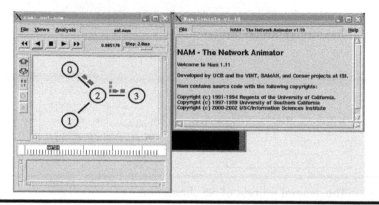

Figure 5.3   NAM display.

Compile the ".Bashrc" of the home directory, and add NS2 related path to the PATH.

export NS_HOME=`pwd`/ns-allinone-2.27

exportPATH=$NS_HOME/tcl8.4.5/unix:$NS_HOME/tk8.4.5/unix:$NS_HOME/bin:$PATH

exportLD_LIBRARY_PATH=$NS_HOME/tcl8.4.5/unix:$NS_HOME/tk8.4.5/unix:$NS_HOME/otcl-1.8:$NS_HOME/lib:$LD_LIBRARY_PATH

export TCL_LIBRARY=$NS_HOME/tcl8.4.5/library

4. Use the examples already existing in NS2 to verify whether the NS and NAM are installed successfully. Enter "startxwin.bat" in the command line. A new window will be created, and we'll enter in this new window:

cd ns-allinone-2.27/ns-2.27/ns-tutorial/examples

ns example2.tcl

The installation is successful if you see what is shown in Figure 5.3.

5.2.5 LEACH Protocol and Its Simulation Process

When the cluster protocol is simulated under NS2, it runs as a routing protocol at the network layer. Depending on the chosen energy model and the underlying protocol, we will make the necessary changes to the corresponding protocols in NS2 to implement specific functions. The general steps of the simulation are as follows:

1. The network scenario configuration mainly includes the generation of node coordinates and the initial energy setting of nodes.
2. Complete the connection of the new protocol to NS2 including the definition of header and the modifying of the NS2 interfaces and classes.

3. The protocol process is split into discrete events, partitioning functions, writing code, and debugging.
4. Run the new protocol and save the output data.
5. Data analysis and draw

Here, we will take the classic clustering protocol LEACH as an example and give the simulation of clustering protocols in the NS2 platform in detail.

5.2.5.1 The Details of the LEACH Algorithm

First, we briefly review the details of the algorithm of the LEACH protocol.

The basic idea of the algorithm is that the clustering process is cyclical and the cluster heads are chosen randomly with probability. The nodes are regarded as cluster heads according to their probability values. Because a cluster head has a heavy burden, after one round of implementation, the protocol reestablishes the process of clustering and each sensor node can average the energy consumption of the network, which can reduce the network energy consumption and improve the overall network lifetime.

The network model of the algorithm:

For the sake of simplicity, the LEACH protocol makes the following assumptions for the network and nodes:

1. The base station is outside the monitoring area of the wireless sensor network (WSN), and all nodes and the base station are fixed.
2. The transmission power of the nodes in the network is adjustable and controllable, that is, the sending power can be adjusted.
3. All nodes in the network are energy isomorphic; they have enough energy to carry on the necessary communication.
4. The computing capability of nodes is sufficient, and two-way communication can be achieved between nodes.
5. The data correlation detected by the close nodes in the network is large. If the data sensed by the nodes in the densely distributed area is merged and processed, the traffic, the routing overhead, and the amount of transmission energy in the network can be reduced.

The energy model of the algorithm:

In the energy consumption of the LEACH algorithm, the formula is the first order radio model, as shown in Figure 5.4.

The LEACH protocol is based on the following assumptions:

1. All nodes in the network are energy isomorphic, and energy is very limited.
2. The signal transmission power in all directions is the same.
3. The base station and all nodes are fixed.

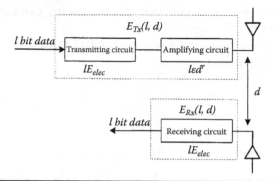

Figure 5.4   Energy model.

If the distance required for the transmission of l-bit information is d, at this time the energy consumption of the sender is

$$E_{Tx}(l, d) = \begin{cases} l * E_{elec} + l * \varepsilon_{fs} d^2 & (d < d_0) \\ l * E_{elec} + l * \varepsilon_{mp} d^4 & (d \geq d_0) \end{cases}, \tag{5.1}$$

where E_{elec} represents the energy consumed by the transmitting circuit. If the data transmission distance is less than the threshold d_0, then power consumption uses the free space model. When the data transmission distance is greater than or equal to the threshold d_0, the multipath attenuation model should be adopted. ε_{fs}, ε_{mp} are energies respectively needed to amplify the power in these two models.

The energy consumption of the nodes is

$$E_{Rx}(l) = l * E_{elec}. \tag{5.2}$$

LEACH needs to carry out the cluster reconstruction process in the course of the operation. Each round is divided into two stages: cluster establishment and data transmission. In order to reduce the overhead of cluster reconfiguration, the duration of data transmission should be much longer than that of cluster establishment, because the reconstruction process of clusters will consume a lot of energy.

5.2.5.1.1 The Cluster Establishment Phase

This stage is divided into four parts: the election of the cluster head node, the broadcast of the cluster head node, the establishment of the cluster structure, and the generation scheduling mechanism.

1. The election of the cluster head node: There are two bases for the selection of cluster head nodes: the total number of cluster head nodes in the network and the number of cluster heads that have been served by each node. Each sensor node randomly selects a value from 0 to 1. If this random value is less than the threshold value $T(n)$, then the node n automatically recommends itself to a cluster head node. The threshold value $T(n)$ is calculated as follows:

$$T(n) = \begin{cases} \dfrac{p}{1 - p(r \bmod 1/p)} & n \in G \\ 0 & \text{otherwise} \end{cases}, \qquad (5.3)$$

where p is the percentage of the cluster head nodes in the network nodes, r is the current number of rounds, and G is the nodes set. The nodes located in this set have not yet served as cluster heads.

2. The broadcast of the cluster head: After the cluster head node is selected, each cluster head node broadcasts the data packet to all nodes in the network with the same probability.

3. The establishment of cluster structure: Each node may receive packets from different cluster head nodes. According to the signal strength of the received packet, the cluster head with the strongest broadcast signal is selected as the cluster head. The nodes send JOIN messages to the cluster head node. A greater signal strength received by the node signifies a shorter distance between node and cluster head and thus the less energy consumed by communication. When all nodes in the network have selected a cluster head, they join the corresponding clusters and become member nodes. Member nodes then inform the cluster head that they have been added as a member of the cluster. In this process, the receivers of the cluster heads remain active and receive JOIN messages from the member nodes.

4. Generation scheduling mechanism: When the cluster head node receives the join information from member nodes, it generates a time-division multiple access (TDMA) slot table, which is the member nodes' scheduling table, and broadcasts the schedule table to all member nodes according to the information of the member nodes (Figure 5.5).

5.2.5.1.2 The Data Transmission Phase

After the cluster structure is formed in the network, the cluster head computes the TDMA slot table and broadcasts it to the member nodes. Then it enters the stable phase of data transmission. The node starts to send data according to the assigned TDMA scheduling slot. That is, only in its own time slot, the node sends

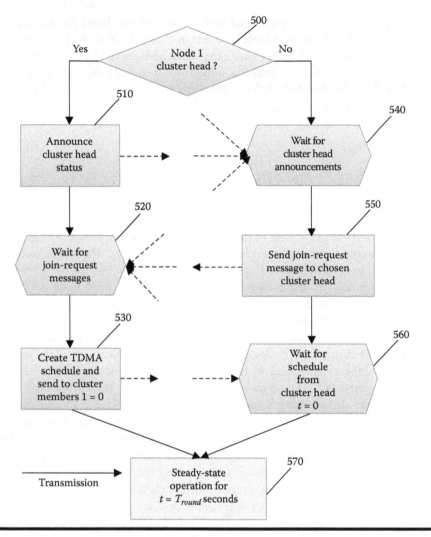

Figure 5.5 Cluster establishment.-From "https://www.google.ch/patents/US7035240".

the collected data to its cluster head node. At other times it can close its communication module and enter a sleep state to save energy. In the transmission phase, the cluster head node must always keep its receiver open, to continue to receive data sent from the member nodes. When a round of data transmission is completed, the cluster head node conducts the fusion process of redundant data sent from member nodes and then sends the fused data to the base station. The long-distance communication between the cluster head and the base station consumes a lot of energy (Figures 5.6 and 5.7).

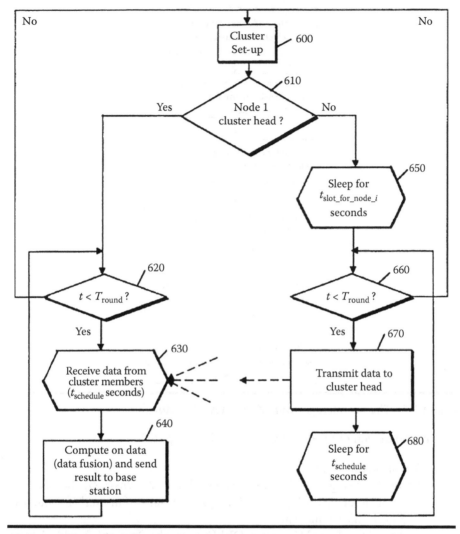

Figure 5.6 **Flow chart of the data transmission phase. From "https://www. google.ch/patents/US7035240".**

5.2.5.2 The Installation of the LEACH Protocol

We have already introduced the installation of NS2. Here we assume that the machine has had ns-2.27 installed. Since most of the clustering algorithms are improved and based on the LEACH algorithm, the implementation model of clustering algorithm using NS2 as a simulation tool should also be based on LEACH mode improvements. This section will focus on the installation and implementation of the LEACH algorithm.

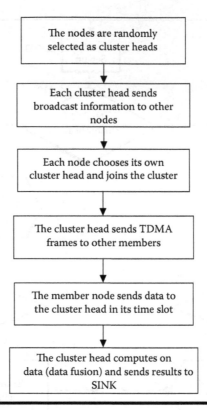

The nodes are randomly selected as cluster heads

Each cluster head sends broadcast information to other nodes

Each node chooses its own cluster head and joins the cluster

The cluster head sends TDMA frames to other members

The member node sends data to the cluster head in its time slot

The cluster head computes on data (data fusion) and sends results to SINK

Figure 5.7   The overall algorithm of the LEACH protocol.

The installation of LEACH requires the following steps:

1. Download mit.tar.gz
2. Put the "mit.tar.gz" in the directory ns-allinone-2.27/ns-2.27, then use the command to unzip the "gunzip mit.tar.gz" and "tar -xvf mit.tar" in sequence.
3. Modify the file of "makefile."

   Add -DMIT_uAMPS after DEFINE in the "makefile"; add -I./mit/rca -I./mit/uAMPS after INCLUDES=\

   Then find OBJ_CC=\ followed by a long list. The end of the string is $(OBJ_STL), filling it with:

   mit/rca/energy.o mit/rca/rcagent.o \
   mit/rca/rca-ll.o mit/rca/resource.o \
   mac/mac-sensor-timers.o mac/mac-sensor.o \
   mit/uAMPS/bsagent.o \
4. Modify the environment variables

   Modify the ".bashrc" file in the directory home\ (username). Set the environment variables of RCA_LIBRARY and uAMPS_LIBRARY

   export RCA_LIBRARY=`pwd`/ns-allinone-2.27/ns-2.27/mit/rca

export uAMPS_LIBRARY=`pwd`/ns-allinone-2.27/ns-2.27/mit/uAMPS
Use "Echo $ RCA_LIBRARY" to look up.

5. "Make clean" in the command line, and then "make." An error may occur during the compilation process of "wireless-phy.cc" in the file "mac" (Figure 5.8).

You can see the error message during the compilation process, find the corresponding file, modify the "min" to "MIN," and then enter the command line, inputting "make." The results appearing as shown below signify "compile completed" (Figure 5.9).

6. If the compilation passes, execute "./leach_test" in the directory ns-2.27.

After running, open the file of "leach.err" in the directory "ns-2.27 \ mit \ leach_sims." The following contents will represent that the LEACH protocol is installed successfully.

```
INITIALIZE THE LIST xListHead
channel.cc:sendUp - Calc highestAntennaZ_ and distCST_
highestAntennaZ_ = 1.5,   distCST_ = 222.8
SORTING LISTS ...DONE!
```

7. Finally, we need to eliminate the existence of the two BUGs.
    1. The warning of the output file about "dst_":
       Open the "leach.out" file in the directory "ns-2.27 \ mit \ leach_sims." The file may contain the following contents:

```
Warning dst_ is no longer being supported in NS. dst_ 0xffffffff
Use dst_addr_ and dst_port_ instead
Warning dst_ is no longer being supported in NS. dst_ 0xffffffff
Use dst_addr_ and dst_port_ instead
Warning dst_ is no longer being supported in NS. dst_ 0xffffffff
Use dst_addr_ and dst_port_ instead
```

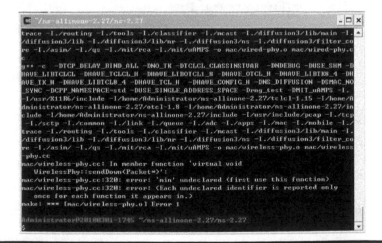

Figure 5.8 Compile error.

```
C ~/ns-allinone-2.27/ns-2.27                                        _□x
make[1]: Leaving directory `/home/Administrator/ns-allinone-2.27/ns-2.27/indep-u ▲
tils/cmu-scen-gen/setdest'
make[1]: Entering directory `/home/Administrator/ns-allinone-2.27/ns-2.27/indep-
utils/webtrace-conv/dec'
make[1]: Nothing to be done for `all'.
make[1]: Leaving directory `/home/Administrator/ns-allinone-2.27/ns-2.27/indep-u
tils/webtrace-conv/dec'
make[1]: Entering directory `/home/Administrator/ns-allinone-2.27/ns-2.27/indep-
utils/webtrace-conv/epa'
make[1]: Nothing to be done for `all'.
make[1]: Leaving directory `/home/Administrator/ns-allinone-2.27/ns-2.27/indep-u
tils/webtrace-conv/epa'
make[1]: Entering directory `/home/Administrator/ns-allinone-2.27/ns-2.27/indep-
utils/webtrace-conv/nlanr'
make[1]: Nothing to be done for `all'.
make[1]: Leaving directory `/home/Administrator/ns-allinone-2.27/ns-2.27/indep-u
tils/webtrace-conv/nlanr'
make[1]: Entering directory `/home/Administrator/ns-allinone-2.27/ns-2.27/indep-
utils/webtrace-conv/ucb'
make[1]: Nothing to be done for `all'.
make[1]: Leaving directory `/home/Administrator/ns-allinone-2.27/ns-2.27/indep-u
tils/webtrace-conv/ucb'

Administrator@20100301-1745 ~/ns-allinone-2.27/ns-2.27
$                                                                   ▼
```

Figure 5.9   Compile completed.

meaning that NS does not support the parameter "dst_." We need to replace the "dst_" with "dst_addr_." To "ns-2.27 \ mit \ uAMPS," two files need to be modified.

a. Open the "ns-bsapp.tcl." Change "dst_" to "dst_addr_" in the following location.

```
Application/BSApp instproc send {mac_dst link_dst type msg
                            data_size dist code} {
    [$self agent] set packetMsg_ $type
    [$self agent] set dst_ $mac_dst
    [$self agent] sendmsg $data_size $msg $mac_dst $link_dst $dist $code
}
```

b. Open the "ns-leach.tcl" and change "dst_" to "dst_addr_" in the following location.

```
Application/LEACH instproc send_now {mac_dst link_dst type msg \
                            data_size dist code} {
    [$self agent] set packetMsg_ $type
    [$self agent] set dst_ $mac_dst
    [$self agent] sendmsg $data_size $msg $mac_dst $link_dst $dist $code
}
```

2. The problem of total energy consumption is greater than the initial energy:

To "ns-2.27\mit\uAMPS," open "ns-leach.tcl." Add "$self GoToSleep" in the "checkAlive."

```
Application/LEACH instproc checkAlive {} {

 global ns_ chan opt node_
 $self instvar alive_ TDMAschedule_
 $self instvar begin_idle_ begin_sleep_
 # Check the alive status of the node. If the node has run out of energy, it
no longer functions in the network.
 set ISalive [[[$self node] set netif_(0)] set alive_]
 if {$alive_ == 1} {
   if {$ISalive == 0} {
     puts "Node [$self nodeID] is DEAD!!!!"
     $chan removeif [[$self node] set netif_(0)]
     set alive_ 0
     set opt(nn_) [expr $opt(nn_) - 1]
     if {$opt(rcapp) == "LEACH-C/StatClustering" && \
         [$self isClusterHead?]} {
       foreach element $TDMAschedule_ {
         if {$element != [$self nodeID]} {
           puts "Node $element is effectively DEAD!!!!"
           $chan removeif [$node_($element) set netif_(0)]
           [$node_($element) set netif_(0)] set alive_ 0
           [$node_($element) set rca_app_] set alive_ 0
           set opt(nn_) [expr $opt(nn_) - 1]
         }
       }
     }
   }
#To solve the Energy consumed > Totle Energy bug
   $self GoToSleep
 } else {
   $ns_ at [expr [$ns_ now] + 0.1] "$self checkAlive"
   if {$begin_idle_ >= $begin_sleep_} {
     set idle_energy [expr $opt(Pidle) * [expr [$ns_ now] - $begin_idle_]]
     [$self getER] remove $idle_energy
     set begin_idle_ [$ns_ now]
```

```
    } else {
    set sleep_energy [expr $opt(Psleep) * [expr [$ns_ now] - $begin_sleep_]]
    [$self getER] remove $sleep_energy
    set begin_sleep_ [$ns_ now]
    }
  }
}
if {$opt(nn_) < $opt(num_clusters)} "sens_finish"
}
```

5.2.5.3 Simulation of LEACH Protocol

1. Node structure

    The internal structure of a common mobile node is shown in the follow-ing figure. The "packet" generated by the application is sent to the agent. The agent has the functions of transport layer and network layer in the pro-tocol stack. The agent passes the packet to CMUTrace, which writes the packet statistics to the trace file. Then, the packet is sent to the connector, through which data link processing is conducted to the Link-Layer. After a short delay, packets are sent to the queue by link-layer. Once the packet is removed from the queue, it enters the MAC. A media access protocol runs on the MAC layer. Eventually, the packet arrives at the network interface, where the packet is sent to the channel at the appropriate power. The channel sends a copy of the packet to all nodes connected to it. The network interface of the nodes at the receivers receives the packet and passes it up to the MAC, queue, link-layer, connector, CMUTrace, and agent. The agent splits the packet and sends its identity to the application (Figure 5.10).

    The nodes in LEACH are resource adaptive. That is, the resource and resource management functions are added to the mobile nodes. The structure of the nodes is shown in Figure 5.11.

    The resource manager provides a usable interface between the application and the independent resources. The resource described here can be anything that needs to be monitored, such as energy and node neighbors. The application updates the state of the resource through three functions of the resource manager:

    Add.
    Remove.
    Query.

    Energy resources are used to track the energy of the nodes. At the begin-ning of the simulation, the initial energy of the node is set. In the simulation

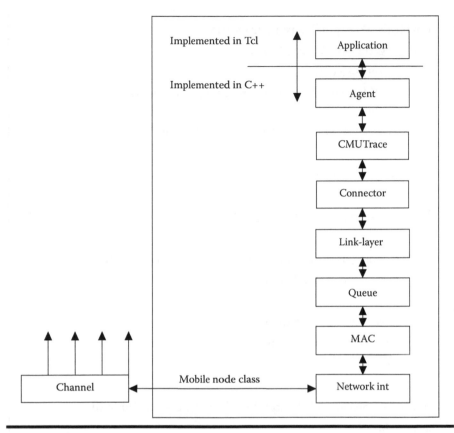

Figure 5.10 The structure of mobile nodes.

process, when the node deals with data, the consumed energy is removed by the application. When the node sends and receives packets, the consumed energy is removed by the network interface. As described earlier, LEACH uses the energy model shown in Figure 5.12 when data is transmitted and received.

This energy model is implemented by the network interface. The specific implementation process and code can be seen in the "wireless-phy.cc" in the directory "\ns-2.27\mac".

```
#ifdef MIT_uAMPS
    hdr_cmn *ch = HDR_CMN(p);
    hdr_rca *rca_hdr = HDR_RCA(p);
    double d = rca_hdr->get_dist();
    double hr, ht;    // The height of the receive and transmit antennas
```

```
double tX, tY, tZ;  // Transmitter location
node_->getLoc(&tX, &tY, &tZ);
ht=tZ+ant_->getZ();
hr=ht;   // It is assumed that the receiving node and the antenna are the
same height
double crossover_dist=sqrt((16 * PI * PI * L_ * ht * ht * hr * hr)
/ (lambda_ * lambda_));
if (d < crossover_dist)
if (d > 1)
Pt_=Efriss_amp_ * bandwidth_ * d * d;
else
// Pfriss_amp_  is the minimum amplifier power during transmission
Pt_=Efriss_amp_ * bandwidth_;
else
Pt_=Etwo_ray_amp_ * bandwidth_ * d * d * d * d;
PXcvr_=EXcvr_ * bandwidth_;
if (energy_)
{
if (energy_->remove(pktEnergy(Pt_, PXcvr_, ch->size())) != 0)
alive_=0;
}
#endif
```

2. The realization of protocols of each layer

Network Interface

Network interface plays the role of the physical layer. When a packet is received from the MAC layer, the transmission power is set according to the approximate distance from the receivers. The appropriate power consumption is subtracted for the packet transmission, and the packet is transmitted to the channel. If the node is exhausted, the node dies and is removed from the channel. The death of the node does not affect the normal operation of the routing protocol. Any packet sent to the dead nodes is discarded.

When data is received, the packet enters the network interface of the node from the channel. If the receiver is in a sleep state, the network interface discards the packet. If the receiver is in a wake-up state, the network interface determines the received power of the packet. If the received power of a packet is lower

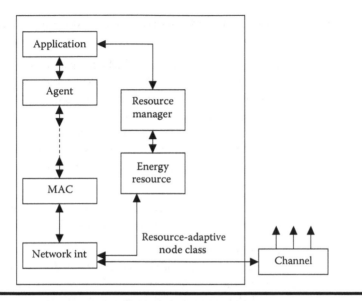

Figure 5.11   The structure diagram of resource adaptive nodes.

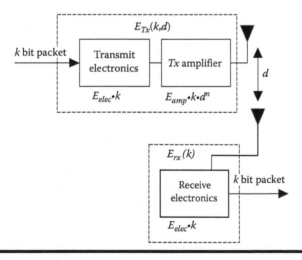

Figure 5.12   Energy model.

than a detection threshold ($p_{r\text{-}detect}$), the receiver cannot detect the transmission of the packet and the packet is discarded. If the received power of a packet is higher than the detection threshold ($p_{r\text{-}detect}$) but below the successful reception threshold ($p_{r\text{-}thresh}$), the packet is marked "erroneous" and enters the stack but cannot be successfully received. Only packets whose received power is higher than $p_{r\text{-}thresh}$ can be successfully received and transmitted to the MAC class.

The implementation of the network interface function is done by "wireless-phy.cc".

MAC

The MAC protocol type of LEACH is called MacSensor. This protocol combines carrier sense multiple access (CSMA), TDMA, and a simple DS-SS model. TDMA is implemented in the application; it controls the application in a specific TDMA time slot for sending data to the agent. CSMA is implemented in the MacSensor class, and the direct-sequence spread-spectrum (DS-SS) is implemented by the application and MacSensor classes.

The specific code can be seen in "mac-sensor.cc" and "mac-sensor-timer.cc."

LEACH

Because LEACH is an application-oriented protocol in NS, it is implemented as a subclass of Application. See "ns-leach.tcl" for specific code.

The function of base station

The base station is not limited by energy and is intended to receive all data. Therefore, the base station must keep track of the received packets to count the packet delay and the amount of data received. The specific function is implemented by the BSApp Application.

Protocol code

The LEACH protocol modifies some of the existing NS files and adds some new features including pp.[cc, h], channel.cc, cmu-trace.[cc, h], mac.cc, packet.[cc, h], phy. [cc, h], and wireless-phy[cc, h]. In addition, mac-sensor. [Cc, h] and mac-sensor-timer. [Cc, h] files have been newly added.

After the installation is completed, enter "ns-2.27 \ mit." There are three subfolders.

1. The rca node resource management directory stores files of achieving the resources adaptive nodes and agents and links function including ns-ranode. tcl, rcagent. [cc, h], rca-ll.[cc, h], resource.[cc, h], and energy.[cc, h].
2. It is the directory that stores the output data files. After the completion of the operation of protocol, the following types of documents will be generated:

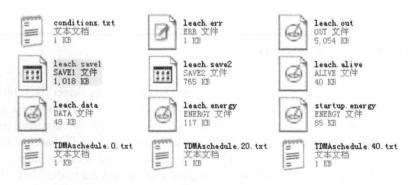

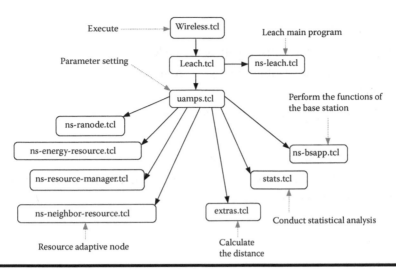

Figure 5.13 Core file.

.save: the detailed output of the execution
.out: Record debugging information
.alive: Record the number of surviving nodes
.energy: Record the energy consumption of each node
.data: The amount of data received by the base station from each node
.err: Error output file
conditions.txt: Output parameter information
"TDMAschedule." outputs cluster information including the cluster head and the TDMA scheduling list of its cluster members.

3. The uAMPS Main Program Directory is the main file that stores the routing protocol. The following figure shows the main function of the file and its call relationship (Figure 5.13).

The process of performing LEACH:
First run the "leach_test" file by the command of "./leach_test." The file contents are as follows:

```
alg=leach
dirname="mit/leach_sims"
filename=$alg
topology_file="mit/uAMPS/sims/100nodes.txt"
num_clusters=5 // the number of expected cluster heads, usually 5% of
the total number of nodes
```

```
eq_energy=1
init_energy=2 //the initial energy of the node
stop=3600   // the deadline of program running
x=1000
y=1000 //the length and width of the monitoring area
bs_x=50
bs_y=175 //the location of the base station
nn=101  //The total number of nodes, which should be one more than the
number of nodes generated in the scene
ns tcl/ex/wireless.tcl \
-sc mit/uAMPS/sims/nodescen \
-rp $alg \
-x $x \
-y $y \
-nn $nn \
-stop $stop \
-eq_energy $eq_energy \
-init_energy $init_energy \
-filename $filename \
-dirname $dirname \
-topo $topology_file \
-num_clusters $num_clusters \
-bs_x $bs_x \
-bs_y $bs_y 2>$dirname/$filename.err 1>$dirname/$filename.out &
```

This file calls the "tcl/ex/wireless.tcl" file to set the parameters. "wireless. tc" is linked to "leach.tcl" as a source. See the "tcl/ex/wireless.tcl" file for details.

Next we find "leach.tcl" in the directory "ns-2.27 \ mit \ uAMPS \ sims." Its contents are as follows:

```
source mit/uAMPS/ns-leach.tcl
set opt(rcapp)     "Application/LEACH"      ;# Application type
set opt(tr)        "/tmp/leach.tr"          ;# Trace file
set opt(spreading)   [expr int([expr 1.5*$opt(num_clusters)])+1]
```

```
set outf [open "$opt(dirname)/conditions.txt" w]
puts  $outf  "\nUSING  LEACH:  DISTRIBUTED  CLUSTER
FORMATION\n"
close $outf
source mit/uAMPS/sims/uamps.tcl
set opt(ra_adv)  [TxTime [expr $opt(hdr_size)+4]]  // RA Time (s) for
CH ADVs
set opt(ra_adv_total) [expr $opt(ra_adv)*($opt(num_clusters)*4+1)] //
Total time (s) for CH ADVs, Assume max 4(nn*%) CHs
set opt(ra_join)  [expr 0.01 * $opt(nn_)]  // RA Time (s) for nodes' join
reqs
set opt(ra_delay)  [TxTime [expr $opt(hdr_size)+4]]  // Buffer time for
join req xmittal
set opt(xmit_sch) expr 0.005+[TxTime [expr $opt(nn_)*4+$opt(hdr_
size)]]]  // Maximum time required to transmit a schedule (n nodes in 1
cluster)
set opt(start_xmit) [expr $opt(ra_adv_total)+$opt(ra_join)+$opt(xmit_
sch)]  // Overhead time for cluster set-up
if {$opt(eq_energy) == 1} {
  puts $outf "Thresholds chosen using original probs."
} else {
  puts $outf "Thresholds chosen using energy probs."
}
puts $outf "Desired number of clusters=$opt(num_clusters)"
puts $outf "Spreading factor=$opt(spreading)"
puts $outf "Changing clusters every $opt(ch_change) seconds\n"
close $outf       // set outf [open "$opt(dirname)/conditions.txt" a]
```

"ns-leach.tcl" is put in the directory "ns-2.27 \ mit \ uAMPS \ sims" and the "uamps.tcl" in the directory "ns-2.27 \ mit \ uAMPS" as shown in the call diagram. The main function of LEACH is achieved by "ns-leach.tcl," a subclass of the application. In "ns-leach.tcl," the whole cluster establishment phase and the data transmission phase are completed by three types of functions.

- The function of distributed cluster establishment
    The process of "decideClusterHead {}"completes the election of the cluster head.

```
Application/LEACH instproc decideClusterHead {} {

global chan ns_ opt node_

$self instvar next_change_time_ round_ clusterNodes_
$self instvar now_ TDMAschedule_ beginningE_ alive_
$self instvar myADVnum_ CHheard_

set CHheard_ 0
[$self mac] set CHheard_ $CHheard_
set myADVnum_ 0
[$self mac] set myADVnum_ $myADVnum_

set ISalive [[[$self node] set netif_(0)] set alive_]
if {$alive_ == 1 && $ISalive == 0} {
  puts "Node [$self nodeID] is DEAD!!!! Energy=[[$self getER] query]"
  $chan removeif [[$self node] set netif_(0)]
  set alive_ 0
  set opt(nn_) [expr $opt(nn_) - 1]
}
if {$alive_ == 0} {return}

set now_ [$ns_ now]
set nodeID [$self nodeID]
set beginningE_ [[$self getER] query]

$self setCode 0
$self WakeUp

set tot_rounds [expr int([expr $opt(nn_) / $opt(num_clusters)])]
if {$round_ >= $tot_rounds} {
  set round_ 0
}// Check the surviving state of the node. If the node has exhausted its
```
energy, it is no longer running, that is, the node is dead.

```
if {$opt(eq_energy) == 1} {
  set nn $opt(nn_)
  if {[expr $nn - $opt(num_clusters) * $round_] < 1} {
    set thresh 1
  } else {
    set thresh [expr double($opt(num_clusters)) / \
      [expr $nn - $opt(num_clusters) * $round_]] // the threshold setting
of cluster head election
    if {$round_ == 0} {
      $self hasnotbeenClusterHead
    }
  }//if round=0, all nodes become cluster heads
  if {[$self hasbeenClusterHead?]} {
    set thresh 0
  }
} else {
  set Etotal 0
  for {set id 0} {$id < [expr $opt(nn)-1]} {incr id} {
    set app [$node_($id) set rca_app_]
    set E [[$app getER] query]
    set Etotal [expr $Etotal+$E]
  }
  set E [[$self getER] query]
  set thresh [expr double([expr $E * $opt(num_clusters)]) / $Etotal]
}

puts "THRESH=$thresh"
set clusterNodes_ ""
set TDMAschedule_ ""

if {[$self getRandomNumber 0 1] < $thresh} {
  puts "$nodeID: ****************************************"
  puts "$nodeID: Is a cluster head at time [$ns_ now]"
  $self setClusterHead
```

```
    set random_access [$self getRandomNumber 0 $opt(ra_adv)]
    $ns_ at [expr $now_+$random_access] "$self advertiseClusterHead"
} else {
    puts "$nodeID: *****************************************"
    $self unsetClusterHead
}

incr round_
set next_change_time_ [expr $now_+$opt(ch_change)]
$ns_ at $next_change_time_ "$self decideClusterHead"
$ns_ at [expr $now_+$opt(ra_adv_total)] "$self findBestCluster"
}
```

The elected cluster head broadcasts its own cluster head message with advertiseClusterHead {}.

```
Application/LEACH instproc advertiseClusterHead {} {

  global ns_ opt ADV_CH MAC_BROADCAST LINK_BROADCAST BYTES_ID
  $self instvar currentCH_ code_

  set chID [$self nodeID]
  set currentCH_ $chID
  pp "Cluster Head $currentCH_ broadcasting ADV at time [$ns_ now]"
  set mac_dst $MAC_BROADCAST
  set link_dst $LINK_BROADCAST
  set msg [list $currentCH_]
  set datasize [expr $BYTES_ID * [llength $msg]]

  $self send $mac_dst $link_dst $ADV_CH $msg $datasize $opt(max_dist) $code_
} // Messages are sent at the maximum power that each node can receive.
```

The "findBestCluster {}" is responsible for completing the construction of the cluster.

```
Application/LEACH instproc findBestCluster {} {

global ns_ opt

$self instvar now_ dist_ myADVnum_
$self instvar clusterChoices_ clusterDist_ currentCH_
set nodeID [$self nodeID]
set min_dist 100000
if [$self isClusterHead?] {
  # If node is CH, determine code and create a TDMA schedule.
  set dist_ $opt(max_dist)
  set currentCH_ $nodeID
  set myADVnum_ [[$self mac] set myADVnum_] // If the node is a cluster head, the CDMA code of the cluster and the TDMA scheduling in the cluster are determined.
  set numCodesAvail [expr 2 * $opt(spreading) - 1]
  set ClusterCode [expr int(fmod($myADVnum_, $numCodesAvail)) + 1]
  $ns_ at [expr $now_ + $opt(ra_adv_total) + $opt(ra_join)] \
     "$self createSchedule"
} else {
  if {$clusterChoices_ == ""} {
    puts "$nodeID: Warning!!! No Cluster Head ADVs were heard!"
    set currentCH_ $opt(nn)
    $self SendMyDataToBS
    return
  }
  foreach element $clusterChoices_ {
    set chID [lindex $element 0]
    set clustID [lindex $element 2]
    set ind [lsearch $clusterChoices_ $element]
    set d [lindex $clusterDist_ $ind]
    if {$d < $min_dist} {
```

```
        set min_dist $d
        set currentCH_ $chID
        set numCodesAvail [expr 2 * $opt(spreading) - 1]
        set ClusterCode [expr int(fmod($ind, $numCodesAvail)) + 1]
    }
    }
    set dist_ $min_dist

    set random_access [$self getRandomNumber 0 \
                    [expr $opt(ra_join) - $opt(ra_delay)]]
    $ns_ at [expr $now_ + $opt(ra_adv_total) + $random_access] \
        "$self informClusterHead"
    $self GoToSleep
    }


    $self setCode $ClusterCode
        puts "$nodeID: Current cluster-head is $currentCH_, code is
$ClusterCode, \
        dist is $dist_"


    set clusterChoices_ ""
    set clusterDist_ ""
    } // If the node is not a cluster head, look for the nearest cluster head and set
    the corresponding CDMA code and distance parameters.
```

In the cluster construction process, an ordinary node it selects the nearest cluster head and joins its cluster by calling createSchedule {}. A cluster head node invokes createSchedule {} to create a TDMA schedule and broadcast the schedule to the member nodes of its cluster.

```
Application/LEACH instproc informClusterHead {} {


global ns_ opt JOIN_REQ MAC_BROADCAST BYTES_ID
$self instvar currentCH_ dist_ code_
```

```
set nodeID [$self nodeID]
set chID $currentCH_
pp "$nodeID: sending Join-REQ to $chID (dist=$dist_) at time [$ns_ now]"
set mac_dst $MAC_BROADCAST
set link_dst $chID
set msg [list $nodeID]
set spreading_factor $opt(spreading)
set datasize [expr $spreading_factor * $BYTES_ID * [llength $msg]]
$self WakeUp
// Note that nodes need to have enough power to allow all nodes in the
network to receive messages, which avoids hidden interrupt problems.
$self send $mac_dst $link_dst $JOIN_REQ $msg $datasize $opt(max_
dist) $code_
}
Application/LEACH instproc createSchedule {} {

global ns_ opt ADV_SCH MAC_BROADCAST BYTES_ID

$self instvar clusterNodes_ TDMAschedule_
$self instvar dist_ code_ now_ beginningE_

set numNodes [llength $clusterNodes_]
set chID [$self nodeID]
if {$numNodes == 0} {
  set xmitOrder ""
  puts "Warning! There are no nodes in this cluster ($chID)!"
  $self SendMyDataToBS
} else {
  # Set the TDMA schedule and send it to all nodes in the cluster.
  set xmitOrder $clusterNodes_
  set msg [list $xmitOrder]
  set spreading_factor $opt(spreading)
  set datasize [expr $spreading_factor * $BYTES_ID * [llength $xmitOrder]]
  pp "$chID sending TDMA schedule: $xmitOrder at time [$ns_ now]"
```

```
    pp "Packet size is $datasize."
    set mac_dst $MAC_BROADCAST
    set link_dst $chID
        $self send $mac_dst $link_dst $ADV_SCH $msg $datasize $dist_
$code_
    }


    set TDMAschedule_ $xmitOrder
    set outf [open $opt(dirname)/TDMAschedule.$now_.txt a]
    puts $outf "$chID\t$TDMAschedule_"
    close $outf


    set outf [open $opt(dirname)/startup.energy a]
    puts $outf "[$ns_ now]\t$chID\t[expr $beginningE_ - [[$self getER]
query]] "
    close $outf


}
```

- Receiving function. The packets from the agent are first received by the
  "recv {args}" function. This procedure determines the packet type and
  passes the packet to the corresponding receive function.

```
Application/LEACH instproc recv {args} {
    global ADV_CH JOIN_REQ ADV_SCH DATA ns_
    $self instvar currentCH_
    set msg_type [[$self agent] set packetMsg_]
    set chID [lindex $args 0]
    set sender [lindex $args 1]
    set data_size [lindex $args 2]
    set msg [lrange $args 3 end]
    set nodeID [$self nodeID]
    if {$msg_type == $ADV_CH && ![$self isClusterHead?]} {
      $self recvADV_CH $msg
    } elseif {$msg_type == $JOIN_REQ && $nodeID == $chID} {
```

```
    $self recvJOIN_REQ $msg
 } elseif {$msg_type == $ADV_SCH && $chID == $currentCH_} {
    $self recvADV_SCH $msg
 } elseif {$msg_type == $DATA && $nodeID == $chID} {
    $self recvDATA $msg

 }
}
```

- The sending function completes the encapsulation of the package and sends the package to the agent.
3. Simulation process of LEACH
    - Scenario Configuration. Open the "genscen" of "ns-2.27\mit\uAMPS\ sims," you can see below:

```
set outf [open "new100nodes.txt" w]
set num_nodes 100
set rng [new RNG]
$rng seed 0
set lim 100
for {set i 1} {$i <= $num_nodes} {incr i} {
  set x [$rng uniform 0 $lim]
  set y [$rng uniform 0 $lim]
  puts $outf "$x\t$y"
}
```

By using the command "ns genscen" to implement the document, we can see the "new100nodes.txt" file in the directory "ns-2.27 \ mit \ uAMPS \ sims." Open the file to see the contents in the following format.

```
65.745973803916002    92.581722416254564
21.008649990432268    92.380389195112684
37.201202259027028    40.606367467253641
..................  .        .................
```

Each row in the file represents a node coordinate, 100 rows in total, indicating that there are 100 nodes in the scene. The two numbers of each row are evenly distributed in the (0,100) interval, that is, the network region is 100×100. Rename the file "100nodes.txt" to replace the original "100nodes.txt" file. That is, conduct the simulation of the new generated scene. When simulating other types of scenes, you only need to modify the "genscen" file to generate the "100nodes.txt" that meets your requirements.

Configuration of simulation parameters. Open the "leach_test" file under "ns-2.27." According to this generated scene, set the parameters such as the area, node number, base station location, the number of cluster heads, and simulation time. The "leach_test" file has the following two lines of code:

eq_energy=1
init_energy=2

eq_energy=1 means that the network is a homogeneous network and all the nodes have the same initial energy. The following line shows the initial energy settings for the nodes in the network. The LEACH protocol is only for a homogeneous network, because it does not consider the heterogeneous network. If you want to simulate the heterogeneous network, you need to modify the "leach_test" and the "uamps.tcl" in "ns-2.27 \ mit \ uAMPS \ sims" in the relevant location to generate your own simulation scenarios.

Run the protocol with the command "./ leach_test." Enter the folder "leach_sims"; you can see that the file "TDMAschedule" grows continuously. Open the "leach.err" file. If there is such a prompt, it means that the program is running (Figure 5.14).

If the file "leach.err" can be normally opened with the following content, this is the normal end of the simulation.

```
INITIALIZE THE LIST xListHead
channel.cc:sendUp - Calc highestAntennaZ_ and distCST_
highestAntennaZ_ = 1.5,  distCST_ = 222.8
SORTING LISTS ...DONE!
```

4. Analysis of simulation results

The simulation of LEACH is mainly for the analysis of the following three documents: leach.alive, leach.energy, leach.data

Figure 5.14   Access denied.

"Leach.alive" records the number of surviving nodes. Open the "leach. alive" file, which has the following format:

```
10 0 1
10 1 1
10 2 1
.........
```

The first column is the simulation time; the second column is the id of the node; the third column is the indicator of whether the node is alive, that is, 1 means survival, 0 means death. For this file, we need to count the number of surviving nodes in each time period. We will write the script file ".awk" to analyze the simulation results. Here, for "leach.alive" we write an ".awk" file named "alive.awk."

```
BEGIN {
  countcyl=0;
  totalleft=0;
  lasttime=0;
  time[0]=0;
  node=0;
  total[0]=100;
}
{
simtime        = $1;
nodeid         = $2;
statenode      = $3;
  if (simtime>lasttime ) {
    countcyl++;
    lasttime=simtime;
    time[countcyl]=simtime;
    totalleft=0;
    }
  if (statenode==1)
    totalleft++;
    total[countcyl]=totalleft;
}
```

```
END {
for(i=0;i<=countcyl;i++)
printf ( "%f %d\n",time[i],total[i]);
}
```

Use the command "gawk –f leach.awk leach.alive>leachalive" to implement the "leach.awk," and then save the results in the file "leachalive." The format of "leachalive" is as follows:

```
0.000000 100
10.000000 100
20.000000 100

........... ......
```

The first column is the simulation time, and the second column is the number of surviving nodes. "Leachalive" will be used for drawing.

"Leach.energy" records the energy consumption of each node. The format of "leach.energy" is as follows:

```
10 0 0.038604391182381334
10 1 0.010892253349204359
10 2 0.010883086512785183

.................................
```

The first column is the simulation time, the second column is the id of the node, and the third column is the energy consumed by the node. According to the different needs, different awk scripts can be prepared to analyze the document. Here are the statistics of the total energy remaining in the network. The analysis script is named "energy.awk."

```
BEGIN {
  countcyl=0;
  totalleft=200;
  lasttime=0;
  time[0]=0;
  node=0;
  total[0]=200;
}
{
  simtime        = $1;
```

```
nodeid          = $2;
statenode       = $3;
if (simtime>lasttime ) {
  countcyl++;
  lasttime=simtime;
  time[countcyl]=simtime;
  totalleft=200;
    }
 if (statenode>0)
   totalleft=totalleft-statenode;
   total[countcyl]=totalleft;
}
END {
 for (i=0;i<=countcyl;i++)
 printf ( "%f %d\n",time[i],total[i]);
  }
```

Execute the command "gawk –f energy.awk leach.energy>leachenergy." The format of "leach.energy" is shown as below:

```
0.000000 200
10.000000 196
20.000000 193
. . . . . . . . . . . . . . . . . . . . .
```

"leach.data" records the amount of data received by the base station for each node. The analysis procedure is similar to the analysis of the two files above. The analysis script "data.awk" is given here for the number of data packets transmitted in the network.

```
BEGIN {
  countcyl=0;
  totalleft=0;
  lasttime=0;
  time[0]=0;
  node=0;
```

```
   total[0]=0;
}
{
simtime        =$1;
nodeid         =$2;
statenode      =$3;
if (simtime>lasttime ) {
   countcyl++;
   lasttime=simtime;
   time[countcyl]=simtime;
   totalleft=0;
     }
if (statenode>0)
     totalleft=totalleft+statenode;
     total[countcyl]=totalleft;
}
END {
for(i=0;i<=countcyl;i++)
printf ( "%f %d\n",time[i],total[i]);
     }
```

5. Drawing. This section draws according to the data from the previous step. We can use the "gnuplot" of NS2 to draw the simulation results for a visual representation. But the visual effect is not ideal, so a separate "gnuplot" is commonly used. The use of gnuplot will be covered in the last section of this chapter. Here's the gnuplot script, named code.gp.

```
set term gif
set output "data.gif"
set xlabel "simulation time"
set ylabel "data in the network"
set size 0.6
plot "leachdata" title "LEACH" with linespoint
exit
```

Run this file with load "code.gp." The following three graphs show the simulation results of the LEACH protocol in terms of node survivability, residual energy in the network, and the amount of data transmitted in the network. The number of surviving nodes in the network changes with the simulation time. That is, it's the testing of the network lifetime (Figure 5.15).

The changes of residual energy in the network with the simulation time (Figure 5.16).

With different simulation time, the statistics of network data packet transmission are in Figure 5.17.

According to the actual situation, we can also display the results of other aspects. The following figure is given for the results of the number of cluster heads generated by LEACH after several experiments. Other aspects of the simulation are not enumerated here. Interested readers can analyze them on their own (Figure 5.18).

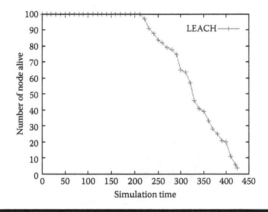

Figure 5.15   Testing of network lifetime.

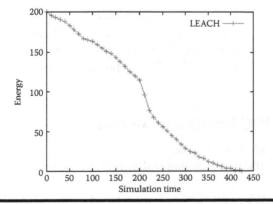

Figure 5.16   Residual energy in the network.

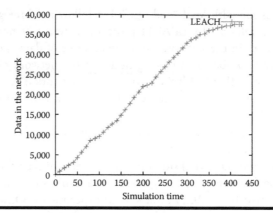

Figure 5.17 **The amount of data transmitted in the network.**

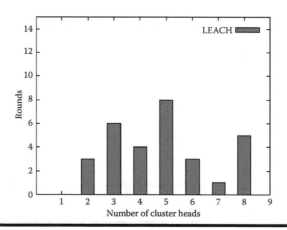

Figure 5.18 **The number of cluster heads generated by the protocol.**

In addition, in some simulations, we compare the simulation results of multiple protocols. At this time, we carry on the simulation of different protocols separately, analyzing the simulation results. The data of different protocols can be painted in the same figure. In Figure 5.19, the LEACH protocol is compared with LEACH-C in the network lifetime.

5.2.6 The EDUC Simulation Example

We select two simulation scenarios.

Sparse Scene: 100 nodes randomly distributed evenly in the 200×200 rectangular area.

Dense scene: 400 nodes randomly distributed evenly in the 200×200 rectangular area.

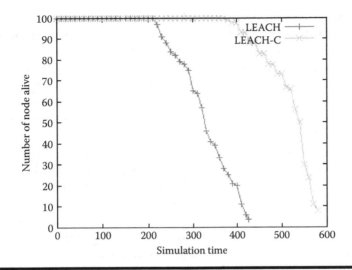

Figure 5.19 The comparison of network life of LEACH and LEACH-C.

The base station is located far from the monitoring area at (250, 100). The values of the specific parameters used in the simulation are shown in the following table:

Table 5.1 Simulation Parameter Configuration

Parameter	Value
Area size	200 × 200 m
Base station location	(250, 100)
Number of nodes	100
Initial energy	0.5~2 J
Packet size	500 bytes
E_{elec}	50 nJ/bit
ε_{fs}	10 pJ/(bit m²)
ε_{mp}	0.0013 pJ/(bit m⁴)
Energy consumption of data fusion	5 nJ/(bit signal)
Energy consumption of node sensing	0 J/bit
R_{max}	120 m

Figure 5.20 shows the distribution of nodes for the two scenarios:

We run EDUC on both of these scenarios. Figure 5.21 shows the relationship between the number of generated cluster head nodes and the maximum contention radius R_{max}. As seen in the figure, when $\alpha=0.5$ the curve is higher than when $\alpha=0$. The reason for this phenomenon is that when R_{max} is fixed, the competition radius α will decrease with the growth. In addition, the values of the curves in the two scenarios are very close, indicating that the density of the nodes has little effect on the number of cluster heads.

We specify that the network lifetime is the time from the deployment of the network until when 90% of the nodes are surviving in the network. In the above two scenarios, we set $\alpha=0.5$ and run EDUC separately. The network lifetime varies with R_{max} in both scenarios as shown in Figure 5.22.

As shown in Figure 5.22, the network lifetime in dense networks is slightly longer than in sparse networks. This shows that increasing the number of nodes can prolong the network lifetime, but the degree of network life extension is not great. In addition, as shown in Figure 5.22, the network lifetime is the largest in sparse networks with R_{max} values of 120–140, while in dense networks, the best value of R_{max} is 90–110.

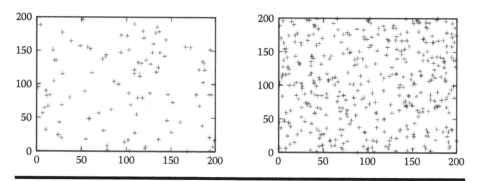

Figure 5.20 Node distribution.

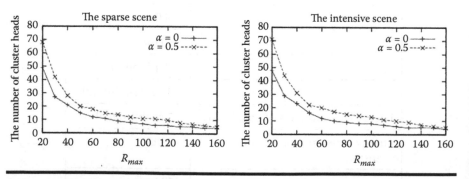

Figure 5.21 The number of cluster heads.

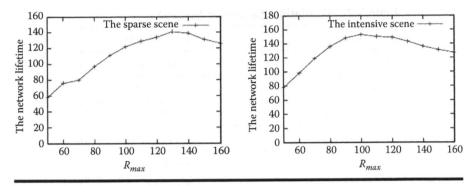

Figure 5.22   The network lifetime varies with R_{max}.

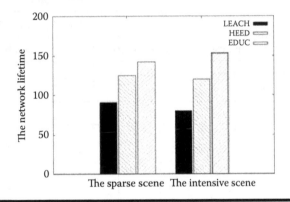

Figure 5.23   Network lifetime.

To measure the performance of EDUC, we compare LEACH, HEED, and EDUC in terms of network lifetime. As shown in Figure 5.23, EDUC can effectively extend network lifetime compared to LEACH and HEED. In EDUC, the lifetime of a dense network is slightly longer than that of a sparse network. While in the other two protocols, the opposite is true: The lifetime of the dense network is slightly shorter than that of the sparse network.

5.2.7 EADC Simulation Examples

The whole experiment is divided into two scenarios:

Scene 1: 100 nodes are evenly distributed uniformly in the 200×200 m square area with the initial energy of $1 \sim 3$ J.

Scene 2: 100 nodes are nonuniformly distributed in a 200×200 m square area with an initial energy of $1 \sim 3$ J.

The values of other parameters in the simulation are shown in Table 5.2.

The topology of the two scenarios is shown in Figure 5.24.

Table 5.2   Simulation Parameter Settings

Parameter	Value
Area size	$200 \times 200\,\text{m}$
Base station location	(250, 100)
Number of nodes	100
Initial energy	1~3 J
Packet size	500 bytes
E_{elec}	50 nJ/bit
ε_{fs}	10 pJ/(bit m²)
ε_{mp}	0.0013 pJ/(bit m⁴)
Energy consumption of data fusion	5 nJ/(bit signal)
Energy consumption of node sensing	0 J/bit

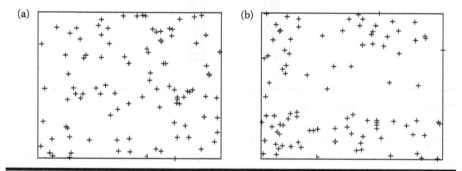

Figure 5.24   Topology of two scenes. (a) random distribution and (b) nonuniform distribution.

5.2.7.1 Cluster Head Distribution

We run our protocol in two scenarios. The contention radius R_c is in the range of 10–200. According to different values of R_c, the number of generated cluster head nodes is shown in Figure 5.25.

It can be seen in this figure that the number of cluster heads in the two scenarios is basically the same under the same value of R_c. This is because the contention radius R_c controls the coverage of the cluster head so that the cluster has a uniform size. Therefore, the number of cluster heads is not affected by the distribution of nodes. In addition, uniform cluster size ensures the balance of energy consumption by the cluster members.

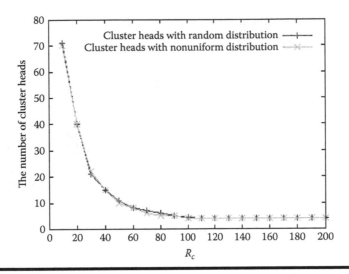

Figure 5.25 Comparison of the number of cluster heads generated by the two scenarios.

In the two scenarios, we take $R_c = 100$ to run EADC and conduct the statistics of the distribution of the number of cluster heads in 30 randomly selected rounds. When $R_c = 100$, the average number of cluster heads of EADC is 4. We take k value as 4 in the LEACH protocol and select 30 rounds of statistics of the distribution of the cluster heads in two scenarios running the LEACH protocol. The distributions in Figure 5.26a and b show the comparison of the number of cluster heads generated by the two protocols in the two scenarios.

It can be seen that, in LEACH protocol, the fluctuation range of the cluster head number is relatively large, because LEACH uses a random number mechanism to generate cluster heads. The generation of cluster heads is more random, so the number of cluster heads fluctuates greatly. In the EADC, the contention radius of cluster heads is adopted, and the nodes compete for the cluster head with the same contention radius R_c, which ensures that there is only one cluster head in the range of R_c and effectively controls cluster head distribution. The cluster head can be uniformly distributed, and the number of cluster heads generated by each algorithm can be guaranteed to be stable. Therefore, EADC has a high stability and reliability.

5.2.7.2 Network Lifetime

Here, the network lifetime is defined as the time from initial network deployment until 90% of the nodes in the network die.

In two scenarios, we let $\alpha = 0.5$ and *DIST_TH* = 80; we test the impact of the contention radius R_c on network lifetime. The test results are shown in Figure 5.27.

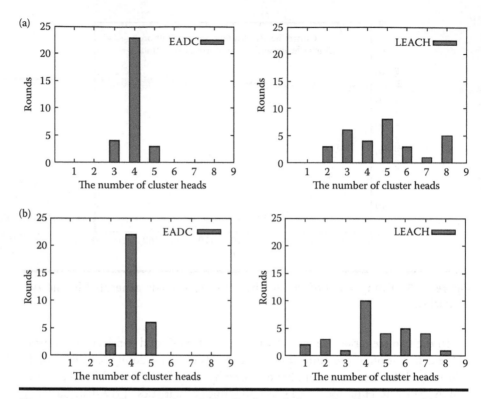

Figure 5.26 (a) The statistics of distribution of cluster heads generated by two protocols in scenario 1 and (b) the statistics of distribution of cluster heads generated by two protocols in scenario 2.

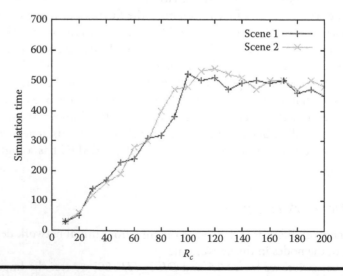

Figure 5.27 The effect of R_c on network life.

In wireless sensor networks, too many or too few cluster head nodes can cause energy waste and affect network lifetime. Analysis of the number of cluster heads in Figure 5.27 with the R_c changes can be seen: With the increase of R_c, the number of clusters in the network is gradually reduced, and the rate of reducing becomes smaller and smaller. Therefore, the network lifetime should also increase with the increase of R_c, and the increase will be smaller and smaller. When it increases to a certain stage, there will be a downward trend. From the analysis of the two curves, it can be seen that when R_c is small, the network lifetime increases gradually with the increase of R_c. When R_c increases to about 100, the network lifetime tends to be stable and decreases slightly, which is consistent with our theoretical analysis. The two curves tend to be stable when R_c increases to about 100, which indicates that the optimal cluster head ratio in the network is 5%–7%. On the other hand, the trend and the value of the two curves are basically the same, which also shows that the distribution of nodes in the two scenarios has little effect on the network lifetime, that is, the inter-cluster routing protocol is well balanced for the energy consumption of the cluster heads.

5.3 Simulation and Example Based on C++

5.3.1 Introduction to VC++

The C++ language is an object-oriented programming language designed to encapsulate data and how data is manipulated as an object. The same type of object is abstracted to form the class. Class connects with the outside world through a simple external interface, and the objects communicate with each other through the message. The relationship between the programs is simple, which has a good protection for the independence of the program module, data security. The program has a high reusability through inheritance and polymorphism.

For the development of the C++ program, after analyzing and abstracting the problem, the problem model is built. Then the model is transformed into a finite sequence of steps. The statement sequence of C++ is composed according to its grammar, that is, the C++ source code. The source code from the keyboard input to the computer is saved as a file of .cpp format. This process is known as editing. Then the source file is compiled into the .OBJ file and then connected to the .EXE executable file. The processed results can be obtained by running the executable file (Figure 5.28).

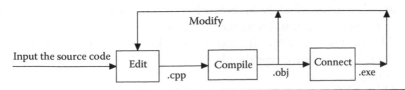

Figure 5.28 The development process of the C++ program.

The basic structure of the C++ program

```
//myfirstprograminC++
#include<iostream.h>
usingnamespacestd;

intmain(){
cout<<"HelloWorld!";
return0;
}
```

The above shows the source code of our first program, whose file name is "hellow-world.cpp." The process of editing and compiling a program depends on which compiler you use. According to whether it has a graphical interface and different versions, the compiled methods may also be different. Please refer to the user instructions of the used compiler.

This procedure is the first program for most beginners learning to write. Its result is to display "HelloWorld!" on the screen. Although it may be one of the simplest programs written in C++, it already contains the basic structure of each C++ program.

5.3.2 The Development Environment of VC++

5.3.2.1 VC++ 6.0

The hardware configuration requirements for the installation of VC++ 6.0 are 486CPU, 100MB of hard disk space, 16 MB of memory, and software configuration requirements: 32-bit operating system. After installation, use the mouse to click "Start" → "Programs" → "Microsoft Visual C++ 6.0". The Visual C++ 6.0 integrated environment interface is shown in Figure 5.29.

The most important thing in the integrated environment is the concept of engineering. The project is a collection of related source files, including source code, header files, and resource definition files, the main venue for programming.

The process of using VC++ 6.0:

1. In the integration environment interface, select "File" → "New" → "Project," and then in the left of the list box, select "Win32Application," enter the name of the new project, and store the project path.
2. Choose "File" → "New File" again, and select the "C++ SourceFile" item in the left list box, then type the file name in the edit box under "File" and click "OK."
3. Click "OK" after the input code, compile, and run.

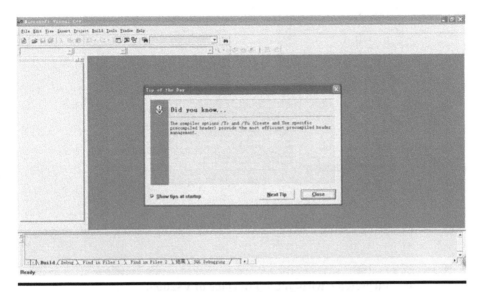

Figure 5.29   Integrated environment interface of VC++ 6.0.

5.3.2.2 VS2005

The hardware configuration requirements for the installation of VS2005 are 486CPU, 100MB of hard disk space, 3G memory, and the software configuration requirements 32-bit operating system. After the installation, use the mouse to click "Start" → "Programs" → "Microsoft Visual Studio2005." Then, the VS2005 integrated environment interface is shown in Figure 5.30.

The process of using VS2005:

1. Select "File" → "New" → "Project" in the integration environment interface, then select "VisualC++" → "General" in the left list box, enter the name of the new project, and store the path of the project as shown in Figure 5.31.
2. Select "File" → "New" → "File" again, select "VisualC++" in the left list box, select the file type to be edited in the right list box, and then type the file name in the edit box. Click "Open" as shown in Figure 5.32.
3. Click "Open" and input the code; then compile and run.

5.3.3 Simulation Example of the EWCDS Algorithm

In this part, we give the simulation of a specific CDS algorithm, to illustrate the simulation method and process of a CDS construction algorithm using VC++. A specific algorithm has been explained in Section 4.3.4.2 in detail. Let's learn the algorithm simulation results.

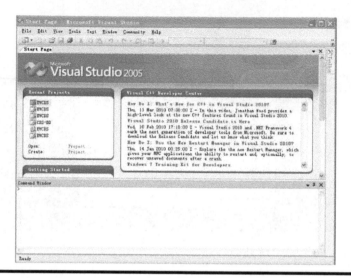

Figure 5.30   Integrated environment interface of VS2005.

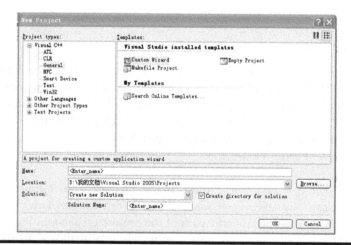

Figure 5.31   The process of "New Project."

5.3.3.1 Simulation Results

We evaluate the performance of the algorithm through specific simulations. This simulation is achieved with the VC++ language, and the whole process is divided into two stages. First, a random network topology is generated. This stage consists of a connected node network generation. The main idea is to randomly generate the required number of nodes in a unit area of a given range. Then, all the nodes are moved to the middle of a given area to generate a connected network. In this

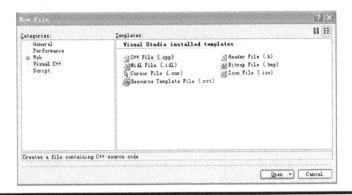

Figure 5.32   The process of "New File."

process, we use a series of data structures for network generation, such as MAP for node location. The second stage of simulation is to construct the EWCDS of the network generated in the previous stage by using the three algorithms. The main idea of this phase is to implement the above three algorithms in a randomly generated network.

Figure 5.33a is a randomly generated network with 200 nodes, each of which has a transmission range of 15 units. Figure 5.33b shows a graph of the random network when the node transmission range is 30. In both topographies, the square node represents the controlled node, and the circular node represents the node in the EWCDS found by the extended region algorithm. A green line between any two nodes represents a link when the distance between them is less than their transmission range r.

We compare the number of nodes found by the three algorithms of EWCDS in two different scenarios. In a scenario, a given number of nodes (the number of nodes changes from 20 to 100 by increments of 10 each time; from 100 to 1000, by increments of 100.) are randomly distributed in the 100×100 and 2-dimensional space. Each node has a fixed transmission range r (15 and 30, respectively). Regardless of the movement of the nodes and the collision of the channels, two nodes are neighbors when the distance between them is less than r. For each fixed number of nodes, we simulate enough experiments (500 times) and average all the simulation results.

Figure 5.34a and b show the simulation results when the transmission range of the node is 15. Figure 5.34a shows the simulation results when the number of nodes in the network is from 20 to 100 (the corresponding network is sparse). Figure 5.34b shows the simulation results when the number of nodes in the network is from 100 to 1000 (the corresponding network is dense). We can see in Figure 5.34a that the three curves increase with the increasing number of nodes. The reason for the increase of nodes in EWCDS is that as the number of nodes increases, the density of the network increases. However, in Figure 5.34b, we find

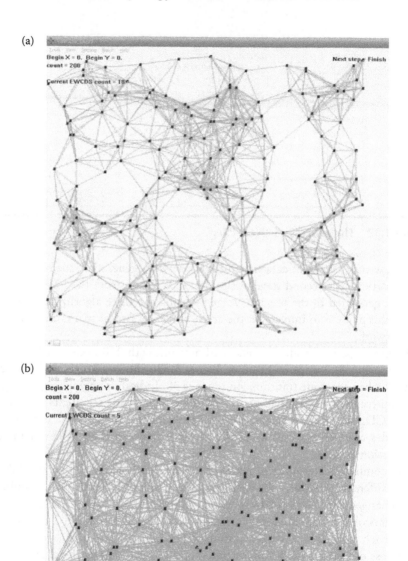

Figure 5.33   (a) *r*=15 and (b) *r*=30.

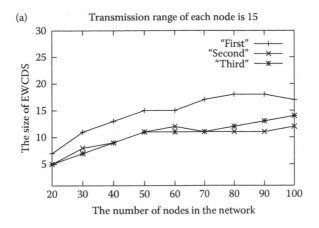

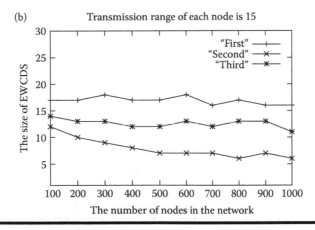

Figure 5.34   The simulation results (the transmission range of the node =15).

that the three curves are in a steady nonincreasing trend, because as the number of nodes increases, the network density increases, and each node can control more neighbors in its transmission range. That is, when the network density increases to a certain degree, the EWCDS size is less affected by node density. We find that these three algorithms can find a smaller EWCDS at $r = 15$, both in the sparse network and in the dense network. The EWCDS obtained by the second algorithm has the smallest scale, and the first algorithm finds the largest EWCDS. Figure 5.35 shows the percentage of nodes in EWCDS (found by the three algorithms for $r = 15$) in the total number of nodes of the network. It can be seen from Figure 5.34 that the number of nodes in EWCDS, which is found in the sparse or dense network, is smaller than that of the other two algorithms. The second algorithm has the optimal EWCDS scale among the three algorithms. From Figure 5.35, we can also see that our three algorithms are more suitable for finding EWCDS in the dense network than in the sparse network.

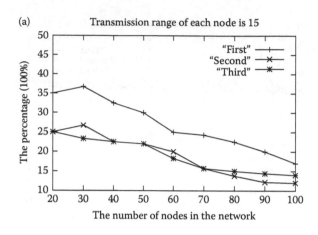

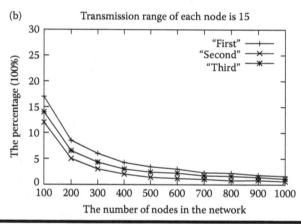

Figure 5.35 **The percentage of nodes in EWCDS in the total number of nodes of the network (*r*=15).**

Figure 5.36a and b show the simulation results when the transmission range of a node is equal to 30, and the number of nodes in the network is from 20 to 100, and from 100 to 1000, respectively. In the figure, we can see that, at *r*=30, the change of the number of nodes in the EWCDS found by the three algorithms is smaller as the network size increases. Because we set the distribution area of the node at 100×100, and the transmission radius of each node is 30, the distribution of nodes can be almost directly connected, so less EWCDS nodes are needed to control the whole network. Figure 5.37 shows the percentage of nodes in EWCDS found by the three algorithms in the total number when *r*=30. From Figure 5.37, it can be seen that the number of nodes in the EWCDS found by the second algorithm is smaller than that of the other two algorithms in both sparse and dense networks. Therefore, the other two algorithms have the best EWCDS scale among the three algorithms.

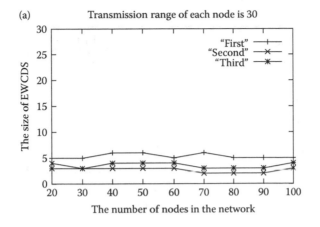

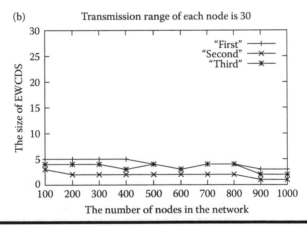

Figure 5.36 **Simulation results (the transmission range of a node =30).**

Comparing Figure 5.34 ($r=15$) and Figure 5.36 ($r=30$), we can see that the size of the EWCDS found by the algorithm decreases as the transmission radius of the node increases. This is because as the node's transmission radius becomes larger, the control range of each node increases. So in order to control the entire network, fewer nodes are needed.

In the second scenario, a fixed number of nodes ($n=100$, 500) are randomly distributed in the same plane. Let's observe the effect of node transmission range on EWCDS size. For each fixed number of nodes, r varies from 10 to 60 (by increments of 10) to perform the simulation.

Figures 5.38a and b show the effect of different node transmission ranges on EWCDS size when the number of nodes in the network is 100 (sparse network) and 500 (dense network), respectively. It can be seen from the figure that the EWCDS decreases in size as r increases. Moreover, when r increases to a certain extent,

(a)

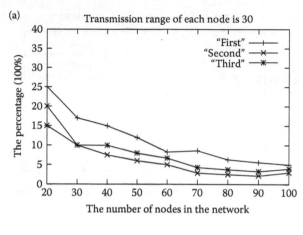

(b)

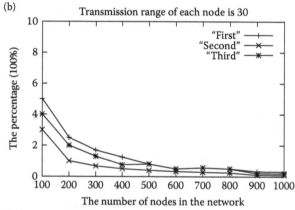

Figure 5.37 The percentage of nodes in EWCDS in the total number (r=30).

EWCDS will no longer change. At this time r is large enough that only a few nodes can control the entire network.

From these simulation results, we can draw the following conclusions: No matter whether networks are sparse or dense, the three kinds of algorithms perform well and can generate a small weakly connected dominating set. Among the three methods, the second algorithm has the best performance in generating EWCDS. These three algorithms are better suited to dense networks.

5.3.3.2 The Specific Implementation Process of Simulation

Simulation is achieved through VC++ language programming; a client terminal is shown in Figures 5.39 and 5.40. The reader can set the size of the network area, the number of nodes, the transmission range, and other parameters according to

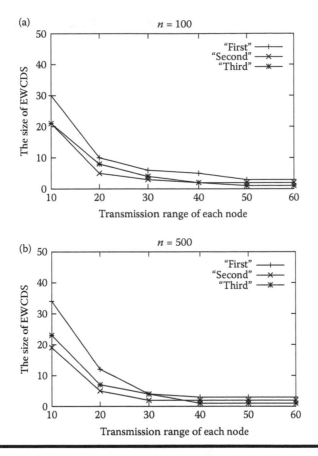

Figure 5.38   The effect of different node transmission ranges on EWCDS.

his or her needs. Under the guidance of the client function buttons, the size of the EWCDS constructed by the three described algorithms can be observed.

5.3.3.2.1 The Implementation Process of Simulation

First, a random network topology is generated. This stage consists of node generation and generation of the connected network. The main idea is to randomly generate the required number of nodes in a unit area of a given range. Then, all nodes are moved to the middle of a given area to generate a connected network. In this process, we use a series of data structures for network generation, such as the use of MAP for node location. The second stage of simulation is to construct the EWCDS of the network generated in the previous stage by using the three algorithms. The main idea of this phase is to implement the three algorithms in a randomly generated network. Figure 5.41 shows the operation flowchart.

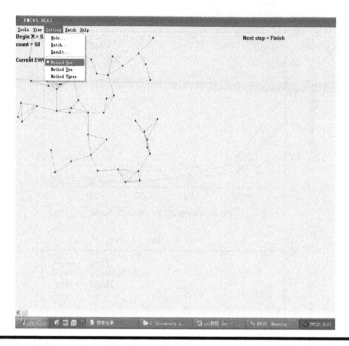

Figure 5.39   Display of graphical terminal.

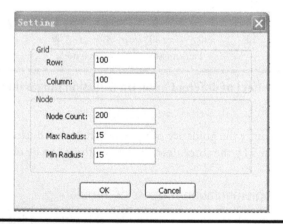

Figure 5.40   Display of parameter configuring.

The following section describes the implementation of specific functions in detail.

1. Node generation
   A specified number of nodes are randomly generated in a given range of cells, and if there are nonconnected nodes, they are moved to the middle until all nodes are connected.

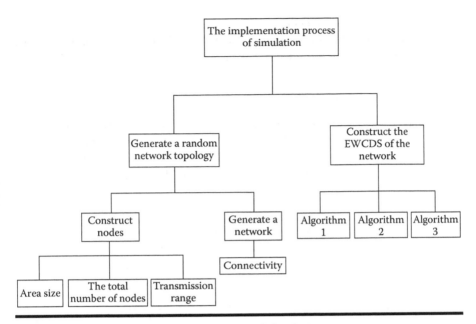

Figure 5.41   The implementation process of simulation.

Specific implementation: First generate a node in the center of the cell. It can be seen that choosing a node is the origin of the topology and does not affect the randomness of the structure (this node does not affect the randomness of the whole graph in the absence of the center). Then generate the remaining nodes by the "for" loop. Each node's X-coordinate is randomly selected from [0, GRID_COLUMN) (GRID_COLUMN is the maximum number of cells). Y coordinate is randomly selected from [0, GRID_ROW]. The node will be regenerated if the node with the coordinates has been generated.

2. Mobile nodes

The mobile node connects all of the nodes. The way to generate the origin graph is to first generate a node at the center point (the reason the first node is at the origin), then generate the second node in the first node coverage area, and generate the third node in the coverage area of the first and second nodes. The problem is that the resulting nodes will be concentrated, which is not a good simulation of random networks. Now the application of the generation algorithm may have the following problems. When generating a few nodes of a network in a very large range, the nodes will be more uniform, and the resulting network seems like a lot of broken lines with an intersection point but not a network. This can be improved by adjusting termination conditions at the mobile node. You can make the nodes move until the network has been connected and then move some distance to improve the generation network.

3. Search for the control node

In the random network diagram generated in (2), three different algorithms are used to find the EWCDS of the network.

5.3.3.2.2 VC++ Implementation

Figure 5.42 shows the implementation of the simulation, the establishment of the project, and its implementation file under VS2005. The authors created a project called "EWCDS" under VS2005, which includes the header files "GlobalDef.h," "EWCDS.h," "EWCDS_DLG1.h," source files "EWCDS.cpp," "EWCDS_DLG1.

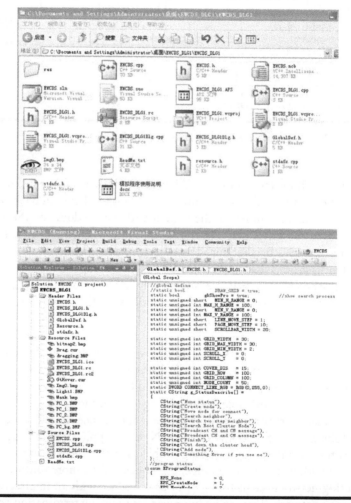

Figure 5.42 The implementation of the simulation; the establishment of the project under VS2005.

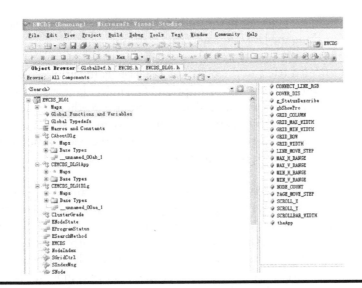

Figure 5.43   **The data structures, variables, macros, and classes in the project.**

cpp," a series of client applications, and other resource files. Figure 5.43 shows the data structures, variables, macros, and classes used in the project.

5.4 Simulation and Example Based on Java

5.4.1 Introduction to Java

Java is a programming language that provides an environment for both application development and deployment. Java language is mainly located in network programming, making the program maximize its network resources.

1. **Good platform crossing**

   The so-called cross-platform refers to the software which cannot be constrained by computer hardware and an operating system in any computer environment. This is the trend of software development and the goal for programmers. All types of computer hardware, operating systems, users, and companies have their own computer environment preferences; therefore, software needs to be independent on platforms to be able to run in these different environments.

   In the Java language, the virtual machine achieves a good platform crossing. Java source code is compiled to generate the binary bytecode, which is platform-independent. However, it is a kind of machine code instruction that the Java virtual machine can recognize. The Java virtual machine provides a barrier from the bytecode to the underlying hardware platform and operating system, making the Java language cross platform.

2. Object oriented

Object oriented refers to the object as the basic granularity, which contains attributes and methods. The description of an object is expressed as an attribute, and the object is manipulated by using a method. Object-oriented technology makes application development easy to use, saving code. Java is an object-oriented language, but it also inherits the many benefits of being object oriented, such as code expansion and code reuse.

3. Security

Security can be divided into four levels, namely, language-level security, compile-time security, run-time security, and executable code security.

Language-level security means that the Java data structure is a complete object. These encapsulated data types are secure. When compiling the Java language, semantics are needed to check to ensure that each variable corresponds to a value. Java classes are generated after compiling. Java classes require the class loader in the runtime; they are validated by the byte verifier before they run. When a Java class is used in the network, its authority is set to ensure that the security of the visited users.

4. Multithreading

Multithreading in the operating system has been the most successful application; it allows an application to have two or more threads to support concurrent transactions and multitasks. In addition to the built-in multithreading technology of Java, a number of classes and methods are defined to build and manage user-defined multithreads.

5. Easy to use

The writing of Java source code does not rigidly adhere to a specific environment; it can be used with Notepad, text editor, and other editing software. The source file is compiled, after which it can be run directly. You can get the desired results through debugging.

5.4.1.1 Download and installation of the Java Development Kit package

Java Development Kit (JDK) is Sun's free software package, which can be freely downloaded from the Sun's Web site http://www.sun.com and downloaded from other domestic addresses. JDK version starts at 1.02 (the current version is 1.4, which achieves backward compatibility from the advanced version to the low-level version). Using this package, you can compile and run Java source code. The JDK package we used is "Javajdk1.6.0.02 virtual machine .exe." Download JDK package and double-click the icon. Then you can install, and the default installation directory is C: \ j2sdk1.6.0.02.

5.4.2 Simulation Example of the EDCDS Algorithm

5.4.2.1 Algorithm Description

A. Edge Dominating Capability

Before introducing the algorithm, we present the concept of Edge Dominating Capability (EDC). EDC is based on the characteristics of the dominating between edges in an undirected graph, which is the main consideration when constructing the dominating set in the ED-connected dominating set (CDS) algorithm.

In the undirected graph $G = (V, E)$, if the node degree of node v is d_v, then there are d_v edges that can dominate the node v, and the dominating probability of this node v is $1/d_v$, that is, each edge dominates the two endpoints. We define the edge's dominating capability as the sum of the dominating probabilities of its two endpoints. As shown in Figure 5.44, the node degree of node 1 is 1, and the degree of node 2 is 3. So according to the above definition, the dominating capability of edge (1,2) to node 1 is 1, and the dominating capability of node 2 is 1/3. So the dominating capability of edge (1,2) is 4/3, that is, the weight of edge (1,2) is 4/3.

According to the nature of the edge dominating capability, we can construct the dominating set. In the actual network, you can choose the node with the largest edge dominating capability as the dominator. Then forward information through the selected dominator, rather than broadcast information. This can greatly reduce energy consumption and information redundancy, so the information can be quickly forwarded to the destination.

B. Algorithm description

According to the definition of edge dominating capability, the assignment on the known undirected graph is conducted. In the following, we introduce an EDC-based dominating set construction algorithm in wireless networks, called the ED-CDS algorithm.

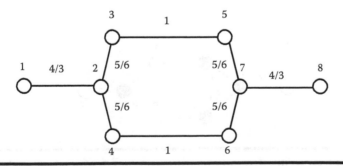

Figure 5.44   The weight of edge.

1. The edge with the highest weight (EDC) is selected as the dominating edge. If there is more than one such edge, then the dominating edge is selected at the same time.
2. Between the two endpoints of the dominating edge, the endpoint with the smallest dominating capability is selected as the dominator. That is, between the two endpoints of the dominating edge, the endpoint with the smallest value of $1/d_v$ is the dominator. If the dominating probabilities of the two endpoints are the same, then the endpoint with the smaller ID number acts as the dominator.
3. If an endpoint of the selected dominating edge is already the dominator, or if both of its endpoints are already under the control of the dominator, there is no need to select the dominator.
4. This process is repeated until each node in the network is controlled by at least one dominator.
5. All selected dominators form the dominating set of the network. Figure 5.45 depicts the whole process of selecting a dominating node using ED-CDS, where the black node represents the selected dominator and the red edge represents the selected dominating edge. Finally, {2,3,4,7} forms the dominating set of the network.

5.4.2.2 Simulation Analysis and Results

We chose the Java language to do the simulation, with development tool of Eclipse, the version of 3.7.1. Nodes are distributed randomly in a 100×100 area with the

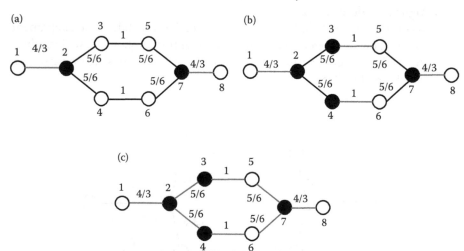

Figure 5.45 (a) In the first iteration, nodes 2 and 7 are chosen as dominators, (b) in the second iteration, nodes 3 and 4 are chosen as dominators, and (c) in the third iteration, each node is controlled by at least one dominator.

number of nodes ranging from 10 to 100. Each node has a fixed range of communication r, ($r=25$ or $r=50$). The nodes are fixed without taking into account the interference generated by the node communication. When the distance between nodes is less than r, they become neighborhood nodes.

5.4.2.2.1 Introduction to Eclipse

1. What is Eclipse?
   Eclipse for Java likes Visual C++ for C/C++. There are more than 10 species of IDE software in Java, such as JBuilder of Borland, IBM's Visual Age for Java, WebSphere Studio, Oracle's JDeveloper, and Sun's Forte for Java. In all of these IDE, Eclipse can be said to be one of the most promising products.

   Eclipse was originally created by OTI and IBM's IDE development teams, starting in April 1999. IBM provided the first Eclipse code base, including Platform, JDT, and PDE. Currently led by IBM, projects around Eclipse have developed into a huge Eclipse Alliance. More than 150 software companies participate in the Eclipse project, including Borland, Rational Software, Red Hat, and Sybase. Oracle recently decided to join in the Eclipse Alliance.

2. The advantage of Eclipse
   Eclipse is an open source software development project; its advantages come from its openness and scalability. According to the Eclipse architecture, through the development of plug-ins it can be extended to any language development and even become a drawing tool. Eclipse has begun to provide the function plug-in for C language development. Even more commendable is that Eclipse is an open source project; thus, anyone can download Eclipse source code and on this basis develop his or her own plug-ins. That is to say, for as long as someone needs in the future, there will appear many development plug-ins for COBOL, Perl, Python and other languages based on Eclipse. At the same time, the functionality of existing plug-ins can be expanded through the development of new plug-ins. For example, the Tomcat server plug-in joined the existing Java development environment. The extendibility, a unified interface, the management of operation and system resource are the potential of Eclipse.

3. Installation of Eclipse
   The latest version of Eclipse is 3.0. We will install Eclipse 3.7.1. Enter the Eclipse interface shown in Figure 5.46. Here are the installation steps:
   1. Before installation, ensure that your machine has installed Java Runtime Environment (JRE).
   2. Enter on the Eclipse project's home page http://Eclipse.org. Click "Downloads," then enter the download page. Supposing you install the Windows version, then the file name should be "Eclipse-SDK-3.7.1-win32.zip." Download the zip file and unzip it directly to the directory you specified.

Figure 5.46   Boot screen of Eclipse.

3. Eclipse SDK has been installed. If you also need to install the Chinese version, then download the language pack: "Eclipse3.7.1-SDK-win-LanguagePackFeature.zip". Unzip directly to the Eclipse directory and overwrite the corresponding files.
4. Now, Eclipse installation is complete. Run "Eclipse.exe" to start the Eclipse workbench.

Under normal circumstances, Eclipse will automatically find your JRE. If it cannot find it, or you installed multiple versions of Java, you can menu "window → Preferences" to set the JRE path, as shown in Figure 5.47.

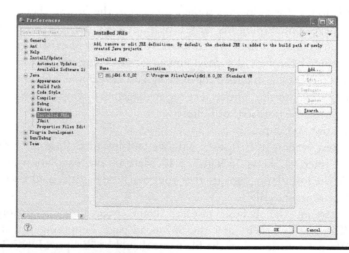

Figure 5.47   Configure the JRE of Eclipse.

4. Eclipse interface

After launching Eclipse, the interface will be as shown in Figure 5.48. The window consists of a menu bar, a toolbar, a workbench, and a status bar at the bottom. Through the menu, we can achieve a lot of features. As mentioned earlier, we can go through "window → Preferences" to configure all the default Java project properties. In the process, you can pop up a context menu at any time by right-clicking. Workbench is an important part of the window. The decomposition of the Eclipse workbench is introduced in detail in the following part.

The Eclipse workbench consists of one or more perspectives, including the following:

■ Resources: for browsing the file structure
■ Debug: for debugging Java programs
■ Java: for browsing the Class structure
■ Java Browse: for browsing the Java project structure

And so on. If you install the relevant Eclipse plug-ins, the perspective will increase.

5.4.2.2.2 Simulation Development of ED-CDS

The development steps for Java programs in Eclipse are as follows:

■ Create a new Java project
■ Create new packages and classes in the project

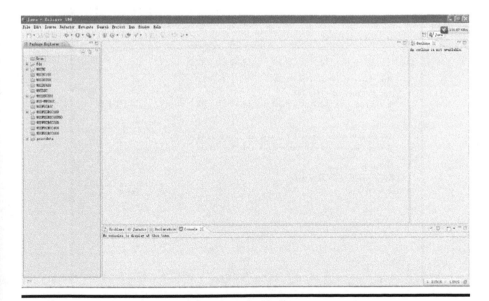

Figure 5.48   The interface after launching Eclipse

■ Write class code
■ Compile, run, and debug

1. New ED-CDS project

   Through the menu or toolbar button, select "new → project," as shown in Figure 5.49.

2. Create a new EDCDS class

   Right-click the new EDCDS project, "new → class" (Figure 5.50); the new class name and project name are the same as in EDCDS.

3. Edit the EDCDS class

   Open the EDCDS class file for editing, as shown in Figure 5.51. Figure 5.52 shows all the files required for the EDCDS project.

4. Run the EDCDS class

   Select "Run → Run as → Java Application" to complete the EDCDS class. The output information is automatically printed to the console window, as shown in Figure 5.53. Or output the required data directly in the text document.

5. Draw

   According to the data obtained, use the gnuplot tool for drawing. The gnuplot work window is shown in Figure 5.54.

Figure 5.49   New project of EDCDS.

Figure 5.50   New EDCDS class.

Figure 5.55 shows the simulation results for a DS-scale with a radius of 25. We compare the ED-CDS algorithm with the MDS and WMDS algorithms. Figure 5.55a shows the trend of the DS scale as the network size increases from 10 to 100 when the communication range of the node is 25. It can be seen in the graph that when the network size increases, the number of dominators obtained

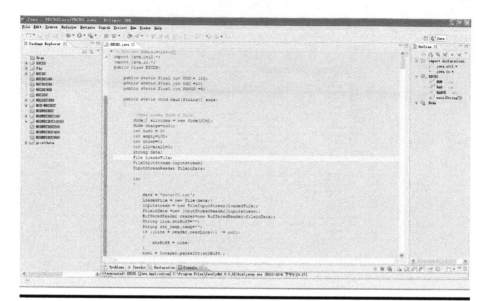

Figure 5.51   Edit EDCDS class.

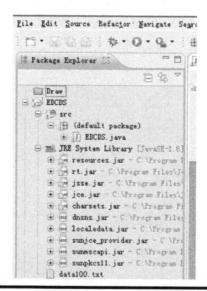

Figure 5.52   All the files contained in the EDCDS project.

by the ED-CDS algorithm gradually increases. However, when the network size increases to a certain extent (the number of nodes being 100), the DS scale will no longer continue to increase; it may even be reduced. The reason is that as the network size increases, the node density increases. So each dominator can control more neighbors. Therefore, when the network density reaches a certain level, the number

Figure 5.53 The console window.

Figure 5.54 The gnuplot working window.

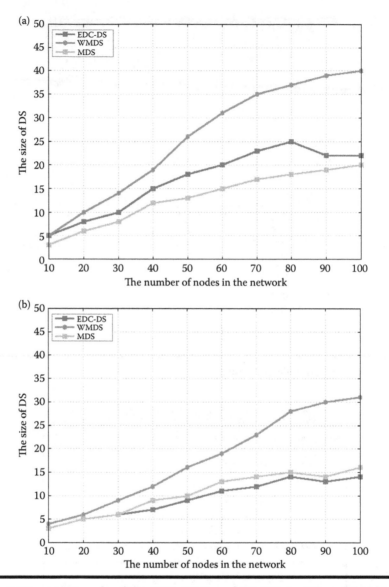

Figure 5.55 **(a) DS scale of ED-CDS, MDS, and WMDS (*r*=25) and (b) DS scale of ED-CDS, MD, and WMDS (*r*=50).**

of dominators will no longer increase. When the network size is the same, the DS scale obtained by the MDS algorithm and the WMDS algorithm is larger than the DS size obtained by the ED-CDS algorithm. Figure 5.55b shows the DS scale when the network size increases from 10 to 100 when the communication range is 50. As seen from the data, WMDS performance is still the worst. And our ED-CDS algorithm is still the smallest scale.

Bibliography

1. G. P. Jesi. PeerSim HOWTO: Build a new protocol for the PeerSim 1.0 simulator [EB/OL]. http://peersim.sourcefo -rge.net/.
2. M. Chen. *OPNET Network Simulation*. Tsinghua University Press, Beijing, China, 2004 (in Chinese).
3. OMNET++ community site [EB/OL]. http://www.omnetpp.org/.
4. B. Yu, B. Sun, N. Wen, H. Wang, J. Chen. *NS2 and Network Simulation*. Posts & Telcom Press, Beijing, 2006 (in Chinese).
5. D. Zhang. *MATLAB Communication Engineering Simulation*. China Machine Press, Beijing, China, 2010 (in Chinese).
6. P. M. Wightman and M. A. Labrador. A3: A topology construction algorithm for wireless sensor networks. *Proceedings of IEEE Globecom 2008*, 2008.
7. P. Santi. *Topology Control in Wireless Ad Hoc and Sensor Networks*. John Wiley & Sons, New York, September 2005.
8. S. B. Lippman, B. E. Moo, J. LaJoie, S. Li. *C++ Primer*. Posts & Telcom Press, Beijing, 2006 (in Chinese).
9. Y. D. Liang, M. Wang, X. Fu, N. Li. *Java Programming*. China Machine Press, Beijing, 2006 (in Chinese).
10. P. M. Wightman. Atarraya: A topology control simulator. http://www.csee.usf.edu/~labrador/Atarraya/, 2012.
11. C.-H. Ke. http://hpds.ee.ncku.edu.tw/~smallko.
12. Z. Ke, R. Cheng, D. Dejun. *NS2 Simulation Experiment: Multimedia and Wireless Network Communication [M]*. Publishing House of Electronics Industry, Beijing, 2009 (in Chinese).
13. The network simulator-ns-2. http://www.isi.edu/nsnam/ns.
14. F. Yu. *A Survey of Wireless Sensor Network Simulation Tools*. http://www1.cse.wustl.edu/~jain/cse567-11/ftp/sensor/index.html.
15. S. Mehta, N. Uilah, M. H. Kabir, M. N. Sultana, K. S. Kwak. A case study of networks simulation tools for wireless networks. *International Conference on Modeling and Simulation, IEEE*, 2009: 661–666.
16. M. Korkalainen, M. Sallinen, N. Kärkkäinen, P. Tukeva. Survey of wireless sensor networks simulation tools for demanding applications. *International Conference on Networking and Services. IEEE Computer Society*, 2009: 102–106.

Index

Milton Keynes UK
Ingram Content Group UK Ltd.
UKHW021849071024
449327UK00021B/1556